The Rabbi's Wife

The Rabbi's Wife

The Rebbetzin in American Jewish Life

Shuly Rubin Schwartz

NEW YORK UNIVERSITY PRESS
New York and London

NEW YORK UNIVERSITY PRESS
New York and London
www.nyupress.org

First published in paperback in 2007

Library of Congress Cataloging-in-Publication Data
Schwartz, Shuly Rubin.
The rabbi's wife : the rebbetzin in American Jewish life /
Shuly Rubin Schwartz.
p. cm.
Includes bibliographical references and index.
ISBN-13: 978-0-8147-4016-3 (cloth : alk. paper)
ISBN-10: 0-8147-4016-2 (cloth : alk. paper)
ISBN-13: 978-0-8147-4053-8 (pbk : alk. paper)
ISBN-10: 0-8147-4053-7 (pbk : alk. paper)
1. Rabbis' spouses—United States—History. 2. Rabbis' spouses—
United States—Intellectual life. 3. Rabbis' spouses—United States—
Religious life. I. Title.
BM652.S25 2005
296.6'1'082—dc22   2005019501

New York University Press books are printed on acid-free paper,
and their binding materials are chosen for strength and durability.

Manufactured in the United States of America

c 10 9 8 7 6 5 4 3
p 10 9 8 7 6 5 4 3 2 1

Contents

Preface

"And what will your role be?" a member of the search committee would invariably ask me, when my rabbi husband interviewed for pulpits. For almost twenty-five years, I lived the life I have chosen to write about. Even before we married, I knew that Gershon planned to become a rabbi. Like so many of the women whose stories fill these pages, I imagined that I would become a Jewish educator as a fitting counterpart to his career as rabbi. After all, this was the model I had grown up with; my dad served as a congregational rabbi for his entire career while my mom taught religious school, reviewed Jewish books, and worked within the congregation to enhance the knowledge and Jewish commitments of its congregants. I knew firsthand what I was getting into when I married a future rabbi, and, over the years, I experienced both the highs and the lows of the role—joys and resentments, feelings of fulfillment and anxiety—just as my own mother had.

In graduate school, I was drawn to Jewish history, and I chose to train professionally in that field rather than to become a Jewish educator. I also became a college dean and carved out a somewhat eclectic rebbetzin role. Though I helped found a synagogue babysitting co-op, delivered Torah talks for Sisterhood Shabbat, and entertained congregants on Shabbat and holidays, I also led lunch 'n' learns, workshops, and scholar-in-residence weekends on topics in Jewish history.

Several years ago, I unexpectedly received in the mail a photo of me taken at a Commencement ceremony. I attend such exercises annually, and seeing a photo of myself in academic garb is hardly unusual. But the envelope read "Rebbetzin Shuly Schwartz," and the photo was sent by a member of my husband's congregation whose niece had graduated that day. What a striking juxtaposition of those two roles! A thoughtful congregant extended herself to me as her rebbetzin, yet her reason for doing so stemmed from my professional identity and not my position as rabbi's wife. This incident best captures the experience of my generation of rebbetzins. Professionals in our own right, we are nevertheless often defined in relation to our husbands' career, an association that I generally enjoyed but one that complicated both my professional and my personal life.

In 2003, my husband, Gershon Schwartz, left the congregational rabbinate and began teaching rabbinical students. For the first time, both he and I began to discover the pleasures of serving the Jewish community without the added expectations of congregational life. Then, tragically, Gershon died unexpectedly less than a year later, and I found myself in the role of rabbi's widow. I reread these pages with new eyes, acutely aware of my new status while struggling to complete revisions to a manuscript that focused on my old one.

The intertwining of personal and professional in my life epitomizes the conundrum I faced in undertaking this project. Initially inspired to examine this topic because of my experiences, I faced the challenge of writing about a topic close to home with the detachment of a historian. Being a rebbetzin myself, I had the insider perspective that gave me special insight into the complicated and multifaceted rebbetzin role. This enabled me to ask my interviewees probing questions and to elicit their honest, unguarded responses. Rebbetzins were eager to share their stories with someone who understood their perspective. Yet my love for rebbetzins as well as my concern for Jewish life also meant that I had to work doubly hard to maintain scholarly objectivity in my research and writing. A tricky balance, but I trust that I have maintained it. In so doing, I hope I have succeeded in telling the story of women whose accomplishments are so richly deserving of attention, both for their own sake and for the light they shed on American Jewish life.

Acknowledgments

This book has been more than a decade in the making, and I am pleased to acknowledge the assistance, encouragement, and support of the many individuals who helped make its completion possible.

First and foremost, I feel privileged to have had the opportunity to learn from many rabbis' wives. My first goal in interviewing was to hear directly from the rebbetzins, and I am grateful to the many women who graciously agreed to speak with me, especially: Joan Lipnick Abelson, Hadassah Carlebach, Janet Chiel, Naomi Cohen, Sylvia Geffen, Rae Goodman, Blu Greenberg, Hilda Greenberg, Zipporah Jacobs, Reba Katz, Maurine Kessler, Eileen Kieffer, Edith Kling, Eudice Lorge, Zipporah Marans, Hadassah Nadich, Eveline Panitch, Louise Reichert, Lilly Routtenberg, Roz Stein, and Miriam Arzt Teplitz. I am also indebted to the women who participated in the Retired Spouses session of the 2000 National Association of Retired Reform Rabbis Convention and the Rabbis' Wives session of the 2000 Rabbinical Assembly Retired Rabbis Convention. To supplement these stories and to learn about rebbetzins who had died, I also interviewed their congregants, family members and associates: Balfour Brickner, Irma and Abraham Cardozo, Judah Nadich, Jack and Jean Stein, David Waxman and Eve Keller, and Mordecai Waxman. I am grateful for the thoughtfulness and candor with which they reflected on the role of the rebbetzin and its place in their lives.

I am also indebted to the many individuals who generously shared personal files, family papers, correspondence, scrapbooks, and photos with me in the hope that I might be able to capture the essence of the rabbi's wife role: Bailey Bloom, Balfour Brickner, Shulamith Elster, Jeremy Goldstein, Hilda Greenberg, Agnes Herman, Zipporah Jacobs, Reba Katz, Edith Kling, Sylvia Lieberman, Michael A. Meyer, Peggy Pearlstein, Marjorie Pressman, Aaron Reichel, Charlotte Rothman, Lilly Routtenberg, Hillel Silverman, Adrienne Sundheim, Helen Tomsky, Jonathan Waxman, and Miriam Wise.

Others also assisted me in tracking down sources, and I am grateful to them for their efforts. J. J. Schacter and Norman Lamm shared materials and insights on Irma Jung. Sara Sager shared recollections and helped me track down contacts on Rebecca Brickner. Joellyn Zollman alerted me to important materials by Miriam Wise. Marjorie Lehman shared materials on Tamar de Sola Pool. Jeffrey Gurock shared valuable sources from Yeshiva University. Mel Scult generously shared unpublished materials on Mathilde Schechter.

I also want to acknowledge the assistance of rabbis' wives, including Annette Botnick, Carol Poll, and Rivkah Lambert, who conducted their own research into the role of the rebbetzin and who openly shared materials and insights with me even as they encouraged me to forge ahead with a full-length study on the topic.

Research on a project that has never been explored before requires ingenuity in uncovering obscure material. For successfully recovering so much rich material, I am indebted to several superb archival professionals who generously aided me in my quest: at the Jacob Rader Marcus Center of the American Jewish Archives, Gary Zola, Kevin Proffitt, Elise Neinaber, and Camille Servizzi; at the Joseph and Miriam Ratner Center for the Study of Conservative Judaism, Julie Miller and Ellen Kastel; at Women's League for Conservative Judaism, the late Edya Arzt and Selma Weintraub; at the Spanish-Portuguese Center, Susan Toben; at the Hadassah Archives, Susan Woodland; at the Yeshiva University Archives, Shuli Berger; at the Jewish Historical Society of Greater Washington, Laura Cohen Apelbaum and Wendy Turman; and at the Cleveland College of Jewish Studies, Jean Letofsky.

I was fortunate to receive the Joseph H. Fichter Research Award, 1999–2000, from the Association for the Sociology of Religion; the Rabbi Levi A. Olan Memorial Fellowship, 1999–2000, from the Jacob Rader Marcus Center of the American Jewish Archives; and a summer fellowship in 1999, from the Myer and Rosalie Feinstein Center for American Jewish History. These grants enabled me to further my research at a crucial point in the process, and I am pleased to acknowledge this support.

I am also grateful to the research assistants who ably transcribed interviews, tracked down materials, and checked sources: Toby Appel, Naamit Kurshan Gerber, Shoshanna Schechter, Aviva Schwartz, Tali Schwartz, Deborah Skolnick, Hadara Stanton, and Lauren Strauss. They not only provided invaluable assistance but also came to share my enthusiasm for the project. Ed Walthall has provided critically important, steadfast administrative support throughout the process.

I am grateful to many colleagues, including Dianne Ashton, Naomi W. Cohen, Jeffrey S. Gurock, Rosemary Keller, Margaret and Michael A. Meyer, Pamela S. Nadell, Riv-Ellen Prell, Jonathan D. Sarna, Mel Scult, and Jenna Weissman Joselit for their friendship and staunch support as well as for many conversations that enriched my understanding of American Jewish life.

Hasia Diner provided tremendous encouragement throughout the project. She read earlier drafts of the manuscript and with her keen editorial eye and deep insight into the American Jewish experience, helped me greatly improve the book as a whole.

It is a pleasure to acknowledge the support and guidance of Eric Zinner, Despina Papazoglou Gimbel, and Emily Park at New York University Press. Eric provided enthusiastic guidance and advice throughout the editorial process, and Despina and Emily painstakingly assisted me through the myriad details of preparing the manuscript for publication. Special thanks to John Dibs for providing a carefully prepared index.

Bernice Cohen offered financial support for the book's publication that has greatly enhanced every aspect of the final product, and I am deeply grateful for her belief in the project and its importance.

Family members have also been invaluable during this process, and I feel lucky to have had the benefit of their know-how as well as their love and support. Alvan and Ruth Ann Rubin opened doors within the Reform Movement that enabled me to secure valuable interviews and materials. Elisheva Urbas generously shared her editorial expertise and provided essential guidance and advice. Peggy K. Pearlstein provided tremendous support throughout the project. Professionally in her role as Area Specialist, Hebraic Section, African & Middle Eastern Division, at the Library of Congress, Peggy discovered many little-known references to rebbetzins. As a rabbi's wife, then a widow, Peggy shared her own firsthand experiences while providing steady encouragement. Ilana Kurshan provided important editorial advice and support. My sister, Alisa Rubin Kurshan, read several drafts of the manuscript and provided vital feedback not only as a rebbetzin and rabbi's daughter herself but also as an astute observer of American Jewish life. She and my brother Jack Rubin, my sister-in-law Leslie Rubin, and my brother-in-law Neil Kurshan, have been a lifeline of essential support throughout my life, but especially during these past difficult months.

I would also like to acknowledge Diane Ajl, Steve and Shelly Brown, Eddie and Anna Edelstein, Benjamin Gampel, Stephen Garfinkel, Carol Ingall, Fran and Michael Katz, Gershon Kekst, Robert S. Lupi, and Burton Visotzky for their immeasurable support and encouragement.

JTS has been a wonderful intellectual home, and I am grateful to faculty colleagues for serving as eager sounding boards for my ideas and for offering constructive suggestions and wise counsel. My students, both in List College and in my classes, have over the years helped me refine my thinking about rebbetzins. JTS provost Jack Wertheimer helped facilitate my sabbatical leaves and provided important guidance throughout the process.

I am particularly indebted to JTS Chancellor Ismar Schorsch, my teacher and mentor for more than thirty years. An enthusiastic supporter of my scholarly pursuits, he granted me the two sabbatical semesters that made it possible for me to complete this project in spite of the heavy demands of the deanship. He has also been a source of great personal encouragement and support through challenging times.

I feel especially fortunate to have such wonderful children: Moshe; my daughter-in-law, Aviva; Tali; and Hadar. As Moshe is studying for the rabbinate, he and Aviva will seek their own balance in the rabbinic lifestyle, and I, God willing, will soon experience firsthand what it's like to be a rabbi's mother! They have both been precious sources of strength to me during this project. Tali provided unconditional and unequivocal encouragement when the project felt too overwhelming to complete. Hadar enthusiastically edited several chapters of the manuscript and offered important insights from the perspective of a "pk" — preacher's kid. I burst with pride for them all and feel so lucky to be blessed with their abundant love. My words of gratitude here are only a fraction of what I feel for each of them.

I end with such heaviness of heart, for I began this project shortly after the death of my father, Mordecai Rubin. I focused initially on the careers of rebbetzins like my mother, Gilla P. Rubin, but, sadly, she died before my first article on the topic appeared in print. As I continued my research into what became this book-length manuscript, I envisioned dedicating it to the memory of both my parents, in recognition of their accomplishments as a rabbinic couple over forty years.

Devastatingly, in November 2003, my adored younger son, Elie, died tragically at the age of twenty-one. With his life cut short at such a young age, Elie never had the opportunity to reach his potential either in a career or in his personal life. A talented, engaging, loving young man, Elie brought great joy to those whose lives he touched. He had great plans for his future, and he inspired me always with his fierce intelligence, creativity, and courage.

Less than six months later my beloved husband, Gershon, also died unexpectedly. Both he and Elie took tremendous pride in this project, and they eagerly anticipated its publication. Gershon, my life partner, my muse, lovingly read and edited every word of the manuscript, except these last. He prodded me to forge ahead when I lost momentum, shared my delight when I discovered new materials, and sharpened the manuscript with his careful eye and literary sensibilities. Gershon also taught me so much about Jewish religious leadership through his rabbinic career, and this, too, deeply infused each page of this manuscript. While he certainly experienced the stresses of the rabbinic lifestyle, Gershon cherished being a rabbi and gave of himself immeasurably to the congregations he served, through his sermons, his counseling, his books, and his presence. His charismatic personality, abundant talents, wit, and thoughtfulness influenced countless men and women to deepen their connection to Jewish life. Both Gershon and Elie overflowed with their love of life, and this continues to inspire me daily. I dedicate this book to their blessed memory.

Introduction

What happened to Box 14? A 1978 inventory of the Jewish Theological Seminary Library's archival holdings listed the thirteen-box collection of Herman H. Rubenovitz. But Rubenovitz, rabbi of Temple Mishkan Tefila in Boston, Massachusetts, from 1910 to 1947, served jointly with his wife, Mignon, in a two-person rabbinate. Their memoirs appeared in one volume as *The Waking Heart*, yet Mignon's papers did not appear in the archives. Twenty years later, cleaning out the JTS tower in preparation for its renovation, archivist Julie Miller discovered Box 14: "Mrs. Rubenovitz Mignon L. Letters, article, memoirs, notes, reviews on her publications etc." This box had been separated from the collection, abandoned in an unused storage area.

Box 14 symbolizes the unique position of the rabbi's wife in American Jewish life. Just as the box went unnoticed for decades, so too have the contributions of rabbis' wives to the American rabbinate largely been ignored. Successful in her own right, Mignon had papers that she thought worthy of preservation. Yet Mignon lacked an official title and position. If they had not been appended to her husband's collection, Mignon's papers would probably never have survived at all. However, without her efforts, his papers would probably not have been preserved either, since Herman predeceased Mignon. She collected and annotated their papers and then, presumably, donated all fourteen boxes to JTS.

This fourteen-box collection, now renamed the "Herman H. and Mignon L. Rubenovitz papers," stands as a poignant reminder of the extent to which the American rabbinate was—for most of the twentieth century—a two-person career. The feminist gains of the last forty years have opened up most careers, including the clergy, to women. But until recently, by both policy and social convention, most careers remained closed to women. As they struggled to find socially acceptable ways to create and sustain meaningful lives, many women discovered that they could expand their opportunities through marriage. Supporting their husbands' careers gave women a consequential focus for their lives. Their "wife of" status opened doors to the public domain, affording them otherwise unattainable access and power.[1]

Scholars have only recently begun to examine these "backstage contributions to public life," which, until the last few decades, were rarely understood or recognized. Generally dismissing this work as "natural" for women, scholars did not view it as deserving of special commen or study. Even when recognized for its supportive function, women's work was not acknowledged for its unique contribution to the building of community. This is understandable, since women often used informal, hard-to-measure techniques. They "helped out" in the absence of other qualified individuals, "pitched in" when more hands were needed, and provided a "shoulder to lean on" for individuals needing private counsel. The success of this status-maintenance or supportive work depended on obfuscation, for societal norms did not easily accommodate women who openly flaunted gender expectations. Also, since these volunteer activities did not fall into the category of formal "work," the critical role women played in the creation and maintenance of community life went unacknowledged and undocumented.[2]

Hanna Papanek, a sociologist, first conceptualized the relationship of a wife to her husband's work as a "two-person single career" in which wives gain vicarious achievement through their husbands' jobs. Identifying this two-person career as a peculiarly middle-class American phenomenon, Papanek demonstrated its power to shift the occupational aspirations of educated women onto a noncompetitive track without overturning the concept of equal educational opportunity. Women gained approval for indirect behavior, while men garnered rewards for individual mastery. Because of this, women often sought to marry men who could provide not only security but also position and status. They then channeled their energies into augmenting their husbands' careers. Such women, including the wives of corporate executives, army officers, physicians, politicians, and academics, have historically enhanced their husbands' work through intellectual contributions, status maintenance, and public performance.[3]

Some two-person careers required spouses to utilize specialized skills or knowledge or to perform functions unique to their husband's profession. Ambassadors' wives, for example, conducted political and social messaging through the symbolic aspects of diplomatic life or through nonofficial channels. This work—though unpaid and without formal title—enabled women to achieve levels of status, authority, and legitimacy they would have been unable to attain on their own, no matter how talented or ambitious they might be.[4]

The frau professor provides a nineteenth-century European paradigm for the pluses and minuses of this two-person career. Shielding him from financial worries, the frau professor enhanced her husband's reputation among colleagues through her social skills. She managed the entertaining deemed essential to her husband's job, smoothing the way for new colleagues through dinner invitations, parties, and discreet inquiries. She also served as her husband's unseen colleague, critic, and editor. She benefited from this aspect of the relationship as well, for she was in an intellectual milieu where she could further her own academic interests. Some academic wives openly collaborated with their husbands on books. Despite the fact that they lacked institutional affiliation in their own right, the wives sometimes received credit as coauthors.[5]

Not all wives were interested in or capable of fulfilling the expectations placed on them by their husbands' careers, and their lack of conformity engendered pain, frustration, and anger. For example, the public expected politicians' wives not only to accompany their husbands on the campaign trail but also to advocate for them publicly. Because of this, the public assumed that politicians' wives possessed the communications and public-speaking skills necessary to do so. But some wives dreaded the limelight and proved to be ineffective campaigners.[6]

The "wife of" role caused difficulties even for those who enjoyed it because it left women in an untenable position. Encouraged to seek out the "wife of" role, women suffered criticism if they succeeded too well. Those thought to have violated gender boundaries were disparaged for speaking their minds or overshadowing their husbands.

Ambivalence about the power women derive through marriage is deeply ingrained in western civilizational attitudes. Aspasia, wife of the fifth-century BCE Athenian statesman Pericles, was said to have taught rhetoric and participated in discussions with Socrates, but she also found herself the target of attacks and jokes for her supposed influence over her husband. Her position brought her fame, but it also provoked controversy. Aspasia was charged with impiety, and some historians blamed her for the Peloponnesian War.[7]

These mixed emotions ingrained themselves into the fabric of the United States through the role of First Lady. The term first came into use in the 1870s among journalists writing about both the first First

Lady, Martha Washington, and the current one, Lucy Hayes. Appearing in dictionaries beginning in 1934, the honorific title described the "wife of the President of the United States, [or] . . . the woman he chooses to act as his official hostess." Gradually, the First Lady role expanded into a more public position that included policy and personnel decisions. This evolution paralleled both the executive branch's ascendancy over the legislative and the growing importance of the United States in the world. Americans were proud of their First Ladies and admired their accomplishments. At the same time, First Ladies never lacked detractors. Over the years, the women suffered criticism for traits that spanned the spectrum of behavior: extravagance, casual entertaining, prudishness, gaiety, excessive grief, advanced age, youthful inexperience, or excessive influence on their husbands or on government.[8]

The unique potential and pitfalls of the role emerge in sharpest relief in the career of Hillary Rodham Clinton. A Yale-educated attorney, Hillary merited praise for her intelligence and abilities. Thus, when Bill Clinton campaigned for the presidential nomination, Hillary promised Democrats that in nominating her husband, they stood to gain a team, not only an individual. Yet as First Lady, Clinton was severely criticized for trying to make good on that pledge. When she led the effort for health care reform, the public brutally attacked her for overstepping her bounds. Several years later, Hillary succeeded in her own run for United States Senate. Yet, she ironically achieved this goal in large measure because, as the *New York Times* columnist Margaret Talbot argued, Hillary derived much, if not all, of her star power not from her own accomplishments but from her First Lady status. After winning, however, Senator Clinton began to solidify her own reputation as a public official.[9]

This study explores the ways in which women succeeded in forging consequential lives through the "wife of" role when direct avenues of power remained largely closed to them. Adopting the life's mission of their husbands, these women worked alongside them to further it. While this phenomenon existed in many careers, it especially characterized the ministry, for this profession most openly embodied a sense of "calling." Moreover, societal expectations of the ministry most explicitly articulated the desire for a spouse who shared the values and activities of her husband. For these reasons, women who heard the call to religious service found that marriage to a minister provided an especially advantageous route to a life of influence.[10]

Some Jewish women—particularly Jewishly educated, motivated, and ambitious women—also felt this calling. Since being a rabbi's wife was the highest status a Jewish woman could attain, it is not surprising that some women coveted the position for its own sake. Priva Konowitz Kohn expressed it best when she explained, "I was a rebbetzin before I married a rabbi."[11] Propelled to a life of service, Priva faced the question only of which rabbi to wed.

For other women, marriage to a rabbi imposed a new set of expectations that willy-nilly became their own. These rabbis' wives gave no prior thought to such a "career." By marrying a man who either functioned as or would become a rabbi, these women grew into the "wife of" role. Some eventually embraced it as their own, gaining the requisite knowledge and skills and growing to love the lifestyle and the work.

Turning a spotlight on the evolving role of the American rabbi's wife will allow her many accomplishments to come to the fore. It will also demonstrate the nuances of marriage as a route to power for women, by revealing the opportunities and limitations marriage placed upon women's own desires for power, status, and meaningful work. Because these women worked both as behind-the-scenes helpmates and as partners with their husbands, this study will deepen our understanding of the fluid boundaries between women's public and private lives. This focus on rabbis' wives will also reinforce the growing recognition of the centrality of women to American religious history, by shedding light on the complexity and significance of the religious leadership role of clergy wives.[12]

Noting the terms used to describe rebbetzins will also help illuminate the significance of the rhetoric used to praise women. Observers initially used imprecise language to describe the accomplishments of female leaders. Using adjectives that stressed feminine virtues of modesty, charm, graciousness, and generosity of spirit, writers often neglected to specify the behaviors and achievements that merited such approbation. Similarly, laudatory compliments based on traditional Jewish texts, such as "fitting helpmate," "mother in Israel," and "woman of valor," abound in descriptions of rabbis' wives.[13] Sorting out what such terms signified will deepen our understanding of the kinds of behavior that merited praise in different eras.

Moreover, highlighting the careers of rabbis' wives will enrich our understanding of American Jewish religious life. Early studies, such as Nathan Glazer's *American Judaism* and Marshall Sklare's *Conservative Judaism*, focused more on the ideologies, institutions, and socioeconomic characteristics of the major religious denominations than on the contributions of individual rabbis or communities. Even the more recent five-volume series, *The Jewish People in America,* edited by Henry L. Feingold, noted the pivotal role that certain rabbis played in the growth of American Jewish religious life in the twentieth century. But these volumes barely mentioned rabbis' wives. Murray Polner, in *Rabbi: The American Experience,* noted how little attention had been paid to rabbis' wives, and devoted eight pages of his 1977 study to enumerating tensions in the role that he attributed to feminism. But Polner, too, neglected to recount the accomplishments of rabbis' wives. Similarly, contributors to the 1985 edited volume *The American Rabbinate* note briefly the potential hardships the rabbinate inflicted on the Conservative rabbi's family, but otherwise, the volume made no mention of rabbis' wives.[14]

Recent works, such as Jenna Weissman Joselit's *The Wonders of America,* Deborah Dash Moore's *To the Golden Cities,* and Karla Goldman's *Beyond the Gallery,* have introduced a gendered perspective to the study of American Judaism. These historians bring to light the critical role women have assumed both as regular worshippers and as pivotal volunteers, particularly through congregational Sisterhoods. Pamela S. Nadell's study *Women Who Would Be Rabbis* reveals the extent to which rabbis' wives played a vital role in the quest for women's ordination. Through these works, the leadership role played by specific rabbis' wives has begun to emerge.

Until now, however, no one has focused primary attention on rebbetzins themselves. This study traces the careers of rabbis' wives from the emerging awareness of a special "wife of" role at the beginning of the twentieth century to the present. It tracks the evolving consciousness of rabbis' wives—as individuals who recognized their potential to be leaders, then as cohorts of leaders who worked together on behalf of American Judaism, and finally, as both individuals and groups who redefined their roles yet again in light of changing gender expectations. In doing so, this study brings to light many achievements never before recognized while also forcing us to think more broadly about what Jewish leadership is and how it has been exercised by American Jewish women.

Finding appropriate sources for this study proved challenging at first. Many rabbis did not preserve their papers; their wives were even less likely to do so. This is not surprising, since as Carla Freedman speculates in her rabbinic thesis, "The Rebbetzin in America in the Nineteenth and Twentieth Centuries," most rabbis' wives would not have considered what they did important enough to document. Even when rebbetzins left a written record, scholars often overlooked such material, as happened with Rubenovitz's Box 14. Moreover, like early feminist historians who ignored the work of clergy wives when seeking evidence of female leadership in the past, most scholars found this "wife of" role too inconsequential to be studied.[15]

This volume brings to light material hidden in rabbis' papers or rebbetzins' closets. Rebbetzins rarely left diaries or memoirs, but some saved speeches, outlines of invocations or lessons, invitations, program announcements, and local newspaper clippings about their career milestones. Condolence notes and obituaries also proved valuable as records of how others viewed rebbetzins. Yet these sources are fragmentary and incomplete, and virtually no national statistical data concerning rabbis' wives exists to help the scholar evaluate how pervasive certain anecdotes or experiences were for rebbetzins as a whole.

Oral interviews with rebbetzins supplemented information gleaned from written sources. As the historian Marc Raphael has argued, oral history is especially useful as a way of learning more about people, trends, or events that "have not received the benefit of conventional documentation." But accuracy in interviewing can be elusive, given the limitations of human memory. Even when conducted with thorough and deliberate technique, oral documentation must be approached warily. To guard against such concerns, I have attempted to verify oral evidence by asking the same questions of many interviewees. I have also attempted to elicit recollections with a minimum of prodding or direction that might influence the outcome, and to guard against conflating contemporary testimony either with what actually happened or with how interviewees felt in the past. Thus the story that follows is based on both extant records and oral interviews and is in no way statistically representative of rebbetzins as a whole. Ultimately, it is the preponderance of data that elucidates the rabbi's wife role. It also suggests individual variations and the way they developed. Taken together, such evidence illuminates the breadth of the role, the ways in which it evolved over time, and the ramifications of those shifts on the wives themselves, on their communities, and on American Jewry.[16]

The *"Rebbetzin"*

In choosing to marry rabbis, American Jewish women assumed a unique position, for they alone among clergy wives stepped into a role with an established title.[17] The Yiddish title "rebbetzin"[18] was the most prestigious one available to a woman in the Jewish community in the era before women could become rabbis. While some Yiddish lexicons define the term simply as the wife of a rabbi or teacher, others note that the term "rebbetzin" also connotes a pious woman, a woman with good lineage, or a woman learned in religious matters. Spivak and Bloomgarten's 1911 Yiddish dictionary includes two sayings that capture essential aspects of the role. The first, "when the man is a rabbi, the wife is a rebbetzin," points to the inevitability and derivative nature of the rebbetzin role—attainable automatically and only through marriage. The second ominously suggests its negative connotations: "Better a son a bath attendant than a daughter a *rebbetzin.*"[19]

Thus, American rabbis' wives assumed a role with longstanding rich, historical associations—both positive and negative. Rabbis' wives, especially in eastern Europe, developed reputations for piety, scrupulous observance, leadership, and concern for the poor. Laudatory stories— though surely exaggerated and embellished—abound in both memoirs and fiction. Together, they constitute a vital part of the collective imagination of eastern European Ashkenazic Jews. A few examples will suffice. Perele, the daughter of Rebbe Israel of Kozienice and wife of Ezra Zelig Shapira of Magnuszew (d. 1849), was remembered for wearing ritual fringes, fasting on Mondays and Thursdays, receiving petitions from her followers, living a life of poverty, and distributing funds to the needy. Lubavitcher rebbetzins became known for their tradition of holding gatherings before the holidays to dispense blessings to Hasidim. Among the most notable Hasidic rebbetzins, Sarah Horowitz-Sternfeld (d. 1939), the "Chentshiner Rebbetzin," daughter of Rabbi Joshua Heschel Frankel-Teonim and wife of Chaim Shemuel Horowitz-Sternfeld, developed a far-reaching reputation for her asceticism, exemplary character, meticulous observance of Jewish law, charismatic leadership, devotion to the poor, and miraculous powers. The Yiddish essayist Moshe Feinkind described her as "the last rebbetsin of the old generation that conducts herself in the manner of a Rebbe in Poland." Contemporary accounts reported that about 10,000 attended her funeral.[20]

Tales of frugality and business savvy also proliferated, since rebbetzins were expected to earn sufficient income to free their husbands for full-time study. Rabbis' contracts often stipulated that the rabbi's wife be given a store with exclusive rights to sell indispensable household items such as candles, yeast, wine for ritual use, salt, sugar, and kerosene. In Czarist Russia, the rebbetzin's burden was even greater, for tax levied on these items was used to support the community, and the rebbetzin was responsible for collecting it. Some rebbetzins also served as executive directors of their husbands' schools. For example, Rayna Batya—granddaughter of Rabbi Hayyim Volozhiner and the first wife of Naftali Zvi Yehudah Berlin (1817–1893), who headed the Volozhin yeshiva for approximately forty years—took responsibility for bookkeeping, loan guarantees, and stipend distribution to local landlords who took in yeshiva students.[21]

The term "rebbetzin" also encompassed women known for their learning and wisdom. This was particularly true of rebbetzins who were rabbis' daughters. By living in a home where rabbinic affairs were conducted, these women absorbed a tremendous amount of traditional Jewish learning and occupied what Wendy Zierler describes as the borderline between traditional Jewish gender divisions. In rabbinic families with no sons, daughters often gained additional opportunities to study with their fathers. This phenomenon was common in general society as well. For centuries, a woman's chances for acquiring education improved greatly if she were a daughter in a family without sons. Serving as surrogate sons for intellectually driven fathers, these women gained their education through informal apprenticeship to their fathers.[22]

Such rebbetzins possessed a breadth of knowledge that included rabbinic texts and fine points of Jewish law, especially concerning dietary laws, family purity, and Sabbath and holiday observances. Among these learned women was Krendel Steinhardt, wife of Joseph ben Menahem Steinhardt (1720–1776), a German rabbi and decisor of Jewish law. In his *Zikhron Josef*, Joseph quoted his wife's comments and novellae. Similarly, Eidele, wife of Isaac Rubin of Sokolow (d. 1876), developed a reputation for delivering discourses. Lubavitcher rebbetzins also gained reputations for their comprehensive Torah knowledge, and stories recount erudition that, in some cases, supposedly manifested itself in childhood. Similarly, the Zionist advocate Sarah Bayla Hirschensohn (1816–1905), wife of Yaakov Hirschensohn, who moved to Palestine from Pinsk in 1848, "was considered a scholar in her own right and was responsible for the administration of yeshivot in both Safed and Jerusalem."[23]

Yaffa Eliach, in her chronicle of the Shtetl of Eishyshok, recalls Rebbetzin Hendl Krechmer Hutner (wife of Zundl Hutner, rabbi of Eishyshok from 1896 to 1919) as an outstanding exemplar of these characteristics. She supported her family as an agent for a Russian dye company and saw to it that her husband pursued his studies with a minimum of distraction. Knowledgeable in rabbinic texts and principles, Hutner merited having students and scholars alike stand up out of reverence when she entered a room—a customary gesture of respect usually reserved for rabbis and teachers. Hutner rendered routine Jewish legal decisions, especially in the area of dietary laws. She comforted the dying and worked with her husband to minister to the sick, old, and poor during World War I. In Eliach's view, Hendl Hutner represents "a group—at least two centuries' worth of Lithuanian rebbetzins—who used their husband's status to gain entrée to the intellectual elite, but [then] secured their place there on their own merits."[24]

These paradigms appear in legends and fiction as well: the poor rebbetzin who struggled to make ends meet, or the rebbetzin whom all the townspeople sought out for counsel and who dispensed profound wisdom. For example, in a popular parable that recounts one woman's desperate efforts to lighten her heavy burdens, one version puts the sage advice in the mouth of a rebbetzin. She encouraged the troubled woman to substitute any other bundle of troubles for her own and helped the woman realize that her own burdens were actually the lightest.[25]

The term "rebbetzin" conjured up a host of negative images as well. Chaim Grade, especially in his novella "The Rebbetzin,"[26] introduced his readers to the full range of eastern European rebbetzins, including those who typified the darker side of the role. He depicted envious, nasty, meddling, haughty, and embittered rebbetzins, enabling the reader to appreciate the extent to which individual personality traits shaped a rebbetzin's experience.

"The Rebbetzin" features Perele, a rabbi's daughter who had heard in her father's house and then in her own "many snatches of Talmudic lore, which she could recite with fluency and ease." Emissaries from distant yeshivas and itinerant preachers who spent the Sabbath with Perele and her husband, Uri-Zvi HaCohen Koenigsberg, rabbi of Graipewo, praised her learning. But Perele was a moody, nervous woman who suffered from headaches and indigestion and resented her rebbetzin role.

She nagged her husband for years to retire from the rabbinate until he finally relented.[27]

Grade peppered this story with other community rebbetzins. Bashka, whom Grade referred to as the "Schloss Street Rebbetzin," manifested a happy disposition. Not fanatically religious, she got along very well with all kinds of people and brooked no qualms about wearing the latest styles. But the wife of the Wolkowysk Street Rabbi complained about her lot because of the poor treatment her husband received. She lamented that it was "'better to be a woodchopper than [a rabbi,] like a public rag everyone uses to dry their hands when they leave the baths.'" She was explicit about the way this treatment affected the rabbi's wife: "They all watch him to see if he's wearing a new hat, and they watch his wife to make sure she isn't buying too good a piece of meat for Sabbath."[28]

Often, individuals employed the term "rebbetzin" with a touch of ridicule or humor. For example, the Zionist activist Shmarya Levin recalled that in eastern Europe "some of the animals have special names. One of them, a large, quiet cow, slow and stately of motion, is called the Rebbitzin, the rabbi's wife." This mocking tone was particularly evident when used to refer to American rabbis' wives who fell short of the eastern European saintly models. As the cookbook author Elizabeth Ehrlich noted, "when applied to a woman of obviously lesser virtue, or newfound virtue, such as my mother's daughter, this term *rebetsin* had the humorous force of a gentle put-down." As Lillian Feinsilver, a rabbi's wife and author of *The Taste of Yiddish,* noted, the term is an "affectionate and slightly disrespectful title" that "combines the loving feeling for the old-time REBBE with a certain touch of light humor." Her husband described a rebbetzin as "'a girl who's foolish enough to marry a rabbi, but smart enough to know what to do about it.'"[29]

Occasionally, rebbetzin stereotypes bordered on the insidious, as the following joke indicates:

A traveler arrives in town and asks the rabbi if he can assemble a minyan (prayer quorum of ten men) so he can say the *Kaddish* for his dead father. With effort, the rabbi assembles nine, then tells his wife to go out and ask the first man she meets to come and be the tenth man. It is pouring outside and the rabbi's wife is a mess. She sees a man and asks him: "Du vilst zein dem tzenta? [Do you want to be the tenth man?]" The man takes one look at her and replies: "Nit dem ershter afileh [I wouldn't even want to be the first]."[30]

The rebbetzin title, then, brought dubious prestige to its bearer, bequeathing an ambivalent legacy to twentieth-century rabbis' wives.

In actuality, the rebbetzin role, in both its favorable and pejorative aspects, predates the Yiddish term. The most famous rabbi's wife in rabbinic literature is Beruriah, wife of the second-century Rabbi Meir. Though elsewhere in the Talmud the rabbis cautioned against teaching women Torah, they described Beruriah as so learned that she "studied three hundred laws from three hundred teachers in a day." About her, rabbis reported, "Rightly did Beruriah say." They also highlighted her high moral character and deep faith, as evidenced by the story in which Beruriah withheld news of her sons' sudden death on the Sabbath from her husband, and then relayed the horrible information to him with a parable about the need to return precious jewels to their rightful owner. Beruriah was also known for teasing rabbis about their negative views of women. Yet these stories of Beruriah's erudition, faith, and boldness are counterbalanced by an anecdote that illustrates how men ultimately outsmarted her. The noted eleventh-century Bible and Talmud commentator Rabbi Solomon ben Isaac [Rashi] quoted a legend that describes Meir's decision to send one of his students to seduce Beruriah. According to this source, she succumbed to temptation and subsequently committed suicide. As a whole, then, the Beruriah stories illustrate both women's ability and potential for religious leadership and the heartbreak that might befall them should they cross the line of gender propriety.[31]

In the medieval period, evidence also exists in Ashkenazic circles of rabbis' wives who developed a reputation for erudition. For example, Miriam, the wife of Jacob Tam, the twelfth-century Tosaphist and grandson of Rashi, possessed the necessary expertise to decide Jewish legal questions in her community. In fifteenth-century Germany, another rabbi's wife and descendent of Rashi, Miriam Spira Luria, was said to have given public lectures and expounded the Talmud and Jewish legal codes. In addition, she was noted for supporting a yeshiva.[32]

In Renaissance Italy, rabbis' wives also merited respect for their knowledge and position. They came to be known by the Hebrew title "rabanit," rabbi's wife, the Hebrew equivalent of the Yiddish "rebbetzin," which referred to both rabbis' wives and widows. These women enjoyed special status. Like their husbands, they merited a seat of honor in the synagogue. Moreover, though the testimony of women was not considered binding in a rabbinic court, some rabbis accepted the testimony of rabbis' wives based on the rabbinic principle that "the wife of a colleague is considered like a colleague."[33]

In the Sephardic world as well, evidence exists of a tradition of learned and respected rabbis' daughters and wives. For example, Asenath (1590?–1670), daughter of Rabbi Samuel Barazani of Kurdistan and wife of Jacob ben Abraham, her father's successor, was a learned woman who succeeded her husband as the chief teacher of Torah in Kurdistan and head of the Mosul yeshiva. Asenath was also known for her letters of exhortation and instruction to various communities and for soliciting aid for the yeshiva.[34]

American Ministers' Wives

American rabbis' wives, then, inherited centuries-old Jewish associations with their position. At the same time, these women also shouldered growing American expectations for clergy wives. In seventeenth-century America, ministers' wives enjoyed an honorific position, similar to their European Jewish counterparts. For instance, the minister's wife and the widow of his predecessor merited special seats in the New England meetinghouse. But the position did not presume a special sense of calling or encompass discrete behaviors until the mid-1800s. As Methodism emerged as the leading Protestant sect, the role of the minister's wife took on definite shape.[35]

The developing role of the clergy wife in nineteenth-century America grew concurrently with the increasingly accepted notion of "domestic feminism," according to which women possessed an innately religious nature that predisposed them to serve as society's moral guardians. This belief justified women's involvement in all kinds of altruistic work in the public sphere. It also gave them more personal authority while reinforcing their social subordination to men. Such a mandate uniquely suited wives to assist their clergy husbands in their work.[36]

This concept made it easier for Methodist itinerant ministers—most of whom had remained single in the previous century—to marry. Marriage enabled them to gain a valued partner in what could be a lonely, challenging career. For women, marriage to a frontier itinerant minister promised broad avenues of religious usefulness either as an assistant or through the possibility of a genuinely shared ministry. Leonard I. Sweet, in his pioneering study of the minister's wife, found that the "most common vocational fantasies of Evangelical women in America involved becoming a minister's or a missionary's wife. . . . Both permitted women a public, assertive form of usefulness. . . . and the wives of ministers functioned as ministers." He further noted that the best way to ensure the realization of those dreams involved being either a minister's daughter, the daughter of parents who ran a "Methodist Tavern," or a student at a female seminary or academy.[37]

Catherine Livingston Garrettson exemplified this type of clergy wife. In 1793, she married Freeborn Garrettson, an experienced Methodist evangelist minister, in order to fulfill her desire to serve God. Six years later, the Garrettsons purchased a home in Rhinebeck, New York, which became known as "Traveler's Rest." While Freeborn continued his itinerancy, Catherine transformed their home into the center of her ministry. She presided over religious services, taught Bible and theology, conducted prayer groups, solicited testimonies of salvation, and served as pastoral counselor and spiritual director.[38]

Catherine Brekus, in her study of female preaching in America, discovered that such marriages became more common after 1830. Clergy wives opened their homes for services, provided hospitality to circuit riders, presented testimony at love feasts, and led prayer meetings. When wives joined their husbands on the circuit, they cared for the sick and dying, prepared bodies for burial, and facilitated conversions. Wives remaining home while their husbands traveled established schools, conducted pastoral visits, provided counseling, and raised funds for church maintenance.[39]

Because they saw themselves assuming an activist role in improving society, many of these clergy wives also came to play an instrumental part in founding women's societies that dispensed charity and served as auxiliaries for Bible and prayer book groups. Such organizations gave ministers' wives a venue for leadership somewhat removed from, yet complementary to, their husbands' congregations. It enabled them to cultivate organizational, executive, political, public relations, financial, and leadership skills and to develop reputations as backbones of religious philanthropy.[40]

Of course, even in the nineteenth century, society was of two minds about this emerging role. In 1877, for example, Hannah Reeves was memorialized with great ambivalence. She was praised for being a "helpmeet" to her husband even though she was "'superior to him in gifts'" and could have demanded her own circuit. Yet Reeves was also described pejoratively as a " 'masculine,' 'indomitable' woman" who sacrificed her children's welfare for her own career.[41]

Ministers' wives suffered from the confining gender expectations of the role. Those who gave up preaching in public after marriage often experienced regret. Others who wanted to continue preaching found themselves unable to do so because domestic chores and childrearing overwhelmed them. They were vulnerable to depression, loneliness, and discouragement, and many ministers' wives felt responsible for alleviating not only their own feelings of despair but also their husbands'.[42]

The restrictions of the role surfaced in clergy advice books of the period. An 1832 manual expected the minister's wife to view herself as " 'wedded to her husband's parish, and to the best interests of his flock.' " In his 1851 *The Itinerant Wife: Her Qualifications, Duties and Rewards,* Herrick Eaton emphasized the wife's need to tend to her husband and children first and then to the church. He acknowledged the unreasonable expectations placed on her by congregants, for "more is expected of her by the public than of other persons, and generally her words and actions are considered with less charity than are those of others." Eaton also admitted that she deserved sympathy for being "the servant of the Church in an eminent, and frequently humiliating sense." Enumerating the rewards for such a life, Eaton suggested that they lay in the knowledge that she served her husband and her children well and that she would experience the glory of her Savior in the future world.[43]

Other frustrations of the clergy wife role can be attributed in part to Methodist ideals concerning poverty and frugality. Methodist ministers received meager compensation for their work, with western itinerants especially living at or close to the poverty line. Not only did they function as unpaid servants of the church, they also struggled to manage household finances on small salaries that were sometimes difficult to collect. Many ministers' wives operated inns where they fed and lodged itinerant evangelists and freeloaders; they also entertained parishioners on the same budget. They endured an especially demeaning form of payment known as the "donation party" or "surprise visit" and, later in the century, as a "pound social." The minister's wife sponsored this party in her home for parishioners who would bring a gift as well as money for an offering. The value of these donations would usually be deducted from what the congregation owed the minister in salary. This deepened the bitterness of ministers' wives, because they were put into the awkward position of accepting as charity what was in fact their husbands' rightful due. Moreover, guests often brought items that the minister's family did not need, which did nothing to alleviate the family's financial worries. If anything, they exacerbated them by absolving the congregation of further responsibility for the minister's salary that year. Moreover, the party gave congregants license to snoop around the parish house, further eroding whatever dignity the family still maintained.[44]

According to Sweet, the ideal of minister's wife as vocational partner or institutional asset declined in the last two decades of the nineteenth century. The minister's wife withdrew to a more behind-the-scenes role that he called the "Companion model," in which the wife primarily served as a psychological support system for her husband. This retreat exemplified a larger trend. By the end of the century, men and women had become deeply concerned about the feminization of American culture, and they mounted concerted efforts to reverse it. This led both to a general decline in the ministry and to changes in the status of women that reinforced patriarchal structures and woman's traditional roles.[45]

American Rabbis and Wives

Though influenced by precedents in the Christian world, the rabbi's wife role in America developed later, emerging at the end of the nineteenth and the beginning of the twentieth century, as the American rabbinate itself came into its own. It was not until 1840 that the first ordained rabbi, Abraham Rice, settled in the United States to serve as spiritual leader of Baltimore Hebrew Congregation. After 1850, larger congregations began to hire European-trained rabbis, but many fledgling congregations struggled to secure stable rabbinic leadership. Disputes between rabbis—many of whom lacked formal ordination—and laity were common, and religious leaders often moved from congregation to congregation. One congregant, Samuel, son of Israel (born in Albany in 1862), recalled that "the rabbis of our congregation played no important role in the community, and I think I can say in all truth that the Jews paid little attention to them. They were 'offish.' We really hardly knew them."[46] Understandably, then, rabbis' wives from the mid-nineteenth century rarely appear in records except to note a congregation's beneficence in granting them some sort of compensation—their husband's salary, a stipend, free housing, or a pension—after their husband's death.[47]

The wives of eminent Reform rabbis Emil G. Hirsch and Kaufmann Kohler, both daughters of the Reform rabbi and ideologue David Einhorn, played supportive spouse roles typical of middle-class women of their time. A clubwoman involved in organizational work, Mathilde Hirsch volunteered with the National Council of Jewish Women from its founding and served several terms as a director on the local Executive Board. She was remembered as a "real and noble person in her own right. . . . Though she avoided the limelight, her influence 'behind the scenes' was never absent. Emil G. Hirsch himself often paid tribute to her wise counsel, her sound advice and her intuitive admonitions."[48]

Johanna Kohler also exemplified the ideals of true womanhood embraced by late-nineteenth-century middle-class women, extending her sphere of influence into the community to promote a variety of religious and benevolent causes. After her marriage to Kaufmann in 1870 and during their years in Chicago, Kohler joined other German-Jewish women in founding the Johanna Lodge in Chicago in 1874, the first midwestern chapter of the Unaghingiger Orden Treue Schwestern (United Order of True Sisters). When the Kohlers moved to New York, Johanna became one of the first board members of the New York section of the National Council of Jewish Women. She also joined the boards of the Kindergarten Association of the Hebrew Free Schools of New York and Temple Beth El's Sisterhood.[49]

When her husband became president of Hebrew Union College in Cincinnati in 1903, Kohler turned her attention to that community, serving in roles that enhanced her husband's position. In her capacity as first Chairman of Religion for the Council of Jewish Women, Kohler invited Henry Englander, professor of medieval exegetical literature at Hebrew Union College, to teach a Bible class. This group, which flourished for more than twenty years, appreciatively remembered through letters Kohler's role as its founder. Years later, Kohler served as chairman of the National Committee on Union Museum for the National Federation of Temple Sisterhoods, the Reform organization founded in 1913.[50] She tried to increase awareness among Sisterhood women of the significance of ceremonial objects and to solicit new objects and funds for the museum, first housed at Hebrew Union College.[51]

Upon her death, the Hebrew Union College faculty remembered Kohler for her "cordial interest in all that pertained to the welfare of the College and its students, her warm personality, her spiritual and cultural interests . . . hospitality . . . devotion to Jewish ideals . . . and the home which she and her distinguished husband established and so richly blessed by their presence and influence. Her life was a symbol of Jewish womanhood at its best." Condolence letters and resolutions issued upon her death call attention to her modesty, refinement, and good works, and praise her for embodying "all the noblest traits of ideal womanhood."[52]

Like the wives of other prominent Reform rabbis, Kohler exemplified nineteenth-century, middle-class ideals for American Jewish women without articulating the contours of a specialized role for rabbis' wives. But Ray Frank, a charismatic preacher and lecturer who studied at Hebrew Union College during its early years, did highlight the potential significance of the rebbetzin role in response to a query posed in 1880 by the *Jewish Times and Observer:* "what would you do if you were a rebitzen?" In her view, the role should be a public one, for even in its present state, the rebbetzin role afforded a woman the opportunity to function as moral exemplar, help establish Jewish women's organizations, and work on behalf of needy congregants.[53]

With the graduation of the first four rabbis from the Cincinnati-based Hebrew Union College in 1883 and the creation of the Central Conference of American Rabbis in 1889 with thirty rabbis, a small cadre of American-trained, English-speaking activist rabbis began to serve congregations around the country. The early graduates of Hebrew Union College, including Henry Berkowitz and his brother-in-law, Joseph Krauskopf, actively labored to initiate a more open Temple, or what historian David Kaufman calls the "classical Reform synagogue-center." They hoped such a synagogue would both model American openness and freedom and incorporate new social and secular functions. These classical Reform rabbis were first and foremost preachers, and the most prominent among them combined oratorical skills with the intellectual capacity to shed light on current issues. But just as they literally opened up their synagogues several days a week—not only on the Sabbath—so, too, did their roles expand to include educator, executive, counselor, and pastor. They exercised a dominant influence in their congregations as they came to exemplify the ideal American Jew.[54]

This broader view of the rabbinate also expanded the horizons of rabbis' wives. For one thing, it created more public venues in which they might serve, both within the synagogue and nationally. For example, rabbis' wives served as delegates to the biennial councils of the Union of American Hebrew Congregations, the lay arm of the Reform

Movement, as early as 1896 because they attended with their husbands. Second, a more expansive rabbinic role opened up opportunities for women to partner with dedicated spouses who both shared their vision and would work with them to implement it.[55]

Soon after, the Conservative Movement set out on a similar path. After its reorganization in 1902 under the presidency of Solomon Schechter, the Jewish Theological Seminary also began to ordain English-speaking rabbis for the American Jewish community. Like their Reform counterparts, early JTS graduates played a crucial role in fashioning a comprehensive view of the synagogue and promoting the American rabbinate. Many came to see their wives as essential to realizing their goals.

American Jewish Women

The beginnings of the American rabbi's wife role coincided with an expansion of opportunities for American women in the latter quarter of the nineteenth century, a development one might expect to deter women from seeking the "wife of" role. The same period that saw a hardening of attitudes about feminization also witnessed an explosion of both careers and volunteer options for women. By 1880, 40,000 women, 34 percent of all students, were enrolled in higher education. Nearly half never married; those who did married later and bore fewer children. This fostered a new class of independent career women who moved into the fields of teaching, nursing, and social reform, with a few rare women breaking the barriers in traditionally male careers such as law, medicine, and the ministry. Middle-class women's groups also flourished, as clubwomen used their leisure time for self-improvement and the betterment of their communities. Women became increasingly aware of their potential to contribute to society, a consciousness that found expression in the World's Congress of Representative Women meeting in conjunction with the 1893 Chicago World Columbian Exposition.[56]

Jewish women grew increasingly aware of the special role they could play not only in American life but also in shaping American Judaism. Reform Judaism had already taken steps in mid-nineteenth-century Germany to ensure the increased involvement of women through the introduction of religious instruction and Confirmation. This trend continued in the United States with Isaac Mayer Wise's establishment of mixed pews and their rapid proliferation in Temples across the country. As

Goldman has demonstrated, Jewish women filled a majority of those pews, and their presence influenced the evolution of liturgy, music, congregational participation, and sacred space.[57]

Jewish women had also come to play an important role as Jewish educators and benevolent workers. Rebecca Gratz was an early example of this impulse, for she effectively channeled her religious devotion and commitment to Jewish life in America into the launching of innovative Jewish institutions for charity and religious education. Through her own example, the Sunday school she founded, and the other schools she subsequently inspired, Gratz also created career opportunities for a whole cohort of Jewish women.[58]

The symbolic coming-of-age of American Jewish women also dates to 1893, when the Congress of Jewish Women convened to represent Jewish women at the World's Parliament of Religions, which met in conjunction with the Chicago World Exposition. As Rosa Sonneschein, editor of the *American Jewess,* the first English-language magazine for Jewish women in the United States, noted, "this is a matter for congratulation, considering that, as a rule, Jewish women have had but little experience in parliamentary rules and public speech." This Congress led to the formation of the National Council of Jewish Women, the first national Jewish women's organization to promote Judaism. Through the Council, Jewish clubwomen channeled their commitments to domestic feminism, civic responsibility, social justice, and the preservation of American Judaism. Rabbis' wives played a role in the founding of the Council, but they did so as middle-class clubwomen, not as rebbetzins.[59]

Glimpses of a discrete rabbi's wife role surfaced more frequently during this decade. A fictional depiction of the rabbi's wife functioning in a distinctive role appeared in an 1892 story about Chanukah. In it, Mrs. Halvick, described as "so grand a person as Rabbi Halvick's wife," reached out to invite a young girl from a poor family to a Chanukah Ball. She recounted the details of the Chanukah story, promising to teach the girl about other Jewish holidays in the future. Enthralled with the holiday and the ball, the girl inspired her father to revive Chanukah observance in their home. The story concluded with his admission that Mrs. Halvick had helped them enrich their lives.[60]

A real-life example of the emerging role can be found in Rosa Sonneschein, one of the most public rabbis' wives of the period. Daughter of the Hungarian rabbi Hirsch Bär Fassel, she was well educated both at home and at a local high school. In 1864, Rosa married Solomon, and four years later they moved to the United States. They settled in St. Louis, where her husband served as rabbi of Congregation Shaare Emeth. Theirs was a discordant marriage, and there is evidence of Solomon's abuse, infidelity, and alcoholism. Despite this, the Sonnescheins were leading figures in the community. Rosa organized two congregational choral societies and "Ladies' Meetings" and founded a Jewish women's literary society, The Pioneers, in 1879. Yet congregants criticized Sonneschein for behavior inappropriate to her position as rabbi's wife, including powdering her face, attending the theater on Friday night in the company of an unmarried man, and playing tenpins.[61]

While she surely launched the *American Jewess* in part to support herself after her 1893 divorce, Sonneschein also hoped it would become a forum to promote her ideas of Judaism, Zionism, and women's rights among middle-class Jewish women. The magazine struggled financially and lasted only through 1899, but during its run Sonneschein used editorials and feature articles to champion her causes to a readership that grew to 29,000. Sonneschein lobbied for the rights of women to participate actively in religious ceremonies, to hold independent congregational membership, and to vote and run for office in Temple school board elections. She highlighted the work of the Council, publicized Ray Frank—the "girl rabbi"—and introduced her readers to the female minister Ella Bartlett. Sonneschein stopped short of advocating women's ordination, but she called for women to become well-educated and well-prepared "preachers."[62]

Sonneschein expressed ambivalence about women's roles, a stance no doubt due in part to her own struggles as a divorcée. On the one hand, she endorsed the female breadwinner who "demonstrated to men her intellectual capacity to a degree which must assure for her perfect equality in the family and in the state." Yet she clung to traditional attitudes, believing that, on the whole, women workers represented a sorry lot and that "to be childless is a misfortune." The goal for her was that the "home woman, at the head of a large family doing her full duty in the narrower sphere of domestic life," be recognized as a true breadwinner.[63]

The same ambivalence characterized her position as rabbi's wife. Sonneschein struggled for decades to extricate herself from her unhappy marriage. She also suffered criticism as a rabbi's wife for insisting on autonomy. Ultimately, Sonneschein established her reputation in an independent arena through her magazine, yet she undoubtedly built on skills and contacts cultivated during her years as the wife of a rabbi. These experiences presage some of the opportunities and struggles rabbis' wives would confront in the twentieth century.

At the 1893 Congress of Jewish Women, similar ambivalence concerning appropriate Jewish women's roles also found expression. Ray Frank brought these issues to the fore by serving as the Congress's "rabbi." Frank expressed compelling ideas both at the Congress and in lectures throughout the country over the next several years that offered new possibilities for female independent religious leadership to a generation of women eager to expand their own roles.[64]

Frank's paper on "Women in the Synagogue" raised the question of women's ordination. Recalling several illustrious women who had played pivotal roles in Jewish life in the past, including Krendel Steinhardt (mentioned above), Frank sought to demonstrate that these women had already earned the right to the pulpit. "Intellectually they were the compeers of their husbands; practically, they excelled them. They built synagogues, controlled colleges, and stipended students." However, she remarked that "with one or two exceptions, they were all wives and mothers, *most of them wives of rabbis,* and in the discharge of their duties no one thing was done at the expense of another." Despite her conviction that women possessed the ability to serve as rabbis and that someday they "may be ordained rabbi or be president of a congregation," she stopped short of advocating women's ordination. Instead she concluded that "every woman should aspire to make of her home a temple, of herself a high priestess, of her children disciples, then will she best occupy the pulpit, and her work run parallel with man's. . . . her noblest work will be at home, her highest ideal, a home." After raising expectations that women might serve as rabbis, Frank articulated an ideal that echoed her 1880 praise of rebbetzins.[65]

Emil G. Hirsch also raised the question of women's ordination in an 1897 symposium on "Woman in the Synagogue" in his *Reform Advocate.* Two-thirds of the twenty-six respondents were open to the possibility. They also argued for equal representation in all aspects of Jewish life. But here too, mixed feelings surfaced. Henrietta Szold, who would come to epitomize the American Jewish female leader, endorsed the concept of women rabbis. However, like Frank and Sonneschein, she repeated the traditional belief that a "woman can best serve the interests of the synagogue by devoting herself to her home."[66]

*

For Jewish women, then, the 1890s ushered in a decade bursting with possibility for women's independent leadership roles yet filled with traditional rhetoric about the primacy of Jewish women's roles as wife and mother. Certain women tested the limits of their autonomy, but the question of how far women should go as religious leaders remained unresolved. As Nadell has shown, such debate disappeared during the first decades of the twentieth century as Jewish women found other vehicles for their talents. As the nineteenth century gave way to the twentieth and as the needs of American Jewry escalated dramatically, one of those outlets—particularly for women who wanted to marry—became the role of rabbi's wife. Jewish women married to rabbis both exemplified the traditional emphasis on Jewish homemaking and contributed to the growth of American Judaism through their own accomplishments. Marriage to a rabbi gave these women the opportunity to satisfy their religious calling; to experience a life of service through teaching, public speaking, and good works; and to gain recognition and status. And they could do so without raising eyebrows about neglecting traditional feminine duties or exceeding limits of appropriate female behavior, for their role built upon solid precedent both in the traditional Jewish world and in American Protestantism. At the same time, marrying a rabbi exposed women to certain risks, for it opened them to public scrutiny, special expectations, gossip, and criticism. For most of the twentieth century, many American Jewish women decided that the benefits outweighed the negatives, and it is these women to whom we now turn to better understand the contours of the rebbetzin role in American Jewish life.

The story of rebbetzins in the United States unfolds gradually over time. Certain discernable patterns emerge in specific eras, and each chapter of this book focuses on how the role developed as well as on specific rebbetzins who epitomize it. At the same time, the role progressed in a fluid manner. New characteristics emerged while older ones persisted; individual rebbetzins emphasized different aspects of the role based on their distinctive personalities, predilections, opportunities, and goals. Thus the chapters represent eras that are fluid and filled with variety even as they illustrate phases in the evolution of the role. Rebbetzins left their mark through each of their myriad activities as well as through the cumulative impact of their evolving role over the decades.

Chapter 1 chronicles the careers of Carrie Simon, Mathilde Schechter, and Rebecca Goldstein, rabbis' wives who founded the national women's organizations of their respective denominations—Reform, Conservative, and Orthodox Judaism—and modeled the role of rabbi's wife for American Jews. Chapter 2 describes the emergence of a discrete rebbetzin role in the 1920s and the way in which rebbetzins, conscious of their position, exercised leadership. Chapter 3 recounts the distinctive achievements of several larger-than-life rebbetzins who illustrated the heights of power and influence attainable during the interwar and postwar period. Chapter 4 traces the growing sense of consciousness among rebbetzins as a group in the postwar period. Even as they became more openly reflective about both the joys and the limitations of their role, they continued to expand the arenas in which they served. Chapter 5 reviews the changing role of the rebbetzin in the wake of dramatic transformations in American life in the 1960s and 1970s. Chapter 6 considers the contemporary rebbetzin in light of both the ordination of women as rabbis and the emergence of rabbinic couples as well as male rabbinic spouses. Looking toward the future, this chapter also reflects on the broader implications of this study for women, for leadership, and for American Jewish life.

1

The Pioneers

Minna, Wife of the Young Rabbi recounts the adventures of a young eastern European girl, tricked by her adoptive parents into marrying a *yeshiva bocher* (yeshiva boy) at the age of thirteen. Abandoning him after their wedding night, Minna searches for her birth mother while raising her son in a completely secular environment. Sentenced to Siberia for nihilism, Minna falls in love with a cellmate who, unbeknownst to her, is her long-abandoned, and now also secular, husband. Ultimately, the two reunite in the United States in true love.

This novel, published in New York in 1905, portrays the rabbi's wife in pitiable terms. Forced as a young woman to marry a *yeshiva bocher,* who is undoubtedly "afflicted with some kind of rash or skin disease" owing to the "filthy and neglected conditions" in which he lived, a rabbi's wife is someone who tends to business and supports her husband. Her fate depends on her husband's, for some *yeshiva bochers* "finally become rabbis and procure good positions; while the others continue their idle life, in addition to making the unfortunate women whom they have married hopelessly wretched and unhappy." The protagonist gains the reader's sympathy and admiration for extricating herself from this thankless life. Like other undesirable memories of eastern European Jewish life, this traditional rabbi's wife role merited being discarded en route to America.[1]

Appearing at the dawn of the twentieth century, *Minna* captures the sense of possibility inherent in Jewish immigration to the United States, where old-world customs did not prevail. But *Minna* recreates the horrors of the traditional religious lifestyle without suggesting a new model to take its place. Such would be the objective of early twentieth-century American Jewish religious leaders. With well over two million Jews entering the United States in the last quarter of the nineteenth century and the first quarter of the twentieth, rabbis faced the monumental challenge of offering these immigrants a compelling religious alternative.

They were also determined to capture the flagging religious sensibilities of American-born Jews. In solidifying an American Judaism to meet these challenges, religious leaders—both male and female—succeeded not only in defining the American rabbinate but also in fashioning a constructive role for the American rabbi's wife.

This role was an attractive one because of the persistence of traditional gender expectations for American women. Despite the efforts of small numbers of dedicated advocates to combine the two, marriage and motherhood in the first decades of the twentieth century continued to be viewed as inconsistent with full-time employment, except for the economically pressed. While the proportion of working women aged twenty-five to forty-four rose from 18.1 percent in 1900 to 30.6 percent in 1940, only 12 percent of wives with husbands present were in the labor force as of 1930. Also during this period, the marriage rate increased while the marriage age declined. Marriage and motherhood overwhelmingly remained a woman's preferred full-time career.[2]

In the first two decades of the twentieth century, more and more American women took advantage of educational opportunities. The female proportion of the total population of college students rose from 39.6 percent in 1910 to 47.3 percent in 1920. Though that figure represented only 7.6 percent of eighteen-to-twenty-one-year-olds, it signified a positive shift in attitude toward women in college. But in the 1920s, women's share of college enrollment declined slightly, as did the number of female physicians. Three-quarters of those who graduated went into the typically female occupations of teaching and nursing. And the vast majority of professional women remained unmarried, as had been the case in the nineteenth century.[3] For most women, then, volunteer work continued to provide the outlet for their interests and talents most consistent with marriage and motherhood. Marriage to a rabbi enabled women working within these boundaries to gain additional status and power. It also gave them a platform from which to speak and congregants with whom to work.

Certain rabbinic couples understood that the challenges of the era necessitated the involvement of both husband and wife. The joint efforts of one such couple at the dawn of the twentieth century illustrate the potential of this two-person career. Anna Myers, a rabbi's daughter, was fluent in Yiddish and educated abroad.[4] After her marriage in 1897 to Isidore Myers, also a rabbi's child, the Myerses moved first to San Francisco and then, in 1905, to Los Angeles, where Isidore served as rabbi of Sinai Congregation. Anna promptly became the founding vice president of the Jewish Women's Foreign Relief Association and a trustee of the Hebrew Consumptive Relief Association. By 1909, she served as interstate representative of the Jewish Consumptive Relief Society of Denver. Responsible for eleven western states, she oversaw fundraising for the Denver hospital. The local press described her admiringly as a cultured woman of ability and energy.

As we have seen, rabbis' wives of the period commonly engaged in such organizational activity. What is unusual about Myers is the public nature of her work before a traditional audience and the way in which she used her learning and position as a rabbi's wife to further her effectiveness. Myers traveled widely to raise funds, and, in many communities, she spoke from the pulpit to get her message across. For example, in Pueblo, Colorado, Myers "addressed the orthodox congregation in their synagogue . . . in Yiddish," interspersing her remarks with biblical and Talmudic quotations. The *B'nai B'rith Messenger* commented that "this is the first time, as far as is known, that a woman has given a *d'rosho* [traditional sermon] in an Orthodox synagogue especially during the Sabbath service."[5] On one of her trips, Myers even assumed the traditional rabbinic role of settling a dispute between different factions of a congregation. Clearly her status as rabbi's wife, coupled with her own Jewish knowledge and talents, greatly enhanced her appeal as a community leader. She also benefited from her husband's support. In a poem written in tribute to her, Isidore boasted of his wife's accomplishments:

> She preaches in Temples and speaks in the Shools [synagogues].
> And gathers the shekels [coins] from wise men and fools.
> She attends to Shool meetings and settles disputes . . .
> When duty is calling, she is ready to go,
> And tramps in the cold through the slush and the snow . . .
> She proves without doubt that she knows how to schnorr [beg],
> Where others got little she's sure to get more.

Throughout her career, Myers modeled the more activist role that many rabbis' wives would eventually come to play during the twentieth century. Living on the West Coast in the early years of the century, Myers did not generate national opportunities for others to build upon. Within a few years, though, three rabbi's wives on the East Coast—

Carrie Simon, Mathilde Schechter, and Rebecca Goldstein—succeeded in establishing national religious institutions essential to the flourishing of Jewish life in America. Each founded the national women's organization of her respective denomination (Reform, Conservative, and Orthodox) and, in so doing, established the infrastructure for women's religious leadership in the United States. These women also embodied for twentieth-century American women a prototype of the American rabbi's wife. By the 1920s, as a result of their efforts and the work of women they influenced, a sense of group consciousness among rabbis' wives emerged. Yet only through the success of these pioneering women could its contours become clear.

Carrie Simon

Carrie Obendorfer Simon (1872–1961) founded the first national organization of synagogue Sisterhoods, the National Federation of Temple Sisterhoods, in 1913. Through her life's work, Simon offered an alternative vision of female leadership to a generation of middle-class Reform Jewish women.

Born in Alabama and raised in Ohio, Simon very much fit the demographic profile of Reform Jewry at the time. She graduated from the Cincinnati Conservatory of Music but did not have access to intensive, formal Jewish education. As a young adult, Simon served as secretary of the local chapter of the National Council of Jewish Women, a chapter her mother had founded. In those years, Simon shared the concern for philanthropy that was so prevalent among middle-class women, extolling its virtues and encouraging Jews to give their hearts and souls to those less fortunate.[6]

In 1896, Carrie married Abram, an 1894 graduate of Hebrew Union College. They had two children, Leo and David. Initially, Simon focused her energies primarily on her husband's congregations, in Sacramento, California, Omaha, Nebraska, and finally, in Washington, D.C., where Abram served as rabbi of Washington Hebrew Congregation, one of the leading Reform congregations of the day, from 1904 until his death in 1938. Involved in many aspects of synagogue life, Simon chaired the women's committee, which sold $104,000 worth of Liberty bonds during World War I.[7]

Simon retained a fond attachment to the Jewish home of her youth,

Carrie Simon. Courtesy of the Washington Hebrew Congregation.

and she worried that such childhood experiences were not being transmitted to the next generation. Over time, Simon grew more and more convinced that Reform Jewish women must move beyond a commitment to universalistic causes toward the goal of enriching Jewish life. Simon grew impatient with the National Council of Jewish Women for its inability to confront religious challenges. Similarly, Simon felt that Sisterhoods of Personal Service and Ladies Aid Societies, then popular among middle-class Reform Jewish women, focused their efforts too narrowly on charity. She wanted Jewish women to channel their efforts also to Temple duties, Jewish education, literature, and art.[8]

By founding the National Federation of Temple Sisterhoods, Simon played an instrumental role in shifting the attention of Reform Jewish women from philanthropic and humanitarian goals toward a concern with preserving Judaism. As articulated in Simon's address to the first biennial session of the National Federation of Temple Sisterhoods, the goal of the organization was to ensure that "the power of our faith shall not grow less, and that the blood coursing its veins shall not only not become anemic but shall even be constantly fed by a new and fresh supply." Two years later, Simon's rhetoric grew bolder: "How easy it is for the mere platitudes of humanitarianism to replace the austere dignity of Jewish obligation and sacrifice. Too well do we know how philanthropic, secular and social service appeals may serve as substitutes for religious sanctions."[9]

In a talk to a joint session of Reform Sisterhoods and Brotherhoods, Simon pleaded with the American Jewish woman to "stand like a solid wall against the forces which may tend to weaken or paganize it." To do so, she explained, women must "graft the religious equality upon the trunk of domestic piety," and strengthen the Jewish home. Hoping to order the priorities of local Sisterhoods, Simon reminded her audience that "it is not the primal business of the Sisterhood to raise money, but to raise Jews in an atmosphere of such religious earnestness and loyalty as will guarantee their allegiance to the synagog." She implored the Union of American Hebrew Congregations to prepare written materials that would imaginatively educate Jewish women, giving them the tools to successfully "toughen the religious fibre" of their children. Simon also called on women to attend services, engage in Bible study, and cultivate congregational singing, and she complimented them on their efforts to maintain religious services even at summer vacation resorts. Simon urged women to involve themselves in synagogue religious schools, believing their influence would ensure the removal of perceived abuses and heighten the educational effectiveness of the schools. Finally, she raised the issue of securing scholarships for young men preparing for the rabbinate by appealing to romantic notions of European Jewish women's self-sacrificing behavior. She recounted the stories from her "sainted mother's lips" about women who made heroic sacrifices so that their men could study in yeshiva—a much more positive image than that conjured up in *Minna*.[10]

According to Simon, anything that stimulated religious feeling fell within the purview of her Federation. She encouraged members to deepen Jewish consciousness in mothers and children and to distribute Jewish objects, such as candlesticks, to increase observance. Especially attuned to the esthetic in Judaism, Simon inaugurated a series of Jewish art calendars that combined information with a high level of artistry. Similarly, she encouraged collecting ceremonial objects, an effort that within a few years resulted in the establishment of the Hebrew Union College Museum.[11]

Sharing her views with synagogue groups around the country, Simon delivered invocations, sermons, and addresses that prodded her audiences to do more for Jewish life. But she faced a steep homiletical challenge, for she addressed largely Americanized audiences who might take offense at her more parochial message. Not one to shy away from this challenge, Simon spoke her mind directly and forcefully. For example, she criticized Reform Judaism for its lax attitude toward Jewish observance:

> I cannot but feel that moral and religious control has slipped from us in the onrushing waves of our progressive religious practice and democratic ideals. . . . We modern Jews have lost Jewish discipline. . . . The Reform synagog hesitates to ask for sacrifices. There should be domestic practices of religion today which should be compulsory.

Simon believed that if women devoted themselves to the "spiritual and refining power of religion" and developed an appreciation for the joy of prayer and domestic ceremonials, they would instill similar dedication in their husbands and would ultimately transform Reform Judaism as a whole.[12]

Simon also challenged Sisterhoods to face the implications of the Women's Movement. For example, in a talk titled "What Can the Women Do for Judaism?" she reminded her audiences that at first "the Jewess was a follower," then with the progress of the Reform Movement, she became a participant. That Reform impulse coupled with the burgeoning women's movement raised "the possibility of the Jewish woman becoming a leader in religion." In that spirit, Simon suggested that "we stimulate our daughters to preach the Jewish religion" so that they too could enter the rabbinate.[13] Simon also lobbied—like Sonneschein before her—to include women on Temple boards, and she personally made sure that she, as Sisterhood president, served on her Temple's board. This led to the anomalous and, no doubt, awkward situation whereby, beginning in 1923, Carrie Simon was automatically invited to Temple board meetings, but her husband, the rabbi, was not.[14]

At the same time, Simon also challenged the feminist ethos of the era. She expressed concern that the "social and economic forces of our age" might engulf the Jewish home. Exhorting the women of Temple Emanuel not to abdicate their primacy of place in the Jewish home, she criticized those who refused "the responsibilities of mothers and no longer rejoice[d] in the privileges of Wifehood" and lamented that "children reared by nurses and outsiders are no longer under the teaching responsibility of their mothers." Warning that "femenism [sic] is replacing womanliness," she extolled Sisterhood as "an organization of Jewish Mothers, by Jewish mothers, and for Jewish mothers . . . come to redeem the Jewish home from sterility and stagnation."[15]

When Simon turned over the reins of leadership of the National Federation of Temple Sisterhoods in 1919, she had indeed established an infrastructure that would direct Reform Jewish women to a life more involved with Judaism. The organization consisted of more than 200 Sisterhoods and 30,000 members. It continued Simon's work in education, fundraising, and Jewish art, providing an outlet for talented women committed to enhancing Jewish life in America. Simon remained involved, chairing committees and delivering invocations or greetings at every biennial convention until her death in 1961. Concerned about providing a home for rabbinical students, Simon personally chaired the committee that raised funds for a student dormitory at Hebrew Union College; within two years, she had procured the entire sum of $340,000.[16]

Throughout this period, Simon also fulfilled the duties of a rabbi's wife. When implored to seek another term as president, Simon reminded her audience that she was " 'still a rabbi's wife,' with its consequent heavy demands on her time and strength." Congregants, too, understood her role as one that obliged her to behave in a certain manner. Some congregants approved of her national efforts and took pride in her achievements, while others found her manner abrasive and criticized "her 'cruel' and biting wit, which she often used to ridicule and belittle people." It is impossible to determine the pervasiveness of such sentiments, but these judgmental attitudes echo earlier appraisals of both clergy wives and European rebbetzins.[17]

A report on Carrie and Abram's twenty-fifth wedding anniversary noted that Carrie "is almost as well known as her husband."[18] Her life's work, nationally through NFTS and locally through her congregation, helped married women imagine the leadership possibilities inherent in the autonomy, self-confidence, and sense of sisterhood that grew out of involvement in organizational work. To a certain degree, these accomplishments paralleled those of other clubwomen leaders. But by focusing her attention on the local synagogue and on Reform Judaism writ large, Simon helped Jewish women realize that the same advantages could accrue from working within Judaism. Most important, her renown embodied the growing public leadership role within Judaism for married women and suggested a more activist role for Reform rabbis' wives as well.[19]

Mathilde Schechter

Mathilde Roth Schechter, wife of Solomon Schechter—the noted scholar, president of the Jewish Theological Seminary of America (1902–15), and leader of Conservative Judaism in the United States—played a role similar to Simon for the nascent Conservative Movement. Just as Simon channeled the focus of Jewish women toward Judaism through the NFTS, so too did Schechter inspire Jewish women to secure the Jewish future through the National Women's League, which she founded in 1918.[20] Both because her husband was the leading figure in the movement and because of her own rich Jewish learning and ambitions, she succeeded in enhancing American Judaism for her largely eastern European audience in several different ways.

Born in 1857, Mathilde grew up in Breslau, Germany. Her father died when she was young, and she received her education in the Jewish orphan home. Quickly distinguishing herself intellectually, Schechter continued her education at the municipal high school for girls. She then entered a teacher's seminary where she received a well-rounded secular education. Schechter taught locally, but, not content to remain the provincial teacher that her education had prepared her to be, she chose to broaden her experiences still further. In 1885, Schechter traveled to England to study at Queens College and "revel in the treasures of the British Museum, the National Gallery and the endless private collections." She also hoped to draw intellectual sustenance by joining the Jewish academic and social circles of Michael Friedlaender, head of

Mathilde Schechter. Courtesy of the Ratner Center for the
Study of Conservative Judaism, Jewish Theological Seminary.

Jews' College. Schechter lived in Friedlaender's home and tutored his
daughter, Lucie. Within a few weeks, Mathilde met Solomon Schechter,
fittingly, in the Jews' College library. They developed a deep friendship,
for he helped her find the right books, while she translated materials for
him from the French. Mathilde coveted a future that would incorporate
the intellectual stimulation that she discovered in the London Jewish
circle, and by marrying the most brilliant member of the group, she
believed she would attain it. Mathilde recalled with pride that her 1887
marriage to Solomon was "a real scholar's wedding."[21]

From the beginning of their marriage, the Schechters conducted their
home as an open forum: "Scholars and literary men came and went as

they pleased, and all day long the hall door was never locked." Assisted by a maid, Mathilde served as hostess, and she and her husband together set a tone she recalled as a "joyous friendly spirit." This mood prevailed despite the fact that the Schechters were burdened with financial difficulties. Mathilde recalled gingerly asking the grocer at one point for some cash to tide her over. To ease their money worries, Mathilde taught German literature and art history to girls and young married women in their homes. She could earn extra money more easily than her husband, for he found writing English a laborious process. By working, she—echoing the role of the eastern European rebbetzin—also made it possible for him to focus on what they both considered to be his "real" work, Jewish scholarship. Despite the stress of this period, Mathilde recalled that "what with the friendly and most interesting circle around us, and the miracle of our first-born, Ruth, this time was probably the happiest in Schechter's life." She wrote this in reference to her husband, but Mathilde could have been speaking about herself, for this was just the kind of life she had been searching for when she first journeyed to Friedlaender's house. As Solomon's wife, Mathilde secured a place at the center not only of a rich Jewish home life but also of Jewish intellectual life.[22]

When the Schechters moved to Cambridge, money matters eased somewhat, though Mathilde again shielded her husband from the extent to which the prominent British Zionist family, the Bentwiches, sustained them. With two maids, Schechter found it easier to maintain a more formal open-house policy. She welcomed university students interested in Jewish studies for classes and Sabbath afternoon tea, an experience that had a profound impact on some of them. Charles Hoffman, who would later be ordained from the Jewish Theological Seminary and whose wife, Fanny, would succeed Schechter as president of the Women's League, recalled that "it was here that Mrs. Schechter shone as the gracious hostess, cheering and heartening both the young men and sometimes also the young women who repaired there from their several colleges. It became, as it were, a second home for them, where Jewish influences, from which they were largely separated, could be retained."[23]

During this Cambridge period, Schechter continued to support her husband's scholarly endeavors. She cared for the children for long periods when Solomon traveled to Egypt, Italy, and the United States. She lived vicariously through his work, which brought her great satisfaction, for she "loved the romance of scholarship."[24] Asked to fill in for her husband at the university in his absence, she met with a scholar who had been invited to receive an honorary degree. Mathilde also devoted her efforts to critiquing and heavily editing Solomon's English writing.[25] These attributes—supporting and advocating on behalf of her husband's work; enhancing his reputation among colleagues through her social graces; serving as colleague, critic, and editor; shielding him from financial worries—exemplified the role of frau professor. Conscious of the nuances of this position, Schechter penned a novel about university wives that considered their social protocol, cultural interests, and romances. Serving as frau professor in England, Schechter honed the skills of supportive helpmate that would undergird her rebbetzin role in the United States.[26]

It was the chance to influence American Jewish religious as well as scholarly life that drew Solomon Schechter to the United States to assume the presidency of the newly reorganized Jewish Theological Seminary. Only in this country did he adopt the title "rabbi"; and in parallel fashion, it was only in the United States that Mathilde Schechter expanded her role as professor's wife to include that of rabbi's wife.[27] They kept up the tradition of their open houses, which not only provided "fitting background" for Solomon's academic interests but also functioned as a perfect setting for Mathilde's work. Just as intellectuals found themselves drawn to the Schechters in England, so too in America did the Schechter home attract members of the Seminary community. As Mathilde later described their partnership, Solomon "brought them and I kept them." Offering solace, a sympathetic ear, and, sometimes, material relief, Mathilde nourished many JTS students in her graciously appointed home. Visually, it modeled her conviction that one ought to incorporate beauty into Jewish life. Jacob Kohn, a 1907 JTS graduate, especially remembered Schechter's brass serving tray. He likened it to an altar, from which flowed not only tea but also the blessings of a "noble woman's heart and mind." In his view, Schechter had a facility "for gathering about her people not usually at home in drawing-rooms." The famed Zionist leader Henrietta Szold went further, noting that, in this gentle, warm milieu, "so many, many of us basked and were transformed."[28]

Schechter's nurturing role did not come at the expense of her own family, and she always took great pride in her children—Ruth, Frank, and Amy. Schechter extolled the virtues of spending time at home with one's children on Sabbath and holidays, believing that this best fostered their spiritual growth. Though she assumed primary responsibility for their three children, Schechter also reveled in the way her husband lavished attention on them.[29]

Yet in New York, in addition to enhancing the mothering, helpmate, and hostessing skills she had honed in England, Schechter also broadened her sphere of interest and activity. Her children no longer babies, Schechter initially plunged actively into charitable work for such organizations as Crippled Children, Young Women's Hebrew Association (YWHA), and the Jewish Women's Council. More important, as a result of Solomon's new position, Mathilde now had the opportunity to complement her husband's work by having her own impact on American Jewish academic and religious life. She still cared deeply about Jewish scholarship, and Alexander Marx went so far as to attribute to her his joining the Jewish Theological Seminary faculty. He claims that she advised Solomon to look Marx up when he went to Europe to recruit faculty.[30]

As a scholar's wife, Schechter had been a "follower and disciple," but in the United States, when Solomon Schechter broadened his scope to concern himself with American Judaism, Mathilde became his equal companion. In Szold's words, "together they led the troops."[31] The blossoming of this more collaborative model was especially gratifying to Mathilde. As she commented:

> One beautiful thing New York has done for Schechter and me, he has more need of me than ever and we can work together in many ways. You see in his scholarly work I remained with my greatest effort but an intelligent outsider. But in his communal work, in his religious endeavors I can be useful to him in many ways. We seem more married than ever, and all my dormant feelings come out. He feels it and is very sweet in his recognition. I am sure we are happier than we were before.[32]

Undertaking vital projects proved satisfying to Mathilde, but not as significant as the need to feel valued by her husband for that work. Mathilde basked in the glow of Solomon's admiration, and secure in that knowledge, she began to blossom as a leader in her own right.

Mathilde expanded her efforts to enrich American Judaism beyond her parlor and into the public sphere. First, she organized the first Seminary sukkah (the ritual booth where Jews eat meals, and sometimes sleep, during the Festival of Tabernacles), enlisting students to help build and decorate it. Second, eager to educate Jewish girls, Schechter worked with the Columbia Religious and Industrial School for Jewish Girls on the Lower East Side, a school that offered both vocational and Jewish subjects. She taught classes and also served as head of religious studies.[33] Finally, coupling her love of music with her desire to strengthen Jewish observance, Schechter turned her attention to congregational singing. In 1905, she organized a Society for Ancient Hebrew Melodies, a choral group that sang melodies harmonized for four voices, and taught free of charge. Schechter's interest culminated in the 1910 publication of *Kol Rinah: Hebrew Hymnal for School and Home,* which she edited with her friend, attorney, and composer, Lewis Isaacs. The publication presented "traditional melodies of the synagogue and the Jewish Home adapted to the needs of young Israel" in order to "further the spread of congregational singing and to increase the interest of the worshipers."[34]

Another focus of Schechter's energies was Hadassah, the Women's Zionist Organization. Schechter first joined Henrietta Szold in the Daughters of Zion study group that proved instrumental to Szold's founding of Hadassah. The two women shared similar interests and concerns and greatly respected each other's work. Schechter's signature graced the invitation to the initial planning meeting. Once Hadassah got off the ground, Schechter served on its first board.[35]

Through her open houses, public speaking, teaching, organizational work, sukkah decorating, and editing, Schechter found many diverse venues to influence American Judaism. But her independent leadership role blossomed most fully after her husband's death in 1915. At that time, the Jewish Theological Seminary invested $10,000 for Mathilde, which freed her "from all material worry." Schechter expressed deep gratitude to the Board of Directors for this arrangement and "for the respect and affection for my Beloved, that dictated your gracious act." Remaining in her home, Schechter maintained her open house tradition, entertaining individuals such as Louis Brush, a family friend and bachelor who had frequently dined in their home. Such contact is thought to have been instrumental in convincing Brush to leave a bequest to JTS for a dormitory facility. According to Hanna Marx, Schechter pleaded with Brush to provide funds for a residence hall after she learned that a gifted Seminary student had undergone minor surgery because he had been overworked and undernourished. When Brush died in 1917, he left JTS $1.4 million dollars for a dormitory, at that time reportedly the single largest gift ever made to a Jewish institution.[36]

In 1918, Schechter addressed the convention delegates of the United Synagogue of America, the lay organization founded by her husband five years earlier. Addressing the group in her husband's memory, she boldly capitalized on the moment to launch an auxiliary branch, the National Women's League of the United Synagogue (later the Women's League for Conservative Judaism). Though her role as "widow of" garnered her the initial invitation, Schechter used that opportunity to advance her own agenda. In a strategic move, she invited representatives of the other women's groups—including the Council of Jewish Women, the (Reform) Federation of Sisterhoods, Hadassah, and the YWHA—to hear her talk. Reassuring them that her organization would not encroach on their territory and asking their cooperation and assistance in initiating her new venture, Schechter shared the frustrations that impelled her to create it: "Whilst we women of conservative homes have done our full share in helping them [Jewish women's organizations] whole-heartedly, we have neglected our own work that is calling to us . . . we wish to serve the cause of Judaism."[37]

Schechter hoped her organization would galvanize the energies of Conservative Jewish women just as Simon's Federation had done for Reform. She implored women to study Jewish literature "to educate ourselves with single-hearted devotion." In so doing, Schechter appropriated for women the traditional value of studying for its own sake rather than for any specific outcome. Of course, Schechter justified this proposal with more conservative rhetoric, reminding her audience that self-education was "only the first step toward the better education of our children."[38]

In keeping with her appeal to a traditional audience, Schechter stressed the importance of observing kashrut, the dietary laws. She suggested that her new organization dedicate itself to developing a system of providing kosher food for Jewish travelers away from home. Finally, drawing on nineteenth-century views of women, she reassured her audience that launching a new organization at this time was essential: "There never was a time, when the religious and moral influence of women was more sorely needed than at the present day of war and misery and social upheaval."[39]

Four months later, Schechter delivered an address outlining the aims and ideals of her new organization. Admitting the growing threats from Christian Science and Christianity as a whole, she pledged that Women's League would aim to save the souls of Jewish women—and through them the souls of their children—by impressing upon them "the beauty and wondrous depth of our religious and literary treasures." Aware that she had no quick remedies, she implored Jewish women to undertake the painstaking task of creating Jewish homes "again." In other words, she believed that Jewish women ought reclaim their historic role as Jewish homemakers, a duty she feared was neglected in the rush toward Americanization.[40]

Determined to promote Jewish ritual, Schechter, like Simon, articulated her concerns about the rampant laxity in Jewish observance. As early as 1905, she had unsuccessfully implored the Council of Jewish Women to form a special religious league open to members who pledged to observe the Sabbath.[41] Now, she sought to make Jewish observance the linchpin of Women's League: "Religious observances are the song of our soul's communion with God. . . . Like wasteful children, we throw away a dear father's inheritance . . . instead, we should get at their meaning . . . we could thus revive and restore a whole treasure-house."[42]

Schechter realized her dedication both to Jewish observance and to students through her Students' House project. She first approached the JTS Board of Directors with the idea, but when informed that they could not take on the responsibility, she made this one of Women's League's first projects. Open to all students in the New York area, the Jewish Students' House was located on 117th Street and Morningside Drive. Initially administered in conjunction with the Jewish Welfare Board for the Students' Army Training Corps, the facility underwent renovation in 1918. Within a year, fourteen students were living there, and many other students joined them for kosher food known "for its wholesomeness and goodness." Cultivating a warm atmosphere by filling lounges with victrolas and pianos, including a "breezy reading room and library" and an "airy" dining room, this house was designed to counter homesickness and "feelings of estrangement." Friday night dinners drew residents together for an unhurried, festive meal. Jewish college groups held meetings there, and the Seminary student organization sponsored lectures. The House was soon replicated at other colleges, including the University of Pennsylvania.[43]

Struck by serious illness in 1919, Schechter lived a curtailed life until her death in 1924. Her funeral took place at the Jewish Theological Seminary, and contemporary reporters remarked on the significance of that honor. According to the *New York Times,* only the most learned and distinguished members of a community merit a synagogue funeral. Schechter was the first woman at JTS "thought worthy of the distinction," and the subheading went so far as to claim that "She Is the First Woman to Be Buried from a Synagogue." Eulogized by many, Schechter was praised for supplementing her husband's great work and serving as his devoted companion. Elias Solomon summed up her character with reference to her husband by offering the high praise that "she was worthy of the illustrious husband whom she cherished and admired so greatly." One account highlighted her independent qualities, noting that "besides" being the wife of an illustrious man, Schechter "was herself a brilliant scholar, a highly cultured woman, and one beloved by all who knew her." Yet by headlining the article "Widow of Famous Scholar Is Dead," the newspaper exposed the gendered assumptions underlying even such effusive praise.[44]

Through Women's League, Schechter succeeded in achieving many of her goals. When she left office in 1919, she could report fifty-seven affiliated sisterhoods with a membership of more than 6,000. She had initiated several projects designed to revive home observances, including the preparation of Sabbath *kiddush* (blessing) cards and a collection of inspirational legends based on Louis Ginzberg's *Legends of the Jews,* titled *Friday Night Stories.*[45] Several pamphlets on Jewish life had already appeared, including *Shabuoth* by Charles I. Hoffman and Elias L. Solomon, *Passover* by Mordecai M. Kaplan, and *The Student's House*; a number of additional booklets were in the planning stages. Most important, the organization stood on firm ground, with young leadership working to further its goals. For decades afterward, Women's League leaders invoked Schechter's memory as they recalled the architect of the vision that continued to guide them. Fittingly, the first JTS residence hall built outside the 122nd Street campus bears her name. Dedicated in 1974, the Mathilde Schechter Residence Hall opened after decades-long fundraising efforts on the part of Women's League members.[46]

Schechter also advanced the role of rabbi's wife, an unexpected accomplishment since her husband never led a congregation. But in combining the roles of frau professor, rebbetzin, and contemporary clubwoman, Schechter modeled a new leadership role for American Jewish women married to rabbis. As a professor's wife, Schechter initially established herself as a supportive helpmate who advanced her husband's career while furthering her own intellectual growth. When Solomon took on the presidency of JTS and they both turned their focus to furthering religious life as well as scholarship, she also assumed many of the characteristics of both a congregational and a yeshiva rabbi's wife. Mathilde kept a traditional Jewish home, tended to the needs of Seminary students, promoted Jewish social and intellectual exchanges through her open houses, raised funds for needy students, and furthered Jewish observances in the areas of Jewish music and holidays. This she did to promote her husband's career as well as her own. Some colleagues especially valued the consciously behind-the-scenes nature of her stance. As Fanny Minkin explained: "It was due to an abundance of modesty, of reverence and admiration for the master of her home and heart, that made her often keep herself in the background."[47]

Yet Mathilde did more than this. Particularly after Solomon's death, she emerged as a public leader by channeling her efforts into organizational work through Women's League. In this way, Schechter combined her previous roles with that of American middle-class clubwoman. Simon already stood out as a successful model of this type of rabbi's wife. By interpreting this public stance as directly related to her role as creator of a nurturing Jewish home for her scholar-rabbi husband and for JTS, Schechter further expanded its definition.

It was precisely this combination of success as both private, home-based role model and public leader that made Schechter especially influential. Upholding prevailing gender assumptions about women's proper roles, Schechter provoked neither anxiety nor opposition among either men or women. On the contrary, she inspired many women to pattern their lives after hers, both as rabbis' wives and as Women's League leaders.

Rebecca Goldstein

Rebecca (Betty) Fischel Goldstein, the wife of Herbert S. Goldstein, rabbi of the Institutional Synagogue in New York City in the interwar period, extended the role of rabbi's wife still further. Working with her husband to forge a distinct path for American Orthodoxy, she founded the Women's Branch of the Union of Orthodox Jewish Congregations in 1923.

Nineteen years younger than Simon and thirty-four years younger than Schechter, Rebecca Goldstein came of age in the twentieth century. American born, Goldstein obtained a rich Jewish upbringing and educa-

Rebecca Goldstein. Courtesy of Aaron I. Reichel.

tion thanks to the efforts of her father, communal leader and philanthropist Harry Fischel. He insisted on home-based schooling for his
daughters and then sent all four to college. Goldstein graduated from
Barnard College in 1912. In that same year, she also earned a teacher's
diploma from the Jewish Theological Seminary's Teachers Institute, having enrolled in its first class. Founded in 1909, the Teachers Institute
was dedicated to meeting the needs of both men and women desirous
of training for careers as Jewish educators. Religious education had
emerged in the twentieth century as a distinctive field among Christians,
and in the early decades of the century, women were involved in equal
numbers with men. As Jewish education became similarly professional-
ized, Jewish women were increasingly drawn to the field. The Teachers

Institute quickly developed a reputation as the premier institution for advanced Jewish education for women.[48]

When Herbert and Rebecca began courting, they spent time together in the JTS library, "he on his sermons, and I writing up texts from books on sermons. I love to work for and with Herbert. That unity of interest is one of the strongest bonds between us." Contemporaries recall that Herbert had initially planned to become an attorney, and they credit Rebecca with inspiring him to change professions. While the extent of her role in this decision remains unclear, it accurately reflects both her desire to assume the role of rabbi's wife and her unwavering dedication to his rabbinate. When she married Herbert in 1915, a year after his ordination from JTS, Rebecca consciously committed herself to the rabbinate as a two-person career.[49]

To Rebecca, marrying a rabbi signified that she would work in partnership with a "kindred spirit" who shared her passion to strengthen Jewish knowledge and observance in America. As soon as they became engaged, Herbert and Rebecca began to work as a team. To spread Jewish knowledge, they translated Moses Haym Luzzatto's *Praise for Righteousness* as a wedding souvenir.[50] Rebecca also joined Herbert on his pastoral rounds. Her diary entries comment that "we are enjoying it immensely." Finally, Rebecca embraced the homemaking aspects of the role. She recalled that when Henry Pereira Mendes delivered the sermon at their 1915 wedding, he told her to make her home a home for the whole congregation. She remembered being delighted, since this was "just as I always intended to do." While there is no evidence that the Goldsteins had direct contact with the Schechters, they studied at JTS during the Schechter years. Whether consciously or not, the life to which the Goldsteins aspired built upon that which the Schechters modeled.[51]

Though a graduate of JTS, Herbert Goldstein devoted his efforts to strengthening American Orthodoxy. He pioneered an expansive view of the Orthodox synagogue similar to that espoused by maverick Reform and Conservative rabbis of the time. With this vision of a synagogue filled with social, recreational, educational, and religious activities, Herbert assumed the position as rabbi of Harlem's Institutional Synagogue in 1917. According to the historian Jeffrey Gurock, this synagogue "constituted the most consciously articulated attempt to approximate within the Orthodox synagogue the activities available in other Americanizing social settings."[52]

Rebecca Goldstein shared her husband's creative views of synagogue life, and she worked with him to realize it. They invited young people for Sabbath dinner on Friday night, and she held Saturday afternoon "at homes"—similar to Schechter's "open houses"—even when other synagogue obligations necessitated her husband's absence from them. In their first year, Goldstein addressed envelopes to prospective congregants in Harlem in an effort to interest them in the synagogue. Over the years, she attended and hosted meetings, brainstormed strategy, invited potential supporters for dinner, prepared for publication a fundraising theater-party brochure, worked at bazaar and rummage sales, and founded the Daughters of the Institutional Synagogue. To lend support to a fundraising campaign, she once dressed up in a green "Dollar Drive" costume adorned with dollar bills. During this period, she also reared their four children. In all of these activities, she saw herself working in partnership with her husband to further their joint goal of strengthening American Jewish life.[53]

Goldstein eventually expanded her involvement into other Jewish organizations and charities. But it is as founder and first president of the Women's Branch from 1923 to 1936 (when she became honorary president) that she left her lasting mark. Like Schechter and Simon, Goldstein used her organization as a vehicle to promote Jewish knowledge and observance for women and children. Similar in purpose and scope to Women's League, the Women's Branch signified the emergence of a distinctly Orthodox female leadership at a time when no clear boundaries yet separated American Orthodoxy from Conservatism. The Orthodox Goldsteins had themselves trained at JTS, and, in the 1920s, members of both camps favored a merger between JTS and Yeshiva University. By founding the Women's Branch, Goldstein secured an anchor for the emerging infrastructure of American Orthodoxy.[54]

While Simon called on Reform to institute compulsory "domestic practices of religion," Goldstein hoped the Women's Branch would inspire women to "re-establish the Jewish home as a sanctuary and to recreate the Jewish mother as the priestess." Even more so than Schechter, Goldstein employed traditional rhetoric—encouraging women to "*re-establish*" and "*recreate*" what had been lost, to *reclaim* their traditional role as guardians of Jewish heritage.[55]

Like her counterparts Simon and Schechter, Goldstein focused on college-age students. She founded the collegiate branch of the Union and served as vice chairman of the Women's Committee of the Yeshiva University Dormitory Fund. Interested in women's religious development,

Goldstein helped launch the Hebrew Teacher's Training School for Girls in 1928, an Orthodox alternative to the Jewish Theological Seminary's Teachers Institute. She also served as director of the old-age Home of Daughters of Jacob and the Hebrew Day Nursery.[56]

Goldstein shared Schechter's commitment to enhancing Jewish rituals through English-Hebrew publications. In addition to their wedding souvenir, the Goldsteins compiled *Avodat haShulkhan: Home Service with Translation and Transliteration*. She hoped it would "enable those who have never had the opportunity of learning Hebrew to follow the reading of the prayers, and to pray to themselves in the Holy Tongue." By making it possible for all Jews to pray, this work would bridge "the gap between the old generation and the new." In this outreach tool as well, Goldstein appropriated traditional rhetoric, hoping the work would succeed in restoring the "old time Jewish Sabbath atmosphere into the home."

Much more so than either Simon or Schechter, Goldstein sought out the role of American rabbi's wife. That she did so suggests that the basic contours of the role had already emerged by the second decade of the century. From her actions, one learns that she understood it to involve entertaining, visiting, educating, organizing, and fundraising. She also saw her role as part of a rabbinic team with husband and wife working together to strengthen American Judaism. A college-educated woman with an advanced degree in Jewish studies as well, Goldstein decided to secure an acceptable outlet for her training and energies by marrying a rabbi.

Through their accomplishments, Simon, Schechter, and Goldstein modeled a route to Jewish religious leadership for educated, motivated, leadership-oriented married women who felt called to strengthen American Judaism in the early years of the century. In the decades to follow, many women would seek that same path. In addition to the many societal influences that made such a role so attractive, one individual—Henrietta Szold (1860–1945)—towered over American Jewish women as the exemplar of female leadership. Szold was never anyone's wife, let alone a rabbi's wife, yet her life story bears examining, for it embodied both the highest aspirations and deepest fears of rabbis' wives. As will be seen below, many rebbetzins were influenced by Szold both directly and by example.

Henrietta Szold

Best known as the founder of Hadassah, the Women's Zionist Organization, Henrietta Szold was often identified—even for this independent accomplishment—in marital terminology, as the "First Lady of Zionism."[57] But her uniqueness preceded and derived from much more than her work with Hadassah or her marital status. Vastly knowledgeable in both Jewish and secular subjects, a visionary as well as an effective organizer, editor, translator, and public speaker, Szold stood virtually in a class by herself among American Jewish women of her era.

Eldest daughter of Benjamin and Sophie Szold, Henrietta received an intensive Jewish education from her rabbi father. Szold became well-versed in Hebrew, Jewish history, German, and French and taught Jewish subjects in her father's congregation, Oheb Shalom, in Baltimore. She also gained a first-rate secular education at the Western Female High School, where she, the only Jew, finished first in her class.[58] At the same time, Szold learned from her mother to distance herself from congregants lest it appear that she was currying their favor. As her sister Bertha recalled, this unfairly constrained their social contacts.[59]

After graduation, Szold taught at Miss Adam's English and French School for Girls. In the 1880s, Szold focused her educational efforts on helping immigrant Jews learn English and civics. She also served as her father's editor and translator, again a common role for the firstborn daughter of a scholar. Drawn to Zionism as a young woman, Szold joined the Isaac Bar Levinson Hebrew Literary Society and was a charter member of the Baltimore Hevras Zion in 1893.[60]

In 1888, Szold combined her secular and Jewish interests in her work for the newly formed Jewish Publication Society. With manifold talents, dedication, and learning, Szold served as the only female member of the publications committee and became the Society's first full-time editor in 1893. Though she held the title "secretary," Szold actually oversaw, edited, and/or translated most of the works the Society published during this period, including Heinrich Graetz's *History of the Jews*, Simon Dubnow's *Jewish History*, and the *American Jewish Year Book*.

When Szold sought to expand her intellectual horizons further, she felt stymied. Her Jewish knowledge surpassed that of her peers, and there were no local institutions that could challenge her academically. After her father's death in 1902, Szold and her mother moved to New

Henrietta Szold. Courtesy of Hadassah, The Women's Zionist Organization of America, Inc.

York in order for her to study at the Jewish Theological Seminary. Though there was no formal way for women to do so, Solomon Schechter granted her permission to take classes with rabbinical students as a special student. Living across the street, Szold studied for three years and quickly became part of the Seminary community. She loved the scholarly milieu of JTS and relished the collegiality of its community.[61]

Szold's prodigious talents inspired awe among students and faculty alike. One student recalled her as "the earliest Jewish woman in America to be known as a savant." Faculty appreciated her literary talents, and she offered informal lessons in English to the foreign-born professors to help ease their transition to English-language instruction and publication. Talmud professor Louis Ginzberg especially esteemed her abilities in Talmud. When Szold inquired as to the propriety of attending a class on the Babylonian Talmud tractate Kiddushin, which deals with marriage laws, he responded: "It is against my character to make any compliments, not even to a lady, but I answer you that I wish I had a class of *Talmidim* [students] like you." In addition to attending his class, Szold translated Ginzberg's lectures, letters, and articles from German into English and eventually assumed the mammoth task of organizing and translating the material that would later be published as the multivolume *Legends of the Jews*.[62]

Then a middle-aged single woman, Szold fell in love with Ginzberg, thirteen years her junior. When Ginzberg became engaged to Adele Katzenstein, Szold suffered tremendously. Shargel suggests that societal mores contributed to the intensity of Szold's devastation, for the asymmetrical gender etiquette that governed male-female interactions at the time made it virtually impossible for Szold to clarify the nature of her relationship with Ginzberg. Women remained dependent on male initiative, and older single women suffered additional indignities because of their age. But Szold also experienced an additional inequity. Members of the JTS community readily welcomed a bright, intellectually oriented woman who shared their values and ideals into their classes, religious services, and homes. Yet Szold's sense of belonging ultimately stemmed from the community's expectation that she and Ginzberg would marry. They shared her view that she had unofficially assumed the role of Ginzberg's "affianced wife." Had Szold indeed become his wife, she would have secured her place in that milieu. Instead, when her romantic dreams shattered, Szold gradually lost her intellectual home as well. Middle-class academic society in the second decade of the twentieth century could not long accommodate the unmarried Szold. She ultimately left JTS not only because of the lingering pain of a "broken heart" but also because once Ginzberg, the only single faculty member, married someone else, Szold no longer had a defined role in its community.[63]

Shortly after Ginzberg's engagement became public, Szold took an extended trip to Palestine with her mother, but she returned to confront the awkwardness of both her continued work on Ginzberg's *Legends* and her unavoidable social encounters with the newly married Ginzbergs. Ultimately, Szold relinquished her work on the *Legends* and turned her energies to Zionism, founding Hadassah in 1912.[64]

Under Szold's leadership, Hadassah became the largest Zionist group in the United States and the most successful American women's volunteer organization. With Szold's steady guidance, the organization established a visiting nurse system, a medical unit, and social services in Palestine. Szold also oversaw Youth Aliyah, an ambitious program to rescue young people from the grip of Nazism. Through word and deed, she influenced thousands of American Jewish women to devote their energies to Zionism. She also demonstrated just how much one educated, motivated, determined woman could accomplish, and, because of this, Szold embodied the best of what American Jewish women wanted to be.[65]

Educated, ambitious women who came of age in the second quarter of the twentieth century joined Hadassah hoping to emulate Szold. But most of them also dreamed of marriage. Szold—extraordinarily accomplished yet single—gave ambitious Jewish women pause, for they did not want to sacrifice marriage for a sense of achievement in their lives. Some found that marrying a rabbi gave them a way to combine their goals.

Simon, Schechter, and Goldstein modeled such a role to twentieth-century Reform, Conservative, and Orthodox Jewish women. Yet they did so as individuals, not collectively. Each was cordial to the other as president of her respective organization. For example, Goldstein sent greetings from her group to the NFTS on the occasion of their biennial convention.[66] But there is little evidence that they identified with each other in any way. Each woman focused on furthering American Jewish life through her own denominational association. Characteristics common to the three women manifest themselves in hindsight, but at the time, these women did not understand themselves to be members of a cohort of rabbis' wives or even of female religious leaders. Only in the 1920s would such a group of rabbis' wives, conscious of their responsibilities and with a distinctive sense of themselves as a group, emerge.

2

The Power behind the Throne

Fourteen years after Minna the *yeshiva bocher*'s wife appeared in fiction, Abram S. Isaacs presented American Jewish families a very different view of the rabbi's wife. Isaacs, a rabbi, scholar, and author of several books for young people, included a story about a rabbi's wife in his collection, *Under the Sabbath Lamp: Stories of Our Time for Old and Young*. Published by the Jewish Publication Society in 1919 to address the dearth of home literature for American Jews, the volume included stories "in the guise of unpretentious fiction," to direct attention "to permanent elements in our social, domestic, and religious life, which are all-powerful in shaping the character of Israel and preserving Jewish ideals." By spotlighting a rabbi's wife as one of his protagonists, Isaacs held up this role among those "permanent elements," thereby demonstrating that the rabbi's wife as a positive religious figure had entered into the consciousness of American Jews.[1]

Isaacs's rabbi's wife, Esther, is bright and studious, possessing "heart and sensibility." With her husband suffering from rheumatism, Esther offers to preach one Sabbath in his stead. The narrator understood that a rabbi's wife not only would be qualified to fill in for her husband but also would be eager to do so. "The golden moment for which she had patiently waited and for whose responsibilities she was amply prepared was now at hand." Esther explains her decision to preach with reference to her special role. "'As I am his wife and helpmate, I deemed it my duty, with his consent, to come.'" But Esther uses the occasion to champion the right of all women to preach, for "the synagogue needed women's influence for its grandest development." Disarmed by her charm, congregants find themselves unexpectedly "awed by her spirited manner and words." The story ends by both reaffirming the expected gender order and endorsing the bold path taken by the rabbi's wife. The rabbi—"man-fashion"—took credit for her success: without his rheumatism she never would have spoken from the pulpit. But he then applauded her efforts, noting their joint accomplishment: " 'We have begun a reformation!' "[2]

Esther embodies many of the qualities of the eastern European rebbetzin—a learned, wise, sensible woman who ultimately gains special admiration for her virtues because of her position. Hoping to inspire an American audience of all ages, Isaacs echoed the positives of the old-world role while utilizing the English-language title, "rabbi's wife." This fictional characterization signaled a decade in which the American rabbi's wife assumed a publicly defined leadership position. Books, lectures, and symposia began to address the role while groups of rabbis' wives banded together for common purpose. All of this signified not only that the role had come into its own by the 1920s but also that sufficient consciousness existed to merit a modicum of introspection by both rabbis and their wives.

The role of the rabbi's wife emerged after 1910, at the same time that the American rabbinate came into its own. This can be attributed in part to the synagogue's evolution from a worship-centered institution into a multipurpose facility designed to meet the social, cultural, spiritual, and educational needs of American Jews. Rabbinical seminaries enhanced their training to cultivate rabbis appropriate for such settings. Solomon Schechter transformed the JTS rabbinical school into a graduate institution. By 1930, HUC also required a Bachelor of Arts for admission to its Collegiate Department. Though Orthodox rabbinical seminaries continued to have varied requirements for the secular education of their students, there was a growing recognition that its congregations also needed well-educated American rabbis at their helm. At the same time, rabbis, at least in larger congregations, began to earn respectable salaries.[3]

Because of these developments, the rabbinate became a desirable career goal, and the number of men training for it increased. In 1924, Hebrew Union College, the Jewish Theological Seminary, and the Rabbi Isaac Elchanan Seminary at Yeshiva College enrolled 231 candidates for ordination. These graduates easily found jobs, for the number of synagogues also grew tremendously during this period—from 1,901 in 1916 to 3,118 in 1926—with most of that growth in Reform and Conservative congregations. For many reasons, then, American-trained rabbis serving the Jewish community during this period saw themselves as a privileged cohort answering the call to deepen the knowledge and commitment of American Jewry.[4]

The Role of the Rabbi's Wife

Rebekah Kohut invited discussion about the rabbi's wife role by writing about it in her 1925 memoir, *My Portion*. Her husband, Alexander Kohut, had served as rabbi of Ahavath Chesed in New York from 1885 until his death in 1894. He was also professor of Talmud and Midrash at JTS, author of the *Arukh HaShalem*,[5] and a staunch defender of traditional Judaism against Reform. But by the 1920s, Rebekah Kohut established herself as a leader in her own right.[6] Founder of the Kohut School for Girls and longtime president of the New York section of the National Council of Jewish Women, Rebekah was a noted lecturer, writer, and teacher. In 1897, she achieved national recognition when she delivered an address on "Parental Reverence, as Taught in Hebrew Homes" at the founding convention of the National Congress of Mothers, the forerunner of the National Parent Teachers Association. Hosted by First Lady Frances Cleveland, about 1,000 mothers assembled in Washington, D.C., to advocate on behalf of children.[7] Kohut's international reputation reached its pinnacle in 1923, when delegates elected her first president of the World Congress of Jewish Women. Because of Kohut's renown, *My Portion* received wide attention.[8]

Through Kohut's memoir, one learns that she fit the European prototype of a rabbi's wife, for she too was a rabbi's daughter. Her father, Albert Bettelheim, served as rabbi in congregations in Philadelphia, San Francisco, and Baltimore after emigrating from Hungary in 1867. When her brother was absent from home, Rebekah spent a great deal of time in her father's library, and, like Szold, she grew close to her father intellectually. Kohut's father also encouraged Rebekah to continue her secular education at the University of California. After an adolescent rebellion against Judaism, Kohut came to the conclusion that "my real mission in life should be as a worker in the front ranks of American Jewish womanhood."[9]

Kohut understood that marrying a rabbi would provide a direct conduit to such a life. Convinced that marriage to an "ordinary" man would thwart her goals, Kohut rejected one marriage proposal because

Rebekah Kohut. Courtesy of the American Jewish Archives, Cincinnati, Ohio.

it would have derailed her from the life she hoped for. "It was a career of service I was dreaming of, rather than a life limited to housewifely duties." When in 1887 she married the widowed Alexander Kohut, a man twenty-four years her senior, and agreed to rear his eight children, Rebekah was "imbued with the thought of spending myself in service, and in leading a life of significance."[10]

Rebekah raised Alexander's children and translated his sermons and lectures for English publication. She learned how to oversee a household of ten people—sewing, entertaining, and welcoming extended family—while managing to "find time to help him carry forward his influence." Eventually taking over Alexander's extensive correspondence,

Rebekah also helped negotiate the contract for the *Arukh HaShalem*. Conscious of her responsibilities as congregational rebbetzin, Rebekah urged her husband to permit the establishment of a synagogue sisterhood after attending several meetings of Temple Emanu-El's pioneering group. "It seemed to be the work that I could do for him, and he consented." She established a Sisterhood of Personal Service in her husband's congregation and served as its first president.[11]

Though Kohut affirmed that attaching herself to a famous rabbi and scholar made her mostly "very happy," the anguish caused by the indignities of the clergy lifestyle spill out onto the pages of her memoir as well. Rebekah keenly recalled the shame she had felt as a rabbi's daughter. She blamed the congregation for her family's poverty and shabbiness and remembered being "pressed into service to teach religious school." Congregants expected her "to appear at the temple Saturday mornings" and criticized her for attending college. They warned her father that "it was dangerous and altogether too radical to allow one of the opposite sex to imbibe the higher knowledge." As an adult, Rebekah still chafed under the glare of such censure, as she came to understand that being a rabbi's wife left her vulnerable to congregants' judgmentalism. For example, she wrote that when Alexander asked for a vacation, he got it, "though I think the congregation attributed the innovation to his American wife and looked rather unkindly upon our going." Kohut also recognized the toll that the role took on her own needs. "It was with no twinge of regret that I put aside, for the nonce, all thought of my own individuality and let myself be absorbed by the lives of my husband and children."[12]

Most difficult for Kohut to bear was the behind-the-scenes nature of the clergy wife role her husband endorsed. He expressed discomfort with her public speaking debut at a protest meeting with the Women's Health Protective Association, "for he felt that I had much to do at home, and was more or less jealous of any time I gave to others." Painfully, Kohut declined an invitation to read a paper at the 1893 Congress of Jewish Women because her husband felt he could not manage without her for a week. "I went to my room and wept. The disappointment was keen. Afterward, when I heard about the gathering of Jewish women . . . I was sorrier than ever that I had not been present." Despite these confessions, Kohut repeatedly concluded, somewhat unconvincingly, that her sacrifice for her husband was worth it.[13]

By 1925, Kohut had come to view her life as worthy of a memoir.

But she also understood that she shared such distinctiveness with a special cohort of women. Commenting on her trip abroad for the World Congress of Jewish Women, she noted the presence of "so many striking and interesting personalities" and found it especially interesting "that there were no less than eleven wives or daughters of rabbis like myself." This growing recognition of the special significance of her roles as rabbi's daughter and wife perhaps emboldened Kohut to tackle the controversial issue of the *agunah* (literally: chained wife; a woman who has not obtained a Jewish divorce and is thus not permitted to remarry). Addressing 300 of the most conservative Jewish Talmudic scholars on the injustice of the *agunah* problem, Kohut began by establishing her credentials as "a daughter and granddaughter of rabbis. I have been the wife of a rabbi and the mother of one."[14]

During this same period, Kohut participated in a symposium on the rabbi's wife that accompanied a larger two-year deliberation on the problems of the Jewish ministry. Conducted by the New York Board of Jewish Ministers, these consultations represented the growing acknowledgment among American rabbis of the special nature of their role, with its ties both to the traditional rabbinate and to the American clergy. Board president Israel Goldstein believed that the rabbinate was a calling, distinctive because of the quality of inspiration that ministers have. But he also recognized that inspiration alone provided insufficient guidance to the American rabbi struggling with contemporary congregational and communal issues. He concluded that the American rabbinate resembled a profession which, like other professions, could benefit from collegial wisdom. The symposium was designed to provide just that. Subsequently published as a book,[15] symposium papers addressed the "main problems with which the American rabbi is likely to deal," including the religious school, administrative chores, pastoral duties, and the sermon. Chapter 10 is titled "The Wife of the Rabbi." Devoting a separate symposium to this topic and including its discussions in the volume suggests that by the mid-1920s, the Board of Jewish Ministers recognized the essential role played by wives in their husbands' rabbinate.

This deliberation provides a critical window into how rebbetzins viewed their role in the 1920s. Just as these rabbis understood the rabbinate as having both historical roots and parallels with Christian ministers, so too did these wives embrace their role's dual dimension. On the one hand, in the symposium, rabbis' wives refer to themselves by the Yiddish title "rebbetzin," thereby directly tying their role to its historical antecedents. Their use of the term is not surprising, for as the makeup of American Jewry shifted from being predominantly of Central European descent to a more eastern European orientation, it began to incorporate many Yiddish terms—and the concepts that they embodied—into everyday vocabulary. The Yiddish term *rebbetzin* had been foreign to most German Jews; they simply used the term *frau de rabbiner* (rabbi's wife). Even when familiar with it, Jews of German descent would not use the title "rebbetzin," for it conjured up an old-world type they strove to extinguish.[16]

During this period, the rebbetzin became the subject of popular Yiddish songs, including "Sha, Sha di Rebbitzen Geyt" (Hush, the rebbetzin is coming), "Di Rebbetzin" (The rebbetzin), and "Di Rebbetzin Hot nit Geheysen" (The rabbi's wife had not meant or intended [that]/given her permission).[17] As nostalgia for their eastern European past grew, more and more interwar American Jews used the term to refer to American rabbis' wives, and they generally did so not with derision but with pride and affection. It became one of many ways in which a growing sentimentality about the past served to bolster Jewish identity in the present. With these positive connotations, it is not surprising that rebbetzins began to use the title themselves.

The term "rebbetzin" first appeared in the *New York Times* in a 1931 review of the *Lexicon of the Yiddish Theatre*. The reviewer described the plot of a "Jewish Hamlet" in which "the Prince is transformed into a 'yeshivah bocher' (seminary student—symbol of the traditional Jewish scholar), and the Queen into a 'rebbetzin.'" While explaining *yeshivah bocher* in parentheses, the author left the term *rebbetzin* untranslated. He evidently assumed that his readers understood its meaning.[18]

On the other hand, though rabbis' wives may have called themselves and were called by others "rebbetzins," they opted to use the English "rabbi's wife" rather than the Yiddish "rebbetzin" in the titles of their articles, talks, and pamphlets. Just as the board of rabbis titled its volume *Problems of the Jewish Ministry* rather than "Problems of the Rabbinate," rebbetzins too often opted for an appellation that paralleled that of their Christian counterparts.[19] Moreover, rabbis' wives saw themselves filling a role that not only evoked the eastern European one but also paralleled that of the American minister's wife. In that vein, the Kohuts attended church services every Sunday evening to hear various ministers preach. Similarly, James Luby, in his *New York Times* review of *My Portion,* admitted with surprise that it read as a very American memoir and not as the parochially Jewish one he had expected. "The story might be that of the daughter and wife of clergymen of any denomination and of, say, New England or Southern origin. . . . the ideals of piety and duty in which the religious impulse asserted itself might be those of any woman of any race or creed who possessed a fine mind and keen sensibilities."[20]

Rebekah Kohut delivered the keynote address at the rabbi's wife symposium. In her address much more so than in *My Portion,* Kohut articulated the duties, responsibilities, and drawbacks of the rabbi's wife role and portrayed its evolution as directly related to the changing role of the rabbi in twentieth-century America. In her view, as the rabbi's position became more financially and politically secure, the spiritual burdens of the job increased. To succeed, a rabbi needed almost superhuman qualities, and he needed a wife who possessed them as well. Because of this, in Kohut's view, a rabbi's ability to choose a "good" wife took precedence over his expertise as a sermon writer.[21]

Kohut bluntly warned women not to entertain false expectations about the role: Don't marry a rabbi for status, glory, or financial security, for one can gain all of this with less pain by marrying a lawyer or businessperson. When married to a rabbi, one must also sacrifice one's privacy. Moreover, the rebbetzin role thrusts women into a no-win situation: if the rabbi's wife "is too forceful she might incur the displeasure of some members of the congregation, if she is too reticent and timid, she might be misunderstood and judged as indifferent. There is no way out of it; whether aloof or in the world, she comes in for public conjecture and appraisal."[22]

However, a woman drawn to lead an active life and prepared to "hide her own ability behind the personality of her husband or to come out openly and undertake work which will keep her continually under public scrutiny" ought to marry a rabbi and "live life as a high duty." Echoing the refrain in her memoir that the rabbi's wife must play a subservient role, Kohut wrote that the rabbi's wife ought to be "consecrated to her husband's calling so that she can and will endeavor to make him happy in his career of self-sacrifice and consecration. The Rabbi's wife, though unheard and unsung, will have played a tremendous part in this immortality, if she will be alive to the mission of her husband."[23]

Kohut outlined three major components of the role: First, rabbis' wives must create an exemplary home characterized not by elegance but rather by "organization, cleanliness, simplicity and culture." Second, rabbis' wives must model straightforwardness, modesty, and praiseworthy motherhood. They should reflect a "deeply moral and religious home influence," rearing exemplary children so that rabbis' families will "truly represent all those desirabilities which the Rabbi advocates week after week from his pulpit." Finally, rabbis' wives ought to involve themselves in the life of the congregation through attendance at services and direct social contact with its members. Rabbi's wives who are college educated, with executive, leadership, or musical abilities, ought to utilize their special skills in the congregation. But just as they ought to take a back seat to their husbands, so too should they serve in an advisory capacity in the synagogue—whether in the choir, the religious school, or the Sisterhood—by taking "second place" behind qualified lay women. Kohut gave this latter advice notwithstanding the fact that she had served as first president of the Sisterhood in her husband's congregation. Presumably, she felt that at that time no qualified laywomen could take on the job.[24]

Kohut then took her explication one step further. She had previously described the rebbetzin role as a desirable one for a well-trained, high-minded woman, but here Kohut advised *every* rabbi's wife to serve in this capacity. Recognizing that all rabbis' wives will automatically gain status from the position, she urged them to earn it. "If she has had no special training for any particular phase of communal service, whether it be social, educational or religious, she should perfect herself so that she can honestly command her rightful place."[25]

Sara Hyamson, who called Kohut "the acknowledged *Doyenne* among English speaking Rebbitzens," served as one of two respondents at the symposium.[26] Tamar de Sola Pool served as the second respondent, and referred to Kohut as "the dean and the noblest exponent in the profession of ministerial wifehood."[27] A much younger rebbetzin, Pool presaged a different view of the role—one that she embodied in the decades ahead, as we will see below in chapter 3.

Hyamson's response[28] expanded on the specific duties of the rebbetzin. Hyamson first established her credentials by revealing that she had been a rabbi's wife for thirty-three years and, like Kohut, was a rabbi's daughter. Particularly intent on establishing the uniqueness of the role, she echoed Kohut's view that, unlike any other wife, the rabbi's wife cannot "arrange her life to suit herself"; her life is lived in the "hurly-burly of congregational activity and community service." In Hyamson's view, the first and paramount duty of the rabbi's wife—before all the functions described by Kohut—involved caring for the rabbi. Though she insisted that rabbi's wives functioned very differently from other men's wives, her elaboration of what this entailed actually paralleled responsibilities common to other professionals' wives: ensuring that one's husband not be overworked or needlessly interrupted; helping him discover his latent, special talents; saving him from diffidence, disappointment, and despondency; and serving as his private censor and critic.

Hyamson then enumerated more specialized tasks that rabbis' wives "are permitted and are practically expected to carry out": visiting congregants, making congregants feel comfortable, serving as friend and confidant to female congregants, encouraging charity, explaining laws of family purity to young women, and preserving peace in the congregation. In her estimation, the rabbi's wife was the "most reliable worker the congregation has." In small towns, Hyamson explained, the rabbi's wife would also commonly teach in the religious school, "particularly if she has special qualifications for such work, and if the congregation is not blessed with too much wealth." This last statement suggests that by the 1920s, congregations presumed their rebbetzin's gratis involvement.

Hyamson believed that as women, rabbis' wives could be even more effective than their husbands in certain areas. For example, preserving the peace required tact and patience, and a rabbi's wife could "often do more in this direction than the rabbi himself." Similarly, women excelled at organizational work, for they could attend to details better than men. Finally, she acknowledged that a rabbi's wife has "greater power than she is conscious of in forming the character and strengtheing [*sic*] the faith of the daughters of Israel." But just as the force of the role stemmed in part from then-current gender assumptions about women's superiority, so too did its limitations. Like Kohut, Hyamson warned rabbis' wives never to forget the derivative nature of the role. A rabbi's wife may "be the power behind the throne, but she must be *behind* the throne and not *apparent.*"

By speaking at the symposium, Hyamson established herself as a public religious leader with a specific set of responsibilities. Perhaps this empowered her a year later to speak authoritatively concerning a delicate issue about which she felt passionately, just as Kohut did with *agunot*. Addressing the Women's Branch of the Union of Orthodox Jew-

ish Congregations, Hyamson challenged the group to confront the laxity in adherence to Jewish marital purity rituals. Since she believed that
the decline stemmed in part from the poor condition of the ritual baths,
she castigated (presumably male) Jewish leaders for focusing on religious education while disregarding the baths.[29]

This depiction of the rabbi's wife as professional takes on special significance in light of renewed interest in the question of women rabbis.
As Pamela Nadell has shown, several women unsuccessfully sought ordination during this period, and the issue, dormant for a generation,
again became the subject of discussion among rabbis. Addressing the
question of the "woman's position in Israel," David Aronson, a 1919
JTS graduate who served as rabbi of Beth El Synagogue in Minneapolis,
Minnesota, from 1924 to 1959, endorsed the concept of a "woman-
rabbi." Yet Aronson admitted that "practically, however, a woman who
wants to live a normal life, will find too many physical difficulties to
prevent her from assuming such an office." Perhaps the role of rabbi's
wife gained enhanced stature at the moment when women rabbis again
became the subject of debate, for it offered a "practical" alternative for
women. Those drawn to the rabbinate who also wanted to marry and
have children—what Aronson called a "normal life"—could have an
acceptable career of service as rebbetzins.[30]

Aronson himself married such a woman. Frequently mentioned as
someone who inspired younger women to take on the rabbi's wife
role,[31] Bertha Friedman Aronson was born in the Ukraine in 1906 and
came to the United States at the age of seven. She graduated from the
University of Minnesota at the age of eighteen and taught high school
French, Spanish, and English in rural Minnesota. She met David in
Duluth, where he was serving as rabbi, and they married in 1927. At
Beth El, Bertha oversaw the religious school, conducted youth activities,
and served as president of the women's group.[32] She later became involved on the national level, serving as one of Women's League's seven
vice presidents in 1950. In that year, when the convention was held in
Minneapolis, Aronson played a quasi-rabbinic role, ensuring kosher
food for the convention by negotiating with the local hotel to purchase
new dishes and ritually wash the silver.[33]

This conscious assumption of the rabbi's wife role also emerges in
Esther Bengis's 1935 memoir, *I Am a Rabbi's Wife.* Like Mathilde Schechter's memoir, Bengis's account is mostly about her husband.[34] A traditional rabbi from a rabbinical family who came to the United States at

the age of twelve, Harry Bengis became seriously ill and blinded as a young man. After serving several congregations, including one in Batavia, New York, he took early retirement.[35] In recounting her husband's career, Esther revealed a great deal about her own.

Bengis characterized her role as gatekeeper, cheerleader, and critic. The Bengises had no children, and together they devoted their full attention to the congregation. They paid hospital and condolence visits. Esther remembered sitting with relatives of dying patients and comforting newly orphaned children. She found this to be enormously time-consuming, for she paid at least one of these visits every day. Corroborating her sense of her special role, Bengis recalled that the Mother Superior of the hospital would call to inform her of the arrival of a new Jewish patient. The Bengises also tried to pay a social visit to every congregant. Bengis recognized that not all rabbis and their wives did this unless there was a special occasion, but "we wanted to keep in touch with our members, and decided on the other course." In later years, Bengis tried to fill this need by hosting an open house at her home at least once a year. She regularly entertained visiting dignitaries, gave charity to needy visitors, and helped her husband conduct and host weddings in their home. Because of what he considered to be her vital assistance, Harry jokingly referred to Esther as his "Shames" [sexton or assistant].

Like Kohut and Hyamson, Bengis understood the supportive, behind-the-scenes nature of the role. She recalled speaking from the pulpit only once—for Hadassah—and commented that "the rabbi used to say jokingly that while he does the speaking in public, I do it at home." Bengis also believed she had chosen this life of "service and sacrifice," and this consciousness increased her satisfaction with it. But her memoir also aches with the reality of its drawbacks. No matter how talented the rebbetzin, her fortunes remained tied to her husband's. This realization weighed down every page of Bengis's book, since her husband's early retirement due to illness effectively ended *her* career as well.

The public articulation of the rabbi's wife role was paralleled in Protestant denominations. Between 1898 and 1928, very few books appeared on the role of minister's wife. Then in 1928, the publication of Gustine Weaver's *The Minister's Wife* heralded a flood of such manuals. Weaver's advice echoes the themes sounded by Kohut, Hyamson, and Bengis. Clergy wives ought to serve as "the power behind the pulpit, the heart of the congregation, the madonna of everybody's children, the refuge of the homeless, the comforter of the broken-hearted, the counsellor of young girls."[36]

As we will see, American rabbis' wives, conscious of their specialized role, sought specific settings for their work. Many were active in their local Hadassah and Sisterhood chapters, with some rebbetzins also extending their involvement to the regional and national levels. Some venues, such as Women's League, NFTS, and *Outlook* magazine, were denominationally based. But especially in the case of Conservative and Orthodox Judaism, denominational boundaries remained fluid. For example, Deborah Melamed's *The Three Pillars,* discussed below, reads as a primer for traditional Jewish observance. Covering such topics as family purity laws and minor fast days, the book is virtually impossible to categorize as "Conservative" rather than "Orthodox," except for its sponsorship by National Women's League.[37] Whatever the venue, rebbetzins found numerous ways to promote their ideas.

Schechter's Legacy

Some rabbis' wives continued along the paths blazed by the pioneers. Mathilde Schechter, especially, influenced future leaders at both JTS and Women's League. For example, Adele Katzenstein Ginzberg, wife of JTS professor Louis Ginzberg, took over Schechter's role at JTS. Adele was awed by Schechter from her first days in the United States. Arriving in 1909 as a newlywed, Adele experienced a difficult adjustment, for she knew no English, did not understand her husband's work, and felt judged for usurping the rightful place of Henrietta Szold. She recalled that Mathilde Schechter, especially, behaved "like a mother to me . . . and through her shining example, I learned a great deal." After both Schechters died, the Ginzbergs became known as "Mr. and Mrs. Seminary."[38] Adele hosted open houses on Sabbath and holidays and invited each member of the Seminary's senior rabbinical school class for Sabbath lunch. Inheriting the Seminary sukkah project from Schechter, Adele for the next several decades raised funds, shopped, and supervised its decoration with fresh fruits, vegetables, and greenery. In her day, the sukkah developed a reputation throughout New York City for its beauty. Louis Finkelstein, as president of the Seminary, annually expressed his gratitude to Ginzberg for her leadership role in decorating

Adele Ginzberg. Courtesy of the Women's League for Conservative Judaism.

the sukkah so magnificently, noting that seeing it so adorned was "among the high points of my life during the whole year." In tribute to her role in heading the sukkah decorating project for so many years, Women's League named it in her memory. To honor the memory of her mentor, Ginzberg also worked aggressively to realize the Mathilde Schechter Residence Hall.[39]

Ginzberg also became closely associated with Women's League. She wrote a monthly column for the League's magazine, *Outlook*, through which she kept members abreast of developments in the larger Jewish organizational world. She was also instrumental in initiating the Girl

Scout project in 1946 that led to the establishment of the Menorah Award for Jewish Girl Scouts.[40]

After Louis's death in 1953, Adele, or "Mama G.," as she was affectionately known, lived for nearly thirty more years. She continued to invite students to her home for Sabbath meals until shortly before her death. Mama G. also gained increasing recognition, for the combination of her vivacious personality and her status as widow of one of the century's greatest scholars made her a formidable leader. In acknowledgment of her talents and influence—beyond rearing her own two children, Sophie and Eli—Ginzberg was honored as New York State Mother of the Year in 1966. Moving beyond this gendered role, Ginzberg also lent support to JTS women fighting for equal rights for women in Conservative Judaism. In 1975, when the JTS synagogue first permitted Seminary women to carry the Torah on Simhat Torah (the "Rejoicing of the Torah" holiday), the community honored Ginzberg by handing her a Torah. Ginzberg was also inducted into the Seminary's Honorary Society of Fellows, and the Women's League's Mathilde Schechter Award was conferred on her posthumously.[41]

Mathilde Schechter also drew rabbis' wives into leadership roles directly through Women's League. Four out of the five vice presidents of Women's League at its founding were rebbetzins: Fanny Hoffman, Augusta Kohn, Rosalie Mendes, and Mignon Rubenovitz.[42] Surely, Schechter included these women because of their leadership potential. But their positions as rabbis' wives influenced her selection as well. According to Fanny Minkin, who served as secretary of Women's League for several decades from its inception, "I was included because of Rabbi Minkin." (Note the formal way she refers to her husband, a common practice that highlighted his title, and, by extension, her position as well.) As Fanny explained, those invited to join were "connected, active members in Sisterhoods, Rabbis' wives, members in the Jewish community who were known." Schechter cultivated this special cohort of rabbis' wives, enlisting them to serve American Jewry through Women's League.[43]

Schechter handpicked one of these women, Fanny Hoffman, to succeed her as president of Women's League. The two had met years earlier in England, for Charles had moved his family there in order to study with Solomon Schechter. The Hoffmans followed the Schechters back to America, and Charles was ordained in 1904. Fanny had exhibited leadership potential even before her marriage. She had helped found and then served as first president of the Philadelphia branch of the National

Council of Jewish Women. She also served as first principal of the Sunday School of Mikveh Israel Congregation in Philadelphia. In 1885, Hoffman established the Young Women's Union as a branch of the Hebrew Education Society, with the goal of creating a free kindergarten for the poor. Hoffman became one of the first Jewish female kindergarten teachers in the United States.[44]

After his ordination, Charles served as rabbi of Congregation Oheb Shalom in Newark from 1906 to 1940 and editor of the *United Synagogue Recorder* from 1921 until it ceased publication in 1929. Charles's choice of the rabbinate benefited Fanny as well, for it gave her a legitimate platform from which to resume the Jewish communal leadership role she had cultivated before her marriage. A colleague explained that Fanny felt that for her, too, "the 'call' had come, and [she] stood by him like a true woman of worth." Fanny paralleled Charles's organizational work in United Synagogue with her work in Women's League. President from 1919 to 1928, she solidified and expanded Mathilde's pioneering work. Gently persuasive, Hoffman complimented women on each step that they took toward increased Jewish learning. For example, like Carrie Simon, she praised those women who spent their leisure time at summer or winter resorts engaged in community service or Bible study rather than "in a recital of one's physical ailments." She added Women's League's endorsement to "the study of those subjects which lead to a finer development of Jewish womanhood in religious life in the home, in the improvement of social standards, in the broadening of the interests and participation in communal activity." She hoped for more intensive Sabbath observance by members through "regular attendance at the synagogue services, and abstaining from shopping and secular pursuits."[45]

Like Schechter, Hoffman tempered the impact of her independent accomplishments by adhering to the model of supportive spouse. One colleague noted that Hoffman worked with her husband "hand in hand . . . joining her efforts with his, and in her charming, modest manner, help[ing] to bring Judaism closer to the Jewish women." Another colleague recalled that Hoffman retained this sensibility in widowhood as well, for she "so completely shared the life and ideals of her pious husband that his presence never left her but remained ever near, even after God had called him from earth."[46] Using conventional phrases such as "ideal Jewish wife" or "modest manner," these descriptions highlight the extent to which Hoffman, like Schechter, succeeded in portraying herself as one who worked within traditional gender boundaries to effect change.

Another woman in Schechter's inner Women's League circle was Fanny Minkin. A rabbi's daughter, she attributed her fine Jewish education to the influence first of her father and then of her husband, describing herself as a "Jewish sandwich." As the filling between the two men, she absorbed Jewish learning from their bread.[47]

Minkin's path to leadership provides an important reminder of the difficult choices women faced at the time when they chose to marry. Drawn to study law by the Talmudic dialogue heard in her home, Fanny graduated from Brooklyn Law School in 1910. Shortly thereafter, she met and married Jacob Minkin, who had been ordained that same year from the Jewish Theological Seminary. Despite her degree, Fanny never practiced law. In this regard, she typified the behavior of other married women lawyers. An increasing number of women trained for the law during this period, and approximately one quarter of them married. But many chose not to practice after marriage, and of those who worked, most helped out lawyer husbands in behind-the-scenes roles, such as managing the office and preparing basic documents.[48] For Minkin, marriage to a rabbi posed additional obstacles to her legal career. Not only was Jacob not a lawyer, he served as rabbi, and Fanny, too, saw the role of rabbi's wife as a job of its own, in addition to the task of running a household. As she explained, "I had to consider being a full time Rabbi's wife. A career would have really interfered and especially since we went to Canada to serve in a Congregation there," where her law degree was not accepted. Minkin later recalled that she enjoyed the "love and attention" that she got as a rabbi's wife and the opportunities it provided for her to become involved in Jewish communal life. She chose to utilize her legal skills in her volunteer work, and one Women's League colleague recalled that "her diction and the reasonableness of what she said made one feel that you were in the presence of a very good lawyer."[49]

After serving in Hamilton, Ontario, for seven years, Jacob Minkin became rabbi of Temple Beth El in Rochester, New York, in 1919. During their years in Rochester, both Minkins played a pivotal role in establishing Conservative Judaism in upstate New York. Fanny Minkin helped organize the New York State Branch of Women's League. She served as president for four years, traveling widely to speak to area Sisterhoods.[50]

Minkin's involvement in National Women's League deepened in the 1930s. She and her husband moved back to New York City, when Jacob assumed the position of part-time chaplain at Fordham Hospital. At that point, she became a regular contributor to *Outlook* on a wide variety of topics. In addition to her ongoing role as secretary, Minkin also worked on the national conventions, serving as co-chair in 1941. When Jacob left the congregational rabbinate for the chaplaincy to gain more time for scholarship, Fanny forfeited her rebbetzin role. But Jacob's career decision also situated Fanny closer to the leadership of Women's League. This, coupled with the fact that the Minkins had no children of their own, increased the importance of Women's League for Fanny. In her view, it served as "one of the greatest forces of my life," providing an outlet to gain "recognition beyond my merit."[51] The impact of Jacob's career on Fanny illustrates one of the important ways in which rebbetzins lived contingent lives. Not only did women play a role secondary to that of their husbands, but they also necessarily depended on them for career venues. Just as Bengis portrayed in her memoir, a rebbetzin's opportunities hinged, in part, on the ups and downs of her husband's career trajectory.

Deborah Melamed, though not one of the original Women's League officers, also owed her involvement to Schechter. The wife of Raphael Melamed, a 1909 graduate of the Jewish Theological Seminary, Melamed wrote *The Three Pillars: Life, Practice and Thought for the Jewish Woman,* which she dedicated to Schechter's memory. Highly educated, Deborah earned a Bachelor of Arts from Hunter College and continued her studies in education, psychology, and English literature at Columbia University until she married. Melamed's Jewish education was equally rich: she studied in the first class of the Teachers Institute, and after moving to Philadelphia upon her marriage in 1915, she continued her education at Dropsie College as a fellow in Semitic languages (1915–17). When Raphael took a position as rabbi of B'nai Israel Congregation in Elizabeth, New Jersey, in 1923, Deborah began her lifelong work with the public schools. One of the few rebbetzins of her era to maintain a separate career while married, Melamed eventually became supervisor of foreign languages in the Elizabeth school district, a position she held until her death in 1954.[52]

The mother of two children, Melamed helped found the Elizabeth chapter of Hadassah. She also played an active role in National Women's League, serving as vice president and chairman of the education committee for many years. Using her skills as a writer, lecturer, and speaker, Melamed sought to motivate modern women to increase their involvement in Jewish life. She argued that the function of Jewish women must move beyond sewing "the tallith bag which the wandering Jew has carried through the ages." Women must be co-managers with men of the Jewish spirit. Melamed's three specific suggestions for how to achieve this goal retained Schechter's basic assumption of a special woman's sphere in their emphasis on educating children and enticing husbands to intensify their Jewish involvement. But Melamed's mission surpassed Schechter's: First, she argued that synagogue schools ought to be given over completely to the Sisterhoods, for these women would work with the rabbi to strengthen the school and ensure that it be complemented by the work of the home. Second, Melamed implored women to fill the pews by attending synagogue themselves and prodding men to join them. She also encouraged women to learn Hebrew in order to more fully participate in congregational singing. Finally, Melamed urged women to organize synagogue social life, for "it is the wife in the congregation who must create the social life of the Synagogue."[53]

Melamed wrote *The Three Pillars,* the first guide book of its kind in English, to provide "a brief exposition of those aspects of Jewish life which have a special significance for the woman." In a simple, easy-to-read style, she reviewed the Jewish life and holiday cycle, from minor fast days to Confirmation ceremonies for girls, which she advocated because "an intelligent Jewish woman bespeaks a certain amount of Jewish training and education." She also emphatically asserted that "nothing ought be permitted to stand in the way of regular attendance at services on Sabbath morning." Melamed hoped that by breathing life into Jewish ritual, she would inspire Jewish women to observe them. Instantly popular, the book garnered excellent reviews. By 1967, Women's League reported that it had gone through nine editions. Women's League received numerous letters praising its utility, and many women wondered how they had managed without it.[54]

Melamed stated her prescriptions boldly without reference to rabbinical opinions or authorities. In her review of dietary laws, including the laws for Passover preparation, she noted what is permitted and what is forbidden. In the Preface, Melamed thanked the members of the Book Committee—five out of seven of whom were rabbis' wives—for their helpful suggestions. She did not mention any rabbis who may have reviewed the manuscript for accuracy. This presumptuousness bespoke

Melamed's confidence in her role. Apparently, she—and others on the committee—understood the rebbetzin role to include the power to interpret traditional Jewish law and shape Jewish practice for the modern woman.

Writing

Like Melamed, many rabbis' wives found that writing gave them a way to reach a broader audience. They could showcase their literary talents and carve out an arena of competence independent of their husbands. This is particularly evident in the Conservative Movement. The *United Synagogue Recorder* in the 1920s and, after 1930, Women's League *Outlook* provided receptive outlets for many rabbis' wives to publish their articles, stories, and poems.[55] Carrie Davidson (1879–1953), founding editor of *Outlook,* the Women's League monthly magazine, served as the primary catalyst for this development. Establishing the magazine in 1930, she served as editor for more than twenty years, shaping the publication that became the principal means of communicating with Women's League members. For many years, Davidson singlehandedly ran the magazine, authoring countless editorials, book reviews, and articles on a variety of topics including Zionism, *agunot,* Jewish holidays, and Jewish education.[56]

Carrie developed her writing and editing talents on her own. The eldest of four, she dropped her formal education after the eighth grade to help care for the household and her younger siblings, but she continued to study and learn independently.[57] After her 1906 marriage to Israel Davidson, an ordained rabbi and instructor (later professor) of medieval Hebrew literature at JTS, Carrie initially portrayed herself as a homemaker. For example, her article "A Jewish Housewife Takes Stock" reviewed the effect of kashrut on a Jewish housewife's budget. But Davidson found the helpmate role uncomfortably confining. She later recalled wistfully that marriage to a scholar meant that *her* day for accumulating books was over; her "own small collection would gradually be crowded out to make way for the rapidly increasing library of the scholar." Furthermore, she noted that she wished she had known that to be a real helpmate, she would have "to acquire the love of scholarship as well as love for the scholar."[58]

Davidson involved herself in the Seminary community by working to establish a Hebrew school for faculty children, for she and Israel had two daughters of their own to educate. (There is some evidence that the school opened, but nothing suggests that it ever affiliated with JTS.[59]) She also helped organize the Women's Institute of Jewish Studies, a three-year course of study for women formed in 1937 and sponsored by five women's organizations—National Women's League, Hadassah, Ivriah, the New York section of the National Council of Jewish Women, and the Federation of Jewish Women's Organizations. In the 1940s Davidson served as National President of Keren Hatarbut (The Cultural Fund), a group that supported the work of Hebrew writers in Palestine. Yet Davidson—like Schechter, Hoffman, and Minkin—channeled her primary energy into Women's League. Involved almost from its inception, Davidson served on the national board and as president of its Metropolitan branch. Especially through *Outlook,* Davidson spread the message of Women's League to thousands of women.[60]

Althea Silverman (wife of Morris Silverman, rabbi of Emanuel Synagogue in Hartford, Connecticut, from 1923 to 1961) is among those rebbetzins who benefited from initial experience as a magazine contributor. She began with a regular column, "The Woman's Field" in the *United Synagogue Recorder,* updating women about Conservative Movement activities and encouraging them to strengthen the Jewishness of their homes. After the founding of *Outlook,* Silverman published articles there as well. Stressing the importance of the mother's role, she reminded women how powerfully they could influence their children by observing the holidays, reading to them, teaching them prayers, playing Jewish games, and singing Jewish songs.[61] She also invented tools to accomplish these goals. For example, Silverman created a board game, *Oasis,* based on life in Palestine. Published by Milton Bradley Company and distributed by the Jewish National Fund, *Oasis* was praised by Jewish leaders who recognized its value in "adopting the principle of letting the child play at business," while bringing in the elements of "philanthropy, education, and even religion."[62]

An involved rebbetzin who, among other things, taught a Sisterhood Bible class, Silverman also contributed independently to the civic life of Hartford, especially through her instrumental role in introducing a children's concert series and music festival. Yet even for this work, Silverman was identified in the press as a rebbetzin: "Rabbi's Wife Says Junior Concerts Evidence Need of Project," a vivid reminder that her stature as community leader derived from her rebbetzin status.[63]

Althea O. Silverman. Courtesy of Women's League for Conservative Judaism.

Silverman eventually expanded her writing beyond magazine articles. Deeply concerned about the dearth of appealing Jewish educational materials for children, Silverman wrote *Habibi and Yow* and *Habibi's Adventures in the Land of Israel*. These stories recount humorous escapades based on Jewish historical moments and values, through the exploits of a little boy and his dog. For young adult readers, Silverman wrote *Behold My Messengers! The Lives and Teachings of the Prophets* (which was also produced as a pageant) and *The Harp of David: Legends of Mount Zion*. Favorably reviewed in Jewish women's publications and the local press, Silverman's books received notice as far away as the *Singapore Free Press,* which quoted her as recommending that housewives "who are too often bored with household routine" ought to try writing books. By giving this advice, Silverman acknowledged the dual significance of her publications. Surely, they provided a much needed service for mothers, but writing them also satisfied Silverman's need for meaningful work.[64]

Silverman also co-authored, with Betty Greenberg,[65] *The Jewish Home Beautiful*. Initially written as a pageant that served as the closing production in the Temple of Religion at the 1939–40 New York World's Fair,[66] this program brought together women from all three Jewish denominational women's organizations—National Federation of Temple Sisterhoods, National Women's League, and the Women's Branch of the Union of Orthodox Jewish Congregations—to celebrate the Jewish home. Subsequently published as a book by Women's League, this enormously popular volume expressed the authors' views on the beauty and spirituality of the Jewish home. Its suggestions were replicated both by Sisterhood groups and by women at home. Together, Greenberg and Silverman inspired a generation of women to apply their artistic sensibilities to their holiday tables, giving them a Jewish outlet for their emerging American views of what constituted good taste, refinement, and proper venues for women's talents.[67]

Even more so than Silverman, Sadie Rose Weilerstein achieved renown for her children's stories. She, too, made it easier for mothers to enrich their children's Jewish upbringing by providing adventurous, age-appropriate stories on Jewish customs and festivals.[68] Weilerstein's stories, many of which first appeared in *Outlook* beginning with its premier issue, were later published in more than a dozen books. Beginning with *What Danny Did* (1928) and continuing for more than fifty years, Weilerstein became best known for the popular series based on the thumb-sized character K'tonton.[69] In 1956, Weilerstein won a special award from the Jewish Book Council of America for her "cumulative contribution to Jewish juvenile literature." In 1980, she won the Sydney Taylor Body-of-Work Award.[70]

Like many women writers, Weilerstein described her career as an outgrowth of her childrearing experiences. As her interviewer recounted,

> like all mothers, Mrs. Weilerstein as a young woman encountered the problem of intriguing her children with things Jewish. . . . At first she told her stories to her children. Later it dawned on her that a story

unwritten is a story lost and thus she was possessed by the first spark of creativity. . . . Now that her children are grown, she tells and writes her stories for her five grandchildren and the countless children in Jewish homes and schools in the United States, Israel and other countries.[71]

Through writing, women like Melamed, Weilerstein, Silverman, and Greenberg influenced a constituency that transcended their husbands' congregations. It also gave them a public platform free of the behavioral constraints prescribed by Kohut and Hyamson. Despite such achievements, Silverman, for one, continued to portray her "wife of" role as primary. When asked by an interviewer in 1956 what among her many projects gave her the greatest satisfaction and presented the greatest challenge, Silverman answered: "keeping up with my husband." She paid tribute to the joys of being a rabbi's wife, ending with "what could be more rewarding?"[72] Perhaps Silverman never lost sight of the fact that the opportunities came her way as a result of her "wife of" status. By portraying themselves as loyal wives and concerned mothers who "merely" provided peers with desperately needed bedtime stories or holiday handbooks, Silverman and the other rebbetzin authors succeeded in extending their influence while remaining squarely within the prevailing gender boundaries of the era.

National Federation of Temple Sisterhoods

Reform rabbis' wives also found meaningful ways to involve themselves in Jewish life. Some did so through their women's organization, the National Federation of Temple Sisterhoods. Like Schechter with Women's League, Carrie Simon paved the way in NFTS. She included the wives of prominent senior Reform rabbis on her first executive board: Johanna Kohler, Ella Philipson, Sybil Krauskopf, and Blanche Stolz. Their involvement not only signaled their husbands' support for the new organization but also heralded the NFTS as an outlet for the energies and talents of rabbis' wives.[73]

Blanche Stolz proved to be a particularly effective board member. Involved with NFTS from its inception, she served as recording secretary from 1929 to 1937. Stolz was best known for her effective chairmanship of the Scholarship Committee, a position she held from 1915 to 1939.[74] Unlike Simon, Stolz had an unusually rich Jewish background.

Her grandparents had been congregants of Isaac Mayer Wise, and both Stolz and her mother had been confirmed and married by Wise. Blanche's husband, Joseph, an 1884 graduate of Hebrew Union College, also studied with Wise. Blanche recalled the "boys", i.e., rabbinical students, as her classmates. "We read and studied together, went to and from school together, 'crammed for exams' together," and belonged to the same literary club. But only Joseph was ordained. Joseph and Blanche married in 1890; they had three children, and Blanche channeled her learning and energies into her "wife of" role.[75]

The Stolzes spent most of their lives in Chicago, and Blanche was the first woman to serve on the board of Chicago's Jewish Charities. She was also one of the founding members, with Hannah Solomon, of the National Council of Jewish Women.[76] As a congregational rebbetzin,[77] Stolz organized the Women's Society of Temple Isaiah (later known as the Sisterhood), serving as recording secretary from its founding in 1896 until 1925. She also helped her husband with pastoral duties. Even in later years when Joseph was incapacitated by illness, Blanche "carried on in his spirit, visiting the sick, comforting the mourners and spreading sunlight wherever she went."[78]

For the National Federation of Temple Sisterhoods, Stolz served as chairman of the Scholarship Committee from 1915 to 1939. The committee raised more than $400,000 in its first nineteen years, and Stolz even enlarged the fund's scope in the midst of the Depression to include raising money for students preparing for careers in religious education as well as the rabbinate. Stolz's effectiveness on behalf of this campaign surely stemmed in large measure both from her intimate understanding of the significance of a Hebrew Union College education and from her passionate desire to "repay the debt of gratitude that I and my family owe our teacher and friend, Dr. Wise" by providing for students at the institution he founded. One of the few females with links to Wise, Stolz invoked his memory to great effect.[79]

In tribute to Stolz's accomplishments, the National Federation of Temple Sisterhoods established a trophy award in her honor, at the fourteenth biennial assembly in 1941. The trophy would be "awarded biennially to that sisterhood which in proportion to its membership had most increased its contribution to the Hebrew Union College scholarship fund and religious education fund during the last biennial period." In acknowledging this honor, Stolz noted that it "places the capstone, as it were, upon my work for more than a quarter of a century . . . always a labor of love for me." Recalling Wise and her husband as inspirations for her work, Stolz—like the other rabbis' wives of her generation—subsumed her independent accomplishments under the rubric of the supportive female role.[80]

Sadie Lefkowitz was also active in the National Federation of Temple Sisterhoods virtually from the beginning. The wife of David Lefkowitz, rabbi of Temple Emanu-El in Dallas, Texas from 1920 to 1947, Sadie came from a distinguished rabbinical family. As a congregational rebbetzin, Sadie followed the blueprint outlined by Kohut. She drew on her earlier music studies to organize both a Music Club and a Choral Club to sing at services, concerts, and Sisterhood fundraisers. Lefkowitz also strengthened the Sisterhood, serving a term as president.[81]

Called "Aunt Sadie" by the congregation, Lefkowitz and her husband were known as "a seasoned rabbinic team." Their partnership—like that of the Hoffmans—extended to the national level as well. David served as president of the Central Conference of American Rabbis. Beginning in 1915, Sadie served on the National Federation of Temple Sisterhoods' Executive Board.[82]

As Chairman of the NFTS Committee on Propaganda, Lefkowitz drew on her experiences as a rabbi's wife in a small Jewish community. She called on members of larger, established Sisterhoods to visit Jewish communities that lacked resources of their own and invite unaffiliated women to join the organization. She hoped that such outreach would inspire these women to adopt Sabbath and holiday observances, Bible study, congregational singing, choral societies, and a simplified Confirmation ceremony. Lefkowitz was confident that the 55,000 members of the National Federation could "wield a chain of such strength as to make our religion, and through it our lives, impervious to all the winds and storms of these changing times. . . . We must work toward that end, that our children, in their generation, shall rise up and call us blessed, and we shall be blessed by them and through them."[83]

By the 1940s, Lefkowitz, like Adele Ginzberg, turned her attention to the Jewish blind. She chaired the National Federation of Temple Sisterhood's National Committee on Jewish Literature for the Blind, overseeing the project of transcribing Judaica books for the blind. In 1944, Lefkowitz appealed to Sisterhood delegates for more transcribers, reminding them that blind men would be coming home from the war in increasing numbers: "We must become Ladies of the Lamp, bringing light again to the dark of blindness."[84] Like her colleagues, Lefkowitz used her status to further causes—both local and national—about which she cared passionately.

During the time she was a rabbi's wife, Ruth Frisch became one of the first women to address the Union of American Hebrew Congregations. The daughter of Rabbi Henry Cohen of Galveston, she married Hebrew Union College graduate Ephraim Frisch in 1916. Ruth Frisch had studied at New York's Damrosch Conservatory and at the University of Chicago; and this, coupled with the Jewish upbringing she had received at home, gave her the necessary training to take on a leadership role in the congregation. When in 1923 her husband became rabbi of Temple Beth-El in San Antonio, Texas, Ruth began to teach ethics, history, and philosophy of Judaism to high-school students as well as to college-age students. These classes were considered innovative since they extended beyond bar mitzvah or Confirmation. Though her death from Hodgkin's disease in 1934 cut short her career, Frisch was perceived by congregants as the ideal rebbetzin. In the spirit of the times, admirers described her as being "a strong right arm to the rabbi, and a ministering angel to the community." Her successor, Helen Gugenheim Jacobson, described Frisch's capabilities in less gendered terms, noting that "she could have been a rabbi."[85]

Other Reform rabbis' wives found outlets for Jewish involvement separate from the NFTS or the UAHC. For example, Louise Wise, wife of the iconoclastic Reform Zionist leader Stephen S. Wise, advanced both relief and Zionist causes. Drawn to charitable work as a teen, she devoted her efforts to improving the care and protection of children and developing communal health care. With an interest in art, Wise also taught in settlement houses. After the Wises married in 1900, they spent six years in Oregon, where Stephen served as rabbi of Temple Beth Israel. During that time, Louise established the Visiting Nurse Association. Upon their return to New York, Louise continued her benevolent work by establishing the Child Adoption Committee in her husband's synagogue (the Free Synagogue), which was the first Jewish agency of its kind. Wise shared with her husband a passion for Zionism, and they also agitated together on behalf of refugees from Nazism. Serving as first president of the Women's Division of the American Jewish Congress, the organization founded by her husband, Louise created the first of several Congress Houses, which sheltered refugees from Nazi Germany free of charge. During the war, she converted this house into the first of several Defense Houses for American servicemen to spend the night. More than a quarter of a million men did so during the war years. After her death, the Louise Waterman Wise Youth Hostel was established in Jerusalem in testimony to her achievements.[86]

On the whole, Reform rabbis' wives played a less prominent role in their organization of Sisterhoods and in their Movement than Conservatives did in theirs. Notwithstanding the rabbis' wives mentioned here, the NFTS counted fewer rabbis' wives on the executive board, as committee chairs, or as authors of educational materials than did Women's League. Similarly, when looking for resources to aid local Sisterhood chapters, Simon did not mention the potential role that rabbis' wives might play; rather, she suggested inviting rabbis to teach the women. A twenty-four-page pamphlet issued by the NFTS in 1916 under Simon lists Mrs. Felix A. Levy as the only woman among dozens of rabbis willing to speak to Sisterhoods without remuneration. Though she was a rabbi's wife, Levy is not identified as one.[87]

Given the lay origins of American Reform Judaism, it is not surprising to find a smaller number of rabbis' wives among its leaders.[88] In addition, the absence of higher educational opportunities at the beginning of the century for Reform Jewish women meant that fewer obtained the knowledge needed to serve comfortably in the role. Finally, the Yiddish term "rebbetzin" may not have appealed to Reform women, whose family backgrounds more likely stemmed from Central Europe. The absence of a Reform rabbi's wife in the 1925 symposium confirms this pattern.

American Orthodoxy

Though American Orthodoxy came into its own only later in the century, certain rabbinic couples played instrumental roles in establishing its foothold during this earlier period. Leo and Irma Jung functioned in this way during Leo's long tenure as rabbi of New York City's Jewish Center from 1922 to 1981. Irma was one of twelve children born to a wealthy European Jewish family in Germany. She studied at the University of Zurich, but after World War I she turned her attention to the plight of eastern European Jews. Irma served as director of the Bureau of the World Congress of Orthodox Jewry in 1919 and of the Central Bureau of Agudat Israel World Organization from 1919 to 1921. She also organized free camps for refugee children in Stansstad, Switzerland, in 1920–21.[89]

After their marriage in 1922, Irma and Leo came to New York, where, in addition to rearing four daughters, Irma became "first lady of the Jewish Center." She accompanied her husband regularly on home visits to congregants and opened her home to them on Rosh Hashanah. Irma ran the book club and sometimes concerned herself with broader congregational matters such as membership. Encouraging congregants to observe Jewish rituals, she taught classes on topics such as kashrut and Jewish family purity laws.[90]

Beyond the synagogue, Jung also supported numerous Orthodox causes, including several in Palestine. Active in the Orthodox Union and especially its Women's Branch, Jung developed a reputation for assisting Yeshiva University students. Chairman of the Yeshiva Dormitory on East Broadway from 1926 to 1928, and vice president and acting chairperson of the Yeshiva College Women's Organization in 1934–35, Jung took a personal interest in students' welfare, delivering weekly stipends and cloth for new suits before Passover. Israel Miller, rabbi and senior vice president of Yeshiva University from 1979 to 1994, reminisced that she made sure "we had warm clothing and something to eat." Jung looked out for congregants in a similar fashion. While the congregation generally attracted a wealthy constituency, in the 1930s refugee families from Germany occasionally appeared in synagogue. When a family arrived without winter clothes for the children, Jung tactfully informed the mother about a fund at the Center designated for just such a purpose.[91]

One of Jung's favorite causes was the Rabbonim Aid Society, a Jewish Center–based group. Jung served as vice president of the group, which raised money for needy rabbinic families. For decades, the Society provided monthly aid for dozens of rabbinic families, many of whom were refugees and Holocaust survivors. Jung hosted meetings and co-chaired fundraising teas, luncheons, and theater parties. She also personally visited the families served by the Society, and she enlisted her husband to speak at the Society's meetings.[92]

Leo understood his wife's accomplishments as stemming from her success as supportive helpmate and role model. He believed that a woman ought to have three roles: beloved lover of her husband, the home's practical esthetic engineer, and the children's living example of goodness, truth, and grace. Because of this, Leo lauded not Irma's intellect or leadership qualities, but "her devotion to our faith, our folk, and above other spheres, to our home."[93]

Rebbetzins Band Together

Heightened awareness of their distinctive role led some rabbis' wives to join forces to enhance their effectiveness. In Yorkville, New York, for example, rabbis' wives from all denominations worked together on an ad hoc basis to strengthen the United Yorkville Joint Passover Relief Fund.[94] A group of Conservative rabbis' wives founded a "Council of Wives of Rabbis" at the 1926 Rabbinical Assembly convention to fill a long-felt need for rebbetzins to "meet one another, to become better acquainted with others holding their own ideals, and to discuss the problems they are confronted with from time to time." The organizers sought especially to offer support to young rebbetzins. As Hyamson had posited in the symposium, these women asserted "that the situation of the rabbi's wife is different from that of any other woman," for they needed to learn not only how to be good housewives but also how to assist their husbands in their work. Those at the meeting acknowledged that even if not committed to the role before marriage, rebbetzins were "irresistibly drawn to communal work after a short time," just as Kohut had hoped would happen. These rebbetzins knew they were expected to play an active role in Sisterhood and understood that they ought to focus on a specific area of congregational work—such as kashrut or youth—in order to leave a lasting mark. The anonymous author reporting on the meeting uses the term "rebbetzin" to describe the women, reinforcing the notion that the women saw themselves filling a unique position that had its own protocol.[95] The group met again at the 1927 convention, where it adopted a resolution advising rabbinic couples to host an open house on the second day of Rosh Hashanah with the goal of "keeping the congregants occupied on that afternoon . . . and fostering a spirit of unity and friendship between the congregation and the Rabbi and his wife."[96]

Choosing a Fitting Mate

Given the increased emphasis on the role of rabbi's wife during the 1920s, one would expect rabbis as well as rebbetzins to reflect more openly on its significance. And many did. For example, in a 1921 talk, Henry Berkowitz explained to his audience of mostly single Reform rabbinical students[97] that "no confidant, no intellectual comrade more unselfish or more devoted to his real well-being can a minister find than the woman who consents to be his wife." Quoting a Jew's College address to students on the question of "Where the Clergy Fail," Berkowitz explained:

> One matter there is upon which turns far oftener than is suspected the success or failure of a clergyman's career. . . . I refer to the minister's choice of a wife. Everybody has heard the old rabbinic adages about "Ezer" and "Kenegdo". . . . True enough in their general application, with no class of the community are they more true than with the clergy. . . . In how many ways can she directly or indirectly help forward her husband's work and contribute to the welfare and progress of his flock! In the social sphere, failure in which may seriously cripple a clergyman's usefulness, who does not know that she is the predominant partner? . . . She can save him, too, from making a fool of himself! Few clergymen who have been fortunate enough to make even a modest success of their careers will hesitate to acknowledge to what human co-operation that success has been in great measure due.[98]

The term *ezer k'negdo* is a reference to Gen. 2:18, where God creates the first woman as an *ezer k'negdo* for the first man. Usually translated as a "fitting helper," the Hebrew words can be understood literally to mean "a helpmate opposite him." This seeming contradiction in terms has inspired numerous rabbinic interpretations. Often invoked to describe the ideal rabbi's wife, the biblical phrase *ezer k'negdo* lends religious legitimacy to the helpmate role. Using a metaphor associated with the first human couple reinforces the notion that the helpmate role is natural and divinely ordained.

Some rabbis wrote that they deliberately sought out potential mates who would fill this role. For example, Stephen Wise knew that his wife could enhance his success as an activist, twentieth-century American rabbi. When they were courting in 1900, he implored Louise to marry him so that she might "do so much for me in my work. . . . You could relieve me of the many small burdens a man in my calling bears so that the one great solemn duty and burden of my life would be borne—I speak in all humility—with greater joy and power."[99] He later elaborated: "With you to help me, I shall be fitted for any station or post of service—you, darling, would adorn and exalt any place! . . . We shall make religious work a moral force, an ethical compulsion."[100]

Similarly, Samuel Rosenblatt, rabbi of Beth Tfiloh Congregation, in Baltimore, Maryland, from 1927 until his death in 1982, recalled that when

> the time had come to look for a companion and partner who would be willing to share with me life and fortune. . . . I was fully aware of the fact that the rabbinate included important social functions. A man cannot minister effectively to the needs of his flock unless he is able to associate himself with them in weal and woe. In the performance of these tasks, the assistance of a real helpmeet is not only invaluable. It is indispensable.[101]

Apparently, he found such a mate. Claire Rosenblatt was later remembered as "the epitome of the Rabbi's other half." She was noted for her active role in Sisterhood, entertaining, open houses, presence at services, and book reviews.[102]

Since many rabbis' wives grew up in rabbinic homes, it is not surprising that aspiring rabbis looking for appropriate helpmates sought out rabbis' daughters. Ira Eisenstein, leader of the Society for the Advancement of Judaism (1931–54) and later president of the Reconstructionist Rabbinical College (1968–81), married Judith Kaplan, the daughter of Mordecai M. Kaplan, the leader of Reconstructionist Judaism and Eisenstein's mentor, in 1934. Recalling the qualities he desired in a wife, Eisenstein explained that he hoped to find a wife who was

> *Jewishly* Jewish, a characteristic lacking in several other young women whom I knew. . . . And, if possible (such requirements!) she had to share an enthusiasm for the kind of Judaism to which I was planning to devote my life. It is thus no coincidence that I thought I found her in the household of Rabbi Kaplan.[103]

Throughout the years, the Eisensteins collaborated on many projects dedicated to furthering Jewish life, including writing several cantatas.[104]

Some rabbis married women who they knew shared similar professional aspirations vis-à-vis Jewish life because these women were already functioning as Jewish educators. For example, Samuel Schwartz, a 1909 graduate of Hebrew Union College, met his future wife, Charlotte Ulmer, in his first congregation, where she was one of his Sunday school teachers. They married in 1917 and spent most of their years with Congregation B'nai Abraham Zion in Chicago (1920–46). A college graduate, Charlotte assisted her husband in his work. As he noted, Charlotte

> entered very diligently into all educational and social functions. We seldom had a free day. . . . I was occupied with temple functions, and she with the Sisterhood, Sunday school, young people and all other congregational activities. Eventually she earned the reputation of being the outstanding *rebbitzin* in town. . . . I can say without hesitancy that nothing went on in Sisterhood without her having a part in it, culturally, socially or financially and the same applied to other functions in the congregation and Sunday school.[105]

Given the commitment of both Schwartzes to the synagogue, how appropriate that in 1958 the congregation dedicated the sanctuary in honor of *both* Samuel and Charlotte Schwartz "as a fitting tribute to your many years of devoted and continuous service" to the congregation.[106]

Just as certain men sought appropriate mates to further their rabbinic careers, so too did certain women seek out rabbi husbands to further their own aspirations. In the 1920s, more and more women believed that they deliberately chose their vocation when they married. Even though motherhood and career continued to be viewed as incompatible during this era, the number of women working increased. Because of this, wife- and motherhood came to be viewed as a choice rather than as a universal prescription. This made the decision to become a rabbi's wife that much more purposeful.[107]

Many who sought out rabbis as mates were—like Kohut, Hyamson, and their European predecessors—rabbis' daughters who had experienced firsthand the opportunities of the rebbetzin role. Their rabbi-and-rebbetzin parents had served as role models of service that they wanted to emulate. They understood from personal experience that a rabbinic lifestyle would facilitate that goal by placing them at the center of Jewish life in their communities.

Reva Epstein was one such rebbetzin. Daughter of Judah Chashesman, the Orthodox leader of Chicago's Congregation Anshe Ticktin, Epstein had been educated Jewishly by her father in their home in Russian Poland from an early age. It was said that by her fifth birthday she could read Hebrew, Yiddish, and German; after World War I, she became the first Jewish girl to attend and then graduate (with honors) from the Suvalki gymnasium. When the family relocated to the United States, Epstein completed her education at the University of Chicago in 1928, just weeks before her marriage to Harry H. Epstein, rabbi of Congregation Ahavath Achim in Atlanta from 1927 to 1982. As her husband's biographer notes, Reva "could have followed a career as a college language and literature instructor. Instead, she chose to use her abilities as the rebbetzin." According to many congregants, she became the "ideal rebbetzin."[108]

Like many talented, Jewishly educated rebbetzins, Epstein supported Hadassah actively, conducted model Hebrew classes and study groups, and helped younger women learn the customs and cooking traditions associated with the Jewish holidays. She was also deeply involved with the Jewish National Fund, the women's division of Israel Bonds, and the congregation's Sisterhood. Finally, Epstein served as her husband's counterpart in counseling. When he would guide a distressed husband in the study, she would listen to the troubled wife in the living room.[109]

Of course, not all rebbetzins were rabbis' daughters. Some married rabbis because of the positive associations with Judaism they had developed in the homes of their childhood. For example, reared in a very Jewishly involved family in London, England, Carmel Bentwich (later Forsythe), wife of Louis Finkelstein (president and then chancellor of the Jewish Theological Seminary, 1940–72), was the tenth child of Susan and Herbert Bentwich, close friends of the Schechters. Trained as a kindergarten teacher at the Froebel Institute, she came to the United States after World War I to help her sister Lillian, wife of Jewish Theological Seminary professor Israel Friedlaender, with her children. Carmel initially met Louis at a Zionist gathering, for he served as chairman of the Intercollegiate Zionist Association. Married in 1922, Carmel taught in the religious school of Congregation Kehillath Israel in the Bronx, where her husband then served as rabbi. Having studied kindergarten education with John Dewey at Teachers College, Carmel also worked with Mordecai Kaplan to develop a kindergarten. Though the Finkelsteins' interests and lives diverged in later years, culminating in their divorce, Carmel remembered their years in the Bronx fondly: "We had an active life developing the congregation."[110]

Similarly, Sylvia Mintz Geffen grew up in New York City in a strong Zionist home, though she had no formal Jewish education as a girl.[111] Geffen was studying at the Art League when she met her husband, Joel

Geffen. He was ordained at JTS in 1926, the year they married. Believing that a rebbetzin ought to help out as best she could, Sylvia learned what she could about Judaism from her husband. In his congregation in Harrisburg, Pennsylvania, she taught Sunday school and attended services every Friday night and Saturday. Later, in Troy, New York, she helped organize the Sisterhood. Geffen felt that as a young Conservative rebbetzin, she played a significant role by demonstrating that the synagogue was a place for young people, and especially for young women, an attitude she felt lacking in Orthodox synagogues of the time.[112]

As we have seen, many of the women who married rabbis had been influenced not only by their families but also by exposure to Zionism. These women often played instrumental roles in establishing and sustaining Hadassah groups, on both national and local levels. Their Zionist fervor fueled their desire to intensify Jewish life in the United States while also contributing to the upbuilding of Palestine. But not all rabbis' wives came from Zionist homes. Some were not driven from their youth to serve the Jewish people, but simply fell in love with men who were rabbis. Many of these women grew up in Americanized families in small cities and towns throughout the United States, and thus were less likely to be Jewishly educated. For instance, because most of the Reform rabbinic students entered Hebrew Union College single, many married Cincinnati women whom they met and dated during their student years. These women may have sought the status and significance inherent in the position of rabbi's wife, but some were unprepared Jewishly to serve in that role. Louise Reichert was one such woman. A graduate of Smith College, Louise had been accepted to medical school, but her Jewish education was minimal. When she married Victor Reichert in 1926, Louise abandoned her plans to be a doctor and channeled her intellect and energy into her role as rabbi's wife. Victor served as rabbi of Rockdale Temple in Cincinnati, Ohio, for his entire rabbinic career, from 1938 to 1962. Like other rabbis' wives in similar situations, Reichert accepted the responsibilities of the role and came to derive great satisfaction from it.[113]

For a few rebbetzins, the burden of the role weighed too heavily, and it damaged their relationships with their husbands. Even before the women's consciousness-raising movement encouraged married women to seek their own independent careers, some rabbis' wives felt stifled by the rebbetzin role. These women married the men they loved *in spite* of their husbands' calling, not because of it. While some managed to sustain lengthy unions based on love and mutual respect, for others, lack of common goals caused tension and discord. For example, Edith Alpert Steinberg, the much younger wife of Milton Steinberg, rabbi of the Park Avenue Synagogue in Manhattan (1933–50), had no interest in religion and no desire to fill the traditional rebbetzin's role. This attitude strained their relationship and complicated Milton's rabbinic career.[114]

Similarly, Toby Lelyveld never felt comfortable with the rabbi's wife role and resented the demands it placed upon her. When her husband, Arthur J. Lelyveld, became rabbi of the Fairmount Temple in Cleveland, Ohio, in 1958, Toby relocated with him. But five years later, she moved back to New York in a separation that eventually culminated in divorce. Toby described this move as liberating her from the duties of a rabbi's wife, noting that on Rosh Hashanah, she would spend her time "not shaking 1,500 hands and not smiling."[115]

Even rebbetzins who relished the role sometimes balked at its constraints. The question of whether a rabbi's wife ought to serve as Sisterhood president highlights the problems. In this instance, Kohut's advice and her example—which directly contradicted each other—closely mirrored the conflicted reality. In the first two decades of the twentieth century, some rabbis' wives, including Carrie Simon, Sadie Lefkowitz, and Bertha Aronson, took the presidency because they believed they were best qualified to lead.[116] In the formative years of their husbands' congregations, as their husbands struggled to establish themselves and to realize a more expansive synagogue, rabbis' wives felt that they could contribute to this vision by establishing the women's auxiliary on a firm footing. This meant acting as Kohut did—serving as president until competent lay leadership could take over. Gradually, as Sisterhoods became more established in congregations, rebbetzins acted in accordance with Kohut's (and Hyamson's) advice: A rabbi's wife should avoid taking on the presidency and whenever possible distribute the work and honors to others while steering her chapter to participate in the national organization of which it was a constituent.[117] The musings of a Mrs. Hermann Cohen illustrate the internal turmoil such decisions ignited:

> It was with considerable reluctance that I first accepted the program chairmanship. As a rabbi's wife, I felt that I should take no office or head any standing committee. I am in accord with the prevailing opinion that Rabbis' wives should be seen and not heard too much. I de-

cided, however, to break the rule, because of my conviction as to the paramount value of carefully prepared programs.[118]

During this period, then, rabbis' wives initially experienced a glimpse of independent leadership, but they soon reverted to the helpmate role, assisting Sisterhood women unofficially in the same way that they supported their husbands. Many soon found this advisory role too confining, and they turned their attention beyond the synagogue to the national arms of Sisterhood groups and other organizations, which provided a welcome outlet for leadership talents that were thwarted on the congregational level.

In general, rebbetzins of the 1920s saw themselves working as their husbands' helpmates to promote common goals. For most, the advantages of the role outweighed the limitations. Their positions as rabbis' wives gave them status that they leveraged to promote the causes they cared about, using means best suited to their talents. It is impossible to know what they would have achieved had they pursued an independent career or had they not married the men they did. But having chosen the "wife of" role, many of these women made the most of it. They transformed the role of the rabbi's wife into a profession, creating a viable alternative for married women desirous of a life of service.

In the 1930s and 1940s, maverick rebbetzins stretched the boundaries of the role in a more public direction. Unwilling or unable to display the reticence and tact required of the behind-the-scenes helpmeet, they took on more independent leadership roles. As they brought the role of the American rebbetzin to its pinnacle, they created new standards that would both inspire and intimidate their counterparts and successors.

3

"Mr. & Mrs. God"

The G's were a lovely rabbinic pair and I loved to visit them. . . .
On one visit, a very long time ago, my host Rabbi descended to
the cellar to take care of the ashes, which at that time meant
caring for the furnace which produced the heat. Calling out to
his wife I heard him say, "Leah, I think I have a wedding today,
please check my calendar." Leah promptly did and reported,
"No, there is nothing on the calendar."

The Rabbi emerged from the basement, clothes covered with
white dust, and decided to look up his own pocket calendar.
"Heavens, yes, a wedding that day." But where? He had neglected
to enter the time and place. Rebbetzin to the rescue.

She called the home of the bride and the mother answered.
The Rebbetzin said, "This is Western Union. We have a telegram
for you. Where is the wedding taking place?" "It will be at the
Rabbi's home at 2:00." Well, the three of us put that house in
order fast. The Rabbi got out of his jeans and into his striped
pants and black jacket. *Nes godol hayo shom*—a great miracle
happened there.[1] My hostess and I set up the chupah [wedding
canopy], prepared a small table with wine and a glass wrapped
in a paper napkin to be stamped on by the groom. And so a
wedding took place and everyone was happy. It was indeed a
miracle that day.[2]

Lilly Soloway Routtenberg, wife of Max Routtenberg, rabbi
in Reading, Pennsylvania (1932–48), and Rockville Centre, New York
(1954–72), penned the above story. She hoped to include it in a book,
tentatively titled *Humor from the Rebbezinate*, which she began writing in retirement.[3] As the "miracle" demonstrates, Routtenberg believed
that rabbis needed the knowledge, dedication, and ingenuity of their
wives to succeed in their careers. The rebbetzin expertly set up the ritual

objects for the wedding, but since her actions fell well within the purview of the homemaking role, they simultaneously reinforced the gendered nature of her position rather than threatening her husband's. At the same time, performing mundane, housekeeping duties in preparation for a wedding enhanced their function by imbuing such work with a larger, sacred purpose.

In many ways, Routtenberg had prepared for such a life from her youth. She remembered being called "rebbetzin"[4] by her parents, in Montreal, Canada, because her devotion to Judaism prompted her to watch over the kashrut of the kitchen when her mother was ill. On marrying Max in 1931, a year before his ordination from the Jewish Theological Seminary, Lilly met weekly with other student wives to educate herself for the role. She recalled everyone taking themselves very seriously, so conscious were they of the significance of the position they were about to assume. After they became congregational rebbetzins, these women continued to provide support for each other through round-robin letter correspondence. One rebbetzin described the goings-on in her community, and the next woman added her own reaction and experiences and passed both on to a third. Annual Rabbinical Assembly conventions became an additional opportunity for the wives to share stories and strengthen each other.

Routtenberg's talents culminated in *The Jewish Wedding Book: A Practical Guide to the Traditions and Social Proprieties of the Jewish Wedding*,[5] which she wrote with her daughter, Ruth R. Seldin. This book, described as "the first of its kind,"[6] wove together American etiquette and Jewish law and custom to guide families through the process of planning a wedding. Summarizing Orthodox, Conservative, and Reform practices on various issues, Routtenberg and Seldin also generalized authoritatively about Jewish practice in the pre-modern period. Their "credentials" for writing are described on the book jacket as: "wife and daughter of a prominent rabbi."

Throughout her life, Routtenberg understood the rabbinate as a two-person career. In her words, "without a wife, it's half a rabbinate." Serving her husband's congregation and Women's League as hostess, educator, writer, and speaker, she recalled with great satisfaction that "*we* had a very happy rabbinate."[7]

It is not surprising that many rebbetzins of the era felt the same way, given prevailing societal attitudes. Women made up approximately 40 percent of all college students in the 1930s and 1940s. More college-educated women entered the professions, and by 1930, almost 25 percent of professional women combined marriage and career. But 75 percent did not. Marriage and family continued to be the primary goal for American women. According to Gallup polls, 82 percent of those surveyed in 1936 felt that wives of working husbands should not be employed outside the home. In a Depression-era economy with few jobs available even for men, this conviction also served to rationalize reality. Even during World War II when women worked, recruiters portrayed women's motivations for working as an outgrowth of their desire to help their men, safeguard their children, answer local needs, and support the national well-being. In this way, working wives did not challenge long-held assumptions about gender, for society viewed their jobs as temporary rather than as nascent careers. Frustrated, many educated, ambitious wives continued to search for acceptable ways to combine marriage and career.[8]

During this period, society came to believe that marriages succeeded more fully when women served as wife-companions who shared an interest in their husband's work. To facilitate this goal, women gave up jobs after marriage in order not to compete with their husbands professionally or financially. They also made an effort to learn more about their husbands' careers. Those women trained in fields that matched their husbands' professions sometimes cemented their relationships by working as nurses or office managers for their doctor or businessman husbands. In this circumscribed way, some women succeeded in maintaining careers after marriage.[9]

In the 1930s and 1940s, women encountered a husband-wife team relationship in the White House. Already in 1930 as a governor's wife, Eleanor Roosevelt had described the significance of this kind of marriage, noting that while women had formerly focused on motherhood, they now increasingly emphasized their roles as partners to their husbands. Roosevelt modeled this shift, for she took on so many activities that reporters described Franklin and Eleanor as a team.[10]

As the First Lady, through her newspaper column "My Day," and through her public appearances in a variety of venues, Roosevelt influenced policy to a degree unparalleled in previous administrations. She also affected thousands of women, and in 1938 *Life* hailed her as the greatest American woman alive. Some rabbis' wives felt a unique affin-

Tamar de Sola Pool with Eleanor Roosevelt. Photography by Hazel Greenwald, Courtesy of Hadassah, The Women's Zionist Organization of America, Inc.

ity with Roosevelt, for they too had a special title that derived from marriage. As community leaders, many had the opportunity to meet Roosevelt. Because they identified strongly with both the special restrictions and the opportunities of her First Lady role, many rebbetzins looked to Roosevelt as an important source of inspiration.[11]

Rebbetzins also saw this activist "wife of" role among their Christian counterparts. Pressed into service during the Depression as unofficial, unpaid staff members and encouraged to take on assistant pastor functions, clergy wives gained increased visibility and importance in the church. Some embraced this more public dimension and happily moved out from "behind the throne." They perceived their marriages as "exalted, rather than intimate," and saw themselves as a "staff member more than as a wife." With this in mind, childrearing became an interruption of their true calling.[12]

During the 1930s and 1940s, then, marriage to a rabbi continued to be an ideal avenue for Jewish women to combine marriage and career in a way that reinforced rather than challenged societal views. These rebbetzins served—albeit it in an unpaid capacity—as the second person in a two-person rabbinate. One young boy depicted this through his recollection of his rabbi and rebbetzin, Samuel and Gertrude Mayerberg of Congregation B'nai Jehudah in Kansas City, Missouri. While Samuel led services, Gertrude led the children's choir, but what the young boy remembered was "Mr. God teaching downstairs and Mrs. God singing upstairs."[13]

The four women profiled below epitomize this activist, partnership rebbetzin role. While they served different denominations—Reform, Conservative, Orthodox, and Jewish Science—all nevertheless had similar experiences as young women that well prepared them for their future roles. They had intensive Jewish upbringings, high levels of secular education, and exposure to Zionism, especially through Szold and Hadassah. These experiences fueled career ambitions that not only enhanced their own reputations but also raised the profile of the rebbetzin position in general. These women rejected a behind-the-scenes role to take on more public leadership positions and saw themselves working in partnership with their husbands in two-person careers. They expanded the boundaries of the rebbetzin role, both by working with their husbands and by building on their own special talents and interests. Mignon Rubenovitz through her art museum, Rebecca Brickner as Jewish educator and "rabbi" of her Sisterhood, Tamar de Sola Pool as editor, writer, and Hadassah leader, and Tehilla Lichtenstein as editor, leader, and pastor—each perfected a niche of public power and influence. Each also outlived her husband, and as a widow, each continued the work to which she and her husband had dedicated their lives. Throughout their adult lives, then, these women exemplified the heights of leadership possible for rebbetzins in the interwar years.

At the same time, these rebbetzins struggled with the frustrations of their position, just as their predecessors had. As we will see, no matter how much they accomplished, they eventually encountered the limitations of the role, for an assistant—no matter how successful—who can never become the boss will inevitably feel constrained. An abundance of sources about and by these four women reveals more completely the contours of such tensions. A closer look at each of their life's stories immeasurably deepens our appreciation of both the individualized achievements of these exceptionally talented rebbetzins and the opportunities and limitations of the rabbi's wife role.

Mignon Rubenovitz

Born in 1884, Mignon Levin Rubenovitz grew up in Baltimore, Maryland, as the youngest of six children. Mignon described her grandparents as learned, religious Jews and her mother as "a pious, orthodox Jewess, rigidly observant of every jot and tittle of the ancient Jewish laws and customs." As an adult, Mignon retained warm, sentimental feelings about her childhood. She received her secular education in the Baltimore schools, but there is no record of her having received any formal Jewish education. The Baltimore Judaica scholar, David Blondheim, introduced Mignon to her future husband at the 1907 Zionist Convention in Tannersville, New York. Herman Rubenovitz, a recent immigrant from Kovno, had been imbued by his father with a lifelong love of Zionism and Hebrew. He was ordained by the Jewish Theological Seminary in 1908.[14]

Growing up in Baltimore, Mignon came under the influence of Henrietta Szold. She recalled being awed by Szold's austere, strait-laced demeanor and her brilliance, and Mignon remembered feeling young and callow in her presence. When Rubenovitz's oldest brother, Louis, married Henrietta's younger sister, Bertha, the ties deepened. Rubenovitz grew to admire Szold immensely: "In all the years of my mature life, I was deeply aware of Henrietta Szold's self-denying quality. . . . Her legacy to American Jewish womanhood was a lofty standard of selfless unfaltering service." As a rebbetzin, Rubenovitz embodied many of the same qualities.[15]

In 1911, Mignon graduated from Columbia University's Teachers College with a B.S. in psychology. She subsequently taught psychology and English literature in teachers' colleges in Baltimore and Brooklyn, but she stopped teaching after her marriage in 1915. In her husband's words, she "turned from the field of general education to serve Zionism, the synagogue and Hebraic culture." Mignon described her change of focus in more gendered terms, explaining that she "entered the rabbinate by way of marriage." Herman Rubenovitz assumed the pulpit of Temple Mishkan Tefila in Boston, Massachusetts, thereby providing a platform for both of them to spread Conservative Judaism and Zionism in New England.[16]

The Rubenovitzes, like the Minkins and Bengises, had no children. There is no evidence either that these couples chose to remain childless or that congregants criticized them for not having children. Since, as we

Mignon Rubenovitz. Courtesy of the Women's League for
Conservative Judaism.

have seen, contemporary expectations of clergy wives celebrated selfless
service to the community over homemaking and childrearing, childless
rebbetzins generally garnered praise for dedicating themselves whole-
heartedly to communal concerns.[17]

In assuming the position of full-time rebbetzin, Rubenovitz emulated
Mathilde Schechter, whom she fondly called "the perfect helpmate."[18]
Rubenovitz hosted guests for Sabbath dinner and opened her home for
congregational and Hadassah meetings and study groups. Like her mentor Schechter, and like many other rebbetzins of her time, Rubenovitz
had household help, which made it possible for her to maintain this full
schedule of activity.[19] In addition to entertaining, she paid condolence

calls, invited strangers for Passover *seders,* shared recipes, presided occasionally at Jewish women's organization meetings, and delivered talks. Outraged that the high point of activity for women was the occasional bridge party, she strove to create an infrastructure of Jewish organizational life that would present an attractive alternative. For example, she was disturbed that congregants did not observe the festival of Sukkot (Tabernacles), and she decided to respond by stringing cranberries, string beans, peppers, and eggplants to decorate a sukkah at the synagogue. Rubenovitz then advertised a reception in the sukkah after services, and, as she later described (speaking about herself in the third person): "At 6:30 a.m. with our parishioners still in bed, the Rabbi and the Rebbitzen could have been seen walking down Elm Hill Avenue and Warren Street, a goodly mile, each carrying a heavily loaded suitcase" filled with necessary items, such as wine, cookies, and silver serving bowls. Rubenovitz noted with satisfaction that as a result of these efforts, the knowledge and joy of the festival grew.[20]

Rubenovitz quickly became a leader to the women in the congregation. She was arguably the most learned woman in the congregation, for at the time most were not college graduates.[21] As her successor, Bernice Kazis, noted, "she knew it and they knew it, and they respected her intelligence. . . . Everyone was so happy to have an educated couple." Because of her position, Mignon had the opportunity to introduce Eleanor Roosevelt when the First Lady came to address the synagogue in 1941. Rubenovitz stressed "her courage, her industry, her constancy," and hailed her as "Teacher and Friend."[22]

In addition to her work in the synagogue, Rubenovitz, like other rebbetzins, expanded her interests into the national arena. One of the original five vice presidents of Women's League, she established its New England branch in 1919 and served as its first president.[23] Rubenovitz joined Hadassah's newly formed Central Committee in 1913, and she served as first president of the Baltimore group. When she moved to Boston, Rubenovitz was asked to serve as president of the fledgling Hadassah chapter there. Initially uncertain about the position, Rubenovitz received a letter from Szold urging her to take it, "provided your duties as Hausfrau and as Rebbitzin are not proving too onerous." Not only did Rubenovitz lead Boston Hadassah for many years, she also channeled her teaching abilities into that organization, establishing and directing the study group that met in her home beginning in 1916.[24]

Rubenovitz's involvement in both Hadassah and National Women's

League continued for many years. In 1923, she was appointed senior adviser to the newly formed National Junior Hadassah, a division established to attract "girls" eighteen and older. She led discussions at Hadassah conventions, and, while visiting Palestine in 1930, reported her impressions back to the Boston chapter. In 1935, Rubenovitz presided over the national Hadassah convention in Cleveland. Through National Women's League, Rubenovitz demonstrated her power as a preacher. For example, in the talk delivered at the 1939 convention, she exhorted her listeners concerning the ominous events in Europe: "We have a great responsibility, we who are the only ones, the greatest aggregation of Jews living in freedom, we who must take that pearl from the broken hands of those who live under the malignant skies of Europe." In her view, Jews must function as "teachers of justice in a world where there is no justice or very little, humane where man has been inhumane to man, peaceful where people are at each others [*sic*] throats."[25]

Ultimately, Rubenovitz succeeded in leaving her special mark through her artistic accomplishments. Her talent initially manifested itself through writing, for like Routtenberg, Silverman, and Davidson, Rubenovitz was a prolific writer. She explained Jewish ceremonies in the Temple cookbook, *The Center Table*.[26] Rubenovitz also wrote historical articles and dramatic stories that appeared in the (Boston) *Jewish Advocate* and Women's League *Outlook*. The latter carried a series in which the wise protagonist was called "Mrs. Rebbitzen."[27] Rubenovitz published several other pamphlets, including *The Boy of Okup: A Day in the Childhood of a Jewish Saint,* about the Baal Shem Tov, the founder of Hasidism. She also wrote *Around the Year in Jewish Ceremonial,* a review of Jewish holidays with a special emphasis on the ritual objects used for each occasion. And she wrote, directed, and produced several pageants, the most ambitious being one on the life of Maimonides. Many of these were performed in the 1930s as fundraisers for Temple Mishkan Tefila or Hadassah.[28] In 1938, she published many of these scripts as *The Light of the Centuries and Other Historical Dramas.*

In a rare glimpse of the gender tension underlying Rubenovitz's leadership role, she included in this collection an amusing script entitled "Hadassah School for Husbands." Based on ironic role reversal, this play celebrated those husbands who willingly assumed the customary supportive wife role for the sake of Zionism. They "sacrifice themselves on the altar of the greatest Jewish cause, the cause of Zion, and Hadassah's achievements are really due to these modest, generous, self-effacing, almost forgotten Hadassah Husbands. May they continue to carry on!" Through this tongue-and-cheek-script, Rubenovitz acknowledged the frustrations inherent in the reticent diffidence generally expected of women. She also affirmed the impossibility of married women taking on leadership roles without supportive husbands.[29]

The most distinctive of Rubenovitz's artistic accomplishments lay in creating the first Jewish museum in the New England area. Inspired to create what she referred to as an "intimate museum" after viewing an American exhibit of works of art made at the Bezalel School in Jerusalem, she proposed establishing a permanent museum in her synagogue in 1920. The "love for what is beautiful, artistic and significant in our Jewish heritage" drove Rubenovitz to attempt on a regional level what Carrie Simon had done on the national level in Reform.[30] Rubenovitz believed that the museum would provide another type of educational resource to help Jewish children better understand and appreciate their heritage. Over the next several years, under the auspices of the Sisterhood, she began to collect "ceremonial objects, art books, paintings and etchings illustrative of Jewish ways in ages past."[31]

Formally dedicated in December 1940, the museum, housed for many years in a separate room in the synagogue's School House, contained ceremonial objects, prints, paintings, and old books. Among its treasures was a copy of the famous Darmstädter Passover *Haggadah,* an early fifteenth-century volume that contained unusually rich, decorated folios. Rubenovitz also included an 1852 Hebrew book written by her grandfather that details the traditional ceremonies of one of the first Ashkenazic congregations in South Carolina. Rubenovitz understood collecting Jewish art in her day as a religious act. As she explained, "while the guns roared in Europe where our people, martyred fed the flames in the concentration camps of the Nazis, we unceasingly pursued our peaceful task of succoring, albeit in small measure, the things they wrought to express their belief in the sacredness of human personality."[32]

The Museum quickly became a valued community resource. Religious school students regularly toured the museum, and other school, church, and adult study groups came as well. When Hadassah and Women's League held their conventions in Boston, their delegates also toured the museum. Visiting dignitaries—most notably the First Lady, Eleanor Roosevelt—also viewed the collection. Rubenovitz personally "conducted" each group through the museum, and in this way the museum became her pulpit, as she sermonically interpreted the significance of each piece in the collection.[33]

In keeping with her desire to promote Jewish education based on visual learning, Rubenovitz also established a museum publications department, which issued several of her books, including *Winecup and Book: The Story of the Darmstädter Haggadah* and *Altars of My Fathers*. These works contained annotated photographs of the museum's holdings, with excerpts initially appearing in Women's League *Outlook*.[34] Rubenovitz's writings, like her tours and lectures, became a forum for promoting her ideas. For example, *Altars of My Fathers* went beyond displaying the museum's holdings to promoting her religious vision. She included photographs of both Temple Mishkan Tefila and the seal of the State of Israel and explained: "That which we presented here tells the oft-repeated story of the Jew persisting in his individuality, of the Jew treasuring the wisdom and grandeur of his Torah."[35]

Creating the museum gave Rubenovitz her own department within the synagogue to showcase not only her artistic sense, but also her fundraising, teaching, and administrative skills. She mounted special exhibits and offered lecture series to the women of greater Boston. She raised funds through the "Museum Guild" to secure the museum's financial stability. The impact of her dedication to the museum continued after her death, for the Rubenovitzes bequeathed $80,000 to the synagogue to support the museum and archives that now bear their names. Mignon's devotion to the museum also affected her successors. When Bernice Kazis married Herman Rubenovitz's successor, Israel Kazis, she took over the museum work. The synagogue had moved from Roxbury to Newton, and Bernice oversaw the establishment of the museum in its new home, bringing Rubenovitz to the synagogue weekly to help with the restoration. Like Rubenovitz, Kazis eventually added new objects to the collection.[36]

A rebbetzin career provided a fruitful outlet for Rubenovitz's prodigious talents. Yet Rubenovitz understood the essential interconnectedness of her work and Herman's. At times, she saw herself as helpmate. She accompanied Herman when he served as "circuit preacher in town after town throughout New England," spreading the philosophy of Conservative Judaism. But more often, she saw them working on parallel tracks, each rushing in and out to meetings and appointments, busily involved in their separate spheres of Jewish life and relying on each other's support. For example, within a few months of their arrival in Boston, Herman Rubenovitz planned a demonstration in the old Boston Theater to protest the poor level of Jewish education in the city. When he learned, the morning of the event, that the theater was about to be condemned, Herman collapsed under the stress. But Mignon "carried on" in his stead.[37] Mignon dedicated one of her books to him: "To My Husband—My Teacher in the Jewish Way of Life"; he lauded her work as a "teacher and interpreter of Jewish values" and admired her desire to "supplement the written and spoken word with the concrete and visual embodiment of Jewish ideals." He expressed gratitude for having been worthy "to win so loving and devoted a companion, co-worker and helpmeet," who "fully shared in my hopes and labors for the advancement of Judaism."[38]

Others echoed these thoughts in congratulatory letters written in honor of Herman and Mignon's eightieth birthdays. Calling them the "spiritual aristocracy," Robert Gordis noted that American Jewry had been "doubly blessed" by the Rubenovitzes. Some attributed their success as a couple to Mignon's helpmate role, describing Herman as the "stellar soloist" and Mignon as the "gifted accompanist without whom his artistry could not have succeeded." Abraham Sachar complimented Mignon for her "lively concern for Jewish culture . . . 'gift of tongues,' and talent with the pen" and noted that these contributions paralleled Herman's. Understandably, the letter of tribute written by the national president of Hadassah primarily applauded Mignon's contributions while also noting the "valuable assistance" of her husband.[39]

That both Rubenovitzes saw her position as part of a joint rabbinate emerges most explicitly in their jointly authored publication, *The Waking Heart*. Herman and Mignon probably began writing separate memoirs, and Mignon combined them into one book when her husband died before either had been published. This book of his-and-hers memoirs and letters appears in two separate sections, each with its own table of contents. Herman's memoirs are first; Mignon's are subtitled "Pages From the Journal of a Rabbi's Wife." Herman and Mignon each review the influences that led them to dedicate their lives to Judaism, but their sections differ stylistically. Herman's includes letters written to him concerning issues of the day, especially the establishment of the Conservative Movement in its earliest stages. Several of Mignon's chapters are edited versions of articles that appeared over the years in the *Jewish Advocate* or *Outlook*.[40]

Given Mignon's commitment to visual representation, it is particularly instructive to examine the book's photographs. They graphically illustrate two professionals busy with their parallel careers: the rabbi in a clerical white robe and high hat; the rabbi speaking on behalf of Conservative Judaism or conducting services; Mignon in a suit with the caption "Mignon L. Rubenovitz, as she appeared at the time of great fulfillment in her life as a rabbi's wife. Busy days and nights with the women of the congregation, interspersed with many active hours spent with Hadassah and the National League of Jewish Women marked this period of her career." Another portrait of her appears with the description: "The author in the early days of the struggle of a rabbi and his wife to gain a foothold for Conservative Judaism in New England." As the book demonstrates, the Rubenovitzes took their ministerial careers equally seriously.[41]

In keeping with the dignified tone of the volume, they refer to each other formally as "Rabbi Rubenovitz" and "Mrs. Rubenovitz" and rarely reveal personal feelings or emotions. Yet hints of frustration emerge. For example, after one of their joint appearances on behalf of the Conservative Movement, Mignon asked Herman: "'Can't we ever leave the propaganda note in the background?'" He responded, no, for "it is our destiny to be pioneers." Together they concluded that despite occasional difficulties and disappointments, "we were committed to this role."[42]

In her eightieth birthday reflections, Mignon again touched on the drawbacks of the role.

> We chose to give up many cheerful sides of life, many hours of comfort and ease, in order that we might travel with our fellow Jews the road of great destiny—the promising, blossoming road of renewed Springtime for our people.[43]

But here too she acknowledged that the benefits of serving in this leadership role ultimately outweighed the limitations.

> How privileged have we been my husband and I, to have been captive to this vision; how privileged to have been the only two among many, in the generation that labored for, and achieved, a Jewish Renascence.[44]

Rubenovitz muted any tensions in this his-and-hers record of their career. Emphasizing the positives, she reiterated how fortunate she felt to have found a way to play a central role in strengthening American Jewish life. Through her museum as well as through the joint memoir, Rubenovitz cultivated her legacy by working, not behind the scenes, but alongside her husband to further American Judaism.

Rebecca Brickner

Rebecca Aaronson Brickner had much in common with Rubenovitz. Both from Baltimore and both influenced by Szold, these women also both fashioned activist rebbetzin roles. Working in different Movements in Judaism—Rubenovitz in Conservative and Brickner in Reform—and in different areas of the country—Rubenovitz in the northeast and Brickner in the Midwest—they each carved out a distinctive career as rabbi's wife. But Brickner's talents and interests as a Jewish educator led her to shape her career differently. Also, a wealth of written material, including sermons, talks, and private letters, provides an even more detailed view of the ups and downs intrinsic to the rebbetzin role.

Born on February 22, 1894, in Baltimore, Maryland, Rebecca Aaronson was one of thirteen children. Though not a rabbi's daughter, she remembered her parents as strong supporters of Jewish education whose home was open Sabbath afternoons to Jewish educators and community leaders. There, Rebecca—like many rabbis' daughters—listened to the men study Talmud and discuss current issues in Jewish education. Brickner attended a German-English school during the day. After school and on the Sabbath, she went to the Jewish school, whose principal was the young Jewish educator Samson Benderly.[45] Studying Bible, prayers, and literature in Hebrew, Brickner was also exposed to Zionist thinking. Brickner recalled loving classes, and she later described the magnetic quality of her early attraction to Jewish education as "soul touched soul." A gifted student, especially of the Hebrew language, Rebecca began teaching in that school by the age of thirteen—though most of the pupils were her siblings and cousins. Jewish educational materials for children were scarce at that time, and she remembered working with Benderly to develop Hebrew stories for her students.[46]

This early association with Benderly proved critical to Brickner's future. When, in 1910, Benderly took a position in New York City as director of the first Bureau of Jewish Education in the United States,

Rebecca Brickner. Courtesy of the American Jewish Archives, Cincinnati, Ohio.

Rebecca moved to New York to serve as his secretary and curriculum writer while attending college.[47] A member of the initial group of Benderly trainees, Rebecca studied at Columbia University with John Dewey and at the Jewish Theological Seminary's Teachers Institute with Mordecai M. Kaplan and Israel Friedlaender. She traveled the boroughs of New York City trying to interest young women in careers in Jewish education, and she then organized a preparatory school through the Teachers Institute to train them by teaching Bible, Jewish history, and modern Hebrew literature. During this period, Brickner also introduced the study of Hebrew into the Sunday School of New York City's Temple Emanu-El. A member of the Jewish Teachers' Association, Brickner, though female, very much belonged to the maverick group of Jewish educators known as the "Benderly boys."[48]

Benderly's wife, Jennie, also had a long-lasting impact on Brickner because she continued to work after her marriage. Serving as secretary, librarian, art and playground director, and teacher, Jennie used novel methods and techniques to teach Jewish subjects. She unwittingly modeled the kind of life Brickner aspired to, for Brickner saw the Benderlys as a "wonderful team. He would spin the ideas, and she would carry them out magnificently."[49]

Henrietta Szold also served as a mentor to Brickner. They grew up in the same neighborhood, and Rebecca admired Szold for her Jewish learning and dedication to education. When Rebecca moved to New York as a young, single woman, she lived next door to Szold and her mother. Rebecca recalled having to check in with Szold daily to give her an accounting of her studies.[50]

These early influences combined to effect Brickner's instrumental role in the founding of Hadassah. Judah Magnes, then president of New York's Kehillah, who had first learned of Rebecca during a visit to Benderly's school, asked her to teach Hebrew to the clubwomen of the Daughters of Zion. Brickner's involvement with this study circle placed her among the nucleus of women who established Hadassah in 1912. In Brickner's recollection, she and her peers had felt out of place among the "old women" of the Daughters of Zion and wanted to start a new association that would appeal to the "younger set." Present at the founding meeting of Hadassah, Brickner was elected to serve on its first board.[51]

Rebecca's future husband, Barnett Brickner, was also a "Benderly boy." A speaker and teacher, and one of the founders of what became the Zionist youth organization Young Judaea, Barnett too studied at both Columbia University and the Teachers Institute of the Jewish Theological Seminary. With last names close together in the alphabet, Rebecca Aaronson and Barnett Brickner met when seated next to each other in class. During that time, Barnett also worked as director of extension education for the Bureau of Jewish Education (1910–15). Drawn to each other like many other rabbinic couples of the era by their commitments to Jewish education and Zionism, the Brickners were married by Israel Friedlaender in 1919, the year of Barnett Brickner's ordination from Hebrew Union College.[52]

After their marriage, both Brickners continued their studies in Cincinnati—he for a Ph.D. at the University of Cincinnati, she at Hebrew Union College. With such an extensive Hebrew background, Brickner later recalled that she knew more Hebrew than most of her classmates and helped them with their Hebrew language skills. There is no indication that Brickner hoped to earn ordination by studying at HUC, as Martha Neumark did a few years later. Rather, Brickner simply took full advantage of the opportunity to advance her own knowledge, a habit she retained throughout her life.[53]

In 1920, the Brickners moved to Toronto, Canada, where Barnett became rabbi of Holy Blossom Temple, and Rebecca began her work as a congregational rebbetzin. In part, she saw this as an extension of her career as a Jewish educator, for she took responsibility for hiring and training religious school teachers. But Rebecca also assumed more typical helpmate duties such as entertaining visitors in her home. She formed the Temple Sisterhood and also founded the Toronto chapter of Hadassah.[54] Yet even at this early stage of her rebbetzin career, Brickner chafed at what she felt were the more frivolous aspects of the role. When she expressed her annoyance to Benderly, he counseled patience: "I can readily understand why you are longing to be among your own people instead of constantly chaperoning the ladies of the Sisterhood. You are still very young and your day may come yet."[55]

In 1925, the Brickners moved to Cleveland, where Barnett served as rabbi of the Euclid Avenue Temple (later called Fairmount Temple) until his death in 1958. Here the Brickners worked in partnership. As their son Balfour later remarked to the congregation: "For thirty years you really had two rabbis. . . . you only paid one; and two rabbis served this congregation alternately for many, many years."[56] With hired help to assist her, Rebecca Brickner focused on her rebbetzin duties. She conducted holiday workshops and contributed explanatory sections on the Sabbath and holidays to the Temple cookbook.[57] She entertained congregants in her home, having guests for dinner on Sunday after the main service of the week. Brickner also took on pastoral duties, paying hospital visits and condolence calls and keeping in touch with congregants by phone and mail.[58]

On Rosh Hashanah, the Brickners hosted a reception for the congregation in their home. Many rabbinic couples adopted this custom,[59] but the Brickners took it to the extreme. First, Rebecca trained those young women whom her husband had married during the preceding year to serve as hostesses. She instructed them on how to dress properly and how to pour tea. Her son, Balfour, recalled that close to 2,000 people lined the streets waiting to enter the Brickner home. When they came through the receiving line, Rebecca stood first, since she remembered names easily. She'd prompt her husband with lines like "Beryl, you remember Chaim."[60]

Rebecca also helped found the Young People's Congregation of the Fairmount Temple. Established after World War II to meet the religious needs of young couples under the age of thirty-five, it boasted four hundred members within the first year. As with many such projects, Barnett provided the original inspiration, but Rebecca's role proved critical to its implementation—just the dynamic she had admired in the Benderlys. After Barnett proposed the idea, Rebecca made phone calls, inviting prospective members to their home.[61]

Through these supportive activities, Brickner enhanced her husband's rabbinate. Yet Brickner also laid the groundwork for a more independent leadership presence in the congregation. In 1926, Brickner read Torah and preached a sermon from the pulpit to 700 women at a mother-daughter service. In subsequent years, Brickner led services many times when her husband was away. She also delivered numerous invocations, talks, lessons, and speeches to the Sisterhood on a wide variety of topics in Jewish life.[62]

Not content with these functions alone, Brickner soon extended her involvement into the larger Jewish community. Ever passionate about her first cause, Jewish education, Brickner played a critical role in founding the Cleveland College of Jewish Studies.[63] She also lectured frequently on Jewish history, Zionism, and Judaism to Hadassah, United Jewish Appeal, Pioneer Women, the Parent Teacher's Association, and ORT groups. When Stephen Wise wanted to form a Cleveland branch of the Women's Division of the American Jewish Congress, he asked Brickner to organize it, and prompted by her longstanding commitment to Zionism, she accepted. Brickner's reputation spread, and she was invited to address Sisterhoods and other women's groups in distant cities. She also attended Biennial Conventions of the National Federation of Temple Sisterhoods, where she focused her interests especially on expanding Sisterhood's role in religious education.[64]

Brickner also got involved in the larger Cleveland community, introducing non-Jews to Jewish beliefs and practices at interfaith gatherings.

Through her civic work, she had the opportunity to meet the First Lady at a small gathering of the leading clubwomen of Cleveland. Brickner recalled that Roosevelt "left a profound impression" on her, for she believed that Roosevelt was "as [triple underlined] capable as our beloved President Roosevelt." She went further, explaining that she looked upon Eleanor Roosevelt as the "Acting [triple underlined] Pres. of our United States. Our Pres. was handicapped and physically could not get around. She covered the country, acting for him with mind with body and with soul and showed great inner strength of courage as well as mind." In lauding Roosevelt's capabilities, energy, and courage, Brickner unmistakably demonstrated her identification with someone she saw as a kindred spirit.[65]

Like the Rubenovitzes, the Brickners often understood themselves as working in separate, complementary spheres, using their individual abilities to further common goals. This was true on an organizational level, but it was also evident on an intellectual one. For example, Rebecca spoke a fluent, literary Hebrew. Barnett, not as comfortable in Hebrew, spoke Yiddish effortlessly. Between the two of them they felt they could go to any Jewish community in the world. Their son, Balfour, recalls that "it was expected that mother handled one part of it, dad handled the other part of it. They lived in a kind of symbiotic way; they lived in each other's heads."[66]

The Brickners' two-person career functioned even when Barnett traveled. When he visited Jewish communities in Europe and Palestine for several months in 1927, Rebecca willingly and capably remained on top of synagogue business. She filled Barnett in on news about various congregants and encouraged him to be in touch with certain people: "Those cards you have been sending to friends mean more than you will ever know. Don't forget—," a reminder followed by a list of couples that she thought he ought to write to. Also: "The girls in the office should hear from you again."[67] Rebecca stopped short of taking on the rabbinic mantle in Barnett's absence. When approached about performing a wedding ceremony, Rebecca demurred.[68] She did, however, take a more activist role in her area of expertise, hiring both a new educational director, Nathan Brilliant, and several teachers for the religious school. Supplying Brilliant with "the curriculum and all the school stuff for his perusal during the summer," she assured her husband that "everything will be running smoothly by the time you get back."[69] This partnership suited the Brickners, and he depended on his wife to fill her part: "I am relying on you to see that Brilliant gets started . . . and also that the Bulletin comes out."[70]

At the same time, the personal correspondence between the two of them during Barnett's trip reveals Rebecca's ambivalence about their roles. His absence gave her increased power and influence in the congregation, which she relished. She also felt a great sense of satisfaction that she had made it possible for him to go. "I have still about two months wait, but I am not lonely. . . . I want you to know that I feel every moment away means wealth gained for you and therefore I am happy." Yet a few weeks later, Rebecca's words hinted at her resentment that Barnett had gone alone to the Zionist Convention, since Zionism was a passion they shared. "Naturally I should like to be with you in Basle. If we had the money to spare I might have surprised you."[71]

Several years later, Brickner redressed that imbalance. She took her own trip to Palestine with her children, Joy and Balfour, from March to August 1932. Certainly she and her husband decided to undergo the pain of a six-month separation in the belief that this would be good for the children, for they wanted the children to learn Hebrew and become devoted to the land. Rebecca's letters to Barnett describe the sorrow and longing of being apart, but they also reveal how essential the trip was for her own well-being. Rebecca insisted in one of her first letters that Barnett ought not to "worry about us one moment. . . . Remember I am the children's mother and they come first and above everything else that I might be interested in or would like to do."[72] But, in reality, Rebecca had high personal aspirations for this trip. Initiating this excursion "for the sake of the children," Brickner also gained a once-in-a-lifetime chance to attend to her own needs.

Once in Palestine, Brickner took full advantage of her time there. She toured the country with her children and gained inspiration from the landscapes, beaches, historic sites, agricultural accomplishments, and medical advances. She hired a private tutor in order to improve her Hebrew, and together they studied Jewish lore and modern Hebrew essays. Taking fifteen hours a week of classes at Hebrew University, Brickner relished being back in an academic environment because it made her feel as though she "were living those Friedlaender days over again."[73] Outside of class, she read works by S. Y. Agnon and Devorah Baron, "the two Iluyim [geniuses] in the land that everyone raves about."[74] She was deeply moved by the poetry of Rahel, which she discovered seren-dipitously in a bookstore.[75] Living among other American Jewish Zionist educators, she reconnected with old friends from her Benderly days, including Isaac Berkson and Bertha Schoolman.[76] Brickner visited with Szold, who at the age of seventy two, continued to inspire Brickner with her energy and creativity. Brickner also got to know Mignon Rubenovitz during this trip, thanks to their common ties to both Zionism and Szold.[77]

Through contacts with her professor, Joseph Klausner,[78] Brickner participated in discussions and lectures, including several with the renowned Hebrew poet Hayim Nahman Bialik. Teachers and scholars who met Brickner expressed great pleasure at her excellent Hebrew. She cherished their praise, repeating it to her husband. For example, Rebecca reported that her Hebrew teacher told her: "I am the most talented student that has ever come to him Michutx La-Aretz [from outside Palestine] and he will hate to give me up." And: "Everybody is simply astounded at my knowledge of Jewish culture and Hebrew. They can't understand how it could have been done in America. Even Dr. Klausner marvels at me." She then admitted that "it was thrilling to find yourself finally acknowledged. When the students saw me taking down my notes [in Hebrew] with accuracy and speed, they didn't believe their eyes." Klausner continued to sing Rebecca's praises a decade later. When Barnett traveled to Palestine in 1943–44, he visited Klausner and reported to his wife: "Well, was he glad to see me! . . . He regards you as one of the best pupils he had ever had."[79]

Satisfied that Joy and Balfour learned Hebrew during those months in Palestine, Brickner realized the ostensible goal of her trip. But she also met her personal goals, for she blossomed in her own right, not merely as a rabbi's wife. No matter how much she had accomplished as a rebbetzin in the United States, she only felt fully satisfied when she was on her own in Palestine. While she never articulated that it was her dependent status that disturbed her, her words betray some awareness of it. In contrast to her life in Cleveland, Palestine gave her the thrilling feeling of being "at home." There she felt herself "rejuvenated every day. Much fresher in spirit and lighter in body and keener of whatever mind I have." Surely, Brickner's exhilaration stemmed in large measure from being in the Jewish homeland for the first time, but she also attributed her newfound vitality to the many opportunities she explored for personal growth. As she explained, "Of course I feel that this trip has already done so much for me. It has opened up new vistas for me and lifted me out of the rut I was falling into." Brickner's words painfully illustrate the toll that restrictive gender expectations took on talented, ambitious women of the era. Being a career rebbetzin gave Brickner a platform from which to realize her goals, but even this position ultimately failed to fulfill her, because it derived from her status as "wife of." Only without her husband and congregation, in Palestine, did she feel fully productive and valued.[80]

As expected, Brickner worried about how she would manage when she returned home. "I don't know how I shall be able to g[o] on without this fresh stream of Mekor Mayim Chayim [source of living waters] when I get back. It will be hard." Her solution involved imagining ways to channel her new knowledge and energy into educating others about Palestine and raising needed funds for it. "Needless to say I come home dejected, but with a firm resolve to do more and more for Hadassah." Once back in Cleveland, Brickner also reasserted her role as "rabbi" of the Sisterhood. She incorporated her new learning and passion into her courses, invocations, and sermons and redoubled her efforts to enhance the Jewishness of the congregation's women.[81]

Brickner was widowed unexpectedly in 1958 when her husband died after a car accident during a trip to Spain. Words of comfort from rabbinic colleagues across the country emphasize her essential role in his rabbinate. As Gertrude and Samuel Mayerberg wrote: "You have been a wonderful helpmate to your husband and you really aided him in achieving a permanent place in the history of Israel." Similarly: "He was a fortunate man to have a wife like you. I can't imagine that he would have achieved all that he did in life without your wisdom and grace to give him constant encouragement and strength." Yet one letter hints at the limitations that this secondary position posed for someone as talented as Rebecca by acknowledging that she had "sacrificed a great personal career to give so much of Barney to his people."[82]

After Barnett's death, Brickner's leadership talents flourished further. Since she remained dependent on her "widow of" position for her power base, Rebecca continued to guide the Fairmount Temple Sisterhood. Addressing Sisterhood members frequently, she grew increasingly accomplished as a speaker. Brickner complimented honorees, celebrated the dedication of women volunteers, and reminded her audiences of the higher religious principles that ought to inform their work. In talks on a variety of topics, she continually educated her audience, including

Hebrew quotes from biblical and rabbinic sources as well as popular citations from American literature and government.[83]

Brickner also took on new causes, devoting herself especially to the World Union for Progressive Judaism, an organization dedicated to strengthening liberal congregations outside North America. By the 1960s, she had joined their governing body and raised considerable funds. So central did she see this among her priorities that she noted that she had "practically become Lady Montagu's heir." Montagu, one of the founders of the World Union, who served as its honorary secretary and chief organizer, was, according to the historian Michael A. Meyer, "the first significant woman in the history of the Reform movement." How fitting that Brickner chose to identify herself with this powerful female religious leader.[84]

Brickner's accomplishments invited comparisons between her and Eleanor Roosevelt, especially since both women attained even wider renown in widowhood. For example, *The Sun Press* noted that "both women gave their husbands firm foundations for family life and solid support in their public service. Later, in their years alone, both women gained prominence for achievements of their own."[85]

Rebecca Brickner also mentored rabbinic couples over the years. One rabbi noted proudly that he counted himself among the rabbis that Brickner "adopted" and guided "through those difficult days of adjustment" in the early years of his rabbinate, "thus softening some of the blows of the active rabbinate."[86] She played an especially important role for Arthur J. Lelyveld, Barnett's successor as rabbi of Fairmount Temple. As he explained:

> She has been over the years a *rebbetzin's rebbetzin.* . . . Rebecca Brickner presided over sessions of teaching for rabbis' wives—how to do it. That's public. What I want to tell you privately is that she also gathered together the rabbis and taught them how to be rabbis. And what's more, we all learned and continue to learn.[87]

Rabbis commonly refer to the best among them as a "rabbi's rabbi." This is the first discovered instance of the use of the feminine counterpart, "rebbetzin's rebbetzin," and it aptly reflects the role Brickner played in mentoring rabbis' wives. Sylvia Lieberman recalled that as a young rebbetzin, she attended a panel for wives at an annual Central Conference of American Rabbis convention. One suggestion that stuck with her was Brickner's advice to have cards printed so that if no one is home when the rebbetzin calls on congregants, she can leave her card at the door, thereby making the visit worthwhile nonetheless.[88]

Yet not all rebbetzins found Brickner's example inspiring. In fact, although Arthur Lelyveld benefited from her guidance, his first wife, Toby, found Brickner's standards daunting, and she recoiled from the rabbi's wife role. Similarly, Louise Reichert, who later helped orient the wives of HUC rabbinic students in the post–World War II era, remembered that she and other wives initially found Brickner intimidating. Brickner's descriptions of hosting Open Houses for thousands of congregants seemed out of reach to young rebbetzins coping with how to serve a few cookies to a small group. At the same time, Brickner modeled the standard to which many young rebbetzins aspired.[89]

In her later years, Brickner gained further public recognition for her accomplishments. For her pioneering role as a Jewish educator, Brickner received the first honorary doctorate in Hebrew letters conferred by the Cleveland College of Jewish Studies in 1971.[90] Brickner earned a Master of Hebrew Literature degree from the College the following spring.[91]

Alfred Gottschalk, president of Hebrew Union College-Jewish Institute of Religion marked Brickner's eightieth birthday with a special citation, which noted that Brickner's accomplishments were "in the forefront of those who have helped indoctrinate a whole generation of Jews with the ideals, the hopes, and the aspirations of our people and our faith." At the same time, the citation paid tribute to her helpmate role, to "the part played by his brilliant Rivkah in helping him [Barnett] achieve a great ministry. She was his strong right hand, advising, sympathizing, always eager to be of service to him, always helpful to every congregant." Sixteen years of widowhood notwithstanding, Brickner continued to garner praise for her "wife of" role.[92]

Like Carrie Simon, Brickner championed causes that foreshadowed the future direction of Reform in the twentieth century. Her commitments to Zionism, Jewish ritual, Hebrew, Jewish education, and women's advancement animated her work as a rebbetzin while at the same time challenging the Movement to embrace them. Brickner's accomplishments illustrate the way certain rebbetzins, working with their husbands, played a critical role in the growth and transformation of Reform in mid-twentieth-century America. These rabbinic couples stood in the vanguard, slowly moving their constituency to embrace ideals, such as Zionism, that gradually became part of mainstream Reform.

Given Brickner's views about women, it is not surprising that her husband Barnett championed the cause of women's ordination in 1955 during his presidency of the Central Conference of American Rabbis. Surely affected by his wife's frustrations at the unjust juxtaposition of first-rate knowledge and ability with secondary status, he exhorted, "Why should we grant women degrees only in Religious Education, qualifying them to be educational directors yet denying them the prerogative to be preachers as well as teachers? They have a special spiritual and emotional fitness to be rabbis." His biographer concluded that the primary reason for Barnett's belief that women were capable of being rabbis is that "he was married to just such a woman."[93]

Would Brickner have preferred to have become a rabbi herself? From the evidence, it appears that, though frustrated at times by her subordinate role, she did not initially aspire to the rabbinate. But in later years, when she reflected on her life, she realized that she would have wanted just that. According to Nadell, after her husband's death, Rebecca continued to champion the ordination issue that Barnett had raised. When Sally Priesand became HUC's first ordained woman rabbi in 1972, Balfour Brickner remembered his mother being angry and resentful, because she recalled completing the course of study at Hebrew Union College so many years earlier without receiving ordination. Because of this, she saw the 1974 Gottschalk tribute as a belated acknowledgment of her learning and accomplishments. Though the word "ordination" does not appear in the citation, Brickner later recalled the occasion as being "in lieu of Ordination," explaining that in her day, women were not ordained. That she came to see herself as a rabbi emerges most vividly in a photograph taken at her son's 1980 installation as rabbi of New York's Stephen Wise Free Synagogue. With Balfour kneeling before her in front of the ark, Rebecca stood above him, arms outstretched to bless him. When asked in 1983 whether she would have been a rabbi had it been possible, Brickner admitted: "I could have conceived of that for myself."[94]

In many ways, Rebecca Brickner's life exemplifies the opportunities and drawbacks of the rebbetzin's role in mid-twentieth-century America. Though Brickner experienced irritation over the confines of the position, she seized the opportunities it presented and made the most of them. By marrying a man who shared her larger vision and goals for American Jewish life and serving as his partner, Brickner had manifold opportunities to shine as a leader. Concentrating on ideals and values

Rebecca Brickner blessing Balfour. Courtesy of Rabbi Balfour Brickner.

most important to her, Brickner shaped her career in a way that best suited her talents and abilities and that got her as far as it was possible to go within the constraints of her time.

Tamar de Sola Pool and Tehilla Lichtenstein

Tamar Hirschensohn de Sola Pool also demonstrated a perceptive awareness of the difficulties of the rebbetzin role early in her career. In 1925, when Pool served as a respondent in the rabbi's wife symposium, she challenged the self-effacement advocated by veteran rebbetzins Kohut and Hyamson. Though bluntly admitting the inevitability of "antimony" between rabbis' wives and congregations, Pool insisted that relying on tact to eliminate friction ultimately proved harmful to the rebbetzin. "We see innocent tact become an instrument of the weakening of the individual personality of, shall we say, the constant tactor? . . . I look upon it as a servile instrument bound to be a destructive force in the long run." In her view,

> The Minister's wife must be free, absolutely free to act and say and do what she thinks is right in a situation without yielding to debasing politics and politicians. . . . An attitude of personal freedom on the part of the Minister and his wife is the only avenue to the ultimate destruction of politics in the Synagogal life. Freedom and truth and the right to one's own individual personality, as against politics, soul-destroying diplomacy, and sanctimoniousness, that is, it seems to me, the way along which we wives of Rabbis must travel to ensure the lasting beauty, nobility and idealism in our lives as human beings, and soul-mates to our chosen companions. This, it seems to me, must be the attitude of the Rabbi no less than that of the Rabbanith [rebbetzin].[95]

Like Brickner, both Tamar and her sister Tehilla lived their lives in this manner, finding avenues to contribute to Jewish life without sublimating their own individual personalities. Since both married rabbis and Tehilla succeeded her husband and served herself as religious leader, a look at both their lives yields special insight into the development of the role in the interwar period.

Born in Jerusalem—Tamar in 1890 and Tehilla in 1893—these two women, like many rabbis' daughters, experienced an intensively Jewish upbringing. Their father, Hayyim Hirschensohn, an outstanding Talmudist, prolific author, and dedicated Zionist, counted himself among the first collaborators of the linguist Eliezer ben Yehuda in the revival of the Hebrew language. Like Ben Yehuda, Hirschensohn and his wife Eva chose to make Hebrew the "Mother Tongue" of their home. Hirschensohn was also particularly supportive of formal education for his daughters. In 1904, the family moved to the United States, where Hirschensohn served as rabbi of Hoboken, New Jersey.[96]

Tamar attended Hunter College, graduating Phi Beta Kappa in 1913. Throughout her life, she remained cognizant of the unique privileges

Tamar de Sola Pool. Courtesy of Hadassah, The Women's
Zionist Organization of America, Inc.

and responsibilities that such an education bestowed on her. As she
later explained to subsequent students: "We have attained a position of
scholarship and general academic standing excelled by no other women's
college in the country. It is our duty to utilize this power to the utmost."
Even in her old age she recalled that she owed Hunter "a debt that takes
a lifetime to discharge, a debt that grows as you discharge it." Two
years later, Tehilla graduated from Hunter as well. Tehilla then continued her education, earning a Master of Arts in literature from Columbia University, and she began doctoral work there in English literature.[97]

Upon her graduation from Hunter, Tamar became the first recipient of an international travel scholarship to France offered to a senior in an American college by the Société Nationale des Professeurs français en Amérique. Upon her return, Tamar joined the faculty of Hunter College, teaching French, Latin, Greek, and Comparative Literature. She also served as faculty adviser to the Menorah Society (1915–17), a Jewish collegiate association. At the same time, she too continued her studies on the graduate level (1914–17) at Columbia University.[98]

Already an activist in her youth, Pool served as president of the New Jersey Woman Suffrage Association (1915–17), but she soon concentrated her efforts on Jewish causes. She first became involved in Young Judaea, and it was at the 1915 Young Judaea convention that she met her future husband, David de Sola Pool, then Young Judaea's president. Since 1907, David had also served as rabbi of Shearith Israel in New York, an Orthodox congregation that was the oldest Sephardic synagogue in the United States. According to Tamar, David sought her out because he had been told that there was a "unique phenomenon" at the convention: a girl who spoke Hebrew. They married in February 1917.[99]

The story of their courtship foreshadowed their future relationship. David was drawn to Tamar because he was impressed by her knowledge and commitments to Zionism and Hebrew language. Tamar was initially intimidated by David's public reputation, learning, and achievements, and she feared speaking or writing to him in Hebrew. By the time they became engaged, David had taken to rewriting sermons to Tamar's high standards, teasing "what a hard taskmaster you are, bless you!" He not only valued her writing skills and logical mind; he had also grown to respect her judgment. Concerning the religious question of whether they ought to fast before their wedding, David wrote that fasting was "only a *minhag* [custom] not a *din* [law]. Nor even is it Talmudic." He explained the reasons mentioned in the *Shulhan Arukh*, but conceded that, despite his being an ordained rabbi, "you know more about the causes and authority of the *minhag*. You may be able to make up your mind about it with more decision."[100]

Their courtship formed the foundation of a partnership that flourished for more than fifty years. So highly were they both regarded that one commentator noted that pre–World War II Jewry admiringly referred to them as " 'Pools of Jewish Scholarship, literature and wisdom' because of their many contributions to Jewish learning and their half century of leadership in a host of Jewish educational and religious movements in some of the great events of 20th century Jewish history."[101]

Upon her marriage, Tamar, like most of her peers, resigned her job and focused on her rabbi's wife career. Pool sought the guidance of her predecessor, Rebecca Rosalie Piza Mendes, wife of rabbi emeritus Henry Pereira Mendes, and the older woman embraced Pool as a "spiritual daughter." Pool welcomed newcomers and put congregants at ease; she became involved in Sisterhood and also served as a representative to the Christian community.[102] The Pools lived with their children, Naomi and Ithiel, in a parsonage physically attached to the synagogue, and they also entertained visitors and guests often, including hosting an open house every Tuesday. Not much of a cook, Tamar kept those gatherings simple. Naomi remembers passing a cookie plate around, while her parents focused on providing spiritual and emotional sustenance.[103]

This hospitality became even more pronounced on Fire Island, where the Pools summered for many years. Until the crowds grew too large, the Pools held religious services in their living room and hosted an *Oneg* (reception) Friday nights. The Pools took advantage of the calm, ocean atmosphere to introduce people to Jewish life in an inviting, unthreatening manner. One woman explained that though she "never became observant in the Orthodox manner of the de Sola Pools," by opening "up their personal and public lives to us without any restrictions," they made her feel comfortable with herself as a Jew.[104]

Writing provided Pool with a separate sphere of accomplishment after marriage, just as it did for many rabbis' wives. Pool published articles and book reviews on a range of topics, from ancient Jewish history to Russian Jewry and Jewish education. These works reveal Pool's commitment to Jewish life in all its facets and her desire to make Judaism accessible to all Jews. This meant creating different ways for Jews to study Hebrew language, Bible, Jewish history, synagogue ritual, and Jewish tradition.

Through her articles, one learns that Pool initially coupled her literary ambitions and her "wife of" role by authoring pieces that highlighted the special insights she had gained as wife and mother. For example, when David served as a member of Herbert Hoover's Food Conservation staff in 1917, Tamar was privy to important information that she shared with her readers. She implored them to study the publications of the Food Bureau and adjust the fatty, heavy Jewish diet accordingly. Similarly, after the Armistice, David joined the First Zionist Commission to Palestine, and the Pools lived in Palestine for three years. Tamar promoted Zionism by writing for American Jewish publications about the way Jewish women managed household duties in Palestine.[105]

Gradually Pool branched out on her own, particularly through Hadassah. Like Rubenovitz and Brickner, Pool came under Szold's influence. The Pools got together with Szold and other friends on Friday evenings. Szold also groomed Pool as a public speaker. Critiquing Pool's early talks, Szold offered suggestions that would help Pool be "direct, clear, and unexceptionable—worth while and needful." Szold apparently succeeded, for Pool was frequently invited to speak on matters pertaining to Israel and Jewish life. In 1929, Pool became president of Hadassah's New York chapter, and from 1939 to 1943 she served as national president. From her niece's perspective, "it was but the logical conclusion" to all that she had done.[106]

In the 1930s, Pool's journalistic and Zionist passions converged when she took over the editorship of the *Hadassah Newsletter*. Under her leadership, the *Newsletter's* circulation exceeded 73,000. Just as *Outlook* had done for Davidson, the *Newsletter* gave Pool an audience for her views while showcasing her writing and editing skills. She loved the work, noting in somewhat exaggerated fashion, "I feel more strongly than ever that we have the opportunity of developing the necessary Jewish woman's journal. . . . I really enjoy the work of the Newsletter and wish I had nothing else to do."[107] When Pool became national president of Hadassah, she temporarily relinquished the editorship. But she continued writing monthly editorial columns that kept her readers informed about world events, especially in Palestine. She also advocated her favorite projects. For example, she exhorted Hadassah women to vote regularly, and she heavily promoted Youth Aliyah. In 1944, after relinquishing the presidency, Pool resumed the editorship of the *Newsletter* and continued in that position until October 1947.[108]

During her years with Hadassah, Pool succeeded in widening its scope. She played an instrumental role in bringing the work of Youth Aliyah into the program of Hadassah and served as an early proponent of the Hebrew University-Hadassah Medical School. Pool chaired its building fund committee and helped initiate its classes during her visit to Israel in 1948. In 1947, she also organized the construction of Ramat Hadassah Szold, a reception center for Youth Aliyah arrivals.[109]

Pool also used her public position to decry the Nazi terror. In the 1930s, she noted ironically that by expelling Jews from Germany, Hitler had given the Jews a gift, for he had returned them to Palestine. But after the outbreak of war, she continually registered alarm and urged her audiences to work through Hadassah to promote justice and peace in the world. "We must fortify ourselves in our ideals by coming together . . . by proving through our own courageous living the transcendence and the power of the ideals in which we believe."[110]

Immediately after the war, Pool dedicated her efforts to improving the lot of child survivors. She visited a Cyprus detention camp for Hadassah and found the living conditions of the children appalling. Deeply moved by the children's spirit despite the horrors they had experienced and the indignities, frustration, and boredom they continued to endure, Pool launched a campaign among Americans to secure for the children textbooks, pencils, paper, and especially, tools for sewing and other handicrafts.[111]

By focusing her Hadassah work on youth, Pool walked a fine line concerning gender roles. On the one hand, she portrayed herself as a mother concerned about her "children," as that image enhanced support for projects such as Youth Aliyah. It also enabled Pool to broaden her involvements to include the presidency of the American Mother's Committee of the Golden Rule Foundation. On the other hand, Pool benefited from an interwar ethos that lauded clergy wives for their focus on community concerns. This attitude made it possible for her to spend Passover in Cyprus, away from her family—with all the neglect of traditional Jewish family duties that this implied. Reports of her trip gave no indication that this decision engendered tension or criticism from her husband, children, congregants, or Hadassah women.[112]

Like her peers, Pool had several opportunities to interact personally with Eleanor Roosevelt over the years. She accompanied Roosevelt when the latter was honored with the establishment of a chair in the history and philosophy of science at the Hebrew University. Fittingly, Pool also corresponded with Roosevelt concerning the Henrietta Szold Centennial. These two outstanding female leaders worked together to honor the memory of a third.[113]

What is unusual about the Pools is that in addition to the remarkable triumphs each achieved singly, they also collaborated on projects in a way that expanded on what either could have accomplished alone. The Rubenovitzes wrote a his-and-hers memoir. But, written in two distinct parts and published after Herman's death, the volume did not represent a true collaborative effort. In contrast, the Pools worked closely on several projects over the years. First, they traveled around the world together, especially to Israel and remote Sephardic communities. During their trips, the Pools sent "Dear Everybody" letters to congregants, relatives, and friends, a tradition Tamar continued after her husband's death. These letters described the various cities, traditions, and people they encountered. Back in the United States, this team reporting took the form of "Duologues," joint lectures in which the Pools spoke to each other and their audiences about their travels. As the duologues grew in popularity, the Pools added new topics to their repertoire. In 1961–62, the Pools went on a joint lecture tour sponsored by the Jewish Center Lecture Bureau of the National Jewish Welfare Board. They spoke on "The Jerusalem Trial of Adolf Eichmann: A Challenge to Civilization and Israel's Answer," "Dilemmas of Our Time—Preview of a Book," "The Swift Clock of Israel: From the Balfour Declaration to the Bar Mitzvah of the State," and "A Look at Jewish History: Why I Am a Jew, an Old Faith in the New World, and Ideas and Ideals." The publicity materials for the tour present them as equals in side-by-side photos: David is identified as "Rabbi, author, community leader," and Tamar as "Hadassah leader, author, teacher."[114]

Finally, the Pools authored several books together, including *An Old Faith in the New World: Portrait of Shearith Israel, 1654–1954* and *The Haggadah of Passover.* The latter, with a "new interpretive" English translation, was originally prepared for use by the Jewish men and women in the United States armed forces. The Pools noted that the *haggadah* inspired in them "a heightened dedication to the ideal of liberty doubly theirs as Americans and as Jews." It first appeared in 1943 and became instantly popular, and the basic text and format have continued to be used through dozens of printings over the decades.[115]

In the early 1960s the Pools co-authored *Is There an Answer?*, "a continuing conversation on questions that do not leave us." This reflective volume drew on the lessons they had gleaned from encounters with their audiences. A typed manuscript of the book contains no clues concerning who wrote which sections or how the authors wove their views together. Perhaps the seamless quality of the manuscript aptly captures the nature of their work. The Author's Note provides a rare moment of self-reflection: they wrote the book to "extend the ministry of our lives,"[116] an acknowledgment not only that they understood their writing to be an extension of their calling but also that they understood the rabbinate to be a two-person career to which both dedicated their lives.

In many ways, these collaborative efforts provided Tamar with the most sustained venue for an equal partnership. The Pools' dual billing on publicity material, their joint writing, and their interactive presentations exemplified their team ministry. Tamar's reaction to one of David's writings reveals by way of contrast the significance of such recognition. Among the works for which her husband became best known was the Sephardic prayer book he edited and translated. After David's death, Tamar protested proposed changes to the prayer book by noting that "while I have only been a junior partner in this undertaking and did not allow my name to appear in the original publication of the Sephardi liturgy, I have worked with Dr. Pool for twenty-five years on the details of the translation." Years after the fact, Tamar resented her invisibility on this project. Perhaps her decision not to appear as coauthor of this project reminded her too painfully of the self-effacing rebbetzin role she had rejected publicly decades earlier, in the symposium.[117]

Though Tamar emphasized her role as equal, others emphasized the more subordinate, helpmate role. For example, a *Jewish Post* article on one of Tamar's speaking engagements in Louisville, Kentucky, included the subtitle: "Wife of eminent rabbi will address Hadassah." Only in the third paragraph did the article note that Pool was a former national president of Hadassah, surely a more significant credential, given her audience. Similarly as a widow, Tamar remained a vital leader particularly in causes she and David shared, such as the Sephardic community. Lauded on many occasions for her own accomplishments, personality, and commitment, Tamar also continued to garner praise with the traditional helpmate metaphor of being an "'ezer kenegdo'[118] [fitting helpmate] in all the innumerable literary and cultural achievements of her great unforgettable husband. With her own work she illuminates in brilliant light his blessed memory."[119]

Pool succeeded in raising the level of Jewish involvement of American Jewish women both through her work with her husband and through Hadassah. Most important, she moved fluidly from one role to the other, modeling the tremendous opportunities available to rebbetzins of the time to get involved both within the congregation and in national organizations, both in partnership with their husbands and in their own spheres. While she experienced certain frustrations with the limitations of her role, Pool generally displayed confidence about and satisfaction with all she had accomplished.

Tehilla Hirschenson Lichtenstein, Tamar's sister, was also a rabbi's wife, yet her path to leadership took her in a very different direction. In 1920, Tehilla married Morris Lichtenstein, one of the first eastern European students to attend Hebrew Union College. Having been ordained in 1916, he earned his Master of Arts at Columbia University three years later. Tehilla's father admired Morris, despite the fact that Morris was a Reform anti-Zionist who lacked the Hebraic background valued by the Hirschenson family. Tehilla left graduate school when she married. She and Morris had two sons, Immanuel and Michael. Morris first served as rabbi in Athens, Georgia; then, in 1922, he founded the Society of Jewish Science in New York City.[120]

Tehilla worked closely with her husband to stem the tide of Jews attracted to the Christian Science movement by demonstrating the appeal of Jewish Science, a unique blend of psychology, spiritual healing, and Jewish teachings. According to the Lichtensteins, Jewish Science was "applied Judaism," the application of Judaism to everyday life. They aimed through their writings, addresses, and counseling to help individuals find inner peace and contentment.[121]

During Morris's lifetime, Tehilla served in the unofficial "assistant pastor" role typical of the period. She was principal of the religious school and editor of the monthly periodical, the *Jewish Science Interpreter*. But after Morris's death in 1938, Tehilla had the rare opportunity to minister on her own. Morris's will had specified that leadership go to one of his sons, or, if neither accepted, to Tehilla. As a widow, she carried on their joint work by becoming the first American Jewish woman to serve as the spiritual leader of a congregation, a position she held until shortly before her death in 1973. The uniqueness of this achievement was not lost on her contemporaries. According to the *New York Times*, more than five hundred people came to hear her deliver her first sermon.[122]

In the decades after Morris's death, Tehilla edited the *Interpreter*, preached on Sundays at the home center in New York City, taught classes, and counseled congregants.[123] Most of her sermons subsequently appeared in the *Jewish Science Interpreter*. Lichtenstein trained a number of members to become practitioners or spiritual healers, and

Tehilla Lichtenstein. Courtesy of the American Jewish
Archives, Cincinnati, Ohio.

in the 1950s she hosted a weekly radio broadcast offering a combination of practical advice and Jewish Science teachings. Lichtenstein also
wrote several pamphlets to popularize the Movement, including *What
It Means to Be a Jew* (1943), *Religion and Medicine* (1945), *Psychology
and Religion* (1948), *A Cure for This Sick World* (1950), and *Choosing
Your Way to Happiness* (1954). Through all of these venues, Lichtenstein promoted the message of Jewish Science.[124]

Lichtenstein illustrated her ideas by weaving together rabbinic
sources, American literature, and the human experience. For example,
in one of her classic Yom Kippur sermons—delivered with slight mod-
ifications in at least three different years—Lichtenstein comforted her

flock by appealing to both the *Shulhan Arukh* (a sixteenth-century code of Jewish Law compiled by Joseph Karo) and human psychology:

> The seed of forgiveness is in the human heart; it flowers quickly when the tears of penitence fall upon it. We forgive others, as God forgives us; we cannot ourselves bear the barrier which resentment and hardness towards another creates between us. It is not others, it is ourselves that some of us, many of us, find hard to forgive; but that, too, we must achieve in order to be spiritually whole, and yes, psychically healthy.[125]

Lichtenstein believed that tradition would survive only if courageous individuals stepped forward to change it. This progressive outlook, coupled with Lichtenstein's own experience in a rabbinic role, led her to support equality for women in Jewish ritual life, including counting them in the *minyan* (quorum required for public prayer) and opening the door to their ordination. Yet in personality, Tehilla, a warm, spiritual person, preferred one-on-one ministering to the public activist role. In that vein, Lichtenstein, harking back to the views of Mathilde Schechter and Carrie Simon, muted her radical suggestions by extolling the traditional homemaker role. Even in her sermon promoting egalitarianism, she conceded that "a woman's greatest career, can be, if she chooses it, and should be, perhaps, the making of the home." Over the years, she highlighted the special influence of Jewish mothers, the unique gifts of womanhood, and the potential of both to strengthen Jewish life. In her words: "a good mother is worth more than a thousand schoolmasters." Despite praising women's employment during World War II for demonstrating to many that women were "just as capable and just as intelligent and just as talented as men," she continued to promote women's roles at home. In her view, after the war, women ought to shift their focus toward running a gracious home and rearing children well.[126]

Lichtenstein also continued to revere her husband as founder of the movement, publicly praising his accomplishments and presenting herself as faithfully carrying on his work. As she explained, "whatever little good I have been able to bring into the lives of others because of the perceptions he gave me . . . whatever part of the structure of my life was built in accordance with the plans he drew and the tools he gave me . . . that is the temple I have built and I dedicate it to him." Yet in the decades after his death, Lichtenstein did adjust the message of Jewish

Science. Over time, her sermons reflected more and more her own priorities. There was a diminished concern with healing—to be expected given the waning attraction of Christian Science for Jews. Her later addresses incorporated the goal of healing into a broader commitment to Jewish life, which included involvement with Jewish teachings, with Palestine and the State of Israel, with achieving inner peace, and with relationships between human beings. By portraying her success as having derived from her husband's guidance and talents, Lichtenstein reassured those who might be threatened by either the new direction of her message or the female promoting it.[127]

Tehilla's role as leader, however unusual at the time, did little to raise expectations that other rabbis' wives might seek to serve as rabbis themselves. In part because the Society of Jewish Science remained outside the mainstream of American Judaism,[128] her tenure had little effect on other rabbis' wives or on American Jewry as a whole. Also, though she served on her own for many years after Morris's death, Tehilla worked in areas—speaking, teaching, counseling, and writing—that fell within the parameters of the rebbetzin role of the time. She also continued to portray herself as carrying on both her own work and her husband's. That is how her sister Tamar viewed Tehilla's accomplishments. Praising the Lichtensteins' work, Tamar noted that "it would take lots to equal Tehilla and the great messages that she and Morris Lichtenstein have brought over these many years to their devoted congregation." Tamar could well have been speaking about any one of dozens of interwar couples who served so ably in two-person careers.[129]

The public nature of the activist rebbetzin role raises several larger questions. First, one is struck by the extent to which housekeeping help and either childlessness or childcare formed essential components of rebbetzins' success. More research is needed to determine the pervasiveness of these factors among rebbetzins at the time and their relationship to prevailing middle-class mores and attitudes.

Second, these rebbetzins shared the expectation of clergy wives of the period that they devote themselves primarily to their communal responsibilities rather than to childrearing. One wonders about the impact of this choice on their children. Pool's daughter, Naomi, felt that she benefited from the public nature of her mother's life. Naomi understood that Tamar's communal interests, obligations, and passions took precedence over childrearing, yet she felt privileged rather than deprived by her mother's commitments. Naomi recalled the excitement of traveling with her mother, and she remembered Tamar instilling high expectations to do the right thing and live up to her potential. Naomi praised her parents for never goading or punishing in order to instill their values, but intead encouraging their children to use their intellects and talents to the best of their ability.[130] Balfour Brickner echoed Naomi's views. So akin were their mothers in their learning, drive, ambition, values, and commitments that it is not surprising that Brickner and Pool inculcated in their children remarkably similar attitudes. Yet Balfour, who became a prominent Reform rabbi in his own right, admitted to feeling much more pressure to live up to high parental standards than Naomi did. At his mother's seventy-fifth birthday celebration, Balfour confessed that though he was a grown man and a rabbi, he still feared reading Torah with his mother in the room without very careful preparation, for she winced at every mistake.[131]

Third, most of these women found outlets for their leadership talents outside their husbands' congregations. Especially through Hadassah, but also through other organizations as well, these women found ways to enhance their skills and confidence free of congregational expectations. These independent venues also enabled them to grow without fear of competing with their husbands.

Finally, all four rebbetzins continued their public lives of service after their husbands died. Lichtenstein especially blossomed most fully as a widow. Given the deeply embedded gender expectations of the era, one can assume that as rabbis' widows these women gained strength from and support for furthering the two-person career goals fashioned with their husbands. But these rebbetzins, having for decades been uniquely situated to observe American Jewish life, had also developed their own understanding of community needs. Then, with the skills, experience, and status they achieved in their rebbetzin years, they felt encouraged as widows to work toward meeting them.

These "career rebbetzins" were larger-than-life women who left their mark not only during the interwar years but also during the postwar period. They exemplified the successful, activist rebbetzin—highly educated, ambitious, and visionary. Each served in partnership with her husband to enrich Jewish life. Then, building on the reputation of her husband, each also used her talents and interests to transform an organization or field of endeavor. Many of these same qualities would also characterize their successors in the postwar era. But the unique challenges facing American Jewry in that period, coupled with contradictory messages to women from society as a whole, would alter the contours of the rebbetzin role yet again. Postwar rabbis' wives would struggle both to measure up to the reputations of their predecessors and to navigate their own paths to leadership.

4

Two for the Price of One

In 1954, the Jewish Publication Society again presented a rebbetzin as fictional protagonist. Margaret Abrams's *Awakened,* written in response to a request for novels on inspirational Jewish themes, featured Ellen Rosen and her husband, Kurt. Refugees from Europe on the eve of World War II, the Rosens struggled to adjust both to their new country and to being an American rabbinic couple. Depicted as a supportive helpmate, Ellen made pastoral calls with her husband, enhanced a wartime wedding with song and refreshment, and befriended a beleaguered convert to Judaism. In the final climactic scene, when an influential congregant's son disappeared just before his bar mitzvah, Ellen alone was able to locate him. Only she understood his anguish and gave him the courage to return home to successfully assume his role. Just as in Lily Routtenberg's account, here too the rebbetzin came to the rescue.[1]

One of the Jewish Publication Society's best-selling titles,[2] *Awakened* succeeded in part because the rebbetzin role continued to be valued and respected during the 1940s, 1950s, and 1960s. Rebbetzins also became more visible as a group during this time, calling attention to the special nature of their roles as both Jewish religious leaders and clergy wives. In contrast to their predecessors, these rebbetzins prepared for their roles more deliberately. They also shared their experiences more openly, cataloguing the joys, expectations, and responsibilities of the role as well as its challenges, limitations, and frustrations. In so doing, rebbetzins increased public awareness of their position, but they also punctured its idealized aura. Abrams sidestepped these realities by choosing a recent immigrant for her protagonist rather than a contemporary American rebbetzin.

In the postwar period, modern American rebbetzins identified closely not only with each other but also with their American Christian counterparts, and the feeling was reciprocated. This coincided with the way

Americans generally came to view Judaism in the postwar period. Signified by the 1955 publication of Will Herberg's *Protestant–Catholic–
Jew*,[3] Judaism gained recognition as one of the country's three great religions. This mutual recognition was anticipated earlier, for in the 1942
edited volume *I Married a Minister*, one of the seventeen selections is
Ruth Wolf Levi's "I Married a Rabbi." The editor, Golda Bader, herself
both a minister's wife and an ordained minister (despite her Yiddish first
name), produced the work during the war years specifically to underscore the role women might play in improving the world by highlighting
"a group who have dedicated themselves through the men they married." As Bader explained, the minister's wife, "like any wife . . . is first
of all a homemaker . . . but the home is only a part of her work. She is
a leader in church and community who concerns herself with matters of
world-wide moment. . . . she is a loyal coworker with her husband in
their labors to bring the Kingdom of God to earth." "Ministers' wives"
—and, in her view, that term encompassed rabbis' wives—"take action
and offer leadership in all human struggles for betterment."[4] Several
years before the war's end, clergy wives recognized the significance of
the challenge the Nazi era posed to religious leaders.

In chapters devoted to various aspects of the role, such as "Her
Privileges," "Her Opportunities," "Her Spiritual Life," "Her Children,"
"Her Appearance," and "Her Avocation," ministers' wives offered insights into the particular challenges of their position. On the question of
how public a leadership role ministers' wives should take, Priscilla Wahl
Stamm offered the same recommendations adopted by rabbis' wives in
the 1920s: "The needs of the small struggling church may make it a
necessity for her to head an organization or a department. . . . [But]
generally speaking, it would seem unwise for the minister's wife to be
at the head of any organization in the church. . . . Her concern should
primarily be to develop leaders rather than to lead."[5] Stamm also cautioned against upstaging one's husband, much the way Hyamson had
done:

> The . . . minister's wife, no matter how gifted for public work she may
> be, or what training she may have acquired, [ought] remember that she
> is still the wife and not the minister of the church. She may crave the
> opportunity to fill the pulpit, and she may even be a better public
> speaker than her husband; but if she desires him to succeed she will
> let him be the preacher. Even when her husband must be away from

his pulpit for a Sunday or two, it would seem far better to secure a pulpit supply than to have the wife in any way appear as a rival of her husband.[6]

Similarly, Grace Tilton Shullenberger, like Kohut a generation earlier, described·"a life that was exacting, that called for tact and understanding and patience in double portion." She ended her chapter by affirming the Proverbs woman of valor as the best guide to the role: "Strength and dignity are her clothing."[7] Finally, on the question of the minister's vacation, Helen Mitchell Gibson described congregants' resentment just as Kohut had done. Gibson counseled that "we must not let them upset us."[8]

In this context, Ruth Levi's chapter "I Married a Rabbi" described the many avenues of involvement open to the rabbi's wife:

> Next to her home activities, the chief obligation of the rabbi's wife is definitely to assist in the work of the synagogue . . . and to interest herself wholeheartedly in the people he serves. This must take precedence over any other cause outside her home. But gone is the day when the rabbi's wife was restricted to the elemental tasks of her household and synagogue. . . . She now has opportunities crowding so thick about her.[9]

Encouraging rebbetzins to take an active role, Levi nevertheless understood that they might easily become overwhelmed by its many responsibilities. Thus, like some of the Christian contributors, she cautioned rebbetzins to develop "an interest in something entirely removed from the routine of the ministerial life. Being engrossed in a secular project will not only enrich life, but keep the minister's wife from being entirely used up by her husband's work and obligations."[10]

Like her 1920s predecessors, Levi enumerated both the satisfactions and the limitations of the role. In her view, the advantages "are outstanding," for the rabbi's wife "knows a large circle of friendly people. . . . [She is the] possessor of an educated, religious, cultured companion who can help her to a higher personal level of development, mentally and spiritually. . . . [She] has the opportunity . . . to use her influence for developing a better understanding of her people, more especially among the women, [and] . . . has the privilege of witnessing the unfolding" of young people's lives.[11]

As for the liabilities, Levi mentioned several. She bemoaned the "lack of privacy . . . living in a goldfish bowl . . . always called upon to be hospitable, amiable, friendly, and above all tactful." The rabbi's wife "may not be part of a single group or develop an intimate circle . . . [and] people are not quite themselves with her."[12] Above all, rabbis' wives found themselves in an untenable bind when it came to their behavior:

> If she is brilliant or militant or persuaded of her ability to be a leader, she is likely to be considered forward, aggressive; if she is timid, hesitant, or just convinced that it is wiser that only her husband's voice should be raised . . . she will be called stupid or lacking in initiative. If she has a keen interest in style and modishness . . . she will be said to be vain and frivolous; if she considers extreme stylishness trivial and unworthy of the time it requires, her criticis [*sic*] will pronounce her dowdy, "old-timey," obsolete. If she naturally has a fondness for social functions and maintains an intimacy with rich or powerful people, she will definitely be called a "climber" and snobbish; if, on the other hand, she prefers people to personages . . . she is sure to be regarded as indifferent or unsocial.[13]

Levi described these frustrations more openly than her Christian co-contributors. Yet ultimately Levi, like her co-contributors, concluded on a positive note. She agreed that

> the difficulties of the position are more than outnumbered by the advantages. . . . To be a minister's wife is an outstanding privilege— a blessed responsibility. To be allowed intimate contact with people in their joys, to be permitted to share in their sorrows, to help comfort the heartsick and dry the tears of grief, to be the confidante of young people in their search for happiness, in their pursuit of personal development or consecration to some unselfish cause—these things enrich life.[14]

Levi's words found echo in many articles written about the role of the rebbetzin between 1944 and 1968. Rabbis' wives opted to share with laypeople the exceptional nature of their position, and editors published such confessional pieces every few years. In contrast to articles written in the interwar years, these pieces almost always featured the specialized Yiddish term "rebbetzin" in their title, as authors signaled the distinctiveness of their position while also demonstrating the pervasiveness of the term.[15]

Like Levi, these authors presented both the role's opportunities for public leadership and its constraints. They wrote with a confidence that illustrated a deep sense of security in the role and an awareness of its influence and power. Like their predecessors, these rebbetzins concluded that the advantages of the position outweighed the negatives and that they enjoyed it. Yet they articulated the drawbacks much more explicitly. Some also touched on the gender limitations of their "wife of" status.

In 1944, Adina Katzoff deplored the fact that, in contrast to the attention given to the rabbi, "little has been said about the function and status of the rebetzin, a regrettable fact since she is frequently called upon for leadership by her sisterhood." Like Levi, she too saw the rabbinate as a two-person career and wrote her piece because she hoped to clarify the relationship between the rebbetzin and synagogue activity in order to secure "her happiness in the rabbinate."[16]

Three years later, an Orthodox rebbetzin, Channa Gerstein, wrote about the sense of continuity with the earlier generation in her "Reflections of a Rebbitzen." Before her marriage, she had read Rebekah Kohut's *My Portion,* "an inspiration that remained as a guiding influence in my life." It is not surprising, then, that Gerstein concerned herself with maintaining gender boundaries and not undercutting her husband's position. She repeated the refrain that the rebbetzin owed her first responsibility to her husband and described a role that derived its power from gender distinctions. For example, she taught the older women Bible every Sabbath afternoon, and "because I and not the Rabbi led the class, a number of the women felt bold enough to discuss, ask questions, and present the fruits of their own reflections." Similarly, Gerstein taught young mothers by appealing to their maternal instincts, convinced that it "would mean a lowering of rabbi's prestige if he were to guide.[17]

By 1950, Shoni Levi provoked her readers with her "Don't Look Now—But She's a Rebbetzin." Exaggerating what she believed were superhuman expectations that rebbetzins faced, she sarcastically explained that upon marriage, the rabbi's wife automatically had to fulfill the ideal prescribed in Proverbs as a "Paragon of Virtue. . . a veritable . . . 'woman of valour.'"[18] Yet even if she were expert in Judaica, "the equivalent or substitute for a Jewish Encyclopedia," that, too, would be insufficient, for "today, she must be, in addition, a combination of Emily Post, psychiatric worker, and public relations expert." Like Ruth Levi, Shoni lamented the "higher criticism"[19] to which rabbis' wives were subject: They can't dress too fashionably; neither can they be "disinterested in the latest vogue." Rebbetzins who befriend the wealthy are "social climbing"; those who befriend the "intellectual, unpretentious, simple-living folk" have "no class." Finally, the retiring type attracts criticism for not helping her husband out with his sermons, but a good public speaker will invite the conclusion that "'surely she must help her husband with his sermons,' and that she is the real 'power behind the throne.'"[20]

This last phrase turned Hyamson's 1925 advice on its head. Hyamson used this expression to encourage women to perfect a behind-the-scenes helpmate role. Not interested in hiding behind anything, Shoni Levi mocked its strictures because she understood the "invidious" criticisms of both rabbi and rebbetzin implicit in the phrase. Having the temerity to suggest that a rabbi's wife might be a physician or executive, she drove home the point that active rebbetzins did not imbibe the role by osmosis, but rather chose to live it because they were Jewishly educated women who saw themselves as "vitally concerned with Jewish survival." Yet Shoni, like Ruth Levi, ended by warning these same rebbetzins to set limits and not "make a career out of your husband's profession!!!"[21]

Outlook's editor hoped Shoni's article would provoke discussion, and she invited other rebbetzins to respond concerning this "challenging theme." One rebbetzin did—anonymously. While agreeing with Shoni's last piece of advice, this rebbetzin felt that the article adopted too negative a tone. "The rabbi's wife is entitled to a life of her own, by all means. . . . But at the same time she should be ready to give part of herself to the work of the Synagogue, as it is expected of any good Jewish woman today." She ended on a more upbeat note: "My horizons have been widened. My life has been enriched because 'I am I' and also a Rabbi's wife."[22]

The next selection, the only to appear in a Reform publication, was written in verse. Helen Wilner, like her Conservative counterparts, half-jokingly—but also half-seriously—reviewed the range of criticism leveled against rabbis' wives.

There is always a great deal of comment in our worship houses
Concerning the activities of the rabbis' spouses.
For the most part 'tis the opinion consensus that ours is a sorry lot,
And that our chances of pleasing our husbands, our congregations, and still
   retaining our sanity are not so hot.
For example, if the rebbitzin's dresses are smart instead of so-so,
Then the whole congregation begins to think the rabbi is getting too much
   dough;
But if, God forbid, she should go to the A & P on a Friday morning
   shabbily,
Then everyone immediately starts treating her crabbily.
And if you should stay at home and tend to your business and your babies,
   and Sisterhood responsibilities should shirk,
The hue and cry goes up: "She doesn't do bit of work!". . .
They say we have no privacy, we live in a glare of publicity;
But let me tell you, any gal who denies she loves it is guilty of flagrant
   duplicity.[23]

As the cheerful ending suggests, Wilner, like her peers, ultimately concluded that the perks outweighed the pitfalls.

In 1955, *Outlook* published a piece by a lay leader titled "How Treat
the Rabbi's Wife?,"[24] an indication that congregants, too, felt unsure
of the role's boundaries. May Kinberg reported on a discussion among
Long Island Sisterhood presidents on the question "where and how
does the rebbetzin fit within the Sisterhood?" Feeling strongly that this
issue deserved wider airing, Kinberg affirmed her belief that the rebbetzin should play an active role as board member, committee member, and
honored guest at all functions. In what sounded like a response to Shoni
Levi's none-too-subtle indictment of congregants' unrealistic expectations, Kinberg cheerfully concluded that "I believe, we usually owe a
vote of thanks to our rebbetzins for giving so freely of their talents,
their earnest cooperation and wise counsel."

A year later, *Outlook* published another sanguine article, this time by
Leona W. Kose. Her "It Feels Good to Be a Rebbetzin" began with the
admission that a woman "is forced into a position of leadership among
women" by marrying a rabbi. But Kose stressed the advantages of a
role "that in some ways seems to parallel the rabbi's role in the congregation." Consciously emulating other rebbetzins, Kose set out to be "of
service when needed." She taught Hebrew language, planned programs,

and held middle- (but never top-) level positions in Sisterhood. Serving as rebbetzin gave her opportunities to grow, particularly as a public speaker. She also felt lucky to gain "the truly religious experience of having all kinds of women turning to you for advice and guidance." Acknowledging the hazards of a fishbowl existence, Kose downplayed its significance, concluding, "How many women are given this opportunity early in life to develop their latent powers for growth, for mature and creative Jewish living—and have the pleasure of being married to a rabbi."[25]

Sylvia Barras, in her "Wraps Off the Rebbetzin," which appeared in *The Reconstructionist* magazine, began by echoing Katzoff's desire for the rebbetzin to be taken more seriously. Barras bemoaned the fact that despite many studies conducted for the tercentenary of Jewish settlement in America, none had investigated the rebbetzin. Then, adopting an irreverent tone similar to that of Shoni Levi, she suggested the variety of talents that rebbetzins possess. She may be an excellent cook and hostess, a strong-willed leader who "all but dons the robe," or a superwoman who "circulates at every meeting, sings solo in the choir, pens the programs, publishes the pamphlets, delivers the speeches, teaches the tots, directs the campaigns, and *paskens* the *shiles* (decides ritual questions)."[26] Describing the rebbetzin's proficiency at invocations, she dared the reader to

> Conjure up in your mind's eye, the podium at the last women's convention or luncheon meeting you attended. Without a doubt a *rebbetzin* added the clerical grace note to the head table. . . . There she sat, publicly ensconced on high, unable to gossip happily or take thirty winks during the main address. Consider with awe and trepidation the millions of words to which she has attentively listened in talks, testimonials, orations, lectures, appeals, harangues, reminiscences, messages, etc. Quantitatively this aural feat is rivaled only by the miles of *kishke* [stuffed derma] which she has gallantly consumed at *Bar Mitzvah* and wedding dinners.[27]

At the same time, Barras echoed Shoni Levi's caution that, however talented, the rebbetzin must "beware of committing the sin of competing with the rabbi." She also bemoaned the necessity of adopting inconspicuous dress and noted the rebbetzin's lack of privacy as symbolized by the extent to which she is the "subject of seasonal interest—is she

Gilla P. Rubin (second from left). Courtesy of the author.

expecting?" But Barras also added a new twist to the conundrum of contradictory expectations: A new rebbetzin might be tested by being told an off-color story by a congregant. If she "laughs loudly and counters with a more pungent anecdote," some will criticize her with: "'*Passt nit* for (it does not befit) a *rebbetzin*.' If, on the other hand, she betrays embarrassment at this public test: 'Well, what did you expect? A rebbetzin!'"[28]

Outlook swung back to a similarly controversial stance in 1957 when it published Dorothy K. Kripke's "Why Rebbitzens Crack Up; or, Pet Peeves of a Rabbi's Wife." Like Shoni Levi, Kripke used humor to underscore the role's difficulties, but she did so primarily to call attention to her main "pet peeve," Jewish apathy. Neither the fishbowl existence nor criticism over clothes truly pained her. Rather, Kripke ached with the knowledge that some Jews saw Judaism as *her* "'business' . . . and are satisfied to let the Rabbi and his family monopolize all the pleasures of Jewish study and Jewish living."[29]

More than ten years later, the Orthodox journal *Jewish Life* published its own tongue-in-cheek parody of the rebbetzin. Libby Klaperman felt compelled to write because of the short shrift author Harry Kemelman had given to the rabbi's wife in his rabbi mystery series.[30] "The fictional Rebbetzin . . . has become lost in the shuffle, overshadowed by her charismatic husband. . . . [She is] a marvelous non-entity easily merged with the Rabbi's book-lined study walls."[31] She encouraged Kemelman to

> reappraise the Rebbetzin and give her her rightful place in the sun. . . . She who is required to be the best dressed, most frugal, best cook, most slender, best speaker, most glamorous, *and* most articulate, charming, talented, relaxed, pleasant, well adjusted, happy partner . . . [and who] usually has to be able also to teach in the Hebrew School and/or lead discussions and youth groups.[32]

To fuel her attack, Klaperman offered Kemelman "private documents," "Dear Rebbetzin" letters, as "background material" for future books. The letters, written in pairs, offered completely contradictory advice that echoed the sentiments about impossible expectations raised earlier in Conservative and Reform publications: The rebbetzin should/ shouldn't cover her hair. She "should have an Open House like other Rabbis' wives do," but then "How do you do so much entertaining on the Rabbi's salary?" "Tell the Rabbi to discuss more contemporary subjects in his sermons," but "You should influence the Rabbi not to speak so much on politics." The one non-paired letter warns: "Don't wear your fur coat to shool [synagogue]. There are plenty people who don't have fur coats and they pay your husband's salary."[33]

Viewed as a whole, these articles reflect the sense of solidarity and camaraderie that had developed among American rebbetzins as a class in the postwar period. As Barras proclaimed: " 'Conservative, Orthodox and Reform *rebbetzins,* one genre, different species.' "[34] These rebbetzins saw themselves as religious leaders committed to an active life, working together with their husbands, despite the judgmental gaze of congregants, to strengthen Jewish knowledge and observance. Their strong sense of self is illustrated by the fact that while many other articles of the era identify female authors by their husband's first names— e.g., Mrs. S. Gershon Levi—each of these articles identified the author by the rebbetzin's own first name. These rebbetzins proudly assumed the mantle of leadership from the previous generation of rabbis' wives. In contrast to their predecessors, though, these postwar rebbetzins lamented the enormity of their task, the disparity between their expectations and those of their congregants, and what they saw as the pettiness of their constituents. Though utilizing humor, no doubt to soften the harshness of their critique, these articles nevertheless reveal pervasive sources of irritation.

Whether postwar rebbetzins experienced more frustration than their interwar counterparts or simply felt more comfortable sharing their views is unclear. However, the contradictory messages with which postwar culture bombarded its women presumably increased the anxiety of these rebbetzins. Following on the heels of rebbetzins who modeled successful activist roles, rebbetzins who came of age in the postwar era felt the added pressure of measuring up to such achievements at just the time when society was urging women to modify their public career goals.

Hints of these contradictory messages can be found in Christian clergy manuals. On the one hand, the more activist model remained, with the minister's wife expected to serve selflessly as teacher, adviser, choir director, hostess, and manifold other roles. But in contrast to earlier works, newer Christian clergy wife manuals re-emphasized the helpmate theme, urging wives to focus on hearth and home first and admonishing them not to take on activist leadership roles but to serve as proper helpmeets. One 1950 handbook redefined the marital relationship of clergy, with husband as captain and wife as service crew, to emphasize that the minister's first priority was to the congregation; his wife's was to her husband. Some manuals invoked humorous asides to describe the irritations of the role, but they nevertheless urged the minister's wife to live up to the task. Postwar clergy wives—rebbetzins included—strove to blaze a meaningful career path within the complicated ethos of the era.[35]

The Postwar Years

As World War II ended, Americans—both returning soldiers and those who had stayed behind—strove to establish themselves by going back to school, finding jobs, moving to suburbia, and especially, marrying. More than 94 percent of all men and women who reached adulthood during and after the war married, most by their mid-twenties, a rate much higher than in previous decades. Women in their twenties had an average of three children. More than ever, marriage and motherhood became the defining characteristic of women's lives.[36]

With this inward shift toward home and family, psychiatrists expressed concern over the masculine ego. Leaving the battlefield and assuming jobs in corporations, men gained security but not necessarily power. Husbands and wives strove for the partnership experts believed made for the happiest marriage, but women also took care to organize their lives in ways that would buttress their husbands' manhood.[37]

Seeing their role as secondary to that of their men influenced women in many ways. Encouraged to go to college, white women were twice as likely to enter college as their mothers had been, and they prepared for a variety of professional careers. By 1950, two-thirds—down from three-fourths—prepared for traditional female careers of teaching and nursing. But only 37 percent of those who entered college graduated. Female college graduates expected to work only until they married or had children, for they were socialized to fulfill their career dreams through marriage and family. Society encouraged them to achieve upward mobility by attaching themselves to highly educated men, finding vicarious achievement, and living "contingent lives."[38] As Rona Jaffe discovered in a study of her 1951 Radcliffe classmates, the prevailing sentiment was "we married what we wanted to be. If we wanted to be a lawyer or a doctor, we married one."[39]

Government policies reinforced such cultural prescriptions. By taxing wives' already lower income at a higher marginal rate, the postwar "married-filing-jointly" provision of the federal income tax code buttressed husbands as primary and wives as secondary earners by compromising the potential for a wife's earnings to gain parity with her husband's.[40] In spite of this, the percentage of women in the work force continued to increase throughout the period, from 24 percent in 1940 to 32 percent twenty years later. Moreover, this number included married women as well as mothers. The number of mothers working increased 400 percent during this period, and by 1960 both parents worked in more than 10 million homes.[41]

Popular culture publicized the contradictory messages that promoted both domestic ideals and individual achievement. On the one hand, marriage and motherhood remained at the center of societal ideals, and the media reinforced these roles with films, television shows, and advertisements that emphasized domestic heroines devoting themselves to their husbands' and children's interests and needs. But the media also showed strong, hard-working fictional heroines and married career women renowned for their successes. These conflicting images converged with Lucille Ball. Ball's television character, Lucy Ricardo, typified the stay-at-home wife in the most popular show of the era. But Ball herself continued to work after giving birth, demonstrating that motherhood need not end a woman's career. Eleanor Roosevelt articulated these contradictions by noting both that the most rewarding activities for any woman involved meeting "the needs of those who are nearest and dearest to her," and that "she will not meet these needs adequately if she has no interests and occupations of her own."[42]

Even non-working homemakers resisted a lifestyle circumscribed by hearth and home. Committing countless hours to a wide rage of organizations, many continued the nineteenth- and early-twentieth-century tradition of female involvement in association work. In the postwar era, women volunteered on both national and local levels, from the League of Women Voters to the neighborhood parish, devoting themselves not only to their own families but also to improving society at large.[43]

Postwar American Jewry

Young Jewish women and their husbands found themselves swept up in these same ideals and expectations. After the war, Jews moved to the suburbs of large established cities as well as to new areas of settlement, such as Miami and Los Angeles, in unprecedented numbers. Suburbanization became the most concrete expression of a rising Jewish middle class, and Jews embraced its ethos. They also flocked to synagogues and temples, for the 1950s witnessed a turn by Americans to organized religion. Many Jews affiliated for the first time, and houses of worship—both Jewish and Christian—became loci of religious activity. From 1945 through the 1950s, some 600 synagogues and temples were built, with Conservative and Reform predominant among them. In this era, the synagogue became the most important American Jewish institution, with 60 percent of American Jews affiliating by 1960. In that year, according to the United States Bureau of Labor Statistics, 2,517 rabbis served congregations.[44]

Rabbinic couples dedicated themselves to intensifying the Jewishness of postwar congregants though education, sharing of life-cycle events, and pastoral duties. As in previous generations, rebbetzins believed that they could play a critical role by focusing especially on the women. Since in their eyes the future of Jewish life rested with the Jewishness of the family, rebbetzins assumed they would succeed best if they motivated women to enrich their homes Jewishly.

Zev K. Nelson captured well the ideal view of the postwar rabbinic couple in his remark that the rabbi "is called upon to Judaize a community, and the help of his wife is invaluable for such a Herculean task." That his remarks were delivered at a 1964 conference on the "Special Problems of the Rabbi's Wife and Children" also demonstrates a growing awareness of the strains this ideal placed on rabbinic families.

In terms of the rebbetzin's function vis-à-vis the synagogue, Nelson depicted an active public leadership role. The rebbetzin

> has a special title . . . and she must not be relegated to K. P. duty or other menial tasks. . . . The Rebbitzin can be of great help to her husband, and can serve the community best, if she devotes her time and efforts to the spiritual and cultural needs of the Congregation. She can help the committees in the planning of sisterhood programs, in determining policy, in arranging courses of study, in strengthening the school, in fostering interest in the regional and national organization of the movement.[45]

As if in direct response to the complaints voiced by rebbetzins in the articles cited above, Nelson noted that by filling such critical functions, a rebbetzin could

> indicate quite decisively that clothes and furnishings are of secondary importance, while the strengthening of Judaism is of primary importance. . . . [T]he Rebbetzin should be dressed smartly, and should more than hold her own in the dignity of her clothing. But, for the sake of her own integrity, she ought not to join the "mink parade" nor compromise her inner spirit for the sake of her outer garb.[46]

Nelson cautioned that a rabbi's wife "must become the 'Ezer' [helpmate], and never the 'Knegdo' [the one opposite him]."[47] His interpretation of this familiar metaphor from Genesis emphasized the rebbetzin as helpmate but not competitor. He reinforced this view by again quoting from the book of Genesis. He advised the rebbetzin

> to strengthen her husband's position, but she must avoid overshadow-ing him. . . . We may recall the inquiry of the visitors concerning [the matriarch] Sarah's whereabouts. The answer: "Hinay V[a]'ohel[48]—be-hold she is in the tent," offers the Rebbitzin of today some practical guidance. If the Rabbi is not the effective and eloquent speaker, the Rebbitzin can be of considerable help by making the home a focal point of religious interest.[49]

Rather than propose that the rebbetzin occasionally speak in her hus-band's stead or assist him with his sermons, Nelson suggested that she deflect attention from his weaknesses by highlighting a safely gendered area of strength—the home. Nelson's ostensibly biblically ordained ad-vice revealed the treacherous waters postwar rebbetzins navigated as they sought fulfill their roles.

Training Rebbetzins

Cognizant of the significance of their task—one that loomed larger than ever in the wake of the Holocaust—rebbetzins began to meet at rabbin-ical conventions to develop guidelines for their work and to learn from one another.[50] At the 1947 Conservative Rabbinical Assembly conven-tion, Leah Treiger[51] explained that rebbetzins must "serve as a demon-stration of what Jewish living is."[52] Miriam Teplitz agreed. "From the rabbi's home should emanate everything that is Jewish. We felt that it was more important to invite people to our home to Seder than to accept invitations to other people's homes. The Seder is a great opportu-nity to influence our guests. . . . In brief, we try to keep a model Jewish home!"[53]

Doris Goodblatt stressed the importance of accompanying one's hus-band to houses of mourning or to life-cycle celebrations and echoed Gerstein in emphasizing the importance of the woman's touch. "I be-lieve she should go as often as she can. It is surprising how much plea-sure a visit from me gives. Often a woman can bring a measure of com-fort which surpasses that which the rabbi alone can render."[54] Decades later, one rebbetzin still recalled how motivated she felt by the enthusiasm and dedication displayed at these meetings by the veteran rebbetzins. "They told us what to do. . . . I went out and tried to do it."[55]

Similar preparation took place among Reform rabbis' wives at Central Conference of American Rabbis conventions. Substantive sessions socialized younger women to the expectations and protocol of their role. Decades later, these initiates recalled feeling a mixture of awe, amusement, terror, and intimidation. They doubted they would ever measure up to what they recalled as the larger-than-life rebbetzins they heard from, but they were eager to learn as much as they could.[56]

Some veteran rebbetzins felt they ought to start even earlier by training the wives of rabbinical students for the challenges that lay ahead. Perhaps the idea for such training programs came from the growing trend in higher education to offer college courses that prepared women for marriage and homemaking. Veteran rebbetzins took this impulse one step further, hoping to teach the younger generation not only how to be good wives and mothers but also how to be good rebbetzins.[57] Similar groups for training wives of Christian ministry students also existed at the time, but there is no evidence that rabbis' wives knew about them.[58]

In the Conservative Movement, Betty Greenberg and Esther Arzt,[59] veteran congregational rebbetzins whose husbands had both joined the administration of the Jewish Theological Seminary, took the lead. In the late 1940s and early 1950s, each invited wives of rabbinical students to her home. When Shoni Levi received such a "Dear Rebbetzin" letter, she envisaged not herself but her grandmother, so unaccustomed was she to her future role. Decades later, rebbetzins still conjured up the essence of these meetings in which Greenberg and Arzt advised young women on the art of entertaining, the necessity of teaching by example, and the goal of inspiring others to Jewish living. Attendees later remembered being told to take their roles seriously and to uphold high standards of etiquette in terms of make-up, jewelry, dress, and behavior. Also, in order to uphold the dignity of their and their husbands' positions, they were directed always to refer to their husbands as "the rabbi."[60]

Attendees also recalled how much Greenberg and Arzt differed in style from each other. Young wives going first to Greenberg's home and then to Arzt's picked up contradictory messages. Greenberg served tea from a silver service set and demonstrated how to hold a teacup properly. One rebbetzin recalled being admonished to always "be prepared for visitors. So at 7 AM, your bed should be made. . . . You should be dressed properly." Rebbetzins remembered that Arzt saw herself as more of a guidance counselor who put the women at ease. She would tell the same women: "Whenever you get up, you get up. Don't worry about whether your bed is made." Years later, one of the attendees recalled that many wives mocked the sessions at the time. But she also admitted that underneath the humor, most women felt "grateful for the help because we were apprehensive."[61] A decade later, JTS student wives initiated a group that met regularly to review the expectations of their future roles. Half-mockingly, these women called themselves FRAU—Future Rebbetzins of America United—an indication that they too were anxious about their future.[62]

These training groups for Conservative student wives and fiancées reached many women, for a good number met their future husbands as fellow students at JTS—the women in the Teachers Institute or Seminary College of Jewish Studies and the men in rabbinical school.[63] In this way, studying at JTS became a form of anticipatory socialization.[64] As Eileen Kieffer recalled, someone once recommended that she enroll at JTS to gain the deeper understanding of Judaism she sought. But the person also remarked, "You know, if you go to the Seminary, you'll end up marrying a rabbi."[65] Similarly, Miriam Teplitz met her husband, Saul, when she attended JTS's Israel Friedlaender night classes in the early 1940s. She recalled such courses as primarily "matchmaking classes for *rebbetzins*," and she remembered seven engagements in one year.[66] This trend also finds parallels among Christian clergy couples. According to a survey of clergy wives, almost one fourth had met their husbands at religion-sponsored colleges and universities. Many others met at church-sponsored rallies or other church-oriented venues.[67]

Similar training occurred in the Reform Movement in the late 1940s and 1950s, with the initial impetus coming from the student wives rather than from veteran rabbis' wives. About ten women banded together and developed a constitution for the "Hebrew Union College Student Wives Club" that delineated three goals: to foster participation in educational activities that would enhance understanding and preparation for their careers as rabbis' wives, to promote unity of social interests, and to encourage cooperation in meeting mutual problems. Sharing recipes, the group jokingly came to be known as the "knives club." Belle Wohl,[68] wife of a local rabbi, and Amy Blank, a faculty wife,[69] served as advisers to the group, and other local rabbis' wives

Hebrew Union College Student Wives Club. Courtesy of the American Jewish Archives, Cincinnati, Ohio.

occasionally addressed the group about their role in the home, the Jewish community, and the community at large.[70] Years later, participants recalled learning how to shield their husbands from problematic situations and shore them up unobtrusively. They were advised never to dress too well or too shabbily. One rebbetzin confessed that learning to play mah jongg was the most useful skill she acquired. Yet like their Conservative counterparts, some remembered these sessions as more intimidating than helpful. One recalled being convinced that all the fourth-year wives except for her knew everything, from raising children to entertaining.[71]

In 1949–50, the Wives Club sent out a questionnaire to what one rebbetzin later referred to as "the most wonderful rabbis' wives in the world," in order to learn from their experiences. Their questions reveal both the parameters within which they understood the position and their anxieties about it. They wanted to know what role these women played in their local Sisterhoods, the frequency with which they accompanied their husbands on pastoral calls or life-cycle events, the extent to which they entertained or gave gifts to congregants, and the way in which the rabbinate affected their personal lifestyle in terms of Jewish observance, friendships, and private time. From their detailed questions, it is clear that these wives understood thè position as encompassing the rebbetzin as educator, adviser to Sisterhood, and partner with her husband in supporting congregants. Their questions suggest that student wives struggled not with these aspects of the role but rather with defining their boundaries. They wanted to pinpoint the right balance between helping their husbands and serving their congregants effectively on the one hand and preserving family life and their sense of themselves on the other. These struggles were more acute manifestations of the general issues American women wrestled with at the time, and the same issues the rebbetzin authors depicted in their whimsical articles.[72]

Tellingly, the responses reveal that the wives, like the rebbetzins of the interwar period, preferred to understand their decision to play an active part in synagogue life as stemming from their free choice, not from any sense of obligation. Student wives shared that perspective. Though they joined the Wives Club in order to prepare for a role that seemed inevitable given their husbands' career decision, they believed that they were consciously opting to serve as rebbetzins. The increased numbers of women working in the postwar era meant that these rebbetzins, even more than their interwar counterparts, could feel that they deliberately elected the rebbetzin role. Christian clergy wives of the period also commonly explained that they filled the role not because it was expected but because they "happened to enjoy doing that kind of thing."[73]

By 1956, the Wives Club had grown more elaborate. While still meeting monthly to "deepen their understanding of their husbands' calling and the problems they will encounter," some women also attended bi-weekly special interest groups such as a Hebrew language class. They also met before each holiday to learn the arts and crafts associated with each festival. These meetings served a social function while also preparing the wives for their future role.[74]

Two years later, wives and fiancées of senior rabbinical students at Yeshiva University also began to undergo such training. Acknowledging that such a program was long overdue, Victor B. Geller, field director of the Community Service Division of Yeshiva University, explained that its purpose was to "fill an important need by providing the women with insights into the social, emotional, and spiritual problems they will be confronted with." Apparently less in need of gaining requisite Jewish knowledge than their Reform counterparts, these women sought guidance more for the intangible aspects of the role. Groups also met monthly in private homes and were led by veteran rabbis' wives.[75]

Some rebbetzins recalled a less formal training process that relied on older rebbetzins who served as role models for them. For example, Bertha Aronson served as a prototype for Maxine Simon, whose husband, Mordecai Simon,[76] served as David Aronson's assistant. She remembered Bertha as "the *rebbetzin par excellence* of the entire world," who "showed me a wonderful example, and I was inclined to follow her." Simon also recalled the rapport between Aronson and her husband, and the profound impact this had on her own vision of the rabbinate. Miriam Wise also pointed to Aronson as exemplar. Wise wanted to emulate Aronson because she saw her as an educator, a good listener, and a warm personality who complemented her husband in the rabbinate.[77]

Helen Tomsky grew up in Minneapolis with Aronson as her rebbetzin. Because of this, when her husband, Mervin, decided he wanted to become a rabbi, she knew she would "be his helpmate—to participate in cong[regational] life as I saw fit."[78]

Reba Katz remembered the influence of Betty Greenberg. Reba knew her as the rebbetzin of her childhood, but she also observed Greenberg as an adult when Reba's husband, Reuben, served as Simon Greenberg's assistant during his student years.[79] As a child, Reba remembered being terrified by Betty's strictness. When Greenberg admonished the Confirmation class girls not to put on lipstick, "we wouldn't dare. We wouldn't have been able to walk up that aisle if we had lipstick on." Like other student wives, Katz remained awed both by Greenberg's graciousness as a hostess and by how special she made her guests feel. "If she served beans, you thought you were getting the most elegant meal in the world because she would take out her finest silverware, and she would bring this thing to the table, and she would serve it with such pomp that you just felt honored to be sitting there eating those beans."[80] Katz strove to emulate Greenberg's sense of dignity and class, hoping to make her congregants feel equally valued.

Rebbetzins who grew up in rabbinic homes learned the role from their mothers. For example, Zipporah Marans remembered her mother,

Libby Mann, entertaining and attending services regularly. Mostly she recalled how much her mother enjoyed being a pulpit rabbi's wife.[81] Jeanette Miller was inspired by the example of her mother-in-law, Francis Miller, who told her that she had given up a law career to serve as a full-time rebbetzin. Jeanette remembered her as a great public speaker and program planner for Sisterhood and other Jewish women's organizations.[82]

By the 1960s, the rebbetzin role had become so firmly established that one Reform rabbi suggested that his Movement grant the degree of rebbetzin. He based this concept on the deaconess position common in Protestant churches, proposing the creation of a "Jewish deaconate" to fill a variety of pastoral functions, such as visiting the sick. This would answer what he identified as a pressing need in the Jewish community while giving women needed professional status. Though he favored ordaining women, he believed that "there are many women who cannot or do not wish to spend as much time as is required in preparation for the rabbinate, but who may want to dedicate themselves to a life of service." What better term for such a role than that self-explanatory title already held by rabbis' wives who exemplified this devotion? There is no evidence that the idea ever took hold, and it is hard to imagine that rabbis' wives would have looked favorably upon it. Making the title attainable on its own terms would have challenged their choices and undermined their status.[83]

Postwar Rebbetzins in Action

With the role deeply implanted in American Jewish life, rebbetzins across the country contributed their expertise to the upbuilding of American Jewish life. They did so, in part, by following in the footsteps of the interwar activist archetypes. But influenced by the postwar climate, they also increasingly emphasized the more traditionally gendered homemaking sphere and strove to incorporate it into their public leadership role. Unfortunately, over time, many also suffered under the weight of their increasingly complex role.

Conservative rebbetzins best illustrate the breadth of the role during this period for several reasons. First, Conservative Judaism emerged as the largest denomination during this period.[84] Second, it experienced the greatest dissonance between the behavior and orientation of its clergy and its laity. Because Conservative rebbetzins had the largest gap to bridge in striving to bring congregants closer to their ideals of Jewish life, the possibilities for both the heights of leadership and the depths of frustration loomed largest for them. Also, the Conservative Movement's National Women's League remained a vital avenue for rebbetzins during this period, just as it had been during the interwar period. Rebbetzins exercised leadership at the regional and national levels and continued to write prolifically on a variety of topics.[85] Particularly drawn to areas like education, Jewish family living, leadership training, and Torah Fund, they developed educational materials, scripts, and programs. For example, out of forty-eight Women's League scripts offered for purchase to affiliated Sisterhoods, almost half were authored or co-authored by rebbetzins.[86] Similarly, rebbetzins continued to utilize *Outlook* as a vehicle for disseminating their ideas. Not only did *Outlook* publish the vast majority of articles on the role of the rebbetzin discussed above; it also published numerous items—both fiction and nonfiction—by rebbetzins during the period.[87] As in the interwar period, neither of the other Movements maintained a comparable publication.

Rebbetzins of this era continued to function in ways similar to their predecessors. They attended services regularly, entertained, and paid bereavement visits. In keeping with the changing nature of American Judaism, which revolved more and more around the synagogue itself, expectations of regular attendance at weekly synagogue services, meetings, and functions grew, while rebbetzins rarely paid routine pastoral or hospital visits. According to rebbetzins' later recollections, the former was rarely done in the postwar period, while the latter continued to be carried out by the rabbis alone.[88]

Like their interwar predecessors, these rebbetzins focused their work primarily around Sisterhood. They did so because, as Rebecca Lang explained, in the postwar period the synagogue would help Jews make wise choices about their Jewishness, and "the sisterhood . . . can through its programs help each member in making her decision."[89] Rebbetzins served as unofficial leaders or chief advisers, and a group of Conservative rebbetzins meeting at the annual rabbinical convention endorsed the view that a rebbetzin accomplished the most by "assisting" and "encouraging" women. Priva Kohn echoed the advice of the minister's wife, Stamm, in her opinion that the rebbetzin should "limit herself to educational activities . . . [and] avoid chairmanships. . . . [F]ar better to do things the hard way and develop leadership."[90] This was also the consensus of the eighty-five rabbis' wives who completed the HUC Student Wives Club questionnaire. The majority favored not taking office in Sisterhood.[91]

Some rebbetzins took this behind-the-scenes mandate to an extreme. Zipporah Jacobs, for example, rarely spoke publicly, but she recalled writing talks for laywomen to deliver: "They get up, they sound good, they like it and nobody tells the other person. . . . It's very pleasing for me to be in the background. . . . I think if you have a *rebbetzin* who asserts herself publicly, then she's taking the place of someone else who could be up there."[92] Perhaps this role suited a rebbetzin with a shy, retiring personality, but others disapproved. On hearing this recollection, another rebbetzin commented that she found this behavior "manipulative" and "sick" but acknowledged that in the postwar period, many women believed it necessary to behave in this manner.[93]

When rebbetzins later thought about their involvement in Sisterhood, they recalled feeling obliged to attend every Sisterhood event and experiencing congregants' resentment and disapproval when they failed to meet those expectations. But rebbetzins also later remembered many of the positive (albeit intangible) aspects of their participation. For example, they noted that by attending meetings, they could keep their husbands better informed about women's concerns. They also believed that their presence ensured the Jewishness of Sisterhood programming by preventing the group from making what they considered to be inappropriate choices. One rebbetzin later bluntly recalled suggesting "intellectual shows, round table discussions. . . . I always said, darling, if there wasn't going to be Jewish content I could stay home and watch television."[94]

Informal work with women congregants sometimes took place outside the framework of formal Sisterhood programs. Ricki Fenster recalled sponsoring regular get-togethers with the women, which she called "Breakfast with the *Rebbetzin*," in her husband's first congregation in Jackson Heights, New York. Similarly, Hilda Schnitzer hosted a Tuesday morning "Open Coffee Pot" to which she invited ten to fifteen women each week for coffee and conversation.[95]

Eager to influence women to enrich their lives Jewishly, some rebbetzins led holiday and Jewish life-cycle workshops. Some taught classes in Hebrew literacy or Bible, while others pioneered adult bat mitzvah classes beginning in the 1950s. Rebbetzins succeeded in large measure because they appealed to young women's desires to create strong Jewish homes and enrich their children's upbringing.[96]

The invocation continued to be a critical tool for rebbetzins. As Barras had humorously described, rebbetzins offered these short prayers before every women's function, and attendees deemed such events incomplete without words of inspiration from a rebbetzin.[97] Hilda Greenberg[98] perfected the formula: Praise God, connect the event to a lofty cause, offer a prayer, quote from the Bible, end with the blessing over bread. For example:

With tender gratitude we invoke Thy name and Thy blessings as we gather in festive mood and attire to mark the 20th Donor Dinner of our beloved Sisterhood. Tonight we proudly proclaim that Sisterhood is a Symphony of Spirit and Service. Keep us mindful, we pray, that we make beautiful music only when Thou art our conductor. Keep us in tune with the highest and in closest harmony with each other. May we make of our lives sensitive instruments which play faithfully Thy gentle melodies of love and piety. May the strings of our hearts ever echo with the tender strains of compassion, charity and reverence. With the Psalmist may we proclaim in joy "Praise the Lord with the sound of the horn. Praise Him with the harp and lyre . . . " motzi [blessing for bread].[99]

Many rebbetzins taught in Sunday schools, afternoon schools and day schools,[100] which raised the question of whether rebbetzins should draw a salary for such work. Teaching in or directing their husband's congregation's religious school challenged societal ideals that wives and mothers serve as full-time homemakers while also testing the boundaries of the two-for-the-price-of-one rabbinate. Postwar rebbetzins were divided on this issue. At the 1947 rabbis' wives session at the Rabbinical Assembly convention, Dorothy Kabakoff argued that the rabbi's wife should not teach in her own congregational school for money, though she could do so as a volunteer. "I supervised my husband's school and taught a group with no compensation, because I knew it was necessary if we were to have a satisfactory school." But Adina Katzoff voiced concern that this would drive rebbetzins to contribute their talents elsewhere in order to earn needed money. She thought rebbetzins should draw a salary in their own synagogue schools as she did: "If one is a good teacher, it is a pity to waste one's services elsewhere. . . . My salary was never a point of issue." Years later, some rebbetzins regretted initial gullibility on this issue. Ethel Rothenberg admitted that when her husband, Tobias, took his first congregation in Roanoke, Virginia (1946–59), she was "young and naïve and, shall we say, a little stupid." She never asked about a salary and ended up teaching for two years gratis. Ruth Nussbaum remembered her husband discouraging her from teaching in his school not because of money, but because of politics. He feared she might cause problems for him if, for example, she failed the child of parents prominent in the congregation. Most rebbetzins who taught in their congregational schools did eventually get paid, mirroring the increasing numbers of working wives and mothers in the country as a whole. But many eventually preferred an independent venue for their talents as Jewish educators. For example, Sarah Lewis became principal of the Solomon Schechter Day School and the Center City Regional Religious School at Temple Beth Zion-Beth Israel in Philadelphia. By choosing this alternate course, rebbetzins set limits on the two-person rabbinate.[101]

Rebbetzins also continued to publish books on Jewish themes to expand the reach of their educational influence. In addition to children's books by Althea Silverman and Sadie Rose Weilerstein and Lilly Routtenberg's *The Jewish Wedding Book* mentioned above, other guidebooks appeared to help women enhance the Jewishness of their lives. For example, in 1959 Sylvia R. Kaplan and Shoni B. Levi authored *Across the Threshold: A Guide for the Jewish Homemaker.* Rebbetzins across the denominations also authored curricular materials. Dorothy Kripke wrote a series of religious school textbooks for children on basic Jewish concepts. *Let's Talk about God* appeared in 1953, followed by *Let's Talk about Right and Wrong, Let's Talk about the Jewish Holidays,* and *Let's Talk about the Sabbath.* Kripke coauthored *Let's Talk about Loving: About Love, Sex, Marriage, and Family* with her husband, Myer.[102]

Similarly, Libby Klaperman coauthored with her husband, Gilbert Klaperman, a four-volume history of the Jews, *The Story of the Jewish People.* She also wrote for young readers *The Scholar-fighter: The Story of Saadia Gaon.*[103] Lillian Freehof, who developed her literary talents editing the works of her husband, Solomon, wrote several books for Reform Movement religious schools, including *The Right Way: Ethics for Youth* and the *Bible Legends* series.[104] She also targeted adults, co-authoring *Flowers and Festivals of the Jewish Year* and *Embroideries and Fabrics for Synagogue and Home: 5000 Years of Ornamental Needlework*. These works sought, like *Jewish Home Beautiful*, to enhance the aesthetic side of Jewish life by illustrating the extent to which chores like gardening and needlework could be imbued with religious meaning.

Serving the Jewish community also involved literally lots of "serving." Like their interwar predecessors, these rebbetzins hosted meetings and study groups and invited congregants for holiday dinners and open houses. They had guests for Sabbath and holiday meals to "show people the joys of Jewish observance." Many rebbetzins recalled relishing the opportunity to display their homemaking expertise. But some rebbetzins mourned the imposition on their families that regular entertaining entailed, and others remembered consciously shielding their children from having to "demonstrate" Jewish living.[105]

Many Conservative rebbetzins devoted their efforts to helping women set up kosher kitchens. In this area, above all others, the leadership talents of rebbetzins dovetailed most closely with gender views that idealized the postwar homemaking role. After teaching women about the importance of maintaining a kosher home, these rebbetzins physically transformed congregants' kitchens. Devorah Rosenberg authored a booklet titled "Have Pots Will Travel, or How to Make Your Kitchen Kosher" as part of her portfolio as National Family Living Chairman of Women's League: "Because I have 'made Kosher' ever so many kitchens, I am listing steps and suggestions for this procedure." Not only did Rosenberg showcase her own know-how in this step-by-step guide, she also elevated the status of all rebbetzins, for in step 2, she advised women to "discuss kashrut with your rabbi and/or rebbetzin, bringing any questions you may have." In her view, rabbi and rebbetzin were interchangeable as religious authorities in the area of Jewish dietary laws.[106]

Eveline Panitch took responsibility for the kashrut of the community one step further. Crossing customary gender boundaries, she served as *mashgiha* (supervisor of dietary laws) for her husband's synagogue kitchen in Milwaukee for fifteen years, a position usually held by a (male) rabbi.[107]

Sisterhood cookbooks, a popular fundraising project undertaken by dozens of synagogues during this era, emerged as an important vehicle for educating congregants about Jewish dietary laws and demonstrating the possibility of maintaining them while cooking a wide variety of foods. The rebbetzin often served as the Judaica expert for these projects, checking the kashrut of recipes before publication and writing an introductory section on the Jewish dietary laws. In *Creative Cooking*, for example, Selma Jacobs authored a detailed section on kashrut in which she offered a Jewish legal ruling on cheeses: "In all recipes where cheese is indicated, only cheese prepared under rabbinical supervision is acceptable." Though she added that when questions arise the rabbi should be consulted, she presented herself as an authority in her own right, signing her piece "Selma Jacobs, Rebbitzen."[108]

Rebbetzins also found new avenues for leadership that coincided with both changes in American life and the expanding role of the synagogue. For example, Edith Kling introduced the "buzz group" technique to her Sisterhood. This method, popularized in the 1960s, involved dividing a large group into small units and posing provocative questions for discussion. Kling challenged her audiences with dilemmas unique to their position as American Jews: "Some people feel that Jews should not be prominent in the current struggle for integration and equality. Others feel that Jews should be in the forefront of the battle. Which position do you take? Why?" or "What should Jews do when New Year's Eve falls on Friday night?" She asked about interdating, religion in the public schools, whether Catholicism should be a factor in electing a United States president, the role of women in synagogue life in light of "Women's Liberation," and whether American Jews ought to make Aliyah (emigrate) to Israel. Occasionally, Kling offered specific responses to the dilemmas posed. For example, she suggested combating intermarriage before it presented itself by inculcating a deeper love for Judaism in the home.[109]

Rebbetzins with an intellectual bent channeled their interests into reviewing books of Jewish content, an opportunity that arose thanks to the increased popularity of American Jewish literature by writers such as Herman Wouk, Leon Uris, Philip Roth, and Bernard Malamud. Writing reviews for synagogue bulletins or Jewish magazines or giving lectures to their own and neighboring Sisterhoods and women's groups, these rebbetzins shared their insights with a larger audience. With their insider knowledge of American Jewish life and customs, they found themselves in great demand among Jews eager to hear their analyses of these authors and their works.[110]

Some rebbetzins played an instrumental part in initiating synagogue gift shops, which became popular in the postwar period as important educational and fundraising tools. Rebbetzins saw this as yet another way to enhance the Jewish living of their congregants. By carrying items necessary for running a Jewish household and enhancing its beauty throughout the annual holiday and life cycle, the gift shop helped Jewish women imagine how they might live more fully Jewish lives while giving them the tools to do so. By carrying art and ritual objects made in the State of Israel, the gift shop also heightened congregants' ties to the newly established State while providing congregations with needed financial support. Miriam Wise, for example, set up a book and gift shop in her synagogue in 1948. To publicize its existence and its wares, she also wrote the "Center Book and Gift Shop" column in the synagogue bulletin for several years. Wise reviewed new books, suggested gift ideas for Hannukah, Passover, and Confirmation, and advertised holiday displays and programs sponsored by the gift shop.[111]

Rebbetzins' aesthetic sensibilities sometimes influenced the physical plant of the synagogue. With so many new synagogues and temples under construction in the postwar era, congregations needed Jewishly knowledgeable individuals to oversee architects' and decorators' plans in order to ensure that they met congregants' religious and aesthetic needs. Some rebbetzins recalled assisting their husbands with this process by reviewing blueprints, choosing the design for stained glass windows, or picking the color of the carpet. Looking back, they understood themselves as providing the "woman's touch."[112]

The career of Libby Polachek Mowshowitz demonstrates just how far one individual could stretch the role during this period without overstepping carefully constructed gender boundaries. Daughter of a rabbi and wife of Israel Mowshowitz (rabbi of the Hillcrest Jewish Center, in Hillcrest, New York, 1949–84), Libby involved herself wholeheartedly in furthering Jewish life in her community. She spoke often in a variety of venues, including Hadassah, United Jewish Appeal, and especially her Sisterhood, delivering talks about Jewish holidays and the weekly Torah portion.[113] Serving—like Brickner—as the unofficial "rabbi" of her Sisterhood, Mowshowitz installed officers annually and delivered so many invocations that she once quipped, "I have had quite a bit of experience in writing prayers. I think that by this time God must be awfully tired of me. I have been invoking Him so much."[114]

Mowshowitz more than adequately fulfilled the traditional homemaking role, though she never made it the hallmark of her "rabbinate." A 1955 newspaper feature of Mowshowitz as "Cook of the Week" captured well the complicated nature of homemaking in rebbetzins' lives in the postwar era. The article featured a large photo of "Mrs. Israel Mowshowitz" smilingly preparing *hamantaschen* for Purim. Sharing her recipe, complete with Mowshowitz's "individual touches," the columnist reported that

> although she's busy with meetings and work connected with the Hillcrest Congregation, she makes time for holiday baking . . . and helping the children with their mathematics lessons. That's a subject on which she's the family's acknowledged master, having received her degree in the subject from Duke University while her husband was serving his first rabbinical assignment in North Carolina.[115]

Featured in the cooking column, Mowshowitz garnered particular praise not for her recipe but rather for her ability to fit her homemaking duties in around her busy schedule of synagogue work. Mowshowitz's success depended on her ability to balance her public activist role with evidence of success as a wife, mother, and homemaker. Similarly gendered messages colored the article's treatment of Mowshowitz's expertise in math. The author acknowledged its value, but not on its own terms. Rather, he noted that it enabled Mowshowitz to help her children with their homework.

For several decades, Mowshowitz faithfully wrote the "Rebitzen's Column" for the monthly Sisterhood newsletter *Hillcrest Hi-Lites*. Even when traveling with her husband, whether for work or for pleasure, Mowshowitz diligently sent in her articles. Her columns illustrate the range of talents that rebbetzins exhibited through this medium. She wrote mini-sermons of inspiration, solace, and celebration that addressed current events, women's concerns, and Jewish issues and that dispensed advice both practical and lofty. For example, one such column, titled "Busy Lines," dealt with the frustration of trying to reach someone whose phone line is constantly busy:

> Pause now and reexamine our ways and our values, our means and our ends. We want a year of continuation of the existence of our world. We want a year of companionship with our friends and neighbors. We want a year of love and understanding with our near and dear ones. We can attain all these by not keeping our "lines busy" all the time, by listening sometimes, instead of talking.[116]

Her columns vividly illustrate how seriously Mowshowitz took her responsibilities. Readers, in turn, took her messages to heart, as seen in the letters of appreciation penned when her collection of columns appeared in book form as *Straight Talk from a Rabbi's Wife.* As one man wrote, "Over the years, on many occasions, Shirley would put a copy of the Sisterhood bulletin on my desk with a note 'read Libby's article.' How often those articles coincided with our thoughts towards family, friends, religion, and the world in general."[117]

Careful to uphold a professional image in her writings and talks, Mowshowitz exuded confidence and autonomy. As a friend noted, "Libby was never the kind of *rebbetzin* who walked behind the rabbi."[118] But in reality, Mowshowitz resented those aspects of the "wife of" role that relegated her to a secondary position. Once, in her response to a 1962 donor testimonial, Mowshowitz candidly shared her views about these constraints. Speaking about her husband, Mowshowitz noted that

> he told you I was his accompaniest [*sic*]. I would very much apreicate [*sic*] it if he would let me know one day in advance, where I am to accompany him. . . . I'll confess I do not deserve all this. But on second thought, I do deserve some sort of medal or purple heart perhaps. To be a Rebbetzen for 25 years is not an easy task, even though it was rewarding and interesting.[119]

This confession bared Mowshowitz's generally submerged frustration over the constraints of the role. Yes, a two-for-the-price-of-one career had its advantages, and Mowshowitz acknowledged them and capitalized on them. Because of it, she succeeded in developing a sphere of influence through Sisterhood, and outlets for her talents through her invocations and bulletin columns. Yet she knew that no matter how much praise she received, her role remained circumscribed because it derived from her husband's and remained secondary to it. And this left her feeling like a martyr deserving of a Purple Heart medal. The two-person career concept allowed others—including her husband—to take her for granted. As her words revealed, Mowshowitz endured, determined to make the most of her position.

Certain rebbetzins not only fulfilled the expectations of their role and stretched its boundaries, but also broke new ground in a way that foreshadowed the independent religious leaders some would become in the next generation. Rose Berman Goldstein exemplified this type of rebbetzin. She grew up in Minneapolis, Minnesota, where her mother, Sarah Berman, played an instrumental part in promoting Jewish life. Berman believed that women could play a critical role in securing the Jewish future, a view her daughter, Rose, came to share.[120]

Born in 1904, Goldstein graduated from the community Talmud Torah and earned her Bachelor of Arts summa cum laude from the University of Minnesota, where she was elected to Phi Beta Kappa. On the urging of her mother, she continued her education at the Teachers Institute of the Jewish Theological Seminary and at Columbia University. There she met and, in 1937, married David Goldstein. When Berman learned that her daughter had decided to marry a rabbi, she acknowledged that "after we educated you to be a first class *rebbetzin*, it were certainly folly to bewail the fact that you will be one." Her mother well understood that giving a daughter an intensive Jewish upbringing and then sending her to study at JTS primed her for just such a role.[121]

Goldstein worked with her husband in congregations in Rockaway Park, New York, and Omaha, Nebraska. Then, in Philadelphia, Pennsylvania, she worked with her husband at Har Zion Temple from 1946 to 1969. Rose taught religious school and Hebrew high school. She also directed many programming and educational projects for National Women's League, the most popular being the Judaism-in-the-Home Project. To make it easier for Jewish mothers to infuse their homes with Jewishness, Goldstein compiled a book of songs and prayers, *Songs to Share,* set to music. She hoped it would lead American Jewish children into "happy participation in religious living."[122]

Goldstein charted new ground with her work in prayer. She shifted her focus away from motivating women to attend synagogue services with their husbands and children in order to benefit the family. Rather, by 1946, Goldstein had undergone what she described as a "religious conversion," and she began to address women's own prayer needs. As she later explained, the trauma of the war years had impelled her to find her own spiritual path. Years of experience as a Jewish educator "had not prepared me in the nineteen-thirties to cope with the surge of grief and helplessness I suffered as reports of Nazi atrocities in Europe came to light. I felt an intense need for spiritual guidance and anchorage and these I found in the Siddur."[123] Goldstein began to lead the religious services at National Women's League conventions. Sharing her insights

Rose Goldstein. Courtesy of the Women's League for Conservative Judaism.

with others, she educated women to the importance of regular prayer. Goldstein also grappled with difficult questions, such as "why pray in Hebrew?" and she was ahead of her time in addressing the issue of women's obligation to pray daily. Her work in this area culminated in *A Time to Pray,* a commentary on the traditional daily prayer book replete with her annotations to the various prayers. In it, Goldstein stated unequivocally that "daily recitation of the *Amidah* is expected of women as it is of men" and suggested ways for women to fit prayer into their daily routine.[124]

Goldstein built on her rebbetzin role to advance her career as a Jewish leader and educator.[125] As Simon Greenberg, David's predecessor at Har Zion, eulogized, Rose and David

> pioneered as Conservative Jewish spiritual leaders in the Middle West. . . . [they were] two distinct personalities who together formed a partnership greater than either of them alone. Rose was an effective, spiritual and intellectual force in whatever community she lived, not merely and not even primarily because she was herself the wife of a distinguished rabbi, but primarily because she was herself an intellectually creative, eminently articulate, piously inclined and passionately devoted Jewess.[126]

Paula Ackerman

Ironically, both the power and the vulnerabilities inherent in the postwar rebbetzin role can best be understood by examining the career of Paula Herskovitz Ackerman, a rebbetzin who also served as rabbi for three years during this period. Born in Pensacola, Florida, Paula Ackerman had a traditional upbringing and later became active in her congregation, Beth El, as both student and, later, teacher. She was confirmed at the Temple and also studied Hebrew privately with a local Orthodox rabbi. Valedictorian of her high school class in 1911, Ackerman hoped to study medicine. She won a full scholarship to Sophie Newcomb College, but her father balked at the idea, insisting that he would allow her to prepare only for a teaching career. Paula stayed home and taught at the local high school. In 1926 she married William Ackerman, who had come to Pensacola to serve as Beth El's rabbi. After two years in Natchez, Mississippi, where their only child, William Jr., was born, they moved to Meridian. William served as the rabbi of Temple Beth Israel from 1922 until his sudden death in 1950.[127]

During her years as rabbi's wife, Ackerman taught the pre-Confirmation class and, with her husband's encouragement, filled in for him in the pulpit occasionally when he was ill or away. Active in Sisterhood, Ackerman served as secretary, program chairman, and "advisor in every capacity." She became involved on the national level through the Na-

Paula Ackerman. Courtesy of the American Jewish Archives, Cincinnati, Ohio.

tional Federation of Temple Sisterhoods. A member of the speaker's bureau, she also chaired the National Committee on Religious Schools. In this latter capacity, Ackerman pleaded with Federation members to become more involved in extending and improving Jewish education on the local level. Reminding her state and local chairmen in the dark years of World War II that religious education is an excellent "battlefront," she exhorted them to ensure that "American Jewish youth is not 'lost' to Judaism." By 1948, Ackerman had become Chairman of the House of Living Judaism fundraising campaign. Building on her experiences in

Meridian, she especially encouraged small Sisterhoods to raise funds. Her appeal drew on the words of Rabbi Tarphon: "The time is short, the need is urgent, the work is much."[128]

Ackerman rose to prominence with her husband's death, for the synagogue president asked her to take William's place as spiritual leader until a replacement could be found. Before accepting, she consulted with trusted friends, especially Jacob D. Schwarz, Union of American Hebrew Congregations National Director of Synagogue Activities, who had been her rabbi and had confirmed her in Pensacola. In explaining her decision, Ackerman noted that it was only in Meridian, where she and her husband had "worked together so happily for twenty-seven years," that she would even consider serving as rabbi. In other words, she saw her tenure as rabbi as the logical extension of the two-person rabbinate that she had already shared with her husband in that community for a generation. Moreover, she explained that she was encouraged to accept because the congregation had confidence in her despite her lack of formal rabbinic training. Finally, she mused that if her actions might "plant a seed for the Jewish woman's larger participation—if perhaps it will open a way for woman students to train for congregational leadership then my life would have some meaning."[129]

Ackerman considered many factors in reaching her decision. On the one hand, she felt confident that she could handle the educational part of the job because she had been teaching religious school since she had been confirmed. On the other hand, she recognized her limitations as a preacher and asked Schwarz to suggest sermon books and story collections to help her prepare. Ackerman also worried about her rudimentary knowledge of Hebrew, for she read the prayers but could not read an unvocalized Torah text. Ultimately, she assuaged her doubts because she realized that despite her weaknesses, she knew more than her congregants. Also, she recognized that what they most wanted was for her to speak from her heart. On a more practical level, Ackerman had to consider the special vulnerability of her "widow of" position. Because she lived in a parsonage, Ackerman could secure her living arrangements, if only temporarily, by taking over as rabbi.[130]

Ackerman's unique circumstances symbolize the conundrum of the rebbetzin position: only as "widow of" would she ever have been tapped to serve as rabbi. Her experiences in a two-person rabbinate had prepared her for it, but only up to a point. Ackerman remained ambivalent about her qualifications but ultimately could not resist the opportunity to serve as rabbi. Yet she may have done so in part to resolve the insecurity over housing that she faced because of her derivative status.

When news of her appointment became public, it spread as far as Tokyo. *Time* magazine called her "the first woman in the U.S. to execute a rabbi's functions." Other papers described her achievement in still more grandiose terms, dubbing her "the first woman spiritual leader in nearly 6,000 years of recorded sacred Jewish history."[131]

Maurice N. Eisendrath, then president of the UAHC, initially supported Ackerman's appointment but later publicly denied having done so. The reasoning behind his change of heart tellingly exposes the extent to which rabbis' wives had become intrinsic to the rabbinate at the time. Eisendrath conceded that Ackerman had unusual gifts that would amply qualify her to serve. He acknowledged that she had had the "opportunity and the privilege of being at his [her husband's] side for many years as a helpmate in every high sense." Yet he withdrew his endorsement because he worried lest her action put ideas into the heads of other rabbis' wives. As he explained, on his trips, he had "been in quite a number of congregations whose rabbis were fortunate enough to have exceedingly able wives. They, however, may not have all the personal and mental qualities that Mrs. Ackerman has, yet you can well understand that if a precedent of this sort is set it may lead to considerable embarrassment in other communities." In other words, Eisendrath recognized that these wives stood only one step removed from being rabbis themselves. Because many served with distinction, Eisendrath feared that only gender conventions prevented them from serving as rabbis themselves. He assumed that if given the opening, they would seize the chance to obtain directly the power they had so long enjoyed only secondarily.[132]

Ackerman served her congregation from January 1951 to September 1953. She led services, preached, performed pastoral duties, officiated at life-cycle events, and represented the congregation at regional rabbis' meetings. In 1962, Ackerman also filled in as rabbi for six months in Pensacola until that congregation could find a new one. Ackerman later recalled these experiences as "wonderful." When asked in 1952—during her tenure as rabbi—if women should be allowed to study for the rabbinate, she answered with an unequivocal "yes." Yet Ackerman continued to insist that she preferred her rebbetzin role. "It was never my secret wish to be a rabbi. My life was very rich and full and satisfying as a 'rebbetzin' and mother. Sabbath school and Sisterhood—local, state and national—gave me an outlet for my intense devotion to Judaism." Even in 1986, she expressed skepticism about a woman rabbi unless "she is married to a rabbi. I can see them working in the rabbinate together, but otherwise, I don't know." The two-person rabbinate remained her ideal.[133]

Despite the unusual opportunity she had to serve as a rabbi in the postwar period, Ackerman resembled her rebbetzin peers more than she differed from them. Eager to make the most of whatever position she filled at a given time, Ackerman fought for the right to serve as rabbi. In so doing, she demonstrated that women possessed the necessary ambition and leadership capabilities to succeed. This also allowed her to champion the right of other women to earn ordination themselves. But Ackerman had gained the skills and confidence to thrive as a rabbi because of her longstanding "wife of" position, and she remained most comfortable in that supportive role.

In Hindsight

Through interviews conducted in the 1990s, rebbetzins echoed the frustrations expressed more than thirty years earlier in articles and talks. For example, one rebbetzin still keenly recalled the pain of trying to meet congregants' expectation in terms of dress.

> I wanted to please everyone in the congregation, have everyone love me. But I found out it was impossible. If I wore the sedate navy-blue dress with the white collar, young people asked me why didn't I get "with it"? When I . . . wore a red strapless velveteen gown to a formal congregational dinner/dance, the elderly matrons almost tore me apart with their disapproving stares.[134]

Some rebbetzins also acknowledged bitterness over the gender disparities of the two-person career. For example, Eveline Panitch recalled that the role differentiation that left women responsible for home and family bred anger and animosity. She remembered that she took on those duties because her husband was busy all the time: "Someone had to hold down the fort at home, and I did."[135]

But hindsight overwhelmingly fostered nostalgia, and rebbetzins generally spoke glowingly about their experiences in the postwar period.

They remembered this as an era in which they made a difference, for they saw themselves as an essential part of a team fighting the battle for Jewish survival.[136] As Elise Waintrup explained, when she and her husband, Harold Waintrup, went to Temple Beth Am in Abington, Pennsylvania, in 1947, they believed they were pioneers: "We came to an area where everything was opening up in the suburbs. . . . So we had a partnership in everything. . . . Since we had no professional staff, my children all sat around on a Saturday night and we all did the bulletin together. . . . We were a unique breed." Similarly, Phyllis Silverman felt that it was just as much her responsibility to help foster positive Jewish experiences as it was her husband Martin's: "I knew that together we were going to do some very, very wonderful things. I really, really felt that way. I was very, very involved. Martin never asked me to do anything. But I just did, because I wanted to be in this creative, this wonderful experience." Lily Kronish agreed. She and others of her generation became active because they felt it was very important, and "we loved what we were doing. We really loved it. I didn't feel like we were sacrificing anything. We felt that we grew and grew and grew." For these women, the postwar rabbinate as two-person career brought them deep satisfaction. As Hilda Greenberg recalled, "*we* had a wonderful, fulfilling rabbinate."[137]

In retrospect, ministers' wives expressed a similar sense of gratitude for having had the opportunity to live "a challenging, growing, changing life." They felt privileged to have had "opportunities that wouldn't have come about in a less vital profession . . . to touch people's lives in such a unique way." As Thelma Grinnin, married for forty-five years to an American Baptist minister, recalled, "more than once we were told it was 'two for the price of one.' I know that some ministers' wives resent this, but I did not." Another clergy wife, married for thirty-six years to a United Methodist minister, reminisced that "for us a team ministry had been very much a pattern that has worked." And another noted that at a minister's ordination, "everyone knew that what *he* promised, *she* also accepted. From that day forward, both of their lives would be governed by the vows he took at ordination." One study concluded that "most ministers' wives wouldn't trade the experience for anything in the world."[138] Given the gender constraints of the era, then, clergy wives—both Jewish and Christian—realized that their role provided an excellent perch from which to construct meaningful lives as wives, mothers, and leaders.

Some rebbetzins focused less on the overall sense of fulfillment they derived and more on the specific perks of the role. For example, they delighted in having had the opportunity to meet visiting dignitaries from all walks of life, including Eleanor Roosevelt and Abba Eban, and they attributed this benefit directly to their rebbetzin status. Still others appreciatively recalled the professional courtesies received from local physicians and businessmen.[139]

Congregants also longingly recalled the essential role rebbetzins played. Frumi Pelcovitz's[140] obituary recalled her "as the Rebetzen of the 'White Shul,'" who "along with the Rabbi were amongst the early pioneers on the south shore of Queens, who blazed the trails of Torah, so that many generations of Jewish families could successfully build Torah-true homes in the area." Many congregations honored both rabbi and rebbetzin with journal dinner dances and evenings of tribute to mark milestone years of their involvement with the synagogue. Temple Sinai in Philadelphia, Pennsylvania, for example, dedicated the sanctuary to both Sidney and Hilda Greenberg in gratitude for fifty years of service to the congregation.[141]

Knowing of their heightened sense of calling, one wonders whether these postwar rebbetzins might have preferred earning ordination themselves. When asked decades later whether they would have wanted to be rabbis, most rebbetzins found the concept too outlandish to consider. As Kling explained, "It never crossed my mind . . . because it seemed like the realm of the impossible. . . . It's not something that was there."[142] Similarly, interviewing rebbetzins for her rabbinic thesis, Carla Freedman could not find one who desired ordination for herself.[143] Yet a few rebbetzins confessed that they might indeed have chosen that route had it presented itself as an option. For example, Maurine Kessler acknowledged that "I never thought about that, but the answer was right there for me. I would have. Definitely."[144] Similarly, Agathe Glaser mused that she and her husband had "met due to common interests in Jewish life. . . . Maybe if I'd lived today, I would've been a rabbi."[145] Some Christian clergy wives also admitted to this desire. As one noted, "if I had been born forty years later, I would probably have felt called to become ordained." But in a manner indicative of the underlying pride clergy wives continued to feel in the supportive roles they filled, that same woman immediately retreated from her claim, concluding that "I doubt we could have done as much in separate ministries as we have done together."[146]

In part, this wistfulness for the postwar role grew in response to dramatic societal changes in the 1960s and 1970s. As Betty Friedan's 1963 critique of traditional gender distinctions found receptive audiences throughout the country, women began to rethink their priorities. This generalized restlessness among women coincided with the feeling among many rebbetzins that they no longer played as essential a role in congregational life as they had a decade earlier. By the late 1960s, many of their husbands led congregations that had grown into full-service synagogues with a large complement of professional staff. The helpmate who taught religious school, decorated the building, edited the bulletin, and infused the Sisterhood with Jewish content discovered that she was no longer indispensable. For both reasons, then—as women and as rabbis' wives—some rebbetzins disengaged, curtailing their involvement in synagogue life and exploring independent career options.[147]

Certain rebbetzins distanced themselves from congregational life reluctantly and regretfully. One recalled the devastation she felt when the congregation gave her husband a gift of a trip to Israel—for one—in honor of his tenth anniversary with the synagogue. She saw this as a slap in the face in light of all the volunteer hours she had contributed to the congregation. This experience led her to warn younger rebbetzins to "be loving and supportive, but don't be a doormat! Pursue your own career or interests—be a Mentch, not an appendage."[148] As the revolutionary changes that swept America in the 1960s began to influence American Jewry in the 1970s, more and more rebbetzins would heed that advice.

5

"Please [Don't] Call Me Rebbetzin!"

"Hearing 'woman of valor' makes me want to throw up."[1] This rebbetzin's lament resonated all too often in the mid-1970s. Though rabbis' wives had begun to express frustration with the role in the previous generation, nothing could have prepared them for the turmoil they would undergo in this one.

The Women's Liberation Movement of the 1960s called into question basic assumptions about how women and men lived their lives. It challenged American women to reexamine their choices, goals, and priorities and to rethink their lives accordingly. By the 1970s, these ideas had gained national attention and broad support. The abortion and Equal Rights Amendment battles politicized not only younger women but also those who had previously been content with a full-time homemaking role. With the founding of *Ms.* Magazine and the introduction of women's studies, dozens of articles and books in both popular and scholarly venues probed many of the beliefs upon which women had based their adult lives.[2] Pioneering works, such as Kate Millett's *Sexual Politics* and William H. Chafe's *The American Woman*,[3] examined gender in society and its impact on the history of women. Feminist theory helped women understand how societal assumptions had discriminated against them and, as a result, how they might alter their lives to seek equity. The sociological perspective, popularized in such works as *Woman in a Sexist Society: Studies in Power and Powerlessness,* edited by Vivian Gornick and Barbara K. Moran, focused attention on gender roles, voluntarism, and the politics of marriage. Other studies, such as Janet Finch's *Married to the Job: Wives' Incorporation in Men's Work,* highlighted the extent to which women sought fulfillment through their husbands' careers.

These new ideas challenged the status quo of many women's lives.

Voluntarism, for example, which had provided a meaningful outlet for the talents and energies of women for centuries, suddenly lost its standing. Feminists discredited it as "pseudowork" and disparaged it as being less about helping out worthy causes and more about giving women "busywork" to fill their empty lives. Declaring any unpaid work exploitative, feminists decried voluntarism as completely antithetical to the goal of women's liberation.[4]

By the 1970s, the postwar supportive spouse found herself under attack from all quarters. Rebbetzins, because they functioned as the unpaid half of a two-person career, understood themselves to be especially easy targets. The derivative nature of a rebbetzin's status offended all that feminists stood for. Moreover, rebbetzins' volunteer duties sapped talents, energy, and creativity that feminists felt ought to have found an independent outlet elsewhere.

All of these influences led to a sustained push by younger women to create a different future for themselves by earning advanced degrees and moving into professional careers. Though marriage and children remained "essential elements of the 'good life'" for both women and men, women became increasingly concerned with controlling and organizing their lives to meet their own personal and career objectives. The proportion of women who graduated from college and the number who entered the professions rose dramatically during this period. Significantly, these women saw themselves preparing for long-term employment and careers.[5]

This phenomenon affected the ministry as well, and by the late 1970s, all the mainline Protestant denominations were ordaining women.[6] Within Judaism, the Jewish Feminist Movement advocated equality for women in Jewish religious life: equal access to both ritual honors and positions of leadership, including ordination. While individual women had pressed for this outcome at various points earlier in the century in both the Reform and Conservative Movements, only in the 1970s did this desire for ordination stem from a sustained movement for change. In 1972, women from Ezrat Nashim, a newly formed group of Conservative Jewish activists, lobbied the Conservative Rabbinical Assembly at its annual convention, calling for women's equality. That struggle proved protracted, and the Jewish Theological Seminary did not ordain a woman until 1985. But in 1972, Sally Priesand became the first woman to be ordained by the Reform Movement's Hebrew Union College. Reconstructionist Rabbinical College ordained its first woman in 1974, in its second graduating class. Only the Orthodox Movement still struggles with the question of women's ordination.[7]

The early years of the ordination battle accent the lingering ambivalence over the issue. On the one hand, American Jewry derived its notion of powerful female religious leadership from its rebbetzins and still assumed this to be the appropriate role for talented women. A 1968 article advocating women's ordination acknowledged that the Jewish community still advised women that "if you are really serious about this, go and marry a rabbi." Similarly, Priesand recalled that many believed she "was studying at HUC-JIR to become a rebbetzin rather than a rabbi." On the other hand, earlier generations had raised the ordination question in part because talented rebbetzins had demonstrated the suitability of women for such a position. Thus, when denied an official forum at the annual Rabbinical Assembly convention to address the rabbis, Ezrat Nashim approached the rebbetzins. The group's leaders found that many of the rebbetzins "strongly identified with the issues raised." Their support makes perfect sense, since rebbetzins better than anyone knew how capably women could serve.[8]

Other rabbis' wives opposed the very concept of women rabbis. Some worried lest women take jobs meant for men—their husbands, sons, or sons-in-law. Others feared that women serving as rabbis would cast aspersions on their decision to serve as supportive spouses. As Tziporah Heckelman complained, "Has vicarious fulfillment and taking turns no place in 20th Century human relationships . . . ?" Women rabbis would deprive rebbetzins of their exclusive status as female religious leaders and threaten their raison d'être, for if women could finally become what they wanted to be, then why take on the rebbetzin role any longer?[9]

Rising disorientation on the part of rebbetzins grew not only out of the Women's Movement but also out of broader consciousness-raising and anti-establishment sentiments of the era. In the 1960s, the public demythologized its leaders—clergy included—viewing them more and more as human beings subject to foibles and shortcomings. A new image of the American rabbi emerged in which "a feeling of familiarity, comfort, accessibility and often of less respect and awe" supplanted the "image of 'otherness,' piety, maturity and paternalism."[10]

In part, this new attitude toward rabbis stemmed from the narrowing educational and status gap between rabbis and their congregants. Earlier in the century, rabbis—with a degree that signified several years of post-college study—stood head and shoulders above most of their congregants in terms of educational credentials and career status. Laity revered rabbis for their learning and title. But in the postwar era, American Jews were the best educated of any major American ethnic or religious group. By the mid-1970s, American Jews averaged fourteen years of education. While less than one-half of Americans went on to college, more than 80 percent of Jews did, and Jews were more likely to attend elite institutions. Many also became professionals. Because of this, congregants no longer instinctively deferred to rabbis on the basis of their superior intellectual attainments or position. This declining level of respect affected rebbetzins as well, since their status rose and fell with their husbands'.[11]

Other seemingly unrelated changes also exacerbated rebbetzins' anxieties. For example, by the 1970s, Americans moved an average of once every seven years. Jews—including their rabbis—gradually approached that statistic, for in this area as well, rabbis came to resemble their congregants. The model, common in the interwar and immediate postwar period, of a rabbi serving one community for virtually his entire career no longer held true. In part, this stemmed from the diminishing reverence for rabbis. Having taken rabbis off the pedestal, congregants could more easily dismiss those who seemed to fall short of their ideals. This increased mobility among rabbis also reflected new realities in which professionals no longer professed lifetime loyalty to a company or institution. Stressful for all, moving affected rabbinic families more often and more deeply, since assuming a new pulpit almost always meant relocating to a new community. Forced to uproot from communities they had embraced as their own, rabbinical families often grew to resent the rabbinate itself. As two-career families became more common, frequent moving caused additional problems, for it caused wives to sacrifice career stability or advancement for the sake of their husbands' rabbinate.

These societal changes left many rebbetzins riddled with self-doubt and resentment. They began to question roles—including surrogate religious leader, wife, homemaker, and volunteer—that they had embraced for decades. Similarly, spouses of rabbinical students graduating in the mid-1970s and 1980s felt rudderless, for the postwar rebbetzin model had been called into question but there was no new prototype to guide them. As one veteran rebbetzin discovered when speaking to the JTS graduating class in 1976, the "'I want my own life . . . you can't buy me as part of a package deal' is coupled with confusion about the role they are expected to play."[12]

Symbolic Exemplar

These mounting pressures heightened worries about the personal toll the rabbinate exacted from rabbis and their families. Like their Christian counterparts,[13] rabbis began to express concern over the high level of stress experienced by all clergy. This, in turn, called attention to the extra burdens carried by their wives and children. Commissioned by the Central Conference of American Rabbis to survey the role of the rabbi, Theodore Lenn found that though rebbetzins remained reasonably active in the congregation, only 40 percent found their lives as rebbetzins fulfilling. Almost half felt the need to develop "potentialities outside the home and synagogue," and 35 percent admitted to being lonely. Interestingly, the questions in this 1972 survey reflect the transitional nature of the era. While Lenn recognized the need to measure rebbetzins' satisfaction as well as rabbis', he did so by asking not whether rebbetzins would prefer that their daughters *become* rabbis, but whether they would prefer that their daughters *marry* rabbis.[14]

Veteran rebbetzin Janice Rothschild[15] attacked Lenn's report for not including the age breakdown of respondents. She saw vast generational differences among rebbetzins, for her generation "formed relationships and habits before women's lib, traffic conditions, mobile society, and the disappearance of domestic help radically changed almost everybody's life." Rothschild felt it critical to isolate the feelings of younger rebbetzins. She endorsed Lenn's findings of rebbetzins' loneliness but believed he had failed to notice other trouble spots, such as divorce and money pressures "it may seem indelicate to mention." She branded Lenn's question about whether rebbetzins would want their daughters to marry rabbis as an "antediluvian stand-by" and expressed longing for a report that might actually illuminate the condition of the "Reform rebbetzinhood," a subject on which she claimed many were "breathlessly awaiting enlightenment."[16] Within a few years, Murray Polner's book on the American rabbinate would quote Rothschild and offer evidence of her claim concerning the generational divide. Polner recounted the views of one rabbi's wife, Anne Lapidus Lerner, who extended Rothschild's critique: "If someone asks me if I had a daughter, would I want her to marry a rabbi, I would answer I'd rather she became a rabbi herself."[17]

The same year the Lenn report appeared, Jack Bloom, who had served as a congregational rabbi for ten years before becoming a psychotherapist, finished his dissertation on "The Rabbi as Symbolic Exemplar." Echoing Kohut's description of the role in the 1920s, Bloom admitted that "every rabbi's wife has married both a man . . . and a symbol. And marrying a symbol always has consequences. . . . That makes a rabbi's public image a hostage to his wife and his family's behavior. This puts a lot more stuff into the marital and family pot that are not items for any other family." He gave contemporary examples of contentious issues, such as the wife who does not want to keep kosher or his own wife, who wore pantsuits to religious services even though the synagogue's Religious Committee had taken a position against it. Because such behavior by a spouse threatened her husband's effectiveness, Bloom concluded that clergy and their wives faced issues unlike those of any other professionals. As he explained, "there is no doctor's wife who expects to be treated by her husband medically. . . . But you just try as the spouse of a rabbi going to another schul."[18]

Bloom's analysis resonated with rabbis, and Reform rabbis invited him to address their convention in 1976. They also responded in other ways. While wives' sessions had been a staple of CCAR annual conventions for a generation, from 1975 through 1979 the Convention offered a full program on the "Rabbinic Family."[19] The Conference also created a task force deputized to sensitize congregants to the fact that "not every woman married to a rabbi accepts the role traditionally imposed." Similar sessions on the stress of the rebbetzin role took place at the Young Israel Council of Rabbis conventions during this period.[20]

At the 1975 Rabbinical Assembly convention, Wilfred Shuchat, rabbi of Shaar Shamayim in Westmount, Quebec, led two sessions on "The Rabbi and His Family," in which he encouraged participants to share their experiences. Focusing on stress in the rabbinate, he specifically noted the additional tensions faced by wives. Shuchat admitted that because of this, many rabbis' wives "resent being referred to as *rebbetzin.*"[21] Mordecai Waxman, rabbi of Temple Israel in Great Neck, New York, echoed Bloom's and Shuchat's concerns about the stresses unique to the clergy in a 1997 volume on the American rabbi. He grumbled about the impossible task faced by contemporary rabbis and wives, the expectation that they be both at a distance and "with it."[22]

The 1980 CCAR Convention devoted a session to "The Personal Equation of a Rabbi's Life,"[23] led by Adrienne Sundheim. Sundheim insisted that the key to happiness rested with acknowledging the human qualities of rabbis and their wives. In her words, "I do not share my life with a rabbi. I share my life with a man whose profession is the rabbinate. I do not love a rabbi. I love a man who is a rabbi." Sundheim candidly illustrated the burdens of symbolic exemplarhood with the following eye-opening anecdotes:

> Once, when I was driving on a busy thruway, a careless driver disregarded a yield sign and almost smashed into me. I slammed on the brakes and demonstrated my anger with an obscene digital message, basically employing one finger. Not only was the driver a congregant, but the wife of a board member.

And then:

> Some years ago, we were serving as faculty members at one of the NFTY [National Federation of Temple Youth] camps. Rooming next to us was another faculty couple. . . . They were also friends and congregants. Although very comfortable, it was not the NFTY Hilton, and apparently the walls were quite thin. After our return home, a mutual friend mentioned that our NFTY neighbor said to her, incredulously, "Rabbis actually do it, don't they?"

Sundheim's advice: congregants needed to stop thinking that occasionally their "rabbis are people"; rather, they ought to remember that "people are rabbis."[24]

The last large-scale study on this issue appeared in 1983. In it, Leslie R. Freedman confirmed much that had already been reported concerning tension in the rabbinate and its effect not only on rabbis but also on their wives. But his conclusions were more alarming, for he noted that the level of stress among rabbis was higher than that of individuals residing within a twenty-mile radius of the Three-Mile Island nuclear power plant in the months following its 1979 accident.[25]

Quality of life concerns worried rabbinical students as well. In contrast to the interwar period, most HUC rabbinic students in the 1960s and 1970s were married. As part of the more introspective mode of the era, they initiated discussions about the role of the spouse in the rabbinate.[26] Michael P. Sternfield wrote his rabbinic thesis in 1973 on "The Rabbi as Family Man"; in it he built on Lenn's findings as well as on similar studies of Protestant clergy in order to "determine the major issues in the home life of the congregational rabbi." According to his findings, rabbis' wives found themselves bombarded by contradictory advice. On the one hand, despite societal changes, the 1973 graduating class was told that "during the first year in a new congregation, wives should plan on devoting their lives entirely to their husband's work." Most congregational rabbis also articulated basic expectations for their wives, such as synagogue attendance. On the other hand, some rabbis in the field claimed that the decision to participate in synagogue life belonged to their wives. As one rabbi explained, "a rabbi's wife today can be whatever she likes to be. . . . The stereotyped rebbetzin is a role I don't think can or should exist anymore."[27]

Among the wives interviewed by Sternfield, some expressed contentment with their rebbetzin role, while others voiced mixed feelings. They enjoyed the status but felt overburdened by the expectations. Sternfield confirmed Lenn's findings of both loneliness (e.g., "my husband is at meetings almost every night and that can be very lonely") and the pain of living in a fishbowl(e.g., "People don't participate in our life but they want to look in and see"). Sternfield isolated younger rebbetzins from older ones and, confirming Rothschild's suspicions, noted that younger rabbinic couples "definitely have more problems than older couples." Like Lenn's study, Sternfield's analysis reflected the uneasy coexistence of both older and newer attitudes.[28]

Steven Fisch built upon Sternfield's findings in his rabbinic thesis to determine whether the attitudes expressed by contemporary rabbis' wives also held true for the wives of rabbinical students. Less ambivalent than rabbis' wives, the student wives were resigned to the fact that their professional and personal goals would be restricted by their husbands' career. Compared to the wives of medical or law students, Fisch found that student rabbis' wives believed they would be more likely to experience emotional stress as a result of their husbands' career. They also expressed feelings of inadequacy and lack of preparedness similar to those that had plagued many postwar student wives. But in contrast to that era, and in keeping with the transformed climate of the 1970s, three-fourths of the student wives interviewed objected to the title "rebbetzin." One described it as "such an old-fashioned sort of 'shtettle' word." Others commented that "the first thing that comes to my mind is a stupid little 'yenta' who walks around with a 'babushka' and knows all of the gossip in town," or "whenever I've heard it, it's been used with a sneer. It's not used with any type of respect implied," and, finally, "rebbetzin" puts "you into a defined role . . . the wife of a rabbi whose whole life revolves around the congregation. . . . it's not *my* profession." Fisch criticized Lenn's more sanguine findings about the term, noting that Lenn's results had been based on a total sample of less than 30 percent of all Reform rabbis' wives. Fisch also felt that Lenn skewed the results by addressing his questionnaire cover letter to "Dear Rebbitzin," a salutation that, Fisch surmised, would have offended younger women and influenced them to not respond to it.[29]

What to call the rabbi's wife became a "hot button" issue in the 1970s, for the "rebbetzin" term represented the burdens of symbolic exemplarhood. At a session sponsored by the HUC Student Association, Leonard Troup, a recently ordained rabbi, explained that if the invitation to address the group had used the word "rebbetzin" rather than "rabbi's wife," his wife would have declined, because it connoted for her a role lacking in individual identity. Troup insisted that he imposed no special expectations on his wife. "I give my wife the same freedom to disregard what the rabbi writes in his bulletin as the rest of the congregation"—the very opposite of what Kohut had counseled fifty years earlier.[30]

Gripe Literature

Debate over the changing role of the rebbetzin spilled out of the seminaries and rabbinical conventions and into the general press in 1975. Revelations touched on new issues and surpassed in openness anything written a generation earlier. In 1975, *Moment,* a new magazine targeted at a broad readership of men and women interested in taking "Jewish possibilities seriously," placed a rabbi's wife on its cover and included a feature story titled "Rabbis' Wives: The Case of the Shrinking Pedestal." Clearly designed for shock value, the article began with a description of Reform rabbi's wife Marlene Schwartz standing in her kitchen where "the breakfast bacon simmers on the stove" next to an article clipping announcing "Restrictions Ease for Clergymen's Wives." Despite the defiant stance, Schwartz admitted to suffering from the tensions of the role. The author, Joan Behrmann, attributed Schwartz's concerns to the pressures of the Women's Movement. Behrmann then proceeded to describe reactions by several other rebbetzins that demonstrate the role ambiguity prevalent in the throes of the feminist revolution.

A veteran rebbetzin with thirty years experience expressed frustration over her initial lack of preparedness for the role, the need for restraint, congregants' judgmentalism, and loneliness. But she also admitted to accepting her role as "vice-president" of a two-person team and claimed that it provided "total fulfillment." In contrast, a younger rebbetzin tried to shake off any expectations, confessing that when asked to bless the bread at a function, she refused, because "I don't have any golden touch with God."[31]

This interchange set the pattern that would characterize debate on this topic for more than a decade. On the one hand, many veteran rebbetzins felt compelled to speak out publicly in defense of the traditional role. These proponents included a small but growing number of Orthodox rebbetzins. As American Orthodoxy came into its own in the 1970s and 1980s, the Movement developed and strengthened a wide range of institutions. Media coverage touted its revival, and American Jewry at large began to acknowledge and admire the renaissance of a denomination once thought incompatible with American life. In this context, Orthodox rebbetzins came to serve as a symbol of this revitalization of traditional Judaism.[32]

On the other hand, other rabbis' wives—usually younger, non-Orthodox ones—boldly flaunted their defiance of traditional expectations and rejected the notion of the rabbinate as a two-person career. In keeping with societal tendencies to demystify authority figures, these rebbetzins insisted on the right to act just like everyone else. Some took special pleasure displaying evidence of their rebelliousness.

The Jewish feminist magazine *Lilith* compounded the confusion with its "Friday the Rebbetzin . . . A Feminist Look at the Rabbi Small Series." Attacking author Harry Kemelman for his inauthentic portrayal of Rebbetzin Miriam Small as Klaperman had done, Ida Cohen Selavan offered what she called an evaluation of Small "from a Jewish feminist perspective." But in actuality, Selavan preached a mixed message. Though she disparaged Kemelman's narrow focus on Small as caregiver to her husband, she praised her "rebbetzin friends," Jewishly and secularly well-educated women who played an active role in their synagogues and communities.[33] Sherry Levy Reiner, herself a rabbi's wife, pointed out that both Selavan and *Lilith* needed their consciousness raised as much as Small and Kemelman did. Exposing Selavan's preference for a two-for-the-price-of-one rabbinate, Reiner revealed her own distaste for the term "rebbetzin," which "identifies a woman by her husband's job."[34]

Debate over the rebbetzin role reached a fever pitch with the publication in 1978 of *Rachel, the Rabbi's Wife* by Silvia Tennenbaum, herself a rebbetzin. Outdoing Marlene Schwartz's simmering bacon in its sensationalism, this novel opens with a description of rabbi and rebbetzin making love on a cold January morning, their post-coital afterglow rudely interrupted by a call from the synagogue. "*Shit!*" the rabbi cursed as he hung up the phone. "They want me for the *minyan.*" Hoping to shatter any remaining illusions that rabbinic couples lived a more godly life, Tennenbaum spotlighted the human side of the rabbinate. Her character, Rachel, found no joy or value in the rebbetzin role, only stigma and stress, and she consistently balked at assuming any of the traditional tasks associated with it. When asked by an elderly rebbetzin if she participated much in congregational activities, Rachel retorted, "Not if I can help it."[35]

While some reviews simply dismissed the book as vulgar kitsch,[36] one particularly revealing review written by a seasoned and satisfied rabbi's wife revisited the rebbetzin role itself.[37] Marcia Weinberg acknowledged that Tennenbaum raised, "however ineffectively," important questions. Conceding the accuracy of the loneliness, marital strains, and injustices of the symbolic exemplar role Tennenbaum depicted, Weinberg especially empathized with the indignities of living in a synagogue house. "When you live in a parsonage, a piece of your self is taken away." But Weinberg provided a contemporary twist to her understanding of the rebbetzin role by admitting that it need not be a full-time career. In her view, the Women's Movement posed no special challenges to it, for "one can be a brain surgeon or a corporate lawyer and still be a good rebbetzin." Weinberg contended that the fault lay not with tensions between the rebbetzin role and feminist values but with the fictional Rachel for refusing to do her part. To illustrate her perspective, Weinberg, like Reiner, contrasted the terms "rabbi's wife" and "rebbetzin."

> Technically it means the same thing, but I perceive it differently. Anyone can be a rabbi's wife. . . . Being a rabbi's wife is the relationship of husband and wife and has many ramifications of its own. . . . [B]ut being a

rebbetzin has to do with the relationship between rabbi's wife and congregation. . . . [I]t has to do with a dimension she brings to the synagogue that would be lost without her.

For Weinberg, the rebbetzinhood continued to offer happiness, fulfillment, and love to those rabbis' wives willing to extend themselves to others.

Outlook, the magazine that had printed most of the articles on the role of the rebbetzin in the 1950s and 1960s, weighed in on the subject in 1980 with its "The Pulpit Rebbitzen: Para-Professional? Wife Support System? Career Woman?"[38] Written by rabbi's wife Lynne Heller, the article asked, "why does the classical . . . Rebbitzen evoke nostalgia, admiration, [and] adulation, while . . . the Rabbi's wife who eschews comprehensive Synagogue involvement, engenders an unsettling, equivocal response?" Heller reviewed the influence of social trends including "women's lib" and the increasing divorce rate, but she didn't fully answer the question. Instead, she devoted the bulk of the article to celebrating the full-time rebbetzin careers of the older generation, profiling such women as Bertha Aronson, Rose Goldstein, Betty Greenberg, and Althea Silverman. In other words, seeking to shore up the increasingly shaky image of the rabbi's wife, Heller looked to the past. She ended with the hope that the lessons of these exemplary rebbetzins' lives might help the contemporary rabbi's wife strike her own balance between her roles as career woman and rebbetzin.

Only in 1983 did the role of the rebbetzin receive full treatment in *Outlook* under the heading "Point of View." Three contemporary rabbis' wives offered their perspective on the role.[39] Sharon L. Cohn, in "Please Don't Call Me Rebbitzen,"[40] began by establishing her feminist credentials: she kept her own name after marriage, and her husband gave his full support to her career ambitions. The title of her article further reinforced her view of herself as one who rejected the traditional role. But though Cohn saw her rabbi's wife role "as somewhat atypical," in fact she mirrored many of her peers in her decision to "select what I want to do, and try to do it well." Cohn taught Sunday school, advised the youth group, and chaired the Education Committee in her husband's synagogue. In contrast, Julie Allender, in "I Married A Rabbi," described her choices with far less ambiguity. A licensed psychologist, Allendar married in her thirties after establishing herself professionally. She and her husband negotiated her level of religious observance, particularly in terms of dietary and Sabbath laws. While not hostile toward the congregation, she explained that "we try to make clear to Congregations when they hire Louis as their Rabbi, that they are hiring one employee. . . . I am not interested in being a full time unpaid volunteer, nor does my schedule allow for it." Allendar also noted the unfair burden that frequent moving from one congregation to another placed on rabbinic spouses. She expressed bitterness at the lack of control over her destiny that rabbinic placement imposed. Indicative of the times, Allendar concluded, "I do not accept a label. I do not call myself a Rebbitzen. I am a person of my own, who married a marvelous guy whose career is being a Rabbi. Nobody calls him a psycholitzen— and I hope no one ever will."[41]

Barbara Kieffer upheld the traditional role in her "Call Me Rebbitzen." She reiterated the view that "being a Rebbizen, a wife, a mother and an individual . . . is necessary and even vital . . . if the rabbinate is to be successful." Kieffer co-chaired the Judaica shop, prepared publicity for Sisterhood, started a choir, and consciously served as a role model for Jewish living. Though she too bemoaned the sense of displacement caused by moving, Kieffer concluded that her own sense of calling kept her focused on providing service to each community in which they lived. As a relatively young, thirteen-year veteran rebbetzin, Kieffer felt the need to justify retaining her traditional stance. She noted somewhat defensively that "my need for professional musical expression has not really taken a back seat in my life. I have simply found it both wise and meaningful to channel my musical abilities into the evolving avenues of my Jewish and rabbinic life."[42]

The next issue printed three responses by other Conservative rebbetzins.[43] In her "I Didn't Marry a Rabbi, But I Answer to Rebbitzen Now," Helen Tomsky, then a twenty-seven-year veteran rebbetzin, acknowledged "identifying with some of the things" that the younger women said, despite the generational difference. She believed that they shared a common bond as a class "because our lives as wives of Conservative Rabbis are quite similar."[44]

Cecile Asekoff, in "Call Me What You Will," denigrated the notion of a rabbi's wife haggling over her level of Jewish observance. Disturbed that *Outlook* did not include the responses of what she called the "'average Rebbitzen on the street' . . . who is herself committed to Jewish values, traditions and education," she presented herself as that prototype. Asekoff noted that all professionals' wives make "certain compromises and adjustments" for their husbands, and she insisted that as a caring Jew, she did "for the Synagogue exactly what I would do if my husband, children and I were just members of the Congregation and not the 'Rabbi's family.'"[45] Like Asekoff, Donna Glazer, in her "Rebbitzens: Supportive and Visible," protested *Outlook's* decision to feature a rabbi's wife who negotiated her commitment to Jewish living. Calling herself a feminist and a rebbetzin, Glazer insisted that "if one were to take a survey, one would find many more women identifying with the traditional views, so eloquently expressed by Barbara Kieffer."[46] Chelly Golderg's 1985 "Understanding Your Rebbetzin" underscored the enormous diversity of Jewish background and attitude that characterized contemporary rebbetzins by concluding that "WE ALL DO IT DIFFERENTLY. Together with our husbands, we are constantly redefining our positions."[47]

In reality, Goldberg's benign view of the range of attitudes among rebbetzins belied the toxic nature of some of the underlying issues. Three of the six rabbis' wives who wrote on the role for *Outlook* subsequently divorced, as did the Troups and Tennenbaums mentioned above, underscoring the extent to which lifestyle stress could cause irreparable damage. While no statistical surveys of divorce in the rabbinate appeared at the time, the general divorce rate doubled between the early 1960s and the mid-1970s, peaking in 1979 at 22.8 per 10,000 married women. The number of divorces approached half the number of marriages per year, and during the 1970s and 1980s, the divorce rate among Jews approximated that of Gentiles. Rothschild and Heller's impressions about mounting divorce rates among rabbis reflected increasing concern among rabbinic families that they too were susceptible to the outside factors that led to divorce. On top of that, rabbis and their wives also worried that the special pressures of their roles made them even more vulnerable than average American couples.[48]

Another strain facing rabbinic families, mentioned by several rebbetzins above, was the lack of job security. This issue became the subject of *The Rabbi's Life Contract*. In this 1983 novel, the author, rebbetzin Marilyn Greenberg, intertwined the specter of moving with the ordeal of contract renewal. The protagonist, Joshua Rosenstock, returned from a year-long sabbatical only to learn that his suburban Chicago synagogue had decided to remove him from his rabbinate despite his life contract. While not dealing directly with the role of the rebbetzin, the novel nonetheless chronicled the wife's mounting pain and resentment.

Myra Rosenstock struggled continually both to make sense of the congregation's behavior and to support her husband through the ordeal. As Joshua explained, "this is very hard on her. . . . She doesn't eat, just smokes. Doesn't sleep." When supporters rallied to help him fight the decision, Myra protested, "and who's helping me. . . . Why don't I have a friend? . . . I don't want to suffer like this. I hate being fastened to all these troubles, to watch him be insulted and robbed of all his work." In an era of confessionals, this fictional tale, like many others, demonstrated rebbetzins' growing willingness to reveal their private agonies to a wider audience. It also poignantly captured the sense among rebbetzins of the 1980s that they continued to share with their husbands the stresses and strains of the rabbinate but they no longer experienced the fulfillment and joys of the two-person career.[49]

The increasingly public debate about the stresses of the rebbetzin role eventually exposed other painful aspects, including retirement and, even more so, widowhood. For some, the transition proved relatively easy. As retirees, adaptable rebbetzins found new volunteer outlets for their skills in teaching, leading book groups, counseling, and performing community service. Some continued to make condolence visits and help out elderly congregants. Others who moved out of the area of the congregation they had served kept in touch with former congregants by mail.[50] But many rebbetzins discovered that they had to renegotiate their relationship with the congregation, and that that could be a painful process. Some found it difficult to let go, and they continued to perform rebbetzin functions, making life miserable for their successors. Others backed away from the role to give the new rebbetzin a chance to succeed. One wisely taught that the retired rabbi's wife ought to model herself after the kabbalistic God and practice *tzimzum* (contraction) to make room for the new rebbetzin. Another retired rebbetzin recalled developing a standard response to requests to do something for the congregation. She would decline, explaining that she suffered from "emereye-tus."[51]

According to a study of widows of rabbis, two-thirds disagreed with the statement that "when a congregation buries its Rabbi, it buries his wife along with him." Most reported a sense of relief at no longer having to live up to the expectations of the role.[52] Some felt free for the first time to develop as leaders on their own terms. But others claimed that widowhood for a rebbetzin triggered a sense of dislocation that intensified their loss. As one rebbetzin explained, "Not only were we suffering a grievous personal loss, but we lost our places in the synagogue, in the community, and—worst of all—in the hearts of our congregants."[53] Rebbetzins recalled the acute sting of no longer being recognized by new business owners, newer congregants, or recently hired synagogue staff. They felt snubbed when they were no longer invited to congregants' life-cycle celebrations, even though they had spent decades fending off such invitations and social engagements. According to Agathe Glaser, this irony pointed up one of the unique challenges faced by widowed rebbetzins. After striving to protect their privacy for so many years, they suddenly needed to reach out to make social connections, and they didn't know how. Some widowed rebbetzins resolved this tender predicament by remarrying another rabbi. Joan Lipnick Abelson noted that marrying Kassel Abelson after the death of her first husband, Jerome Lipnick, reinstated her as a public Jewish figure.[54]

For some rebbetzins, the sense of dislodgment took literal form, since retired rabbis and widows were often forced out of a parsonage. After living in a community for decades, they suddenly found themselves without either a home or equity to purchase one. For example, only a month after Nathan Rosenbaum, longtime rabbi of Temple Beth El in North Bellmore, New York, died in 1978, the congregation asked his wife, Shirley, to move out of the parsonage.[55]

Concerned about the solvency of the rabbinic lifestyle in the face of mounting discontent, Reform rabbi Sylvan Schwartzman argued that the solution was not to be found in abandoning outdated role expectations for rebbetzins. On the contrary, in light of the competing pressures of the era, female rabbis, and the need for two incomes among rabbis, Schwartzman proposed upgrading the status of the rebbetzin, "to accord as much status . . . as we do to the role of the female rabbi." He praised it as one of the most skilled professions, one that had the added benefit of strengthening the marital bond between husband and wife. Though Schwartzman claimed, as others had, that the rabbinate differed little from other professions, he illustrated his point by noting that "a friend of mine is a skilled pediatric surgeon; his wife is a superb surgical nurse." For Schwartzman, then, the ideal remained the "assistant pastor" model, though he neglected to note the disparity between the paid nursing position and the unpaid rebbetzin role—let alone the status differential between nurse and doctor. In a subsequent letter to the editor, one female Reform rabbi chided Schwartzman for his "anachronistic" view.[56]

Schwarzman's regressive proposal found echoes in Alex Goldman's 1987 novel, *The Rabbi Is a Lady*, a fictional account of the experiences of a woman rabbi. The plot hinged not on a recently ordained rabbi but rather on a widowed rebbetzin asked to serve as rabbi after her husband's death. Reverting to the stereotypes of an earlier era and building on the 1951 experience of Paula Ackerman, the author explained that "it had been natural for her to marry a rabbi. And through the years, she had lived the role vicariously by helping, guiding, and assisting in sermons. But for herself the urge [to be a rabbi, which she had expressed as a child] had been suppressed."[57] Goldman explored some of the unique difficulties faced by women rabbis, but the plot device itself undermined this more progressive goal by reinforcing traditional stereotypes.

Debate about the rebbetzin role persisted throughout the 1980s. Rabbis and rebbetzins continued to bemoan unrealistic expectations, while congregants expressed both support and criticism of the traditional role.[58]

Ministers' Wives

Ministers' wives grappled with the same issues beginning in the 1960s.[59] National church organizations commissioned studies to better understand the challenges and determine how best to resolve them. Clergy wives wrote books, hoping to expose the problems and offer support to their colleagues.[60] Ruth Truman's *Underground Manual for Ministers' Wives* addressed the dilemmas head-on: "The bras are burning, the flags are waving, and pins and bumper stickers burgeoning to announce the dissatisfaction of woman. . . . The libbers are upon us, and we must come to terms with them—and ourselves." Truman advised the minister's wife to "begin by knowing the person you actually are . . . not the preacher's wife, which may be the role you play." She acknowledged that though "the seminary told you that people don't think of the minister's wife as special or unique anymore. . . . The seminary goofed again!"[61]

Truman emphasized the particular indignities of living in a parsonage, empathizing with those who "live in a house whose exclusive ownership is of the church, by the church, and for the church . . . and is overseen with exquisite care by a parsonage committee that either never quits or never starts." She also soberly recounted the toll that frequent moves took on a minister's family.[62] Truman encouraged ministers' wives to think about going back to school or work, but she cautioned them not to expect sympathy from the congregation, and she endorsed retaining some pastoral duties even after taking a job.[63]

To address such tensions, Ministers Life & Casualty Union printed a brochure with a haunting photo of a white, artificially cheerful female face-mask capped by a halo. The heading read "How does it feel to be a minister's wife? Imagine wearing this. Almost everywhere. Almost all the time." The same graphic also appeared on a full-size, six-sided brochure with the heading, "Despite appearances, ministers' wives are only human." After listing the special challenges faced by ministers' wives, including loneliness, being underappreciated, and feeling married to the congregation, the brochure promoted the formation of support groups for ministers' wives. Clearly, the mental health of clergy wives had become widespread enough that this insurer of ministers felt compelled to take action.[64]

Rebbetzins Respond

Many avenues of response emerged to counter mounting societal pressures. Initially, some rebbetzins reacted to criticisms and strains by rededicating themselves to working in partnership with their husbands but finding new ways to do so that established a more equal balance of power between them. This reflected sentiments of the era, which came increasingly to value the notion of couples redefining their marriages on their own terms.[65] Rabbinic couples led synagogue Israel trips and cross-country youth tours, work that enabled them to serve together as group leaders.[66] Jewish Marriage Encounter provided the best outlet for this impulse, since the equal involvement of both husband and wife was intrinsic to its success.

Jewish Marriage Encounter based itself on the Christian Marriage Encounter Movement, itself a corollary of marriage and family enrichment programs based on T-group and sensitivity-training movements of the 1960s. Major Christian denominations created Christian Marriage Encounter to respond to feelings, widespread at the time, that marriage and family needed support. By the early 1970s, Jewish couples who had experienced Christian Marriage Encounter sought rabbinic couples to better serve them in ongoing Encounter activities. Bernard Kligfeld, then chairman of the Family Life Committee of the CCAR, responded. He and his wife, Julia, attended a weekend as observers to learn more about the techniques and determine if they might be applicable to Jewish families. Given their shared interest in strengthening Jewish life, the Kligfelds' decision to become involved is not surprising. Both were ardent Zionists in their teens and graduates of JTS's Teachers Institute. Bernard served as rabbi of Temple Emanu-El of Long Beach, New York (1950–81), while Julia taught Hebrew in the School of Education at Hebrew Union College-Jewish Institute of Religion. On their Encounter weekend, they unexpectedly found themselves transformed. With the support of the Catholic Encounter Movement, they developed Marriage Encounter—The Jewish Expression.[67]

The Kligfelds recruited colleagues to serve as rabbinic couples on Encounter weekends, and they worked with them to develop topics for discussion. In 1974, Jewish Marriage Encounter, as it came to be known, became an independent organization under the umbrella of the National Marriage Encounter organization. Couples served together on the national board and worked to promote Jewish family life by strengthening marriage. Rabbinic couples undertook this work not only to enrich the lives of Jewish couples but also "to achieve the satisfaction of having worked together as a couple in a meaningful activity." By mid-1974, thirty rabbinic couples in twelve states, nine on Long Island alone, functioned as rabbinic team leaders. More than 10,000 Jewish couples participated.[68]

Jewish Marriage Encounter became an important vehicle for rabbis' wives, since their involvement was essential. Rabbinic couples attended Jewish Marriage Encounter board meetings as a unit, and they co-chaired committees. Together they developed the scripts for their Encounter weekends. For example, Reuben and Reba Katz prepared type-written notes of their remarks on each area covered. Seeking to put their audience at ease and to model Encounter communication techniques, they first confessed doubts and insecurities. As Reba admitted:

> For many years I had a very difficult feeling that I was afraid to reveal to Ruby. This was a feeling that I had about funerals. . . . Before my marriage to Ruby I could handle my feelings about funerals since I simply didn't have the need to go to any. But suddenly I found that with being a rabbi's wife, I had to attend more funerals in one year than the

number of funerals the average person attends in a lifetime. . . . I had always tried to be a good rebbetzin. If I told Ruby that I dreaded funerals, would he think that I was shirking my responsibilities as a rabbi's wife? . . . After Ruby and I began to dialogue, I decided to have confidence in him and tell him about my dread and fears regarding funerals. He not only accepted my feelings, but he shared with me his own discomfort and the fact that he had a difficult time dealing with this important area of his professional life.[69]

Katz's rebbetzin role exacerbated her fears, but it also enabled her both to confront them and to influence others through Marriage Encounter. Such open reflection by rabbinic couples within a Jewish framework characterized the essence of the Encounter weekend.

Attendees valued the honesty of their rabbinic leaders and expressed profound gratitude to them for sharing of themselves so intimately. As one appreciative couple wrote to the Kligfelds, "So many, many times Joe and I have tried to put in a reflection to you, what your sharing does for us and each time we fear it will come across reading like 'idol worship.' You both mean so very much to us, we love you both so dearly. . . . To us, you are the Ideals of Living True Judaism." Another confessed that "You gave us a taste of what Judaism is. . . . Thank you for opening our eyes. We are now searching for more. We want to enrich our lives with Judaism." Such positive feedback must have provided rabbinic couples with a tremendous sense of satisfaction.[70]

While Marriage Encounter and other ventures gave some rabbis' wives the opportunity to strengthen their partnership roles, other rebbetzins needed special support mechanisms to cope with the stresses of the era. By the early 1980s, the Conservative Movement established the "RA Care Line," a twenty-four-hour hotline for rabbis and their families. In 1984, the Reform Movement formed the Spouse Connection as a way for wives and husbands of rabbis "to share common experiences and offer mutual support." It offered a semiannual newsletter, *SpouseConnection*; SpouseLine, a telephone "warmline" for feedback and advice; and workshops and study groups at regional meetings and conventions.[71]

Rebbetzins also formed local support groups, influenced in part by the self-help movement proliferating in the United States during this period. Gathering regularly in each other's homes, they shared stories, offered advice, and confronted dilemmas in an atmosphere of mutual respect and confidentiality. At least one of the groups also gained strength by joining forces on behalf of Soviet Jewry.[72]

Others continued to respond to feminist pressures by bolstering the traditional role. Orthodox leaders, especially, promoted the traditional rebbetzin role in contradistinction to that of the female rabbi. In 1978 the Wurzweiler School of Social Work of Yeshiva University enhanced its legitimacy through a Clergy Plan, a new course of study open not only to clergy, but also to spouses "if they hold a bachelor's degree and function as clergy in that they perform a specific role in giving service to their communities."[73] The Orthodox also began increasingly to refer to rabbi's wives by the rebbetzin title to reinforce the view that Orthodox Jewish women leaders did not need to take on the title "rabbi." For example, as part of its ArtScroll Judaiscope series, Mesorah Publications included a section on "Great Women" in its collection of biographies of Torah luminaries. Three of the four women profiled were rebbetzins, and they are identified by that title. Similarly, Lubavitcher publications such as *Di Yiddishe Heim—The Jewish Home* identified rabbis' wives, including the editor, Rachel Altein, by the title rebbetzin.[74]

Certain older rebbetzins responded to the challenges of the day by parlaying skills honed during the postwar years into paid careers in the Jewish and non-Jewish worlds. In many ways, they found themselves better prepared than their non-rebbetzin peers to take on these roles because they had had many opportunities to develop marketable talents—as public speakers, teachers, writers, organizers, and counselors. When feminist thinking transformed society's attitudes toward married women's employment, these rebbetzins found themselves with the resources to step into careers of their own.[75]

Blu Greenberg

Blu Genauer Greenberg is one example of such a rebbetzin.[76] Noted author and lecturer and founding president of the Jewish Orthodox Feminist Alliance, Greenberg is often described as the "spiritual mother of Orthodox feminism."[77] Daring the Orthodox establishment to respond to the unique challenges the Women's Movement posed to tràditional Judaism, she boldly asserted what has become her widely quoted mantra: "Where there's been a rabbinic will, there's been a *halakhic* way."[78]

Blu Greenberg. Courtesy of Ina Furst.

Greenberg was born in 1936, in Seattle, Washington, to Sam and Sylvia Genauer. Both parents were committed to intensive Jewish education for their daughters, and the family moved to New York in part to take advantage of the more extensive educational opportunities there. After completing yeshiva high school, Blu entered Brooklyn College, while continuing her Jewish studies in the evenings at the Teachers Institute for Women of Yeshiva University. After earning both a Bachelor of Arts (1958) and a Bachelor of Religious Education (1957), Greenberg completed a Master of Arts in Clinical Psychology at the City University of New York and a Master of Science in Jewish History at Yeshiva University's Bernard Revel Graduate School of Jewish Studies (1977).[79]

Like many young women of her era, Greenberg prepared for a career in teaching. In her mother's view, it would be her "insurance," for Jewish mothers at the time commonly saw teaching as a sensible route for women to achieve economic security and status in case they ever needed to work.[80] Greenberg had taught religious school part-time in various synagogues wherever she lived, beginning while she was still in high school. She recalls loving her work as a teacher, gaining great satisfaction from educating children. When Blu and her husband Irving (Yitz) moved to Washington Heights, New York, in 1959, two years after their marriage, Blu taught adults Hebrew language and holidays at the local synagogue.[81]

One year after moving to Riverdale, New York, Yitz Greenberg became rabbi of the Riverdale Jewish Center, a position he held for seven years (1965–72). During these years, Blu functioned as a traditional postwar congregational rebbetzin. First and foremost, she reared five children—Moshe, David, Deborah, J. J., and Goody. She later recalled this stage of life giving her great joy and satisfaction; yet, like the women Betty Friedan described in *The Feminine Mystique*, Greenberg experienced occasional moments of conflict. She recalled that one morning as her husband was about to set out for work, leaving her to tend to their five children all day, she fantasized lying down and blocking the door so that Yitz would be unable to leave the house.[82]

As a rebbetzin, Greenberg invited guests for Sabbath and holiday meals, as well as for Saturday-night and week-night dinners. She also hosted the synagogue's guest lecturers. Greenberg recalled feeling obligated to attend synagogue dinners and bar mitzvah receptions, and she remembered going to every *shiva* (condolence) visit and paying many hospital visits, though not as many as her husband.[83] Serving as a sounding board for her husband's sermons, Blu gave Yitz feedback on ideas and formulations and took pride in his accomplishments. She recalled that

> in sermon preparation and relationships with people, he often sought my advice. . . . I also gave him a lot of unsolicited advice. There's one person who always says, "Oh my favorite rabbi." . . . I know why. Because I suggested to Yitz to do something for him . . . that made a big difference to this man at that moment in his life. I used to remind Yitz

to call people or go visit them or do special things for them. And so ninety percent of those pastoral duties, he did on his own, but ten percent I helped along—and that's a pretty big percentage for an unpaid second career.[84]

When Blu began to exercise religious leadership in traditionally male areas, she also did so initially to help out her husband. Though Greenberg had studied Talmud in the late 1960s at Yeshiva University, she had never taught it. In the Orthodox world, religious power was anchored in Talmud teaching, a traditionally male preserve. Greenberg moved into this territory in a serendipitous and unofficial way. Recalling this incident with surprise twenty years later, she explained:

> I did something that was really *chutzpadik* [brazen] now that I think about it. He [Yitz] taught a regular Gemara [Talmud] class in our home on Shabbat afternoons. He was going away, and he asked me [if I would teach it]. Many times I would do things when he had to go away for Shabbat or something. He asked me if I would do it, and I said: "Yes, I'll do it." I can't understand [now] how the men accepted it even. It's really startling [now], and it was just matter of fact [then].[85]

This opportunity came her way because of her "wife of" status. It also protected her by masking, under the guise of "helping out," her radical move into this traditionally male role.

Greenberg maintains that her years as a rebbetzin gave her invaluable experience in interpersonal relationships. It allowed her to become central to people's lives rapidly, because she related to congregants intensively at peak moments of the life cycle. For example, she felt that *shiva* visits as a rabbi's wife felt qualitatively different from those paid before she served as rebbetzin because they "engaged people at extraordinarily deep levels of emotion, and the trust was there because of my special role."[86]

For many reasons, then, Greenberg valued her years as a congregational rebbetzin, a term that she always loved. In her view,

> There's room to be both an enabler and to be your own person at the same time. . . . I was lucky to have had the opportunity of being an enabler in that kind of position. It was rich and very rewarding. . . . And in the ways that I was able to serve—and it was a service role . . .

it made my life very much richer. . . . There's something fortunate about being in that auxiliary role . . . something lucky to being the second person sharing that career.[87]

Greenberg's role in this two-person rabbinate eventually opened the doors to her independent career. She recalls that she began teaching college as a direct result of her husband's reputation. Approached to teach a course on Judaism at the College of Mount St. Vincent, Yitz Greenberg found himself too busy to take it on and proposed co-teaching it with his wife. As she explained: "We finished one semester and then he turned it over to me, and I stayed there for eight years, and I loved it."[88] Blu readily acknowledged her debt to her husband:

> In all those years whatever I was doing was helped along by his reflective glory and status. . . . The way I got into most things in my life was really through his connection. . . . That's how I got into Jewish-Christian relations dialogue work, which has been a major part of my life for the last twenty-five years. . . . And the Jewish feminist work—the Jewish feminist interfaith dialogue—well, just the fact that I was recruited into Jewish feminism at all came through my being there as his wife.[89]

In 1973, Arlene Agus and Toby Brandriss, pioneering Jewish feminist leaders, asked Blu to deliver the keynote address at the First National Jewish Women's Conference. The women had come to the Greenberg home to discuss the conference and invite Yitz to participate in the Sunday panel. Blu chatted intermittently with them in be-tween getting the children ready for bed. By the end of the evening, they had decided to invite *her* to speak at the conference. When asked re-cently why she had chosen Blu, Agus gave several reasons. One was that Blu already had a public reputation, in part, as the wife of a prominent rabbi.[90]

Agus realized the irony of her decision to choose the main speaker for a feminism conference on the strength of her husband's reputation. But Blu's mixed feelings about her role undoubtedly intrigued Agus as well. As a rebbetzin and mother of five young children, Greenberg embraced her traditional role with enthusiasm. Yet as feminist thinking began to affect her, Greenberg became increasingly sensitive to the restrictions placed on women within traditional Judaism. It was precisely her ability to see both sides so passionately that enhanced Greenberg's effectiveness. Her rebbetzin status and personal satisfaction with an Orthodox way of life reassured traditionalists that she would not over-turn the world view they revered. At the same time, Greenberg had gained invaluable know-how as a teacher, leader, counselor, and orga-nizer by functioning one step removed from the pulpit. These experi-ences whetted her appetite to succeed in a more public, independent manner and to challenge the gendered assumptions that underlay the very role that she loved.

Greenberg's involvement at the conference marked the beginning of her personal quest to determine "what position can we as committed Jews take toward feminism?" Her first book, *On Women and Judaism,* represented the fruits of close to a decade of exploration on the topic. In it, Greenberg boldly invoked both *halakhic* precedent and process to advocate for full women's equality within Judaism. Addressing a topic that most of her Orthodox peers preferred to leave unexplored, Green-berg again straddled both worlds. She remained wedded to her identity as a "mild-mannered yeshiva girl" with impeccable Orthodox creden-tials who was unwilling to break the chain of tradition. Yet she also ex-panded her thinking to embrace radical ideas, challenging the rabbinate to respond to the ethical demands of feminism.[91]

Greenberg's move into the public arena bred controversy, in part, because the views she espoused deeply threatened the Orthodox status quo. It is not surprising, then, that for her next book Greenberg re-treated to a topic that highlighted her role as a traditional rebbetzin. In *How to Run a Traditional Jewish Household,* Greenberg reviewed modern Orthodox practice in the areas of Jewish holidays, daily ritu-als, life-cycle stages, and general behavior. As other rebbetzins had done in previous generations, Greenberg recounted Jewish law in the name of "the Rabbis," and told her readers to consult a contemporary rabbi concerning such questions as whether one is permitted to use a dish-washer for both meat and dairy.[92]

Greenberg wrote in the somewhat self-deprecating style of a har-ried housewife, interspersing chatty anecdotes to explain how she and her family prepared for and celebrated holidays and life-cycle events. Though she acknowledged larger cultural feminist trends, Greenberg downplayed their effect in this paean to traditional Jewish practice. For example, recounting a Shabbat experience with a group of young re-newal Jews, she recalled them chiding her and her husband for perpetu-ating what feminists had come to disparage—the ritual of a husband reciting Proverbs 31, *Ayshet Chayil* (Woman of Valor), to his wife. Greenberg wrote that "they could not convince me that it was sexist, nor could they convince me that I didn't enjoy having it sung to me every Friday night." Similarly, she admitted that some people think the custom of a bride encircling the groom seven times under the *huppah* (wedding canopy) is sexist, but to her "it has always seemed a most wonderfully sexy ritual, as if she were wrapping him up in the train of her gown to take him home with her."[93]

Detailing Jewish observance in this 500-page book, Greenberg popularized traditional views on a topic about which Jewish women—especially rebbetzins—were expected to have special expertise. About a dozen years after the book appeared, Greenberg confessed that, though the publisher had initiated the project, she had probably taken it on as her way of making amends and stymieing those who would rob her of her Orthodox legitimacy.[94]

Greenberg was not entirely successful in this regard, because she did not fully mute her feminist voice, opting, for example, "reluctantly and cautiously" to include a liberal view of abortion:

> Thus it can be said that abortion on demand is not permitted, but in cases where carrying to term would aggravate a stressful condition or would place the mother in a situation where she could not cope, some authorities would interpret the law to permit an abortion. . . . Thus the traditional position is such that it [Jewish law] gives neither a blanket veto on abortion nor unfettered license to a woman to decide what to do with her own body. . . . Abortion is a sensitive and private subject, and it is difficult to say whether Orthodox women who terminate a pregnancy do or do not consult a rabbi. I know some women who did. And some who didn't.[95]

Over the years, Greenberg's reputation as leader of Orthodox feminism grew. She continues to remain an important role model for Orthodox Jewish feminists who admire her forthright endorsement of the notion of Orthodox women rabbis and her ongoing challenge to the Orthodox rabbinate to resolve *halakhic* (Jewish legal) issues that discriminate against women. In February 1997, Greenberg chaired the first Conference on Feminism and Orthodoxy, attended by more than 1,000 women from across the country. Six months later she became founding president of the Jewish Orthodox Feminist Alliance, a position she held until February 2003. This organization, dedicated to increasing awareness among Orthodox women of feminist issues, coordinates efforts to share information and advocate on behalf of common interests.[96] Greenberg's talents have taken her in other directions as well, even to co-authoring a children's picture book, *King Solomon and the Queen of Sheba.*

Moving from traditional rebbetzin to independent leader of the Orthodox Feminist Movement, Greenberg found herself readjusting her relationship to her husband. Dedicating her first book *On Women and Judaism* to Yitz, Blu noted that the book reflected his thinking but also includes "a good deal that reflects my new ability not to back down in the face of his critique."[97] She recognized the need to articulate her own distinctive views and to distinguish them from her husband's. But, as she became more confident in her independent leadership role, Greenberg came to appreciate anew the benefits that accrued from her partnership with her husband. Writing in *Black Bread: Poems, after the Holocaust,* Greenberg explained:

> It is not in one manner of meaning alone that I say without him these poems would never have been written, much less published. It was through his interest that I first became open to the Shoah and through his work and friendships that I came to know many survivors and scholars of the Shoah. . . . He helped me through numerous versions of each poem. And when my confidence in this work flagged, he pressed me forward, a constant story of our lives together.[98]

He returned the compliment in his book, *The Jewish Way: Living the Holidays,* which he dedicated to her:

> My wife, Blu, has been my intellectual companion and best friend, inspiration and early warning system, source of constant appreciation and most honest critic. I have learned to depend on her judgment and to ignore her wisdom only at my peril. Her humanness and love, her religious model, her ability to juggle the contradictions of life without self-pity or resentment have been the anchor of my life for more than thirty years. The dedication of this book to her is but a grain of sand on the shores of a boundless sea.[99]

As this interchange demonstrates, rebbetzins and their husbands continued to offer each other critical support even when the two were no longer bound by the conventions of the two-person career.

Ruth Waxman

Like Greenberg, Ruth Bilgray Waxman also built on her rebbetzin skills —in Waxman's case, in her later career as editor of *Judaism*. Daughter of Chaim and Bertha Bilgray, Ruth Waxman was born on February 22, 1916, in Palestine. Her family left Palestine when she was four and settled in Chicago. Cultural Zionists and Hebraists, Ruth's parents provided her and her older brother, Albert, with a rich Jewish upbringing. A family rule mandated that everyone speak only Hebrew at home after 5:00 P.M. Ruth also attended Kehillat Jacob Talmud Torah, an intensive, ten-hour-a-week educational program that taught *ivrit b'ivrit* [Hebrew language in Hebrew]. While attending the University of Chicago, she continued her Jewish education at the College of Jewish Studies.[100] Ruth also studied piano for many years and considered playing professionally, but after graduating college in March 1937, she chose to pursue graduate studies at the University of Chicago in Comparative Literature. She received her Ph.D. in 1941. Mordecai Waxman grew up in the same social and cultural circles in Chicago, and their paths crossed numerous times—in their parents' Hebrew-speaking cultural group, at the university, and in a youth group called *Haskalah*. They married in 1942.[101]

In 1947, the couple moved to Great Neck, New York, where Mordecai Waxman accepted a position as rabbi of Temple Israel. That same year, Ruth Waxman secured a job in the English department at Adelphi College. She recalled that there had always been an assumption between her and her husband that she would work, and this continued even after the birth of their three sons. The couple engaged a housekeeper who remained with the family for more than thirty years and helped maintain the household.[102] In addition to her teaching duties, Waxman attended services regularly, went to bar and bat mitzvah receptions and congregants' weddings, entertained company regularly, and visited the sick. As a Jewishly educated rebbetzin, Waxman also felt comfortable answering religious questions, especially on kashrut.[103]

Waxman's involvement in Sisterhood was unconventional from the start, since she taught during the day and was unable to attend regular

Ruth Waxman. Courtesy of the Waxman family.

meetings. Yet, according to Helene Schachter, president of Temple Israel Sisterhood from 1972 to 1975, "when we called on her through Sisterhood for installations, etc. she was wonderful. She was always there for us." In addition to assisting the women with programming for Shabbat, Kashrut, holidays, and prayer, Waxman gave frequent book reviews and lectures on Jewish topics.[104]

In the formative years of the congregation, Mordecai Waxman initiated informal discussion groups that met in the evenings in people's homes. Such couple-oriented get-togethers were typical of the suburban scene, and they were a social and intellectual outlet for the rabbi and rebbetzin as well. The initial idea for the synagogue's monthly magazine, the *Temple Israel Light,* grew out of these conversations, and Ruth's interests led her to become particularly active in launching it: "She was a bright woman who was Jewishly educated, with editorial skills, and something to say—therefore she was a significant force in the small group that created the *Light.*" Waxman, with her leadership and editorial talents, proved instrumental to the success of this award-winning publication.[105]

Like most rebbetzins, Waxman served as a sounding-board for her husband's sermons. "He'd pace around the house with his yellow pad and test things out with her." Yet Waxman's value went beyond this. Her particular editorial skills made her a decisive force in shaping the material in Mordecai Waxman's *Tradition and Change*; according to one of her sons, the title was hers.[106]

More than any of her other activities, it was the institution of the "Saturday salons" that showcased Waxman's strengths as a rebbetzin. A tradition that dates back at least to the days of Mordecai Waxman's parents and that recalls the Schechters' open houses, these Saturday salons provided company and conversation. A regular group of about a dozen couples would be supplemented by occasional attendees as well as visiting dignitaries. Waxman's home-baked treats were a particular attraction, but Waxman was also a vital part of the intellectual give-and-take: "Reflecting both her acuity and her extensive reading, she could be counted on for special contributions to a conversation on any subject." Discussion ranged from politics—synagogue, Israeli, and American—to the weekly Torah portion. These salons became an intrinsic part of the Waxmans' shared rabbinate and exemplified its strengths.[107]

By her own account, Ruth Waxman found her duties as rebbetzin to be unremarkable, likening them to the demands placed on wives of other professionals. Yet she also confessed to enjoying the special status the role carried "both vicariously and personally." Waxman was flattered by the many invitations she received and found it rewarding to share in congregants' milestones. In short, Waxman concluded: "I like it. As a matter of fact, I suspect that I flourish on it."[108]

For more than twenty-five years, Waxman continued her college teaching at Adelphi College, C. W. Post, the State University of New York at Stony Brook, and Queens College.[109] Waxman's identity as a professor was formative both for her and for her family; her eldest son recalls:

My sense of my mother is that relative to what other *rebbetzins* were like, she was relatively unique. She did Sisterhood, the *Light,* yet she had a life outside the synagogue. That's much more memorable to me, seeing her sitting at the dining room table marking papers, typing on her Remington portable typewriter. . . . She was a tough grader. We didn't want her to be our teacher; if she gave two A's that would be a lot.[110]

Waxman also took on freelance editing over the years and served as chairman of the publications department of United Synagogue of Conservative Judaism for twenty-five years.[111]

Waxman's Jewish, academic, and career interests converged in her work at *Judaism,* a free and nonpartisan quarterly journal sponsored by the American Jewish Congress and dedicated to the creative discussion and exposition of the religious, moral, and philosophical concepts of Judaism and their relevance to the problems of modern society.[112] Surely her teaching had prepared her for this role, but the experience she gained as a rebbetzin—interacting with congregants, hosting Jewish national leaders in her home, and launching the synagogue's magazine —also contributed to her success. After taking a break from college teaching to accompany her husband to Los Angeles during his sabbatical in the spring of 1972, Waxman assumed the new position of managing editor of *Judaism.* This gave her a platform for Jewish leadership independent of the congregation, for she had the opportunity to influence Jewish public opinion on a wide range of issues. The American Jewish Congress noted that Waxman "brought intelligence, discernment and taste to our publication, as she did to every aspect of her life." Similarly, her assistant editor, Lippman Bodoff, recalls her as an excellent editor—accurate and thorough, with a fantastic feel for a good product and a bad product. Yet even in the 1970s, gender disparity prevailed. Though she took responsibility for reviewing manuscripts and preparing them for publication, Robert Gordis, the general editor, had final say. As one colleague noted, "for a long time she must have felt that she did a lot of the work, and he got the glory." Despite these tensions, Waxman "hit her stride with *Judaism.*" She used her education and previous work experience as well as the editorial, negotiation, and social skills honed as a rebbetzin to thrive in an independent career that brought her considerable recognition.[113]

Esther Jungreis

The careers of Greenberg and Waxman illustrate some possibilities for independent leadership positions that built on earlier experiences as a rebbetzin. Esther Jungreis, founder and president of Hineni, represents the pinnacle of what rabbis' wives could attain through this avenue.

For almost thirty years, Esther Jungreis has stood virtually alone among American Jewish Orthodox religious leaders not only as a woman but also as an evangelical leader. Both the Lubavitcher rebbe, Menachem Mendel Schneerson, and Shlomo Carlebach were charismatic leaders who drew Jews closer to God. Today, Jungreis alone continues to influence large numbers of Jews in this fashion. And she derived both her initial standing and her skills from her years as a congregational rebbetzin.

Jungreis launched her national career in the 1970s at precisely the time when many neo-evangelical ministries of the electronic church also rose to prominence. Responding to counterculture movements of the 1960s that underscored the crisis of meaning in the modern world, neo-evangelical movements of the 1970s and 1980s preached social and moral conformity. Their religious leaders had learned from the counterculture just how powerful a role the electronic media could play in promoting massive social and cultural changes, and they mastered the medium to great effect. During this period, which historian William McLoughlin has called the Fourth Great Awakening in American life, religious leaders arose who both articulated the cultural crisis and offered ready solutions through revitalization movements enhanced by the power of technology.[114]

Count Jungreis among such leaders. Her imagery, goals, and message differed, yet her methods and techniques have much in common with the electronic ministry. In recounting her family background and upbringing, Jungreis explained that she believed herself to be chosen to lead a Jewish revival movement. Born in Szeged, Hungary in 1936, the only daughter of Avraham and Miriam Jungreis,[115] Esther Jungreis understood that she represented a link in a long chain of devoted servants of God dating back to the biblical King David. This awareness is dramatically portrayed by the large framed Jungreis family tree hanging prominently on her office wall. The tree trunk represents King David, with selective branches connecting the trunk to prominent religious leaders throughout the centuries. Several branches of the family tree link the generations not from rabbi to rabbi but rather through the female rebbetzin line.

A survivor of the Bergen-Belsen concentration camp, Jungreis recounted that of the more than eighty-five rabbis named Jungreis in Hungary before the war, only a handful survived, her father among them. According to Jungreis, her father charged his children in the aftermath of the war: "This, then must become our task, to teach our people to kindle the Sabbath lights. That is why we have survived." Reportedly mesmerized as a child by stories of miracles performed by her Hungarian ancestor Asher Anshel Jungreis, the rabbi of Csenger, Jungreis recalled being taught that this ability to perform wonders passed to his descendants; she came to believe that she had inherited it.[116] This combination of special *yichus* (lineage) and Holocaust imagery formed an important part of Jungreis's self-presentation and appeal. Jungreis portrayed herself as being plucked from the ashes of the Jewish past in order to realize the special mission of saving the Jewish future.

Arriving in New York in 1947, Jungreis received a yeshiva education at the Bais Yaakov School for Girls. In the early 1950s, she spent several years in Israel, studying and teaching. Upon her return in 1955, she married her fifth cousin, Meshulem Halevi Jungreis. By marrying him, Jungreis not only attained the title rebbetzin but also succeeded in retaining the last name "Jungreis" after marriage. Thus, she both upheld the tradition of taking her husband's last name and kept this visible evidence of her distinctive lineage. In 1963, she and her husband established an Orthodox congregation, Ohr Torah, in Woodmere, New York. That she saw the rabbinate as a two-person endeavor can be seen in her description of this period. She noted that "my husband could have entered almost any profession, but *we were both* determined to follow in the path of our fathers and continue in the rabbinate." She characterized their efforts to establish the congregation using the plural, e.g., "*we* gathered a small group of dedicated friends . . . *we* wanted them to become learned."[117]

Based on later recollections, it appears that Jungreis, like other rebbetzins in the postwar period, involved herself with educational activities for women and children. She organized "Tiny Tots" for women with small children and a kitchen class for girls. In her "Cultural Encounters for Teens" group, Jungreis attempted to fortify teens Jewishly before they left for college. Her success with this group likely heightened the interest in working with young adults that eventually grew into Hineni. Together with her husband, Jungreis also spoke to couples before marriage and took brides to the *mikveh* (ritual bath). In addition, she taught classes for Sisterhood and led luncheon discussions. Jungreis also entertained guests for Sabbaths and holidays.[118]

During this period, Jungreis found additional outlets for her talents and attention. She reared four children, Chaya Sora, Yisrael, Slovie Chana, and Osher Anshil; and in 1963 she began contributing a column to the recently launched, Brooklyn-based *Jewish Press*. Tying this independent venture to her traditional role and capitalizing on her title, Jungreis called the column the "Rebbetzin's Viewpoint." She claimed to want to restore luster to the position of rebbetzin and dreamt of the day when young girls would want to play "not only nurse, teacher, or actress, but rebbetzin as well."[119] Using this platform to praise the role, she wrote that "it is essential that the non-observant Jew *see* Judaism in action, and certainly there can be no better 'showcase for Torah life' than the Rabbinical home. . . . I myself have succeeded in persuading more women to keep a kosher home in the intimacy of my kitchen than in the most awe-inspiring lecture hall."[120]

Initially found on a short-lived "For Women Only" page, Jungreis's column appeared in a question-and-answer, Dear-Abby-type format in which individuals, usually women and children, would ask about matters such as child-rearing and becoming more observant. But this column also provided Jungreis with her own pulpit. Over the years, she continually called on her readers to return to Jewish observance, stressing the need for a step-by-step, gradual approach.[121] She also commented on timely matters that she believed affected Jewish interests, especially Israel. For example, writing about the Six-Day War, she called it a miracle from God, "equal to that of the exodus from Egypt." And Jungreis early on identified the need for an Orthodox matchmaking organization to help young people find suitable mates in a dignified manner, a concern that emerged fully in the 1990s through Hineni.[122]

The origin of Hineni dates to 1972. In addition to tying Jungreis's rise to prominence to the neo-evangelical ministries of the electronic church, one can also trace her success to a growing hysteria within the Jewish community concerning cults. Experts claimed that between 1965 and 1976 more than 1,300 new religious groups appeared in America, while other observers estimated 1,000 to 3,000 such groups in the United States alone. They believed that in 1970 about two and a half million Americans belonged to these new religions and that, in the latter part of 1970, as many as a million people sought answers to what they saw as a frightening world. Although Jews made up only about 2.5 percent of the population, experts estimated that they constituted between 10 and 15 percent of all cult members. Subsequent research has revealed such figures to be wildly exaggerated, with scholars later branding much of the controversy "a hoax, a 'scare' in the truest sense of the word." Yet at the time, the Jewish community panicked over the attraction such groups held for young Jews.[123]

Jungreis launched her initial plan in a Labor Day weekend address to the Young Israel Collegiate Youth Convention. She chided her audience of several hundred young observant Jews for remaining smugly religious while thousands flocked to "alien cultures and strange gods." Openly admitting her desire to emulate "the most successful of religious revivalists—Billy Graham," Jungreis proposed countering the lure of such cults by staging a mass Jewish revival in Madison Square Garden.[124]

Jungreis wisely modeled herself after the media master Graham.[125] Billy Graham rose to fame in the 1950s with a direct preaching style characterized by intense, flowing sermons peppered with biblical quotations that he believed offered insights into contemporary crises and personal problems. He launched a major, international crusade from New York's Madison Square Garden and used the autobiographical format to describe his religious calling. By 1954, his weekly show "Hour of Decision," drew an audience of more than 15 million, the largest of any religious program. His Evangelistic Association annually sent out more than 100 million pieces of literature. Graham's popularity rested in part on his espousal of traditional family values, exemplified by his own marriage to a devoted partner who shared his goals. Furthermore, he projected a consistently clean image of honest finances and morals. Jungreis aspired to all these facets of Graham's success.[126]

Jungreis linked her proposed revival meeting to the creation of a new organization. As she exclaimed in her column, "A new movement was born; 'HINENI—I AM HERE!' B'ezras Ha-Shem—with the help of G-d, twenty thousand Jewish kids will call out 'HINENI' in Madison Square Garden!" Already emerging as a savvy businesswoman, Jungreis ended with a direct fundraising pitch: "Money is needed—at least a hundred thousand dollars. Pls answer the call. Write your checks to 'HINENI.'"[127] She spoke in synagogues and other Jewish organizations to generate interest and raise funds. By April 1973, Jungreis's efforts caused enough of a stir that one of her speaking engagements prompted a lengthy article in the regional Sunday edition of the *New York Times*.[128]

Jungreis also imagined Hineni igniting Jewish awakenings on college campuses—then understood to be hotbeds for cult recruitment. She dreamed of reaching "the Kevins, Bruces and Scotts who would discover that they are really Moshe, Yaakov and Dovid,"[129] and expressed the hope that this would hasten the coming of the Messiah. Lest her audience disapprove of her unconventional tactics, Jungreis assured them that she had received the blessings of famous Orthodox rabbis including Joseph Henkin, Moshe Feinstein, and Joseph Soloveitchik.[130]

Jungreis's revival took place at the Felt Forum of New York's Madison Square Garden on November 18, 1973. The auditorium filled beyond its seating capacity of approximately 5,600, with additional people sitting in the aisles and standing in back. Jungreis dubbed the event the "homecoming of the American Jew."[131]

Scores of Yeshiva students, enlisted to offer guidance, gave everyone who attended a plastic shopping bag to stock up on "Jewish soul food." This soul food consisted of ten educational pamphlets on different as-pects of Jewish life. Trying to compete with cults that appealed to young people by offering community, meaning, and spiritual direction, Jungreis's booklets covered such topics as "Kosher: A Diet for the Soul," "Women's Lib: A Jewish View," and "[Shabbat:] A Day to Turn On." These materials attempted to dispel misconceptions about Judaism and highlight ways in which it promoted Jews' physical, emotional, and psychological well-being. Filled with flowery rhetoric and glowing descriptions, the booklets encourage alienated Jews to view Judaism in a more positive light and to give it a chance to transform their lives.[132]

Though she continued to serve as a congregational rebbetzin for another twenty years until her husband's death in 1996, this Garden event marked the beginning of Jungreis's independent leadership role as president of Hineni. Speaking around the country on behalf of the organization, she further refined her own revivalist preaching style. For example, Jungreis told the riveting tale of rescuing a young woman from the Jews-for-Jesus Movement at one of her "happenings." During the event, a student Jews-for-Jesus group infiltrated the audience to distribute literature to the crowd. According to Jungreis, she transformed the crowd "from the torpor of indifference." One youth approached with an extended arm to be shown how to don *tefillin* (phylacteries). With heightened drama, she described a young woman saying, "I am afraid that

Esther Jungreis. Courtesy of Yeshiva University Archives.

after you leave my mind will become confused again. . . . There is so much that I would like to know, but where will I learn?" Jungreis related her decision to take the young woman, Lisa, home with her. In her words, "my daughter Chaya Sora is close to you in age. She will accept you as her sister. She will help you study. I, too, will teach you, and my husband, the Rabbi, will teach you."[133] After her religious transformation and marriage, Lisa was subsequently honored at a Hineni Annual Dinner. Stories like this became staples of Hineni's revival meetings, publicity materials, and fundraising efforts.[134]

In 1982, Jungreis opened the Hineni Heritage Center at 223 West End Avenue between Seventieth and Seventy-first Streets in Manhattan. Every week, individuals flock down a short corridor to a sanctuary to hear a Torah lesson from the rebbetzin. Overflow crowds watch her on closed-circuit television in the downstairs auditorium. Jungreis stands alone on the *bima* (raised platform) in front of an imposing stone ark shaped in the form of the Ten Commandments and capped by a round seal with the words of the *Shema*. Using a handheld microphone for dramatic effect, she teaches the weekly Torah portion. There is not a man in sight on the *bima* as Jungreis engages the "congregation" and offers a relevant message. A master of voice and tonal modulation, Jungreis holds court as effectively as any charismatic rebbe.

In the 1990s, Jungreis established a Young Leadership division. According to one account, this began as an intimate Torah class for Patricia Cayne, wife of Bear Stearns Chief Operating Officer Jimmy Cayne, and her friends. As word spread of how inspiring the classes were, their size increased dramatically. When overflow rooms and closed-circuit televisions proved inadequate to the needs of growing numbers of students, the class relocated in December 1996 to the sanctuary of Manhattan's Congregation Kehillath Jeshurun. There, young Jewish singles, mostly ages twenty-five to forty-five, gathered on Tuesday evenings to hear Jungreis's Torah lectures. Estimates of the number of participants range from 500 to 1,000. Jungreis repeated the message she had offered twenty years earlier in battling cults: Why look elsewhere for meaning when "the Torah is an instruction manual for life?"[135]

Jungreis added a new spin by criticizing the materialism of contemporary society. "You can have all the material things. . . . But if you don't have inner peace, you have nothing."[136] These devotees saw themselves as refugees not from the cult movements but rather from anxiety, in the post-AIDS era, about the New York dating scene and finding a suitable marriage partner. Well integrated into American life, they admitted that monetary success still left them wanting. Addressing that need directly, Jungreis offered what her adherents found to be a successful formula to meet their contemporary needs, just as she had done in the 1970s for young people attracted to cults.[137]

Some attendees remained skeptical of her style; one felt that Jungreis went "a little bit overboard" and was too emotional.[138] A reporter noted that he found it difficult not to think of her as a "kind of Jewish Tammy Faye Bakker (minus the false faith and false eyelashes)."[139] But Jungreis continued to draw crowds, and her lectures remained popular not only on the singles scene, but also as a news item. In 1997, articles in the *New York Times*, *New York* magazine, and the *Forward* featured Jungreis and her work.[140]

Jungreis also found additional avenues to spread her influence. She personally led annual trips to Israel and hosted *shabbatonim* (Sabbath retreats).[141] Hineni also initiated a newsletter that features testimonies by individuals who describe how their previously unsatisfying lives became filled with Jewish spirit after being exposed to the rebbetzin.[142] In 1982, Jungreis published her autobiography, *Jewish Soul on Fire,* an account of her life with inspirational stories—both traditional and contemporary—designed to engage and convince readers to return to Judaism. By bringing Jews back to Judaism, Hineni would, in her view, prevent the Holocaust that Jews are bringing on themselves through assimilation. In *The Committed Life: Principles for Good Living from Our Timeless Past,* Jungreis followed a similar pattern, incorporating stories to illustrate the wisdom of Torah values. Hoping to inspire readers to gain control over their lives, the book encourages individuals to become more compassionate and hopeful and to lead Jewish lives.[143] *The Committed Marriage: A Guide to Finding a Soulmate and Building a Relationship through Timeless Biblical Wisdom* shares the wisdom gained from Jungreis's years as a matchmaker to help others find and sustain marital happiness.[144]

Jungreis continually harnessed the latest technology to further her goals. In 1982, she launched a weekly twenty-eight-minute television program on the National Jewish Television cable network.[145] In 1996, Hineni created a website to extend the organization's reach. In addition to publicizing its activities, the site includes a question-and-answer section: ask the rebbetzin a question, and she will respond. This medium is one illustration of the rabbinic mantle Jungreis has assumed, for rabbis generally address the religious needs of their constituents through this question-and-answer-format.[146]

Jungreis's tradition of female religious leadership continues with her daughters and daughters-in-law—all rebbetzins themselves—who work at Hineni. They teach classes in Hebrew reading, prayer, and the prophets; they also offer one-on-one tutorials and facilitate young marrieds' groups. One responds to parenting questions on the website. They also work with Jungreis to arrange marriages.[147]

In all of these endeavors Jungreis acted on her own accord, not as one half of a two-person career. And yet she did so as a rebbetzin, using that title to legitimate her independent leadership status. Initially, she rationalized her ever-expanding slate of activities as an extension of her rebbetzinhood. Moreover, she insisted that her husband urged her on by telling her that "G-d gave you the gift of speech. You must try and reach the people in every community." Even after Meshulem's death, Jungreis continued to connect her success to her husband by invoking his memory in her work. For example, when honored by Temple Ohr

Torah Sisterhood in 1997, she demurred, noting that she had never taken honors for herself but would do so in her husband's memory. She then proceeded to give a passionate sermon about his rabbinate to further her goal of bringing people closer to Torah.[148]

Jungreis's obfuscation of her formidable leadership acumen in favor of a more traditional reading of her career is striking. Jungreis consciously built a large, well-financed, sophisticated organization. Yet she continually couched her independent accomplishments in helpmate terminology. In this way, though functioning as a religious leader in her own right for decades while her husband was alive, she nevertheless retained the imprimatur of the traditional Jewish world. When Orthodox Jewish law necessitates a male leader, for instance, in leading religious services or other rituals, Jungreis now calls upon one of her sons. Yet from the sermons in her columns to the exhortations at her weekly classes, from her counseling sessions to her public lectures to her web responses, Jungreis serves as pastor, teacher, and preacher in her own right. She lacks only the official title "rabbi." It is hard to imagine Jungreis succeeding so fully had she not amassed the requisite skills, confidence, and legitimacy during her years as a congregational rebbetzin.

As we have seen, rabbis' wives reacted in vastly different ways to the challenges of the feminist era. Some stubbornly defended the traditional role while others found themselves unable to sustain a meaningful "wife of" role without denying their commitments to feminism. Some marriages disintegrated in the process, while other rabbinic couples shaped a transformed rebbetzin role. For certain rabbis' wives, early experiences as traditional rebbetzins in two-person careers coupled with spousal support for moving in new directions enabled them to strike out on their own to create consequential independent careers as Jewish leaders. But by the 1990s, more and more talented Jewish women who felt called to serve the Jewish people became rabbis themselves. Women rabbis, by their very existence—let alone by their accomplishments, insights, and contributions to American Jewry—cast doubt on the future of the American rebbetzin. At the end of the century, American women no longer needed to fill a "wife of" role to satisfy their own ambitions. Though women continue to marry rabbis, it remains to be seen whether the rebbetzin role will survive in the twenty-first century.

6

They Married What They Wanted to Be, but What Does That Mean for the Future?

Since the mid-1980s, hundreds of women have been ordained.[1] These women have, in many ways, taken rebbetzins' dreams of rabbinic leadership and partnership to their logical conclusion. Some serve congregations with the help of supportive husbands. Some are married to rabbis, and they both work in the Jewish community professionally in complementary arenas as teachers, pastors, or administrators. In rare cases, dual-rabbinic couples serve as rabbis of the same congregation. Women have made great strides in the rabbinate in the last generation, yet gender imbalances continue to plague them. A recent study of Conservative rabbis found that while 25 percent of men hold senior rabbi positions in congregations, no women do. Moreover, a significantly larger percentage of the women work in part-time pulpit positions or non-pulpit positions, and they earn an average of $40,000 less than men. Finally, the women are three times as likely as the men to report being unmarried, a statistic that confirms the fears of rebbetzins generations earlier that independent female public leadership would preclude marriage. Though these women can now become what they want to be professionally, serious obstacles continue to impede their full equality.[2]

At the same time, despite the growing numbers of women rabbis, the female rebbetzin role has endured, and, in some quarters, even flourished, throughout the 1990s and into the twenty-first century. Rebbetzins continue to capture people's imagination, and local and national newspapers continue to feature articles by, and about, rebbetzins. Some romanticize the traditional role, and stories, especially those about rebbetzins preparing for Passover, read like throwbacks to the 1950s.[3]

Others highlight veteran rebbetzins reflecting on the joys of their career or younger wives commenting on the role and its specialized title, some positively and others dismissively.[4]

Rabbis' wives continue to write about the role, in both nonfiction and fiction, and by the 1990s these works were being read by an ever-widening audience. For example, Carolyn Hoyt recounted the indignities of a fishbowl existence and her impatience with the expectations of the rebbetzin role in *Woman's Day*, which, with a circulation of approximately four million, is the largest general-interest women's magazine in the United States.[5] Similarly, a fictional tale by "the former wife of a rabbi" featured a rebbetzin trying to solve the mystery of her husband's murder. One character exclaimed that expectations for a rebbetzin are no longer appropriate, for "this is the nineties, remember?" But Ruby, the rebbetzin/detective, concluded ruefully that even after her husband's death, she retained the title, with all the obligations associated with it. "I've learned that being a rabbi's wife is not something you graduate from in this life. . . . No such luck." Just as with Hoyt's article, one finds no new disclosures about the rebbetzin role, but Scribner published the book, and Book-of-the-Month Club chose it as an alternate selection.[6]

Noted religion author Paul Wilkes gave the woes of rebbetzinhood further exposure through his study of the life of one congregational rabbi. Shadowing Jay Rosenbaum, rabbi of Congregation Beth Israel in Worcester, Masssachusetts, Wilkes also gained insight into the life of the rabbi's wife. As Janine Rosenbaum achingly explained, when she became a rabbi's wife, she realized that "what you did before out of conviction and a pure desire becomes expected of you. . . . Being the rabbi's wife has bled religion out of me."[7]

Rebbetzins remained the butt of jokes as well, though here, too, the readership broadened. In the following contemporary joke—reaching the infinite audience of the Internet—the humor incorporates a contemporary awareness of homosexual Jews.

> Just before Rosh Hashanah, a man hears that in San Francisco there's a gay shul. He's very excited, as this sounds like what he's been yearning for. He gets there, and sure enough, there's a gay chazzan and a gay rabbi, and the congregation too is mostly gay. He joins in the service, but is terribly distracted by the handsome young man sitting next to him. (There's really no good place to put a mechitzoh in a gay syna-

gogue.) Finally, he gives into temptation and puts his hand on the young man's knee. Immediately two large men wearing leather jackets under their talleisim rush over, pick him up, carry him out of the sanctuary, and toss him down the stairs onto the street. "Why did you do that?" he cried. "I thought this was a gay synagogue." "It is," replied one of his ejectors, in a deep voice. "But nobody messes with the rebitzen."[8]

In part, continuing publicity about rebbetzins stems from increased interest in the comparatively new phenomenon of rabbis' husbands. Sometimes, articles by or about male and female spouses appear side-by-side in the same issue. But despite the parallel treatment in the press, the experiences of rabbis' husbands are not comparable to rebbetzins'. For example, Michael Kline explained that, like many rebbetzins, he was well prepared for the rabbinic spouse role because Judaism had played an important part in his upbringing. He confessed to serving as sounding board, critic, comforter, and informal secretary for his wife. Yet Kline believed himself freer to define the role because of its novelty. Interestingly, he found himself combating a reverse bias that left him feeling like "Rabbi Pell's little boy rather than her husband." Similarly, James Meier recalled that when he accompanied his wife, Judith Edelstein, to her part-time pulpit, congregants made rebbetzin jokes and "didn't know what to do with me," leaving him free to invent his role. Historian Michael A. Meyer dealt proactively with the role by learning how to conduct "educated discourse on the Super Bowl and the Americas Cup" in order carry on casual conversation with male congregants at Temple functions. He went so far as to suggest a specialized title "rebbitz" for rabbis' husbands, and he has used this as his vanity license plate since 1987, a year after his wife, Margaret, was ordained from Hebrew Union College. But there is no indication that this title has caught on, and male rabbinic spouses consistently report fewer expectations and greater freedom to determine their roles than do rebbetzins.[9]

Use of the term rebbetzin has also declined. According to Nina Salkin, editor of *SpouseConnection,* the word rebbetzin itself has become taboo in Reform Jewish circles. It has been replaced by the gender-neutral term "rabbinic spouse," which, as Salkin explained, connotes that spouses are "free to have careers, even free to opt out of synagogue life." The same sentiment was echoed at the New York Board of Rabbis when a new member requested that the rabbis banish the word rebbetzin from their vocabulary. "That noble and distinguished role belongs in

Michael A. Meyer's license plate. Courtesy of the American Jewish Archives, Cincinnati, Ohio.

the past; to allow for the change, the designation 'rabbi's spouse' must henceforth be used."[10]

This decline aptly captures the changing reality, for few full-time rebbitzes or rebbetzins exist today in the liberal denominations. Many rabbis' spouses work full-time, and they take on limited and circumscribed roles in the synagogue. Congregants by and large have come to accept the fact that they can no longer expect two-for-the-price-of-one. They have hired full-time professionals to assume many of the functions once filled by rebbetzins, including assistant rabbis; principals; social workers; and preschool, Hebrew high school, and youth directors. One congregant actually suggested creating a "professional paid rebbitzen [not the wife of the rabbi] to work closely with the rabbi and assume much of the burden that the rabbi carries." Some rabbis' wives may, in fact, fill professional positions in congregations, but they do so because of their own credentials, and not because of their rebbetzin position.[11]

Though it is too soon to tell, anecdotal evidence suggests that younger liberal rabbis' wives feel distant from the traditional rebbetzin role and have no frame of reference through which to understand it. They don't view themselves working in partnership with their husbands, nor do they feel the need to consciously disassociate themselves from that model as their 1970s predecessors did. Women with careers of their own, they don't worry that congregants' expectations might compromise their identity. When they contribute to the synagogue through a specific activity of their choosing, they do so as their way of giving back to their community.[12] Of course, not everyone has come to terms with this shift. Some among the older generation lament the loss of the traditional rebbetzin. One Conservative rabbi went so far as to declare the contemporary American Jewish community an orphaned generation because it lacks such leaders.[13]

Only among the Orthodox—who encompass about one fifth of affiliated American Jewry today—does the rebbetzin role thrive today. As the sole de-nomination to limit ordination to men, Orthodox Judaism continues to assign great weight to the rebbetzin role, revering exceptional rabbis' wives who distinguish themselves through lives of service. This emphasis manifests itself in many ways, from the publication of hagiographic studies, such as Raichel Horowitz's *The Bostoner Rebbetzin Remembers* or Malka Schwartz's *In Her Own Right a Great Woman: Rebbetzin Rivkah, Wife of the Fourth Lubavitcher Rebbe,* to the publication of young adult books, such as *The Brookville C.C. Series: Getting Started,* in which traditional rebbetzins abound.[14] A study of yeshiva high school girls found that their school socialized them to reject the rabbinate as an appropriate avenue of leadership and to embrace the rebbetzin role as a worthy one for them.[15]

Certain Orthodox women have gained special renown. For example, Rebbetzin Faige Teitelbaum was admired for establishing, with her husband, the largest Hasidic school system in the United States and for raising millions for charity. Teitelbaum was also known for her small acts of kindness, such as taking kosher meals daily by subway to hospital patients. After the 1979 death of Faige's husband, Joel Teitelbaum, the Satmar rebbe, many Satmar Hasidim turned to Faige as a spiritual leader and a symbol to preserve his memory. Until her death in 2001, Faige dispensed blessings regularly to Satmar followers.[16]

Rebbetzin Judith Friedlander, the first Orthodox woman certified as a hospital chaplain, received the Chaplain of the Year Award and the Zagelbaum Family Prize of the New York Board of Rabbis in 1997. She gained recognition for "her many years of devoted service and compassionate concern for patients and their families in the upper East Side neighborhood and in the hospitals servicing that area," including Mount Sinai Medical Center, New York Hospital-Cornell Medical Center, and Memorial Sloan-Kettering Cancer Center.[17]

Among modern Orthodox rebbetzins, the contemporary role best manifests itself through the pages of *The Rebbetzin's Letter*, a supplement to *The Rabbi's Letter*, a project of the National Council of Young Israel and the Young Israel Council of Rabbis. This newsletter, launched in 1998, demonstrates that Orthodox rebbetzins, like their Conservative and Reform counterparts a decade earlier, recognize the need for a support mechanism to help them cope with the special challenges of the role. As the editor, Judi Steinig, explained in the first issue, "I think that many suffer from stress. . . . Creating a support system is an important way for the rebbetzin to alleviate her tension and anxiety. . . . *The Rebbetzins' Letter* is available to share experiences, offer guidance, and exchange information and has the potential to fulfill many of the needs for rebbetzins throughout the world."[18] But what also emerges from these pages is the recognition that the Orthodox rebbetzin's role is expanding even as its liberal counterparts' role contracts. As Abby Lerner explained:

> The 'job' has become much more. . . . Rebbetzins can have an invaluable function as liaisons in the area of *taharat haMishpacha* [family purity]. . . . So much anguish can be alleviated if the rebbetzin intervenes. When her knowledge of halacha is more comprehensive, she can do an even better job. . . . It is natural for a woman to feel more comfortable speaking to a rebbetzin. Our involvement can make a serious and important contribution to the well-being of the families in our communities. Our new roles are much more taxing—but so much more significant and that much more rewarding.[19]

Other rebbetzins reinforce this view. A 1994 article in *Yeshiva University Review* on "Reinventing the Role of Rebbitzin" featured five active rebbetzins who described the extent to which they welcomed the opportunities and added responsibilities of the role.[20] At "The Rebbetzin's Role" forum at the 1998 International Conference on Feminism and Orthodoxy, rebbetzins enthusiastically described their roles as teachers, counselors, and leaders of their congregations' women.[21] One year later, the Annual Rabbinic Conference of the National Council of

Young Israel and Young Israel Council of Rabbis included a session on "The World of the Rebbetzin: 21st Century Challenges."[22]

This renewed emphasis on the power of the rebbetzin role in Orthodoxy can be understood in part as a reaction to the Jewish Feminist Movement. The ordination of women in the other three denominations challenged Orthodoxy to identify female leadership roles of its own. Interestingly, modern Orthodoxy also created quasi-rabbinic positions —"congregational interns"—for women, but some rabbis and rebbetzins took offense at these new roles. They argued that establishing these new positions implied that there was a female leadership void. In their view, the work that interns performed, including teaching and counseling, simply replicated what "every Orthodox rebbetzin in the United States does."[23]

Of course, not all Orthodox rabbis' wives embrace this enhanced role. For example, Rebbetzin Rhanni Herzfeld, a physician, admires the traditional rebbetzin role, though she herself does not model it. A working mother, Herzfeld spends her free time with her children. When honored by her synagogue, Herzfeld praised the congregation for their respect. She recognized that her congregants' acceptance freed her to devote herself to career and children rather than to serving the congregation.[24]

The largest area of expansion of the rebbetzin role today can be found among the Lubavitcher Hasidim. Known for their aggressive outreach work, Chabad sends out husband-and-wife rabbinic teams to far-flung Jewish communities and college campuses to spread Judaism. First launched by the Lubavitcher rebbe in 1950, this effort today includes more than 3,800 emissary couples who serve in sixty-one foreign countries and forty-five states. The role of emissary offers Hasidic women an unrivaled opportunity to serve as spiritual leaders. Those who aspire to such work will often date only like-minded men, since only through marriage to such a man can these women have this life for themselves.[25]

Emissary work includes varied ways for Lubavitcher rebbetzins to fulfill their sense of calling. For example, Rivkah Slonim prepares and serves dinner to more than 150 college students each Friday night at the Chabad house she and her husband Aharon established at Binghamton University. She serves as surrogate parent, counselor, and teacher to the students. Additionally, Slonim lectures around the country on women's issues in Judaism, and she edited a volume on *mikveh* to broaden her reach still further. Serving a different population, Doba Levin spends five hours a day in her Brooklyn office working with Russian immigrants who seek advice on "the laws of family purity, on where to get a mezuzah, on what their children should wear to Lubavitcher day camp." Adept at the guitar, Chaya Teldon tours the country, singing in Yiddish and Hebrew and telling stories to Jewish groups, "dispensing what she calls 'chicken soup for the Jewish soul.'" She also works with her husband, Tuvia, to enhance Jewish life in Suffolk County, Long Island. As she explained, "I knew what I was getting into. . . . I'm not schlepping along. This is a team."[26]

The rebbetzin role remains alive and well, then, within Orthodoxy, evolving to satisfy a sense of calling among traditional women in this century just as it did for so many rabbis' wives in previous ones. Flourishing in the one community that denies ordination to women, Orthodox rebbetzins today are the exception that proves the rule. "Marrying what they want to be" remains an effective and satisfying strategy for those unable to attain such power or position on their own.

For more than a century, then, the rebbetzin role has provided American Jewish women with access to power and status that they then solidified and extended through their own accomplishments. Looking at American Jewish religious life through the lens of this role has brought many remarkable women to the fore. Some were virtually unknown beyond their congregations, while others have simply been underacknowledged. Beginning with a spotlight on Simon, Schechter, and Goldstein, we saw the American rebbetzin emerge as a formidable player in the creation and maintenance of American Jewish religious life. Establishing the denominational women's organizations, these three rabbis' wives created the infrastructure that has anchored women's religious organizational efforts for more than a century. Modeling the rabbi's wife role, they also influenced their peers and followers. By the 1920s, a small cohort of rebbetzins understood themselves as working together to further common interests. In the decades that followed, many rebbetzins, in partnership with their husbands, played principal roles in bringing Jewish life to numerous regions, communities, and towns throughout the United States. They also found arenas of Jewish leadership outside their congregations through writing, speaking, and organizational work. Affected by second-wave feminism, rebbetzins precipitously lost both status and self-esteem. Yet many transferred their dedication and skills to independent careers that offered them great satisfaction while also en-hancing American Jewish life.

These insights illuminate the importance of hidden careers for women themselves. Obscured because women entered them through marriage and received no monetary compensation, these careers nevertheless pro-vided women with opportunities for meaningful work. They offered women status and position as well as a built-in audience for their tal-ents. Despite the drawbacks that inevitably accompanied this deriva-tive role, the rebbetzins we have looked at generally felt fulfilled by this vocation.

Reviewing their lives and accomplishments has deepened our under-standing of the impact of these rebbetzins on the communities they served. We have seen the rebbetzin role accelerate the expansion of American Jewish synagogue life. Rabbis may have called the meet-ings, but rebbetzins addressed the invitations, made the follow-up calls, served the cake, and warmed up the crowd. Similarly, rabbis spoke from the pulpit, but rebbetzins talked to congregants at Kiddush, meetings, and at-home gatherings. They filled the expected roles of hostess, enter-tainer, and supportive spouse, but as we have seen, they also did much more. They served as rabbis to the women—teaching, demonstrating Jewish living, kashering homes, providing them with tools to live a fuller Jewish life, and dispensing advice, support, and comfort. As reb-betzins, they educated and socialized female congregants to an Amer-ican Jewish lifestyle that encompassed Jewish holidays and life cycle, prayer and learning. Many rebbetzins reached an even wider audience with their books, music, and lectures. Through all of these efforts, reb-betzins intensified the involvement and commitment of American Jewish women—and through them, American Jewish men and children—to Judaism. While this book does not attempt a full-fledged impact study, the preponderance of evidence over time suggests that many rebbetzins left an indelible mark on their congregations.

Of course, not all female volunteer leaders were rebbetzins. The vast majority of women who held positions of leadership in national Sis-terhoods, Hadassah, and the National Council of Jewish Women were not rabbis' wives. Other talented women wrote educational materials, taught, and lectured. Where, then, lies the uniqueness of the rebbetzin role? It rests precisely with the additional power and status intrinsic to it. Simply by virtue of being married to rabbis, rebbetzins automati-cally gained a measure of public recognition, standing, and visibility in the larger community that empowered them to influence others. Those married to congregational rabbis also acquired a constituency through Sisterhood that gave them a base from which to preach, teach, and write. Rebbetzins were uniquely situated to utilize their specific talents to galvanize others to live a fuller Jewish life.

As long as scholars assumed that religious life developed from the top down, they focused their research on rabbis and other prominent leaders. Their studies paid little attention to the constituents, the majority of whom were women. They also neglected the female leaders who taught or worked with women. Most female leaders went unnoticed for decades, for they rarely held top positions in national organizations—unless they were women's organizations—and they often performed in unofficial and unpaid capacities. Thus, to the extent that women remained marginal figures in American religious life, so too did their female leaders. But just as recent studies have established the centrality of women to American religious life, so too has this study demonstrated that the leaders of these women—many of whom were rebbetzins—played pivotal roles in fostering and strengthening American Jewish religious life.

Similarly, this study also suggests new ways of thinking about periodization in American Jewish history. For example, rebbetzins' sermons and writings from the 1930s reveal their awareness of the need to mobilize American Jewry to ensure Jewish survival in a precarious age. They began laying the groundwork for intensifying Jewish life before the end of World War II. This suggests a greater link between the interwar and postwar periods, a pattern that confirms the conclusions in Jonathan Sarna's recently published *American Judaism*. Sarna describes the mid-1930s as a period of spiritual and cultural revival in which women played a prominent role.[27]

Similarly, today's polarization among denominations often leads one to assume that stark differences always existed among Reform, Conservative, and Orthodox Jews. Yet this study reveals that at least for rabbis' wives, commonalities have outweighed differences. Rabbis' wives of all denominations shared comparable opportunities, frustrations, and goals. Distinctions among them had more to do with their relative knowledge of and commitment to traditional Jewish living and their personal inclination toward religious leadership than with their denominational affiliation.

This focus on rebbetzins has also deepened our understanding of the characteristics that foster female religious leadership. Though we have certainly seen individual differences, definite patterns have emerged. First, ambitious, activist rebbetzins often had positive, serious secular and Jewish learning opportunities in their teens and young adulthood. Whether they studied in colleges, Jewish teachers' seminaries, or at home, these women found themselves taken seriously for their intellectual capabilities. They felt privileged to achieve such advanced learning, and it convinced them that they were destined to play leadership roles in society. Second, most could point to a strong female leader who had served as a role model to them, whether it was Eleanor Roosevelt, Henrietta Szold, their mother, a specific teacher, or a rebbetzin. Rabbis' wives often admired this one special woman, and they sought to emulate the leadership qualities this individual epitomized. Third, most of these rebbetzins volunteered in one of the burgeoning women's groups, often in its formative years. The experience of building an organization together with other women bolstered both their skills and their confidence. It also profoundly shaped their views of how much women could achieve together. Fourth, many of the rebbetzins profiled found arenas for leadership separate from their husbands' congregations. While they gained their initial status and arena for leadership through their husbands' congregations, they did not fully shine as leaders until they developed their own spheres of influence and their own competencies, whether through writing, speaking, or programming. Finally, this independent streak blossomed even further in widowhood, and many rebbetzins reached their peak of creativity and accomplishment after their husbands died. As widows of rabbis, they retained their status but no longer felt bound by the restrictions of the role. This enabled them to take on new challenges and responsibilities that broadened their impact.

Rebbetzins' accomplishments also underscore the fluidity of women's leadership roles in public and private realms. For example, rebbetzins who drew on their homemaking expertise to write nationally acclaimed books designed to aid other homemakers conflated the boundaries between those spheres. Rebbetzins who excelled at both intimate home gatherings and national public addresses further confounded them. Rebbetzins moved comfortably between the spheres, and experience in one area enhanced their effectiveness in the other. The use of formulaic phrases such as "Woman of Valor," "loyal helpmeet," and "Mother in

Israel" to praise rebbetzins blurred the lines still further, for these epithets anchored the modern rebbetzin role to the traditional one, and, in so doing, blended the behind-the-scenes roles with the more radical, independent, and public ones.

Recognition of rebbetzins' singular position in American Jewish life also sheds light on the broader experience of clergy wives in general. Having uncovered so many parallels between the lives of Jewish and Christian clergy wives in America, this study demonstrates the broader significance of the clergy wife role as an outlet for women who felt called to serve their faith communities. One can only hope that this study of rebbetzins will inspire a comprehensive parallel study on the development of the American Christian clergy wife role and its impact on American Christianity and on American religious life as a whole.

At the same time, delving into the lives of rabbinic couples has uncovered hints of the effect of the clergy lifestyle on children as well as wives. These "PKs," or preacher's kids, as they are affectionately called, also experienced both its advantages and its hardships. Born into the limelight, some grew up with deeply conflicted feelings about their roles. Interviews with children about their rebbetzin mothers provided glimpses of the complexity of these feelings. Surely, a full study of these children would further illuminate the impact of the ministry on family life and the effect of parental career choices on the lives of their children.

Looking at rebbetzins has also inspired a rethinking of the effects of gender stereotyping and expectations, for it has revealed that contemporary assumptions about gender inequality distort our understanding of the past. Though operating with gender constraints that limited their direct access to power, rebbetzins gained confidence, skills, autonomy, and power that they would not otherwise have had. Because of this, many loved their roles, believing that the opportunities far outstripped the restrictions. Recognizing their views enables us to understand the impact of gender distinctions in a much more nuanced way.

How might women's leadership evolve in this most recent era, when women can become what they want to be? It is too soon to tell whether the impact of women's equality will ultimately erode the rebbetzin role even among Chabad. More important, women rabbis have only just begun to confront the lingering gender differences—in pay, marital status, and expectations—that circumscribe their success. It remains to be seen whether women rabbis will affirm—as their rebbetzin predecessors did earlier in the twentieth century—that the advantages of their roles ultimately outweigh the liabilities. Time will also reveal both the ways in which women rabbis will shape their own leadership styles and the arenas in which they will leave their most profound marks.

Taken as a whole, the manifold roles assumed by rabbis' wives in the twentieth century reveal to us how doubly blessed American Jewry has been. Rebbetzins "served" the Jewish people—both literally and figuratively—and, in so doing, lived lives that they generally found satisfying and meaningful. When these talented, motivated, capable women joined forces with their rabbi husbands, the American Jewish community gained more than two for the price of one. Overwhelmingly, the resulting rabbinic team proved greater than the sum of its parts. The landscape of American Jewish life has been immeasurably enhanced by the contributions of its rebbetzins. By studying their lives, our perspective on American Jewish religious life has been indelibly enriched as well.

Notes

NOTES TO THE INTRODUCTION

1. Finch, *Married*, 152.

2. Daniels, *Invisible Careers*, 270; idem, "The Hidden Work of Constructing Class and Community: Women Volunteer Leaders in Social Philanthropy," in *Families and Work*, ed. Gerstel and Gross, 228–34; and Finch, *Married*, 153.

3. Papanek, "Men, Women, and Work," 852–72; Nieva and Gutek, *Women and Work*, 97–98; and Epstein, *Woman's Place*, 40. I am grateful to Dr. Carol Poll for helping me clarify this concept with reference to rebbetzins.

4. Finch, *Married*, 7, 101; and Hochschild, "Ambassador's Wife," 73–74.

5. Fowlkes, *Successful Man*, 67–75.

6. MacPherson, *Power Lovers*, 50–51.

7. *Oxford Classical Dictionary*, 3rd ed., ed. Simon Hornblower and Antony Spawforth (New York: Oxford University Press, 1996), s.v. "Aspasia."

8. Caroli, *First Ladies*, xv, xviii, xxi, 117, 361n7.

9. Germaine Greer, "Abolish Her: The Feminist Case against First Ladies," *New Republic*, 26 June 1995, 27; http://www.whitehouse.gov/history/firstladies/hc42.html; Caroli, *First Ladies*, 356; and Margaret Talbot, "Here Come the Wives," *New York Times Sunday Magazine*, 14 March 1999.

10. Martha R. Fowlkes, "The Myth of Merit and Male Professional Careers: The Role of Wives," in *Families and Work*, 347–48.

11. Heller, "Pulpit Rebbitzen," 13. S. Joshua Kohn served as rabbi of Temple Beth El in Utica, New York, from 1930 to 1946. Among other things, Priva was known for teaching and supervising elaborate religious school holiday celebrations. When she and her husband moved to Trenton, New Jersey, Priva served as Women's League National Chairman of Leadership Training. In this capacity, she authored an extensive guide to help Sisterhoods train future leaders. "Women's League Notables," *Outlook* 27 (December 1956): 18; Kohn, *Utica*, 67, 108, 184; and "How Beautiful Is Our Heritage," 9–13 November 1952, 4–8, box 2, WLA.

12. Braude, "Women's History *Is* American Religious History," 87–107.

13. "Fitting helpmate" is taken from the creation story, Genesis 2: 18, where God states that "it is not good for man to be alone; I will make a fitting helper for

him." "Mother in Israel" describes the prophet Deborah. "Deliverance ceased, Ceased in Israel, Till you arose, O Deborah, Arose, O mother, in Israel!" (Judges 5: 7). "Woman of valor" comes from Proverbs 31: 10–31 which begins "What a rare find is a capable wife!" but is often translated "A Woman of Valor, who can find?"

14. Polner, *Rabbi*, 154–61; and Marcus and Peck, eds., *American Rabbinate*, 159–60.

15. Freedman, "Rebbetzin," 145; and Brekus, *Strangers & Pilgrims*, 7.

16. William Cutler III, "Accuracy in Oral History Interviewing," 79–81; Sherna Gluck, "What's So Special about Women? Women's Oral History," 222–23; and William Moss, "Oral History: An Appreciation," 96–99, in *Oral History: An Interdisciplinary Anthology*, ed. David K. Dunaway and Willa K. Baum (Nashville, Tenn.: American Association for State and Local History, 1984); and Marc Lee Raphael, *Jews and Judaism in a Mid-Western Community: Columbus, Ohio, 1840–1975* (Columbus: Ohio Historical Society, 1979), 436–44. The quote is on 437.

17. In sixth-century Christianity, clergy wives obtained their own title when they took a vow of continence at their husbands' ordination. They received a special vestment and could be addressed by female forms of the honorific titles "*deaconissa, presbytera, episcopa.*" These wives functioned as assistants to their husbands, caring for the church and undertaking a pastoral ministry with women. Yet after the twelfth-century reform movement, the church strove to marginalize clergy wives, and they were officially defined as concubines. Rosemary Radford Reuther, *Christianity and the Making of the Modern Family* (Boston: Beacon Press, 2000), 6–7, 48, 56.

18. Since rebbetzin is not an English word but is taken from the Yiddish, there is no standard spelling. I have adopted the generally accepted and most common spelling while retaining variant spellings in citations and direct quotations.

19. Ronald Lötzsch, *Jiddisches Worterbuch* (Leipzig: Bibliographisches Institut, [n.d.]), 149; Siegmund A. Wolf, *Jiddisches Worterbuch* (Mannheim: Bibliographisches Institut, 1962), 159; Nahum Stutchkoff, *Der Oytser fun der Yidisher Shprakh* (New York: Yidisher Visenshaftlekher Institut, 1950), 913; Alexander Harkavy, *Yiddish-English Dictionary* (New York: Hebrew Publishing, 1910), 814; and C. D. Spivak and Sol Bloomgraten, *Yiddish Dictionary* (New York: n.p., 1911), 241 (translation mine).

20. Tzvi Rabinowicz, *Hasidism: The Movement and Its Masters* (Northvale, N.J.: J. Aronson, 1988), 343; Shaul Shimon Deutsch, *Larger than Life: The Life and Times of the Lubavitcher Rebbe Rabbi Menachem Mendel Schneerson*, vol. 1 (New York: Chasidic Historical Productions, 1995), 139–40; Zalman Alpert, "The Rebbetzin who Became a Rebbe: The Chentsiner Rebbetzin," *Chasidic Historical Review* 1 (April 1996): 8–9; and Nehemia Polen, "Egalitarianism in

Hasidic Thought," *Modern Judaism* 12 (February 1992): 10–11. Polen quotes Feinkind from his 1937 *Froyen Rebeyyim un Berihmte Perzenlikhkeiten in Poylen* [Women-Rebbes and Famous Personalities in Poland].

21. "What Is a Box Tax?" *Avotaynu* 12 (summer 1996): 39; Yaffa Eliach, *There Once Was a World: A Nine-Hundred-Year Chronicle of the Shtetl of Eishyshok* (Boston: Little, Brown and Co., 1998), 95; and Meir Berlin, "The Rebbetzin of Volozhin," trans. Yaacov Dovid Shulman, *Wings of Morning* 3 (June 1999).

22. Wendy Zierler, "The Rabbi's Daughter In and Out of the Kitchen: Feminist Literary Negotiations," *Nashim* (fall 2002): 84–85; Lerner, *Feminist Consciousness*, 28; and Solomon, *Company*, 2.

23. *Encyclopedia Judaica* (New York: Macmillan, 1972), s.v. "Steinhardt, Joseph Ben Menahem"; Zolty, "Learned," 215–16, 256; Eliach, *Once Was a World*, 94–95; Rabinowicz, *Hasidism*, 344; Aharon Zev Mendelsohn, *The Rebbe: A Biography*, vol. 1 (Brooklyn, N.Y.: Mendelson Press, 1995), 121–28; and Jennifer Breger, "Hebrew Printing in Jerusalem in the 19th Century," *Bookman's Weekly* 97 (20 May 1996): 2014. Hirschensohn was also the grandmother of Tamar de Sola Pool and Tehilla Lichtenstein, two of the rabbis' wives profiled in chapter 3. So powerful is this association of rebbetzins with learning that in recent years, as the numbers of Jewishly learned women in Israel grew, Israelis first tried to appropriate for them the term "rabbanit," the Hebrew equivalent of "rebbetzin." Gershon Bacon, Remarks, "Jewish Religious Leadership: Image and Reality" Conference, Jewish Theological Seminary, 5 November 2001; and Debra Nussbaum Cohen, "A New Orthodox Vocabulary," *Jewish Week,* 19 February 1998, 8.

24. Eliach, *Once Was a World*, 101–10.

25. See, for example, Eve Penner Ilsen, "A Tale of Reb Nahum Chernobler —and a Tikkun," 167–68; and Helen Mintz, "The Pekl Story," 222–25, in *Chosen Tales*, ed. Schram.

26. Chaim Grade, "The Rebbetzin," in *Rabbis and Wives*, 1–118.

27. Ibid., 3–5.

28. Ibid., 35–36.

29. Shmarya Levin, *Childhood in Exile*, trans. Maurice Samuel (New York: Harcourt, Brace & Co., 1929), 56; Ehrlich, *Miriam's Kitchen*, 297; and Feinsilver, *Taste of Yiddish*, 28, 259–60.

30. Joseph Telushkin, *Jewish Humor* (New York: William Morrow, 1992), 87.

31. *EJ*, s.v. "Beruriah"; Rachel Biale, *Women and Jewish Law: An Exploration of Women's Issues in Halakhic Sources* (New York: Schocken Books, 1984), 35; Judith Hauptman, *Rereading the Rabbis: A Woman's Voice* (Boulder, Colo.: Westview Press, 1997), 57n26; and Emily Taitz and Sondra Henry, *Written Out of History: Our Jewish Foremothers* (Sunnyside, N.Y.: Biblio

Press, 1988), 54–58. Brenda Bacon offers a more favorable interpretation of Beruriah's end by introducing the alternative narrative of Rabbenu Nissim b. Rabbenu Jacob. See Brenda Socachevsky Bacon, "How Shall We Tell the Story of Beruriah's End?" *Nashim* (fall 2002): 231–39.

32. Aron Shimon Shpall, "Genealogy Scroll of My Mother Hannah Toiva" (Hebrew), [1915?], mimeograph, personal files of author, translation mine; and Zolty, "Learned," 178–79, 186–87.

33. Zolty, "Learned," 159; Robert Bonfil, *Rabbis and Jewish Communities in Renaissance Italy*, trans. Jonathan Chipman (Oxford: Oxford University Press, 1990), 76–77, 168–71; and David Nirenberg, "A Female Rabbi in Fourteenth Century Zaragoza?" *Sefarad* 51 (1991): 179–80.

34. *EJ*, s.v. "Barazani, Asenath Bat Samuel"; and Zolty, "Learned," 140.

35. Sweet, *Minister's Wife*, 18; and Douglas, *Feminization*, 23.

36. May, *Great Expectations*, 18–19; Jeffrey, "Ministry," 143–44; Blair, *Clubwoman*, xii; and Ginzberg, *Benevolence*, 8.

37. *Women in American Protestant Religion*, intro., n.p.; Jeffrey, "Ministry," 144–45; and Sweet, *Minister's Wife*, 91–92.

38. Diane H. Lobody, "'A Wren Just Bursting Its Shell': Catherine Livingston Garrettson's Ministry of Public Domesticity," in *Spirituality*, ed. Keller, 28–29.

39. Brekus, *Strangers & Pilgrims*, 132–37, 298–300; Jeffrey, "Ministry," 145, 153–55; Sweet, *Minister's Wife*, 3, 99, 114–21; and Mary Orne Tucker, *Itinerant Preaching in the Early Days of Methodism, by a Pioneer Preacher's Wife* (Boston, 1872), 9-160, in *Women in American Protestant Religion*.

40. Sweet, *Minister's Wife*, 148, 154, 172–83; and *Women in American Protestant Religion*, intro., n.p.

41. Brekus, *Strangers & Pilgrims*, 297–98.

42. Jeffrey, "Ministry," 147–48, 156–58.

43. [Anon.], *Hints for a Clergyman's Wife; or, Female Parochial Duties*, quoted in Boyer, "Minister's Wife, Widow, Reluctant Feminist," 257; Herrick M. Eaton, *The Itinerant's Wife: Her Qualifications, Duties, Trials, and Rewards* (New York, 1851), 9–10, 55, 86–96, in *Women in American Protestant Religion*; and Jeffrey, "Ministry," 146–47.

44. Sweet, *Minister's Wife*, 70–75, 96; and Jeffrey, "Ministry," 151, 155–56.

45. Sweet, *Minister's Wife*, 3, 221, 224; and Douglas, *Feminization*, 326.

46. Hasia Diner, *A Time for Gathering: The Second Migration, 1820–1880*, in *Jewish People*, ed. Feingold, vol. 2: 120; *Kehilath Anshe Mayriv*, n.p.; and Gordon, *Jews in Transition*, 282.

47. For example, upon Abraham Rice's death in 1862, the congregation resolved to provide his bereaved spouse, Rosalie, with his salary for the current year and then an annual pension of $300 for life. While the author comments that this resolution represents the congregation's acknowledgment of his rabbinate and "her role as the first *rabbetzin* in the land," the minutes indicate only

that this gesture honored the rabbi: "As a further tribute to respect the memory of the lamented deceased." Sharfman, *First Rabbi,* 710–11; and Raphael, *Profiles,* 130–31. Even before there were ordained rabbis in the United States, evidence exists that widows of those who served in that capacity were treated with dignity. For example, when Jacob Raphael Cohen, hazzan, rabbi, and shohet of Mikveh Israel in Philadelphia, died in 1811, the synagogue granted a continuation of Cohen's salary to the widow and allowed her to live rent-free in the house provided for the hazzan. Edwin Wolf II and Maxwell Whiteman, *The History of the Jews of Philadelphia* (Philadelphia: Jewish Publication Society, 1956, 1975), 247.

48. Extracts from Dr. Mann's eulogy, 13 December 1949; and Nannie A. Reis, "Emil G. Hirsch—His Life," Emil Hirsch, nearprint box, AJA. Emil Hirsch served as rabbi of Chicago's Har Sinai Congregation from 1880 to 1923.

49. Kaufman Kohler served as rabbi of New York City's Beth El Congregation from 1879 to 1903 and as president of Hebrew Union College from 1903 until his death in 1926. May, *Great Expectations,* 18–19; "Mrs. Kaufman [*sic*] Kohler Dies in New York," *Reform Advocate,* 19 March 1932, 146; and *American Hebrew,* 18 March 1932, 465. These published accounts state her age at death as 83. The *American Israelite,* 17 March 1932, claimed she was 80. Evans, *Born,* 140–41; Katz, *Beth El Story,* 84; *Constitution and By-Laws of the United Order of True Sisters, Inc.* (New York: n.p., 1941), 7; and Diner, *Time for Gathering,* 109, 113. The UOTS, founded in 1846 in New York to render "moral and material aid" to its members, included at meetings secret rituals, dress, and other kinds of paraphernalia. It served, in many ways, as the female counterpart to the larger, male B'nai B'rith Organization.

50. For more on this organization, see below, chapter 1.

51. Henry Englander to Johanna Kohler, 3 May 1931, 6 November 1931, and 12 February 1932; Resolution from the Council Bible Class (Cincinnati), 17 March 1932, 3/2 "Kohler, Johanna (A-L) 1908; 1926–32," series A, subseries 2, Kaufmann Kohler Papers, AJA; and Kohler to every local chairman, Committee on Union Museum, 24 May 1917 and 2 October 1917 series e, box 26, circular file VII: Union Museum, 1916–1932, Women of Reform Judaism, AJA [WRJ].

52. Resolution of the HUC Faculty, 25 March 1932; Sara and Siegfried Geismar to Rose and Lili, March 17, 1932; and Michael Potter to Max Kohler and Edgar Kohler, 14 March 1932, 3/2 "Kohler, Johanna (A-L) 1908; 1926-32," series A, subseries 2, Kohler papers.

53. Frank, "If I Were a Rebitzin," *Jewish Times and Observer,* 20 June 1880, http://www.jwa.org/archive/frank/rfreb1.jpg.

54. http://huc.edu/aja/berk.htm; http://huc.edu/aja/JosephKrauskopf.htm; David Kaufman, *Shul with a Pool: The "Synagogue-Center" in American Jewish History* (Hanover, N.H.: Brandeis/University Press of New England, 1999), 12–36; Raphael, *Profiles,* 38; and Michael A. Meyer, *Response to Modernity: A*

History of the Reform Movement in Judaism (New York: Oxford, 1988), 280–81. Berkowitz served as rabbi of Philadelphia's Rodeph Sholem Congregation from 1892 to 1921. Krauskopf served as rabbi of Philadelphia's Congregation Keneseth Israel from 1887 to 1923. For more on Berkowitz, see below, chapter 2.

55. Meyer, *Response*, 285.

56. For a contemporaneous review of career options for women, see *Woman's Work in America*, ed. Annie Nathan Meyer (New York, 1891). Sweet, *Minister's Wife*, 224; Evans, *Born*, 145–50; Drachman, *Sisters in Law*, 253–54; Blair, *Clubwoman*, xii–xiii; and Nadell, *Women*, 24–28.

57. Meyer, *Response*, 139–40; and Goldman, *Beyond the Synagogue Gallery*, 4.

58. Dianne Ashton, *Rebecca Gratz: Women and Judaism in Antebellum America* (Detroit, Mich.: Wayne State University Press, 1997).

59. *JWA*, s.v. "National Council of Jewish Women"; and Rosa Sonneschein, "Editorial," *American Jewess* 4 (December 1896): 139. For more on the National Council of Jewish Women, see Faith Rogow, *Gone to Another Meeting: The National Council of Jewish Women, 1893–1993* (Tuscaloosa: University of Alabama Press, 1993).

60. Cousin Cynthius, "Mrs. Halvick's Chanukah Ball and Its Results," *Sabbath Visitor*, 9 December 1892, 250. My thanks to Dianne Ashton for sharing this reference with me.

61. *Jewish Women in America*, ed. Paula E. Hyman and Deborah Dask Moore (New York: Routledge, 1998), s.v. "Sonneschein, Rosa"; David Loth, "Notes on the Marital Discord of Solomon and Rosa Sonneschein," in "Sonneschein, Rosa, Three Articles," sc #11770, AJA; idem, "The American Jewess," *Midstream*, February 1985, 44; Kessner, "Rosa Sonneschein," 326–28; Porter, "Rosa Sonneschein," 125–31; Nadell, *Women*, 47; and Olitzky et al., *Reform Judaism*, 200–201.

62. Rosa Sonneschein, "Editor's Desk," *American Jewess* 2 (October 1895): 63–64; "Editorial," *American Jewess* 4 (December 1896): 138; and Myrna Goldenberg, "Rosa Sonneschein and 'The American Jewess,'" *Tenth World Congress of Jewish Studies*, Division B, 2 (1990): 333.

63. Rosa Sonneschein, "Women as Breadwinners," *American Jewess* 9 (May 1899): 4–6; and Goldenberg, "Rosa Sonneschein," 335.

64. *Papers of the Jewish Women's Congress* (Philadelphia, 1894); and Nadell, *Women*, 41–44.

65. Ray Frank, "Women in the Synagogue," excerpted in Ann D. Braude, "The Jewish Woman's Encounter with American Culture," in *Women and Religion in America*, vol. 1, 186–87. Emphasis mine.

66. "Woman in the Synagogue," *Reform Advocate*, 20 February 1897, 7–9, and 27 February 1897, 24–25; and Nadell, *Women*, 50–56. For more on Szold, see below, chapter 1.

NOTES TO CHAPTER 1

1. Wittigschlager, *Minna*. The quotes are on 25 and 29.

2. Cott, *Public Vows*, 167; Chafe, *American Woman*, 56; and May, *Great Expectations*, 7, 117.

3. Evans, *Born*, 142, 147–48; Solomon, *Company*, 62–63; and Caroli, *First Ladies*, 153.

4. The following information, including the quotations, is drawn from Kramer and Stern, "Woman Who Pioneered," 335–45.

5. This claim appears in numerous places. Many congregations insisted that *their* rebbetzin was the first woman to preach from the pulpit. For example, this claim was made about Rebecca Brickner when she spoke at her husband's temple in Cleveland. See below, chapter 3.

6. *JWA*, s.v. "Simon, Carrie Obendorfer"; Olitzky et al., *Reform Judaism*, 194–96; and *Universal Jewish Encyclopedia* (New York: Universal Jewish Encyclopedia Co., 1939–1944), s.v. "Simon, Carrie Obendorfer."

7. Ibid.; and "Honor for Mrs. Simon," unidentified newspaper clipping, ca. 1917, 1/6, Abram and Carrie Simon Papers, AJA.

8. Unidentified newspaper clipping, 1/6, Simon papers; Carrie Obendorfer, "Philanthropy," *American Jewess* 2 (July 1889): 545–48; Felicia Herman, "From Priestess to Hostess: Sisterhoods of Personal Service in New York City," in *Women*, ed. Nadell and Sarna, 152; and "Four Presidents on the N.F.T.S. Silver Jubilee," *Topics and Trends of the National Federation of Temple Sisterhoods* (January-February 1938): 3.

9. "The President's Message," *Proceedings of the First Biennial*, 46–51, and "The President's Message," *Proceedings of the Second Biennial Meeting*, 25, box 1, vol. 1, WRJ.

10. Simon, "Women's Influence," 7688–92.

11. "The President's Message," *Proceedings of the First Biennial*, 46–51, box 1, vol. 1, WRJ.

12. "What Can the Women Do for Judaism?" 1/3; and untitled, undated address to Rodeph Shalom Sisterhood, Pittsburgh, 1/3, Simon papers. In these suggestions, Simon was ahead of her time, anticipating the direction Reform would take decades later.

13. "What Can the Women Do for Judaism?" 1/3, Simon papers. Pamela S. Nadell identifies this as having appeared in the *Union Bulletin* (October 1921), 12ff. See her *Women*, 70–71, 239n. 34. Nadell also points out that the timing of Simon's remarks suggests that she was lending support to Martha Neumark's bid for ordination. "A Message to Temple Emanuel Auxiliary"; and untitled, undated address to Rodeph Shalom Sisterhood, 1/3, Simon papers.

14. Marc Lee Raphael, "'Training Men and Women in Dignity, in Civic Righteousness, and in the Responsibilities of American Citizenship': The

Thought of Rabbi Abram Simon, 1897–1938," *American Jewish Archives* 49 (1997): 73–77.

15. "A Message to Temple Emanuel Auxiliary," 1 March 1923, 1/3, Simon papers.

16. Report of the National Committee on Programs, Eighteenth Annual Report, 31 October 1930, 81–82; Nineteenth Annual Report, 31 October 1931, 83–86, *Proceedings of the National Federation of Temple Sisterhoods* [*PNFTS*], box 1, vol. 11, WRJ; and Mrs. Joseph [Blanche] Stolz, "The Hebrew Union College Yesterday and Today," *Union Tidings* 10 (March 1930): 9, in 1/7, Joseph Stolz Papers, AJA.

17. "Honor for Mrs. Simon," unidentified newspaper clipping, ca. 1917, 1/6, Simon papers. For earlier examples of such attitudes, see the Introduction.

18. "Silver Wedding Is Planned by Rabbi, Sept. 5," unidentified newspaper clipping, [1921?], 1/6 Simon papers.

19. Blair, *Clubwoman*, xiii; and Raphael, "'Training,'" 73.

20. Women's League dates its founding to 1918, but the Women's Religious Union of the United Synagogue with Schechter as president had actually been founded two years earlier. *They Dared to Dream,* 10; and Jack Wertheimer, "JTS and the Conservative Movement," in *Tradition Renewed,* ed. Jack Wertheimer, vol. 2, 408–9. Some of this material appears in slightly different form in Schwartz, "Mathilde Schechter."

21. *JWA,* s.v. "Schechter, Mathilde"; Louis Marshall to Frank Schechter, 5 September 1924, reprinted in Mel Scult, "Mrs. Mathilde Roth Schechter: Her Life and Letters," unpublished manuscript, 123–24; Ollendorf, "Mathilde Schechter," 7; Marx, "Life," 10–11; Scult, "Baale Boste," 1–27; and Mathilde Roth Schechter, memoir, undated, Solomon Schechter Papers, Jewish Theological Seminary of America [JTSA], New York, N.Y. (hereafter referred to as "Schechter memoir"). The pagination is very confusing, and because of this, I have not cited page numbers. Though mostly about her husband, Solomon, Mathilde's memoir provides important glimpses into her life and thinking. According to Mel Scult, the memoir was written between 1916 and 1919. He refers to it in his unpublished manuscript as "LondonCambridge Fragments," since most of it deals with this period. I am grateful to Scult for sharing his work-in-progress with me.

22. Schechter memoir; and Karp, "Mathilde Schechter," 30. Mathilde records in her memoir Joseph Jacobs's lament that once the Schechters left London, he could not keep the old circle together.

23. Mathilde Schechter to Mrs. Bentwich, 4 September 1899, Bentwich Papers, Central Zionist Archives, Jerusalem [CZA]; and Charles Hoffman Papers, JTSA, both quoted in Scult, "Mrs. Mathilde," 70, 12; Badt-Strauss, "'Aunt Mathilde," 4–5; and *EJ,* s.v. "Bentwich."

24. Szold, "Lineaments," reprinted, 10; and Scult, "Mrs. Mathilde," 16–29.

Mel Scult correctly notes that one finds no trace of unhappiness or envy in Schechter's memoir.

25. Mathilde Schechter to Israel Zangwill, 5 September 1896 and 3 January 1898, CZA, reprinted in Scult, "Mrs. Mathilde," 38, 40.

26. The German manuscript of this unpublished novel can be found in the Mathilde Schechter Papers, JTSA. Karp, "Mathilde Schechter," 31. This European paradigm of the frau professor became common among university wives in twentieth-century America as well. A comparative study of the wives of physicians and academics demonstrates that many wives of academics in the United States strove to fulfill roles similar to that of the frau professor. One wife noted that "academics puts me into a setting where I could then further my own interests." Fowlkes, *Behind*, 102.

27. On Solomon Schechter's attitudes, see Robert S. Liberles, "*Wissenschaft des Judentums* Comes to America: A Chapter in Migration History, 1890–1935," in *Tradition Renewed*, vol. 1, 338–39. Mathilde was initially ambivalent about the move. Though eager for financial security and the opportunity America might present to her husband professionally, she was reluctant to leave cherished friends in England. Mathilde Schechter to Mrs. Bentwich, 4 September 1899, in Scult, "Mrs. Mathilde," 68–70.

28. [Althea Silverman], "Woman's Field," *United Synagogue Recorder* (October 1924), 26; Minkin, "Mrs. Solomon Schechter," 2; Rubenovitz, *Waking Heart*, 19, 268–69; Kohn, "Beauty," Hoffman, "Helpmeet," and "From the Funeral Tribute of Dr. Elias L. Solomon," *United Synagogue Recorder* (October 1924): 6–7; Joselit, *Wonders*, 151–53; Schechter memoir; and Henrietta Szold to Frank Schechter, 31 August 1924, reprinted in Scult, "Mrs. Mathilde," 125–26.

29. Both Schechters drew children to them. Solomon stocked up on candy to share with children after synagogue services. Mathilde was remembered for both her children's parties and the English, French, German, and Hebrew children's songs she loved to sing. Eli Ginzberg, son of Louis and Adele Ginzberg, fondly recalled her generous gifts. As a child, he thought of her as a "very important person" who sat on an elevated, queen-like chair; he was taken to visit her right after his bar mitzvah. Schechter memoir; Scult, "Mrs. Mathilde," 23–24, 44–46; Kohn, "Beauty," 6; and Eli Ginzberg, interview with author, 25 October 1994, New York, N.Y.

30. Mathilde Schechter to Susie Bentwich, 3 September 1903, Bentwich papers, CZA, reprinted in Scult, "Mrs. Mathilde," 83; and Marx, "Life," 12.

31. Szold, "Lineaments," reprinted, 10.

32. Mathilde Schechter to Susie Bentwich, 16 February 1904, Bentwich papers, CZA, reprinted in Scult, "Mrs. Mathilde," 86.

33. Solis-Cohen, "Mathilde Roth Schechter," 5; "Mathilde Schechter: Founder of Women's League," brochure, "Mathilde Schechter file," WLA; Scult,

"Mrs. Mathilde Roth Schechter," 54; and http://www.jewishgen.org/wconnect/wc.isa?jg~jgsys~ajhs~r!!220. Solis-Cohen and the Women's League brochure both identify Schechter as the school's founder, but the school dates to 1888, long before Schechter arrived in the United States. Scult calls it the Columbia Street Religious and Technical School for Girls.

34. Mathilde Schechter to Susie Bentwich, 3 September 1903, Bentwich papers, CZA, reprinted in Scult, "Mrs. Mathilde," 83; Mathilde Schechter, interview with Mrs. Morris (Althea) Silverman, in "Woman's Field," *United Synagogue Recorder* (April 1923): 17; Mathilde Schechter, "Problems of Religious Observance," talk delivered ca. 1905 to National Council of Jewish Women, reprinted in Scult, "Mrs. Mathilde," 129; "Hebrew Choral Society Planned," *Globe,* 10 February 1905, 21, in "ephemera M.S.—Newsclips" folder, box 20, "Schechter, Mathilde Correspondence", arch. 101–20, Mathilde Schecter papers, JTSA; *Kol Rinah*; and Scult, "Mrs. Mathilde," 50–52. Isaacs also worked with Schechter on the Columbia Street School. Mark Slobin believes that the growing interest in congregational singing and music was one aspect of the American synagogue's expanding scope in the early 1900s. Mark Slobin, *Chosen Voices: The Story of the American Cantorate* (Urbana: University of Illinois Press, 1989), 68–69.

35. Bernard A. Rosenblatt, "Beginning of Hadassah," *American Zionist* (January 1960), 6; Rose G. Jacobs, "Beginnings of Hadassah," in *Early History of Zionism in America,* ed. Isidore S. Meyer (New York: American Jewish Historical Society, 1958), 233–34; and Scult, "Mrs. Mathilde," 54–56. Rebecca Brickner was one of the younger women involved at this initial stage. For more on Brickner, see below, chapter 3.

36. Mathilde Schechter to Louis Marshall, 30 December 1915, reprinted in Scult, "Mrs. Mathilde," 110–11; Louis Marshall to Mathilde Schechter, 6 January 1916, arch. 101–20, Mathilde Schechter papers; Marx, "An Appreciation," 5; Scult, "Mrs. Mathilde," 82n77; Kohn, "Beauty," 6; and Jenna Weissman Joselit, "By Design: Building the Campus of the Jewish Theological Seminary," in *Tradition Renewed,* vol. 1, 279–80.

37. Schechter, "Task," 1.

38. Ibid.

39. Ibid.

40. Mrs. Solomon (Mathilde) Schechter, "Aims and Ideals of the Women's League," May 1918, "Mathilde Schechter" file, WLA.

41. Schechter, "Problems of Religious Observance," 126–31; idem, "Plea," 5, 17; and Solis-Cohen, "Mathilde Roth Schechter," 5.

42. Schechter, "Plea," 5–17.

43. Cyrus Adler to Mathilde Schechter, 20 May 1918, arch. 101–20, Schechter papers; Mathilde Schechter to Felix Warburg, 15 July 1918; Herbert Cottage to Mathilde Schechter, 16 July 1918; Mathilde Schechter to Felix War-

burg, 17 July 1918; Mathilde Schechter to Felix Warburg, 10 December 1918; Felix Warburg to Mathilde Schechter, 11 December 1918; and Schechter, "Address," 103–5, in Scult, "Mrs. Mathilde," 114–19; Scult, "Mrs. Mathilde," 63–66; "Women's Field," *United Synagogue Recorder* (April 1927): 25; Samuel Diamond, "The Jewish Students' House at the University of Pennsylvania," and Louis M. Levitsky, "Five Years at the Students' House," *United Synagogue Recorder* (January 1925): 7–9; and Joselit, "By Design," 276–77.

44. "Mrs. Schechter's Funeral," *New York Times,* 29 August 1924; and "Widow of Famous Scholar Is Dead," *Jewish Chronicle* (Detroit), 5 September 1924, arch. 101–21, Schechter papers.

45. *They Dared to Dream,* 11. Sulamith Ish-Kishor adapted *Friday Night Stories* from Ginzberg's *Legends of the Jews.*

46. Ibid.; Schechter, "Address," 108; "A Valorous Woman" (editorial), *Outlook* 2 (September 1930): 2; Minkin, "Mrs. Solomon Schechter," 2; and Mrs. Moses Hyamson, "Mrs. Samuel Spiegel: An Appreciation," *Outlook* 15 (December 1944): 3.

47. Evans, *Born,* 135–42; and Minkin, "Mrs. Solomon Schechter," 2.

48. *JWA,* s.v. "Goldstein, Rebecca Fischel"; *American Jewish Year Book* [*AJYB*] 63 (1965): 359; "Alumni/ae Seminary College of Jewish Studies-Teachers Institute," *Jewish Theological Seminary of America Register, 1977–1982* (New York: Jewish Theological Seminary of America, 1982), 118; *Who's Who in American Jewry* [*WWIAJ*] (1928), 246; David Kaufman, "Jewish Education as Civilization: A History of the Teachers Institute," in *Tradition Renewed,* vol. 1, 578–84; Lindley, "*You Have Stept,*" 308–9; and Reichel, *Maverick Rabbi,* 50. JTS was the second teachers college founded in the United States; Philadelphia's Gratz College was established in 1897. Louis Hurwich, "Origin and Development of Jewish Teacher-Training Schools in the United States: A Brief Historical Survey," in *The Education of American Jewish Teachers,* ed. Oscar I. Janowsky (Boston: Beacon Press, 1967), 4.

49. Reichel, *Maverick Rabbi,* 34–35, 37.

50. Goldstein and Fischel, trans., *Lah-y'-shaw-riem T'hie law.*

51. Reichel, *Maverick Rabbi,* 59, 41.

52. Jeffrey S. Gurock, "The Orthodox Synagogue," in *American Synagogue,* ed. Wertheimer, 58; and *Orthodox Judaism,* ed. Moshe D. Sherman, 79–81.

53. Reichel, *Maverick Rabbi,* 59–60, 110, 111, 131, 174, 177, 181, 192–93; and Saul Bernstein, *The Orthodox Union Story: A Centenary Portrayal* (Northvale, N.J.: Jason Aronson, 1997), 90–91. Similarly, Joseph Lookstein, rabbi of Kehillath Jeshurun in New York City (1923–79), and his wife, Gertrude, also held numerous "at homes" as they worked to create a positive image of a modern Orthodox rabbinic family. Joselit, *Jewish Jews,* 67.

54. Gurock, *Men and Women of Yeshiva,* 60–66.

55. *WWIAJ* (1927), 218–19; Selma Freedman, "The Women's Branch: 25

Years of Achievement," *Jewish Life* 15 (June 1948): 51–56; and Mrs. Herbert S. [Rebecca] Goldstein, "Women and Orthodox Judaism," *Synagogue Light* 1 (August 1934): 5.

56. *WWIAJ* (1928), 246; *AJYB* 63 (1965): 559; and Goldstein, "Women and Orthodox Judaism," 6. The Hebrew Teacher's Training School became part of Yeshiva University in 1952 as the Teachers Institute for Women. Hurwich, "Teacher-training," 7; and Gurock, *Yeshiva*, 196–98.

57. See, for example, "Hadassah Celebrates Founder's Day," *American Jewish Times* (Greenwood, S.C.), January 1940, n.p., in 1/1, rg 13; and Tamar de Sola Pool, "Zionism's First Lady," 7/74, rg 7, Henrietta Szold Papers, Hadassah Archives, New York, N.Y. [HA].

58. Attending a separate women's high school in Baltimore in the 1870s, Szold would have followed a curriculum that included literature, modern languages, history, and teacher preparation rather than classical studies. John Rury has demonstrated that Baltimore educators at the time were committed to preparing women for a variety of nurturing functions as teachers, nurses, organizers of charitable organizations, or participants in Reform movements—all lessons that would serve Szold well in her career. Rury, *Education*, 6–7, 21, 39–40.

59. Bertha Szold Levin, "Manuscript Notes on the Early Life of Henrietta Szold," 61/7, rg 7, Szold papers.

60. There is an extensive bibliography on Szold, including Joan Dash, *Summoned to Jerusalem: The Life of Henrietta Szold* (New York: Harper & Row, 1979); Fineman, *Woman of Valor: The Life of Henrietta Szold, 1860–1945* (New York: Simon and Schuster, 1961); Elma Ehrlich Levinger, *Fighting Angel: The Story of Henrietta Szold* (New York: Behrman House, 1946); Marvin Lowenthal, *Henrietta Szold: Life and Letters* (New York: Viking Press, 1942); and Baila Round Shargel, *Lost Love: The Untold Story of Henrietta Szold* (Philadelphia: Jewish Publication Society, 1997). Basic biographical and bibliographical information can be found in *JWA*, s.v. "Szold, Henrietta." On the long and deep Zionist feeling in Baltimore see S. Schaffer, "Zionism," in *The History of the Jews of Baltimore*, ed. Isidor Blum (Baltimore: Historical Review, 1910), 39–48.

61. Johns Hopkins University did not admit women as undergraduates until 1969. http://webapps.jhu.edu/jhuniverse/information_about_hopkins/about_jhu/frequently_asked_questions/index.cfm; Jonathan D. Sarna, *JPS: The Americanization of Jewish Culture* (Philadelphia: Jewish Publication Society, 1989), 47–94; Shargel, *Lost Love*, 3–14; and Nadell, *Women*, 54–59.

62. Rubenovitz, *Waking Heart*, 23–24; and Shargel, *Lost Love*, 9–10, 40–41. The quote is from Ginzberg to Szold, 10 October 1904, 41.

63. Shargel, *Lost Love*, 19 December 1908, 192, 24 December 1908, 193–94, 30 December 1908, 207, and 24–26. Finding an adult community proved particularly difficult for unmarried American women at the time. As Eleanor

Stebner demonstrates, women were drawn to the social settlement movement in part because it provided acceptable living arrangements. It gave bright, well-educated, reform-minded, single women a sense of home and community as well as vocation. Perhaps, Szold eventually settled in Palestine not only to pursue her vocation more effectively but also to find the home that had been displaced by the Ginzberg incident. Eleanor Stebner, *The Women of Hull House: A Study in Spirituality, Vocation and Friendship* (Albany: State University of New York Press, 1997), 17–19.

64. Dash, *Summoned*, 78–107. Fineman's *Woman of Valor* is the first biography to make use of Szold's journal in recounting the details of her unrequited love and its impact on her.

65. *JWA*, s.v. "Szold, Henrietta," and "Hadassah."

66. Transcript of proceedings, 8th Biennial Assemby, 1929, 11, 2/3, WRJ.

NOTES TO CHAPTER 2

1. Isaacs, *Sabbath Lamp*, 7; and Sarna, *JPS*, 24, 170, 395.

2. Isaacs, *Sabbath Lamp*, 161–71. Italics mine.

3. Abraham J. Karp, "Overview: The Synagogue in America—A Historical Typology," in *American Synagogue,* ed. Wertheimer, 17–23; Henry L. Feingold, *A Time for Searching: Entering the Mainstream 1920–1945, Jewish People,* ed. Feingold, vol. 4, 92–93; Mel Scult, "Schechter's Seminary," in *Tradition Renewed,* vol. 1, 76; *Hebrew Union College-Jewish Institute of Religion at One Hundred Years,* ed. Samuel E. Karff ([Cincinnati]: Hebrew Union College Press, 1976), 97; Gurock, *Yeshiva,* 112–15; and http://www.yu.edu/admissions.

4. Feingold, *Time for Searching,* 90–93; Karp, "Overview," 23–24; and Deborah Dash Moore, "A Synagogue Center Grows in Brooklyn," in *American Synagogue,* ed. Wertheimer, 305–10.

5. A lexicon of Talmudic terms in eight volumes (Vienna, 1878–92).

6. *JWA*, s.v. "Kohut, Rebekah Bettelheim"; *AJYB* 7 (1905–6): 76; *AJYB* 54 (1953): 539; Nadell, *Conservative Judaism,* 165–68; and *EJ*, s.v. "Bettelheim, Albert (Aaron) Siegfried."

7. James Luby, "Romantic Career of a Vicarious Mother in Israel," *New York Times Book Review,* 26 April 1925, 5; unidentified newspaper clipping, 2/4, George A. Kohut Papers, ms collection #381, AJA; and http://www.pta.org. Luby puts attendance at 1,000. According to the website, 200 were expected, and 2,000 attended.

8. Several unidentified newspaper and magazine clippings among Kohut's son's papers indicate that *My Portion* was covered in both the Jewish—including the Yiddish—and the general press. For example, see Sulamith Ish-Kishor, "Rebekah Kohut's Self-Portrait," *Jewish Tribune,* April 3, 1925, 74. A publicity brochure includes a review quote from the *Cincinnati Times-Star.* In the *New*

York Times Book Review, James Luby wrote a glowing review: "Romantic Career," 5.

9. Kohut, *My Portion,* 72–76. The quote is on 74.

10. Ibid., 89, 118–19.

11. Ibid., 154–55, 173.

12. Ibid., 46, 50, 71, 135, 154–55.

13. Ibid., 133, 180–82.

14. Ibid., 283; and Marcel Vavin, "Mrs. Kohut, Leader of Her Sex and Race, Wants Jewish Law Changed," unidentified newspaper clipping, [1929?], 2/4, Kohut papers.

15. *Problems of the Jewish Ministry.*

16. Feingold, *Time for Searching,* 62–89; and Michael A. Meyer, conversation with author, 9 July 1999. For more on the traditional eastern European rebbetzin role, see the Introduction.

17. Feinsilver, *Taste,* 7; and "Di rebbetzin" (1928) and "Di rebbetzin hot nit geheysen" (1929), in Irene Heskes, *Yiddish American Popular Songs 1895–1950* (Washington, D.C.: Library of Congress, 1992), 307–16.

18. William Schack, "A New Spotlight on the Jewish Stage," *New York Times,* 5 April 1931, 105.

19. Ruth Levi also refrained from using the term rebbetzin in her article, "I Married a Rabbi." The title of her article paralleled that of the book in which it appeared—*I Married a Minister,* ed. Golda Bader. But this practice changed, particularly in articles written for a Jewish audience in the postwar period. See below, chapter 4.

20. Kohut, *My Portion,* 156–57; and Luby, "Romantic Career," 5.

21. Rebekah Kohut, "The Wife of the Rabbi," *Problems,* 210, 217.

22. Ibid., 210–11.

23. Ibid., 211, 215.

24. Ibid., 212–16. For more on this issue of rebbetzins serving as Sisterhood presidents, see below.

25. Ibid., 216.

26. Hyamson's husband, Moses Hyamson, was an Orthodox rabbi who served Orach Chaim Congregation in New York City from 1913 to 1949. He also served as professor of codes at JTS, vice president of the Union of Orthodox Jewish Congregations of America, and co-editor of the *Jewish Forum. UJE,* s.v. "Hyamson, Moses"; and David Golinkin, "The Influence of Seminary Professors on Halakha in the Conservative Movement: 1902–1968," in *Tradition Renewed,* vol. 2, 472n26.

27. Kohut, "Wife of the Rabbi," 217, 222.

28. Hyamson's remarks also appeared in the *Jewish Forum,* an Orthodox Jewish monthly journal that rarely published articles by women. Mrs. Moses

Hyamson, "The Rabbi's Wife," Jewish Forum 8 (December 1925): 583–85. The quotes in the following paragraphs are taken from this article.

29. Hyamson, "Ritual Baths (Mikvaoth)," 22–25.

30. Nadell, *Conservative Judaism,* 35–36; idem, *Women,* 61–80, 174–75; and David Aronson, "Woman's Position in Israel II," *Jewish Forum* 5 (October 1922): 380.

31. See below, chapter 4, for some of the rebbetzins who describe Aronson as their role model.

32. *A Cantorial Odyssey,* 1 April 2001, personal files of Helen Tomsky.

33. "National Women's League Proceedings of the Biennial Convention, Minneapolis, Minnesota," 12–15 November 1950, box 1 (1919–1950), WLA; and Mrs. David [Bertha] Aronson, "National Women's League Convention Brings *Kashrut* to Minneapolis," *Outlook* 21 (March 1951): 8.

34. The information in the following paragraphs, unless otherwise noted, is drawn from Bengis, *Rabbi's Wife.*

35. Jacob Rader Marcus, *The American Jewish Woman: A Documentary History* (New York: Ktav, 1981), 777.

36. Gustine Weaver, *The Minister's Wife* (Cincinnati: Powell and White, 1928), 111, quoted in Kirkley, "'Mrs. God,'" 11.

37. Gurock, *American Jewish Orthodoxy,* 241–43. Regina Stein found evidence of similar fluidity between Conservatism and Orthodoxy in the pre–World War II period in her study of gender issues in American Judaism. Stein, "Boundaries."

38. *JWA,* s.v. "Ginzberg, Adele Katzenstein"; Ginzberg, *Keeper,* 243–46; "Quotable Quotes," *Scope* (February 1964): 2; "Presentation of Mathilde Schechter Award," *Women's League Biennial Convention Proceedings* (1980), 75–76; Carrie Davidson to Adele Katzenstein, 30 October 1908, box 3, "Israel Davidson" folder, Louis Ginzberg Papers, JTSA; Eli Ginzberg, interview with author, 25 October 1994, New York, N.Y.; "Irrepressible," 4, 20–21; and Eisenstein, *Reconstructing Judaism,* 84–85. In her later years, Ginzberg always carried an address book listing the whereabouts of "her boys"—Conservative rabbis—and visited them whenever possible.

39. Ginzberg, interview; Ginzberg, "Seminary Family," 117–26; Louis Finkelstein to Adele Ginzberg, 19 October 1945, rg 1C-47-49, JTS records, JTSA; and "Irrepressible," 20–21. I was privileged to be among the students invited to Ginzberg's home on several occasions. She continued to bake her own apple pie —from scratch—into her nineties.

40. *They Dared to Dream,* 63; and "Presentation of Mathilde Schechter Award," 74. Ginzberg's monthly column was titled "Cooperation with National Organizations." Ginzberg's son, Eli, suggested that her zeal for Women's League may have been fueled in part by her lack of enthusiasm for Hadassah,

an understandable reticence given the tensions between her and Szold. Ginzberg, interview with author.

41. Ginzberg, interview; Shenker, "Adele Ginzberg"; "Publicity and Public Relations" folder, file 5a, WLA; and "Presentation of Mathilde Schechter Award," 74–75.

42. "Early History" folder, WLA. The fifth, Racie Adler, was a JTS faculty wife whose husband, Cyrus Adler, was not an ordained rabbi. H. Pereira Mendes served as rabbi of Congregation Shearith Israel in New York City from 1877 to 1923. Rosalie Mendes played an instrumental role in creating the Young Women's Hebrew Association in New York City in 1902, serving as its first vice president and religious guide. David de Sola Pool, *Shearith Israel Bulletin*, 29 February 1929, quoted in "An Evening of Reminiscences," 20 November 1975, 9–10, "Mrs. Pool Corres. and Misc." box, David and Tamar de Sola Pool papers, Sp.-Port.; and *JWA*, s.v. "Young Women's Hebrew Association." Jacob Kohn served as rabbi of Anshe Chesed in New York City from 1911 to 1931. Augusta Kohn had an impact on her husband's rabbinate through her efforts as hostess and Sisterhood president. Like many of her peers, she was involved in the founding of Hadassah. Lebeson, *Recall to Life*, 256. For more on Fanny and Charles Hoffman, see below. For more on Mignon and Herman Rubenovitz, see below, chapter 3.

43. Fanny Minkin, interview with Shoni Levi, [1973], "Oral History file," WLA.

44. *JWA*, s.v. "Hoffman, Fanny Binswanger"; *EJ*, s.v. "Binswanger, Isidore"; Minkin, interview with Shoni Levi; and Althea Silverman, "Women's Field," *United Synagogue Recorder* (October 1923): 20. The information about Hoffman's father in *JWA* is incorrect. He was a businessperson and philanthropist, not a rabbi.

45. Nadell, *Conservative Judaism*, 142–43; *They Dared to Dream*, 12–13; Silverman, "Women's Field," 20; and Hoffman, "Use of Leisure," 2–3. Silverman also encouraged women to incorporate Judaism into the summer months: "A vacation should be recreational, but it should also be re-creational," *United Synagogue Review* (July 1923): 16.

46. Silverman, "Women's Field," 20; and Sarah Kussy, "Fanny Binswanger Hoffman," *Outlook* 19 (December 1948): 5.

47. Minkin, interview with Shoni Levi; and Jacob S. Minkin, *The Shaping of the Modern Mind: The Life and Thought of the Great Jewish Philosophers*, with an introductory appreciation by Fanny R. Minkin (New York: Thomas Yoseloff, 1963), 18.

48. Drachman, *Sisters in Law*, 101–5, 254, 257.

49. *Outlook* 13 (December 1942): 2; Minkin, interview with Shoni Levi; and Solomon, *Company*, 131. This pattern continued for other rabbis' wives as well. According to her daughter-in-law, Jeannette Miller, Francis Miller had also

graduated from law school in the 1920s. When she married Joseph Miller, she gave up the law profession because she too felt that a rabbi's wife ought to serve as a full-time helpmate. RA session.

50. Nadell, *Conservative Judaism*, 190–91; and *United Synagogue Recorder* (April 1921): 13, (June-July 1924): 22, and (April 1927): 29.

51. For examples of her articles, see *Outlook*, "Our Convention," 6 (March 1936): 1; "Lag B'Omer: Scholars' Festival," 8 (May 1938): 2; "The High Holidays," 22 (September 1951): 4, and "Happy Anniversary to Us," 26 (September 1955): 4; "1939–46 folder," box 1 (1919–50), WLA; Nadell, *Conservative Judaism*, 190–91; and Minkin, interview with Shoni Levi.

52. *JWA*, s.v. "Melamed, Deborah Marcus"; and "Women's Field," *United Synagogue Recorder* (February 1926), 28.

53. Deborah M. Melamed, "The Modern Woman and Traditional Judaism" (January 1921): 9–10; and "Woman's Opportunity in the Synagogue" (April 1921): 12–13, both in the *United Synagogue Recorder*.

54. Melamed, *Three Pillars*, Preface, 34–35, 74; Emily Solis Cohen, "*The Three Pillars*," book review (April 1927): 28; "*The Three Pillars*" (February 1928): 29; "Book Corner of Special Interest of Our Women" (January 1929): 23; and (February 1926): 28, all in *United Synagogue Recorder*; and *They Dared to Dream*, 43.

55. Many examples abound and can be seen in articles cited throughout. The National Federation of Temple Sisterhoods' *Topics and Trends* appeared in the 1930s as a newsletter that did not regularly print literary material. The Union of Orthodox Jewish congregations' *Jewish Life* did not appear until 1946. Even then, it rarely included articles by women.

56. Articles on these topics can be found in almost any issue of *Outlook*. Before *Outlook* appeared, Davidson wrote on these themes for *United Synagogue Recorder*. See, for example, "The Education of Deborah" (April 1924): 9–10, and "The New Jerusalem: A Free City" (January 1927): 27–28. Her articles also appeared elsewhere through the Jewish Telegraphic Agency. See, for example, "Unjust Laws Affect Jewish Women," *Jewish Advocate* (Boston), 7 March 1930, and "A New University on Old Soil," which appeared in the *Jewish Exponent* and *Hadassah Newsletter*, undated clippings, 1/2, Carrie Davidson Papers, AJA.

57. Jessica Davidson, "Carrie Dreyfuss," 1/2, Davidson papers; *JWA*, s.v. "Davidson, Carrie Dreyfuss"; *AJYB* 56 (1955): 569; and *New York Times*, obituary, 19 December 1953.

58. Nadell, *Conservative Judaism*, 65–66; Fanny Minkin, "Carrie Davidson Appreciation," *Outlook* 24 (March 1954): 17; *American Jewish World*, 25 March 1932, 1/2, Davidson papers; and Davidson, *Endless Yearnings*, 63–64.

59. Cyrus Adler, "Report of Acting President to Board of Directors," 16 May 1920, JTSA Board of Directors minutes, JTSA. I am grateful to Ira Robinson for sharing this reference with me.

60. "Carrie Davidson," *Bloch's Book Bulletin,* 1946, 43, 1/4, Davidson papers; Kaufman, "Jewish Education," in *Tradition Renewed,* vol. 1, 612; and Minkin, "Carrie Davidson Appreciation," 16.

61. *United Synagogue Recorder* (January 1923): 2, (April 1923): 17–18, (July 1923): 16, and (April 1924): 19; and *Outlook* 6 (March 1936): 7.

62. *Oasis* flyer; and Louis Finkelstein to Althea Silverman, 27 April 1937, personal files of Hillel E. Silverman.

63. Hillel E. Silverman, phone conversation with author, 20 March 2000; Shoni B. Levi, "Author Has Her Say," 28; citation, Harry Truman to Althea O. Silverman, n.d.; undated clippings, *Hartford Times;* Jennie C. Grossinger to Althea Silverman, 24 August 1959; Berthold Gaster, "National Women's League of United Synagogue to Honor Mrs. Ribicoff and Mrs. Silverman," *Jewish Ledger,* 15 October 1959; and citation, Mathilde Schechter Luncheon, 9 November 1959, in personal files of Silverman.

64. "Original Pageant Set by Sisterhood," *Hartford Times,* 1 November 1955; Review of *Behold My Messengers!, Hartford Courant Magazine,* 25 December 1955; *Hartford Times,* 31 December 1955; Review of *Behold My Messengers!,* by Jacob Neusner in Women's League press release; "Singapore Diary," *Malay Mail* (incorporating the *Singapore Free Press*), 8 May 1963; and other undated clippings, personal files of Silverman. According to her son, Hillel, Althea applied her literary skills to her husband's work as well. Hillel claims that Althea translated some of the material into English and especially helped improve the English translations of the poetry in Morris Silverman's *Sabbath and Festival Services* (Hartford, Conn.: Prayer Book Press, 1936; rev. 1937). Hillel Silverman, conversation.

65. Her husband, Simon Greenberg, served as rabbi of Har Zion Temple, Philadelphia, Pennsylvania, from 1925 to 1946, when he left to assume the position of provost at JTS. For more on Betty Greenberg, see below, chapter 4.

66. Silverman had also written *My Country Tis,* a pageant that was chosen to open the Temple of Religion at the Fair. Levi, "Author Has Her Say," 28; *My Country Tis,* program, 29 August 1939; National Women's League Board, Minutes 1939; and *Chicago Sentinel,* 18 May 1939, in "World's Fair 1940," folder, WLA.

67. Greenberg and Silverman, *Jewish Home Beautiful;* "Joint Sisterhood Program," *Topics & Trends* (May-June 1940): 1, personal files of Silverman; and Joselit, *Wonders,* 161–63. Lilly Routtenberg recalled implementing these ideas in her own Sisterhood. Routtenberg, interview. For more on Routtenberg, see below, chapter 3.

68. B. Rubin Weilerstein served as rabbi of Beth Judah Congregation in Atlantic City, New Jersey. Heller, "The Pulpit Rebbitzen," 12, 23; *They Dared to Dream,* 56; and Jenna Weissman Joselit, "'A Set Table': Jewish Domestic Culture in the New World, 1880–1950," in *Getting Comfortable in New York:*

The American Jewish Home, 1880–1950, ed. Susan L. Braunstein and Jenna Weissman Joselit (New York: Jewish Museum, 1990), 51–53.

69. Weilerstein's books include *The Adventures of K'tonton, K'tonton in the Circus, K'tonton in Israel, K'tonton on an Island in the Sea,* and *K'tonton's Yom Kippur Kitten.* For the story of JPS's initial rejection of her K'tonton manuscript, see Sarna, *JPS,* 171–72.

70. Nathan Ziprin, "Conversation with a Writer," December 1968, "Publicity and Public Relations folder," file 5A, WLA; and http://www.jewishlibraries .org/ajlweb/awardsscholarships_files/taylor_book.htm.

71. Ziprin, "Conversation." Even Henrietta Szold was touched by Weilerstein's stories. Though she had no children of her own to read to, Szold still took delight in the adventures of K'tonton. Szold admired Weilerstein for succeeding in recounting Jewish traditions to Jewish children in such a charming way. Henrietta Szold to Carmel Finkelstein, 9 February 1936, 1/6, "Weilerstein, Sadie" folder, WLA. On the concept of women's professions as an extension of women's spheres, see Woloch, *Women and the American Experience,* 283–87.

72. Levi, "Author Has Her Say," 28. Given Silverman's larger-than-life accomplishments, it is not surprising that Roberta Sigoloff Smotrich had a difficult time adjusting to the rebbetzin role when she married Althea's son, Hillel Silverman, in 1981. Roberta recalled the intense pressure she felt to be the kind of rebbetzin her mother-in-law had been. Roberta eventually found a successful niche that utilized her talents as a folk dance instructor. Roberta Silverman, conversation with author, Miami Beach, Florida, 5 January 2000.

73. "1915–1917, National Federation of Temple Sisterhoods: Officers and Executive Board," n.p., *PNFTS,* box 1, vol. 1; and Sybil F. Krauskopf to Local Chairman, Committee on Religious Schools, 7 December 1915, 24 February 1919, and 10 March 1919; box 26, vol. 8, WRJ. David Philipson, a member of the first graduating class of HUC, taught at the College and served as rabbi of Bene Israel Congregation in Cincinnati, Ohio, from 1888 to 1949. For more on Blanche and Joseph Stolz, see below. For more on Johanna and Kaufman Kohler, and Joseph Krauskopf, see the Introduction. Sybil Krauskopf, in her capacity as chairman of the Committee on Religious Schools, encouraged Sisterhood members to support free religious schools in their communities. She wanted to make it possible for all Jewish children, including the poor, to receive a Jewish education.

74. Blanche R. Stolz to Mrs. Benesch, 10 February 1950, 1/7, Joseph Stolz Papers, AJA.

75. "Introduction, Story" [1929], autobiographical sketch; and "Message Delivered by Mrs. Stolz at Executive Board Luncheon in Chicago, June 18, 1933," 1/7, Stolz papers.

76. Untitled address to Council of Jewish Women [1938]; and Blanche R. Stolz to Mrs. Benesch, 10 February 1950, 1/7, Stolz papers. As expected—given

their visibility as community leaders and their interest in Jewish life—other rabbis' wives of this period also took leadership roles in founding National Council of Jewish Women sections in their communities. For example, Gussie Woolner Calisch, wife of Edward Calisch, rabbi of Beth Ahabah in Richmond, Virginia, 1891–1946, headed the Richmond section at its inception. Berman, *Richmond's Jewry,* 261–62.

77. Joseph served as the assistant to Bernard Felsenthal at Zion Temple in Chicago from 1887 to 1895. He then became rabbi of the newly formed Isaiah Temple in Chicago, where he served until 1929. *Reform Judaism,* 207–8.

78. Felix A. Levy, "Joseph Stolz," memorial address, *CCAR Fifty-Second Annual Convention* 51: 253.

79. Mrs. Joseph [Blanche R.] Stolz, *Report of the National Committee on Hebrew Union College Scholarships,* National Federation of Temple Sisterhoods; Mrs. Joseph [Blanche] Stolz, "The Hebrew Union College Yesterday and Today," *Union Tidings* 10 (March 1930): 9; Blanche Stolz, "Hebrew College Scholarship Fund," *Sisterhood Messenger* (West Virginia), March 1925; and "Message Delivered by Mrs. Stolz at Executive Board Luncheon in Chicago, June 18, 1933," 1/7, Stolz papers; Blanche Stolz to co-worker, 6 March 1931, and 9 September 1936, 36/3; and Blanche R. Stolz to co-worker, 7 January 1936, 28 February 1936, and 10 April 1936, 31/2, WRJ.

80. Transcript of Proceedings, Thirteenth Biennial Assembly (1939), 224, *PNFTS,* 3/2; Transcript of Proceedings, Fourteenth Biennial Assembly (1941), 127–31, *PNFTS,* 3/3; Proceedings of the Fourteenth Biennial Assembly, 202–3, *PNFTS* 4 (1942–47); and Albert J. May, "Presentation of Blanche R. Stolz Trophy," Proceedings of the Fifteenth Biennial Assembly, 105, *PNFTS* 4 (1942–47), box 1, WRJ.

81. In terms of her civic work, already in Dayton, Ohio, Sadie had served as president of the Visiting Nurse Association. She founded the Dallas Visiting Nurse Association in 1934, to provide adequate health care for the poor, especially for mothers delivering babies at home. She also launched a Women's Exchange that met monthly to bake goods and sew decorative items for sale downtown during the Christmas holidays. Transcript of Proceedings, Eleventh Biennial Assembly (1935), 176, *PNFTS,* 2/5, WRJ; http://www.huc.edu/aja/lefkowitz.htm; Cristol, *Light in the Prairie* 261, 94–95; and Weiner, *Jewish Stars,* 221.

82. Weiner, *Jewish Stars,* 219–21; "1915–1917, National Federation of Temple Sisterhoods: Officers and Executive Board," n.p.; "Report of Committee on Nominations," 26, *PNFTS,* box 1, vol. 1; 1919–1931 National Standing Committees, n.p., box 1, vol. 2; Reports of National Standing Committees, Eighteenth Annual Report, 71–73, *PNFTS* 11 (1931), box 1; Transcript of Proceedings, Ninth Biennial Assembly (1931), 202–3, *PNFTS,* 2/4; and Transcript of Proceedings, Eleventh Biennial Assembly (1935), 180, *PNFTS,* 2/5, WRJ.

83. Http://www.huc.edu/aja/lefkowitz.htm; Reports of National Standing

Committees (1933), Twenty-first Annual Report, 55–56, *PNFTS* 11 (1931), box 1; Transcript of Proceedings, Eleventh Biennial Assembly (1935), 178–82, *PNFTS* 2/5; and Mrs. David [Sadie] Lefkowitz, "Let Us Question Ourselves," *Topics and Trends* (May-June 1936), 3, 69/2, WRJ.

84. Report of the National Committee on Jewish Literature for the Blind, *PNFTS* 4 (1942–47): 199–202, box 1, WRJ.

85. Weiner, *Jewish Stars,* 163–74.

86. *JWA,* s.v. "Wise, Louise Waterman"; *EJ,* s.v. "Wise, Stephen Samuel"; *The Personal Letters of Stephen Wise,* ed. Justine Wise Polier and James Waterman Wise (Boston: Beacon Press, 1956), 24; Wise, *Legends of Louise,* 13, 27–29, 67, 71, 86–87; Stephen S. Wise, *Challenging Years: The Autobiography of Stephen Wise* (New York: G. P. Putnam's Sons, 1949), xiv; and Lebeson, *Recall to Life,* 300.

87. Report of the National Committee on Programs, 31 October 1930, 83; and 31 October 1931, 81, *PNFTS,* box 1, vol. 11; and *The Sisterhood Lecture Bureau* (Cincinnati, Ohio: National Federation of Temple Sisterhoods, [1916?], box 25, circular file 4, WRJ. Felix Levy served as rabbi of Congregation Emanuel in Chicago from 1908 to 1955.

88. Though Women's League grew out of the United Synagogue of America, the lay arm of the Conservative Movement, both stemmed from the mandate of JTS's president, Solomon Schechter.

89. *JWA,* s.v. "Jung, Irma Rothschild."

90. Arthur G. Degen, remarks, *The Jewish Center Annual Dinner in Honor of Rabbi and Mrs. Leo Jung,* 8 June 1987, 4; *Jewish Center Bulletin,* 29 May 1957, 6; Meeting of the membership of the Jewish Center, minutes, 7 December 1932, Jewish Center Archives; Gertrude Cohen, phone conversation with author, 18 June 2000; Jenna Weissman Joselit, conversation with author, 11 May 2000; Norman Lamm, phone conversation with author, 30 May 2000; and Martin Schwarzchild, remarks, *The Jewish Center Annual Dinner in Honor of Rabbi and Mrs. Leo Jung,* 8 June 1987, 11.

91. *JWA,* s.v. "Jung, Irma Rothschild"; and Schwarzchild, remarks, *Jewish Center Annual Dinner,* 11.

92. *Jewish Center Bulletin,* 10 May 1940, 3; 18 September 1942, 12; 16 October 1942, 4; 13 November 1956, 5; 3 April 1957, 6; 4 December 1953, 4; 18 December 1953, 3; 19–20 February 1954, 5; 11 November 1955, 5; 2 March 1956, 5; and Degen, remarks, *Jewish Center Annual Dinner,* 4. The quote is from the *Jewish Center Bulletin,* 5 June 1964, 4.

93. Leo Jung, "Woman's Threefold Role of Education," *Jewish Center Bulletin,* 3 January 1964, 1; and idem, *The Path of a Pioneer: The Autobiography of Leo Jung,* The Jewish Library, vol. 8, ed. Leo Jung (New York: Soncino Press, 1980), 55–56.

94. Jung, *Path of a Pioneer,* 221.

95. "Council of Wives of Rabbis," *United Synagogue Recorder* (October 1926): 33.

96. *United Synagogue Recorder* (October 1927): 23.

97. Raphael, *Profiles*, 69.

98. Http://huc.edu/aja/berk.htm; and Henry Berkowitz, *Intimate Glimpses of the Rabbi's Career* (Cincinnati, Ohio: Hebrew Union College Press, 1921), 121–22. See below, chapters 3 and 4, for other examples of the use of this term. Henry Berkowitz's wife, Flora Brunn, whom he married in 1883, did fulfill those roles for him. Mabel Lyon, "Rabbis at Home," *Jewish Criterion* (Pittsburgh), 20 September 1957, 32.

99. *Personal Letters of Stephen Wise*, 25–26.

100. Ibid., 41.

101. Rosenblatt, *Days of My Years*, 62.

102. Ibid., 62–63, 128; Jan Kaufman, e-mail correspondence with author, winter 2000; and Judy Chernak, e-mail correspondence with author, 13 June 2000.

103. Eisenstein, *Reconstructing Judaism*, 118.

104. Judith and Ira Eisenstein published a number of cantatas; she wrote the music and he the words. See, for example, *What Is Torah? A Cantata for Unison Chorus and Piano* (New York: Jewish Reconstructionist Foundation, [1943]); *Our Bialik: A Cantata for Unison Chorus and Piano* (New York: Jewish Reconstructionist Foundation, 1945); *Reborn: An Episode with Music* (New York: Jewish Reconstructionist Foundation, 1952); and *Thy Children Shall Return: A Cantata* (New York: The Reconstructionist Press, 1953).

105. Schwartz, *Tell Thy Children*, 63, 72.

106. Ibid., 84.

107. Cott, *Public Vows*, 167.

108. Nadell, *Conservative Judaism*, 78–79; and Bauman, *Harry H. Epstein*, 99.

109. Bauman, *Harry H. Epstein*, 101.

110. Carmel Forsythe, taped interview with Jack Wertheimer, 22 December 1922; and Carmel Forsythe to Ismar Schorsch, 8 March 1996, Ratner.

111. Geffen, interview.

112. Geffen, interview.

113. Reichert, interview; and *WWIAJ* (1938–39): 844.

114. Noveck, *Milton Steinberg*, 47–51.

115. Joseph Lelyveld, *Omaha Blues: A Memory Loop* (New York: Farrar, Straus and Giroux, 2005), 171–72. For more on Arthur Lelyveld and on the Fairmount Temple, see chapter 3.

116. For example, in 1910, Mrs. Morris Newfield served as president of the Ladies Aid Society, an auxiliary to her husband's Temple Emanu-El of Birmingham. Mrs. Abraham P. Hirmes, whose husband became rabbi of Congregation

Ahavath Achim in Atlanta in 1919, formed its Sisterhood. Mrs. Julia Feist Solomon, wife of George Solomon (rabbi of Congregation Mickve Israel, in Savannah, Georgia, from 1903 to 1945), served as president of the reorganized Temple Guild, the forerunner of the congregation's Sisterhood. Augusta Kohn, wife of Jacob Kohn, rabbi of Ansche Chesed in New York City (1911–31), served as president of her Sisterhood. A certain Rebbetzin Schwartz was "honored with the presidency of her Sisterhood" in 1926, while Rabbi Dr. J. Leonard Levy's wife served as president of the Rodeph Shalom Sisterhood in Pittsburgh from 1909 to 1911. Elovitz, *Jewish Life in Dixie,* 46; Bauman, *Harry H. Epstein,* 52; Rubin, *Third to None,* 225–26, 237, 295, 318, 326; Lebeson, *Recall to Life,* 19; "Council of Wives of Rabbis," 33; and *Jewish Criterion* (Pittsburgh), 20 September 1957, 33.

    117. Hyamson, "Rabbi's Wife," 585.

    118. Mrs. Herman Cohen, "The Sisterhood's Share in Creating a Jewish Environment," *Outlook* 9 (September 1938): 17.

NOTES TO CHAPTER 3

    1. This expression is commonly used to describe the miracle of the Hanukkah story.

    2. Personal files of Lilly S. Routtenberg.

    3. Nadell, *Conservative Judaism,* 212–14. Personal information and quotes, unless otherwise noted, are taken from Routtenberg, interview.

    4. Similarly Naomi Greenberg Cohen, whose husband, Seymour Cohen, served as rabbi of Anshe Emet in Chicago, Illinois, from 1961 to 1991, was active in Jewish life before her marriage. Because of this, family and friends teased her that she ought to marry a rabbi. Cohen, interview.

    5. Previous to this, Routtenberg had written invocations, poems, skits, and plays for her local Sisterhood and for Women's League. See, for example, "Ode to Spring," *Outlook* 30 (May 1960): 8; idem, "Once Upon a Rabbinate," 12; and *Leket Divray Torah,* 83.

    6. *The Jewish Catalogue,* comp. and ed. Richard Siegel, Michael Strassfeld, and Sharon Strassfeld, is generally acknowledged to be the first comprehensive English-language how-to book on Jewish life. It did not appear until 1973.

    7. Emphasis mine. Routtenberg further explained that her experience as a rebbetzin "stood her in good stead" even in her old age. In the assisted-living facility where she lived when I interviewed her, Routtenberg felt she succeeded as an unofficial resource for her peers because of her experience as a rebbetzin. She died in 1998.

    8. Solomon, *Company,* 62–64; Brown, *Setting a Course,* 68, 247; May, *Homeward Bound,* 49–53; Chafe, *American Woman,* 107–9; and Cott, *Public Vows,* 186.

9. May, *Homeward Bound,* 54–57.

10. Caroli, *First Ladies,* 191, 195; Chafe, *American Woman,* 42–43; and Ware, *Holding Their Own,* 171–72.

11. Chafe, *American Woman,* 42–43.

12. Kirkley, "'Mrs. God,'" 14–15, 19.

13. Mayerberg, *Chronicle,* 44; and Adler, *Roots,* 159. Samuel Mayerberg served as rabbi of B'nai Jehudah from 1928 to 1945.

14. "Ancestral Beginnings," "A Teenager's Friday Night in the Late 90's"; "Memoirs 1890" folder; "Biography"; and "Biographical data folder," box 14, Herman H. and Mignon L. Rubenovitz Papers, JTSA; Rubenovitz, *Waking Heart,* 172; Israel J. Kazis, eulogy delivered 29 November 1968, reprinted in *Temple Topics* [December 1968], Mishkan Tefila Archives, Chestnut Hill, Mass.; and Miriam Feinberg, phone conversation with author, 8 February 2000.

15. Rubenovitz, *Waking Heart,* 203, 208; Mrs. Herman H. [Mignon] Rubenovitz to Anne Kapell, 23 June 1961, "Boston Chapters," folder, rg 15, HA; Mignon L. Rubenovitz, "Henrietta Szold, My Teacher and Friend," n.d., Mishkan Tefila Archives; "Biography"; and "Biographical data folder," box 14, Rubenovitz papers; and Feinberg, conversation.

16. "Biography"; "Biographical data folder"; and *Jewish Advocate* (Boston), 15 August 1957, box 14, Rubenovitz papers; Rubenovitz, *Altars,* 8; Feinberg, conversation; Rubenovitz, *Waking Heart,* 26, 104; and Mignon L. Rubenovitz, "Condolence Call," *Outlook* 22 (December 1951): 8. The Rubenovitzes did for Conservative Judaism in New England what Fanny and Jacob Minkin had done in upstate New York and Bertha and David Aronson had accomplished in the Midwest. Heller, "Rebbitzen," 12–13, 19–20. For more on Minkin and Aronson, see chapter 2.

17. Kirkley, "'Mrs. God,'" 14–15, 19; and Bernice Kazis, phone conversation with author, 8 February 2000.

18. Rubenovitz, *Waking Heart,* 19, 265–70.

19. Rubenovitz's mother had also had regular household help, and Rubenovitz undoubtedly expected to have a similar lifestyle. Rubenovitz, *Waking Heart,* 232; Bobbie Richards, phone conversation with author, 8 February 2000; and Feinberg, conversation.

20. Rubenovitz, *Waking Heart,* 98, 244, 263, 266–69, 271, 275, 284; Rubenovitz, "Condolence Call," 8; Dorothy Crandall, "Jewish Homes Hum in Preparation for Passover," unidentified newspaper clipping, Mishkan Tefila Archives; "Mignon Rubenovitz . . . Remembered," "Mignon Rubenovitz" folder, rg 10, HA; Mignon L. Rubenovitz, "Museum within a Temple," *Jewish Advocate* (Boston), 11 December 1958, 7; and Jen S. Margolis, "Mignon L. Rubenovitz 75 Years Young," unidentified newspaper clipping, box 14, Rubenovitz papers.

21. Kazis, conversation. Ruth Wolf Levi, whose husband, Harry Levi, served

as rabbi of the neighboring Reform congregation, Temple Israel, from 1911 to 1939, was also highly educated and active as a rabbi's wife in her congregation and community. Educated at Mount de Chantal Academy, in Wheeling, West Virginia, she also graduated from the Cincinnati College of Music. Levi, "I Married a Rabbi," in *I Married*, ed. Bader, 192. For more on Levi, see below chapter 4.

22. In 1945, Rubenovitz's keynote address to the New England Branch of Women's League, titled "Two Great Women of Our Times," focused on Schechter and Szold. "Women's League Holds Conference," *Jewish Advocate* (Boston), 15 November 1945, n.p., box 14, Rubenovitz papers.

23. "Early history" file, WLA.

24. Rubenovitz, *Waking Heart*, 57, 98, 103, 205–6; Jacobs, "Beginnings of Hadassah," 232; Mrs. Herman L. [Mignon] Rubenovitz, "The Pursuit of Knowledge," *Hadass-A-Gram: The Voice of the Boston Chapter of Hadassah* (December 1954): 1, Mishkan Tefila Archives; and Kazis, conversation.

25. Carol Bosworth Kutsher, "The Early Years of Hadassah: 1912–1921" (Ph.D. dissertation, Jewish Brandeis University, 1976), 42; Judith G. Epstein to Mrs. Herman H. [Mignon] Rubenovitz, 29 October 1929, "Epstein, Jacobs, Greenberg correspondence," folder; and Mrs. Herman H. [Mignon] Rubenovitz to Board of Directors, 17 December 1930, Boston Chapters, rg 15/Chapters, HA; Rubenovitz, *Waking Heart*, 104; and "Jewish Preparation for Community Living," box 1 (1919–50), WLA.

26. Mrs. Morris [Althea O.] Silverman, ed., "Woman's Field," *United Synagogue Recorder* (April 1943): 16.

27. See, for example, "The Synagogue Pilgrim on a Long Trek," 1 January 1953, n.p.; and "The Fabulous 'Marcus the Africaner,'" 14 March 1957, n.p., both in *Jewish Advocate* (Boston); "Candlelight," *Outlook* 14 (December 1943): 4–5, and "Living Waters," *Outlook* 9 (May 1939): 9–10.

28. "Donor Luncheon Program to Feature Dramatic Play and Address by John Haynes Holmes," unidentified newspaper clipping; and Sisterhood Fortieth Anniversary Program, 24 March 1949, box 14, Rubenovitz papers.

29. Rubenovitz, *Waking Heart*, 281–83; and idem, *Light*, 166.

30. Rubenovitz, "Museum within a Temple," 7; and *Bulletin of Temple Mishkan Tefila*, undated, in Mishkan Tefila Archives. A Jewish museum for the Conservative Movement had been proposed many years earlier by Mayer Sulzberger, but it was not until 1931 that such a museum was dedicated at JTS. Julie Miller and Richard I. Cohen, "A Collision of Cultures: The Jewish Museum and the Jewish Theological Seminary," in *Tradition Renewed*, vol. 2, 311–16.

31. "Museum Dedication: Sisterhood Temple Mishkan Tefila," 25 December 1940, Mishkan Tefila Archives; Rubenovitz, "Museum within a Temple," 7; Rubenovitz, *Waking Heart*, 248–52; and idem, *Winecup*, n.p. Other rebbetzins exhibited similar aspirations in later years. For example, Sylvia Plotkin, wife of

Albert Plotkin of Temple Beth Israel in Phoenix, Arizona, founded the Judaica Museum in that city in 1966. She hoped it would enable her to foster a better understanding of Judaism and illustrate the role of Jews in Arizona. Like Rubenovitz, Plotkin considered her work as director to be the most fulfilling part of her life. *Arizona Republic/Phoenix Gazette*, 25 April 1996, obit.

32. Rubenovitz, "Museum within a Temple," 7; *EJ*, s.v. "Haggadah, Passover"; and Rubenovitz, *Waking Heart*, 252–53.

33. Rubenovitz, *Waking Heart*, 250–53; Rubenovitz, "Museum within a Temple," 7; and Kazis, conversation.

34. For example, excerpts from *Altars of My Fathers* appeared in *Outlook*, May 1952 and June 1954.

35. Rubenovitz, *Altars*, 79.

36. "Museum Dedication: Sisterhood Temple Mishkan Tefila," 25 December 1940, Mishkan Tefila Archives; *Jewish Advocate* (Boston), 11 November 1948, box 14, Rubenovitz papers; Mrs. Israel Jewish [Bernice] Kazis, "The Past as Prologue," in *Our Congregation 1858–1973: Temple Mishkan Tefila* (Boston: Temple Mishkan Tefila, 1973), n.p.; Richards, conversation; and Kazis, conversation.

37. Rubenovitz, *Waking Heart*, 94–96, 230–31, 264.

38. Rubenovitz, *Light*; and "Capacity Crowd Fills Auditorium of Temple Mishkan Tefila in Tribute to Rabbi Herman H. Rubenovitz," *Jewish Advocate* (Boston), 27 September 1945, box 14, Rubenovitz papers.

39. Robert Gordis to Abraham Bloom, 30 March 1964; Judah Nadich to Abraham Bloom, 13 April 1964; Abraham Sachar to Friends, 16 April, 1964; and Mrs. Siegfried Kramarsky to Mignon Rubenovitz, 28 April 1964; in *A Tribute to Rabbi Emeritus and Mrs. Herman H. Rubenovitz on the Occasion of Their Eightieth Birthdays*, 10 May 1964, Mishkan Tefila Archives.

40. Rubenovitz, *Waking Heart*; and Israel J. Kazis, eulogy, *Temple Topics* [December 1968]. Herman died in 1966. The book appeared a year later. The Foreword, written by Louis Finkelstein, reads as if he wrote it only for Herman's section. An editorial note for the article "Then a Spark Was Kindled," 7 September 1961, *Jewish Advocate* (Boston), box 14, Rubenovitz papers, explains that the selection is taken from a "forthcoming volume of memoirs by Mrs. Rubenovitz under the title 'Pages from the Journal of a Rabbi's Wife.'"

41. Rubenovitz, *Waking Heart*, 71, 95, 106,166, 189.

42. Ibid., 264.

43. Ibid., 167.

44. Ibid.

45. Brickner's mother was herself Jewishly knowledgeable. Suspicious of Benderly's school at first, she chose to send only her daughters and not her sons. Brickner, "As I Remember," 53.

46. Interview with Rebecca Ena Aaronson Brickner, 23–24 February 1983,

American Jewish Committee Oral History Collection, New York Public Library; Notes for "B'nai B'rith Great Books Series" talk, undated, 7/1, Barnett and Rebecca A. Brickner Papers, AJA; Silver, *Portrait*, 13; and Brickner, "As I Remember," 55–56. Benderly early on recognized the potential of young women for the field of Jewish education. As the *Jewish Comment* noted of his early experiments: "He wisely chose Jewish girls . . . who are able intelligently to grasp his ideas . . . and they are now pursuing advanced studies." Rebecca Brickner was one of those "girls." Quoted in Fein, *Making*, 189.

47. Brickner used a Hebrew typewriter that she claims had been made especially for Benderly by the Remington Co. She believed it to be the first Hebrew typewriter in the world. Brickner, "As I Remember," 57.

48. Interview with Rebecca Ena Aaronson Brickner; Notes for "B'nai B'rith Great Books Series" talk, undated, 7/1; and "Biography—Rebecca A. Brickner," 8/7, Brickner papers; *The Jewish Communal Register of New York City 1917–18* (New York: Kehillah of New York City, 1918), 459; Jacob Kohn to Herman Rubenovitz, 18 February 1914, in Rubenovitz, *Waking Heart*, 135–36; Scult, *Judaism*, 392n56; Alexander M. Dushkin, *Living Bridges: Memoirs of an Educator* (Jerusalem: Keter, 1975), 10n11. Dushkin lists the "boys" and then, after an "also," he lists the women; and Kaufman, "Jewish Education," in *Tradition Renewed*, vol. 1, 584–85.

49. Brickner, "As I Remember," 54.

50. Interview with Rebecca Ena Aaronson Brickner; and Notes for "B'nai B'rith Great Books Series" talk, undated, 7/1, Brickner papers.

51. Jacobs, "Beginnings of Hadassah," 242; Rosenblatt, "Beginning of Hadassah," 6; Kutsher, "Early Years of Hadassah," 42, 125; Notes for "B'nai B'rith Great Books Series" talk, undated, 7/1; and "How Hadassah Was Born," 20 April 1950, 6/8, Brickner papers.

52. Silver, *Portrait*, 13. Aviva Friedland Polish also shared with her husband David (rabbi of the Free Synagogue, now called Beth Emet The Free Synagogue, in Evanston, Illinois, from 1950 to 1980) a fervent commitment to Zionism, Jewish life, and the Hebrew language, and this is what initially drew them to each other. NAORR session.

53. Interestingly, Brickner's name does not appear on any student roster of the period, though Martha Neumark's name does. Boxes B-14 and D-12, Hebrew Union College Papers, AJA; and Nadell, *Women*, 62–72.

54. Interview with Rebecca Ena Aaronson Brickner; Balfour Brickner, interview; Invitation to Ladies Meeting, 10/3, Brickner papers; and Silver, *Portrait*, 26.

55. Samson Benderly to Rebecca Brickner, 14 September 1923, 6/2, Brickner papers. He wrote the letter to "Tobacco," his nickname for Rebecca. The two remained in close touch throughout their lives. Brickner, "As I Remember," 58.

56. Balfour Brickner, remarks, "Rebecca Brickner: Luncheon in Honor of

Her Seventy-fifth Birthday," Fairmount Temple, 28 January 1969, tape recording, AJA.

57. *The Fairmount Cookbook,* ed. Irene Rousuck (Cleveland, Ohio: Fairmount Temple Sisterhood, 1957). Brickner contributed many recipes for traditional holiday foods, including *kreplach,* sweet and sour cabbage, and matzo balls. Though she described how to observe the holidays and included relevant blessings, she did not explain the laws of kashrut. At the same time, the recipes did not call for any non-kosher ingredients and did not entail mixing milk and meat. Fairmount Temple rabbi Lisa Eiduson recalls her grandmother relying on Brickner's Passover almond torte recipe from this cookbook. Arlene Fine, "Rebbetzins Rev Up," *Cleveland Jewish News,* 30 March 2001, 38.

58. Helen-Rose Klausner to Rebecca Brickner, 13 February 1964, 8/8, Brickner papers; and Brickner, remarks, "Rebecca Brickner: Luncheon." According to Balfour, Rebecca did much more pastoral work than her husband.

59. For example, note the following invitation: "Rabbi and Mrs. Samuel J. Abrams extend hearty New Year greetings to the members and worshippers of Temple Ohabei Shalom. In accordance with their annual custom, Rabbi and Mrs. Abrams will be pleased to receive all callers at their home, 24 Fuller St., Brookline, to exchange New Year greetings on Sunday afternoon, September 20." *Temple Ohabei Shalom Bulletin,* September 11, 1925, 2, in 1/5, A. Irma Cohen Papers, AJA.

60. Brickner, remarks, "Rebecca Brickner: Luncheon"; Brickner, interview; and NAORR session.

61. "Y.P. C.s 15th Anniversary," 8/ 2; and "YPC Celebrates 15th Anniversary on March 21st," *Mosaic* (March 1964): 1, in 9/2, Brickner Papers.

62. "Mrs. Brickner Tells of Her Faith in Girls of Today," *Cleveland News,* 25 April 1926, in 9/3; and 7/1-6, Brickner papers; and Brickner, interview.

63. Beginning in 1926, the community worked to create a College of Studies. Brickner was a founder and, in 1952, first acting chairman of the Cleveland Institute of Jewish Studies, a precursor to the College. The College was established and accredited in 1963. Convocation of the Cleveland College of Jewish Studies *Proceedings,* 13 December [1971]; and Louis Hurwich, "Origin and Development of Jewish Teacher-training Schools in the United States: A Brief Historical Survey," in *The Education of American Jewish Teachers,* ed. Oscar I. Janowsky (Boston: Beacon Press, 1967), 6.

64. Lauren B. Tishkoff, "Jewish Scholar Rebecca Brickner leaving Cleveland," *Cleveland Press,* 25 October 1981; "Biography—Rebecca A. Brickner," 8/7; 7/1-6; 8/5; Stephen S. Wise to Rifkahleben, 27 April 1936, 6/10; and "How Hadassah Was Born," 20 April 1950, 6/8, Brickner papers. Rebecca incorrectly recalled this convention occurring in 1934; Katz, *Beth El Story,* n.p.; and Transcript of Ninth Biennial Assembly (1931), 2/4, *PNFTS,* WRJ.

65. "Biography—Rebecca A. Brickner," 8/7; 7/1-6; 8/5; Katz, *Beth El Story,*

n.p.; and Notes for "B'nai B'rith Great Books Series" talk, undated, 7/1, Brickner papers.

66. Brickner, interview.

67. Rebecca Brickner to Barnett Brickner, 15 July 1927, personal files of Balfour Brickner, New York, N.Y. For more on the letters between Barnett and Rebecca Brickner, see Shuly Rubin Schwartz, "Rebecca Aaronson Brickner: Preacher, Teacher and Rebbetzin in Israel," *American Jewish Archives* 54 (2002): 64–83.

68. Rebecca Brickner to Barnett Brickner, 3 August 1927, personal files of Brickner.

69. Rebecca Brickner to Barnett Brickner, 15 July 1927, personal files of Brickner.

70. Barnett Brickner to Rebecca Brickner, 10 August 1927, personal files of Brickner.

71. Rebecca Brickner to Barnett Brickner, 15 July and 3 August 1927, personal files of Brickner.

72. Rebecca Brickner to Barnett Brickner, 25 March 1932, personal files of Brickner.

73. Rebecca Brickner to Barnett Brickner, 17 May 1932, personal files of Brickner.

74. Rebecca Brickner to Barnett Brickner, 2 May 1932, personal files of Brickner. Shmuel Yosef Agnon (1888–1970) became a renowned Hebrew writer who won the Nobel Prize for literature in 1966, the first granted to a Hebrew writer. The first edition of his collected works appeared in four volumes in 1931. Devorah Baron (1887–1956) was one of the few female Hebrew fiction writers of the era. Rahel Bluwstein (1890–1931) was a Hebrew poet whose clear, uncomplicated style made her very popular with the public. In the early 1930s, these writers were virtually unknown in the United States except among a select group of Jewish studies scholars and Hebraists. Conversation with Avraham Holtz, conversation with author, 17 February 2000; and Gershon Shaked, "Judaism in Translation: Thoughts on the Alexandria Hypothesis," in *Hebrew in America: Perspectives and Prospects,* ed. Alan Mintz (Detroit, Mich.: Wayne State University Press, 1993), 291–92.

75. Rebecca Brickner to Barnett Brickner, 14 June 1932, personal files of Brickner.

76. Isaac Berkson (1891–1975), another "Benderly boy," was a Jewish educator and philosopher. He was in Palestine from 1928 to 1935, having gone in response to an invitation from Szold to survey its Jewish schools. Bertha Schoolman (1897–1974), Brickner's classmate at both Hunter College and JTS's Teachers Institute, was a well-known Zionist and Jewish educator. She taught at the Central Jewish Institute in New York and worked with her husband, Albert, founding director of Cejwin Camps, on Cejwin's educational program-

ming and administration. She also held various positions of national leadership in Hadassah.

77. Rebecca Brickner to Barnett Brickner, 12, 15, and 18 April 1932, personal files of Brickner. Their paths also crossed in 1935 at Hadassah's Cleveland convention when the group decided to assume responsibility for Youth Aliyah. Tamar de Sola Pool played a pivotal role in convincing Hadassah to undertake this project. For more on this, see below. Dash, *Summoned*, 253.

78. Joseph G. Klausner (1874–1958), literary critic, historian, and Zionist, settled in Palestine in 1919. When Hebrew University was established, he assumed the chair of Hebrew literature. Klausner was especially interested in the transformation of the Hebrew language into a modern spoken tongue.

79. Rebecca Brickner to Barnett Brickner, 10 and 13 April, 2 and 17 May, 6 June 1932, personal files of Brickner; and Silver, *Portrait*, 67.

80. Rebecca Brickner to Barnett Brickner, 10 April and 2 and 8 May 1932, personal files of Brickner.

81. Rebecca Brickner to Barnett Brickner, 6 and 28 June 1932, personal files of Brickner.

82. Harry Ettelson to Rebecca Brickner, 2 May 1958, 6/13, Brickner papers; and Joseph I. Weiss to Rebecca Brickner, 27 May 1958; Aryeh Lev (rabbi) to Rebecca Brickner, 19 May 1958; and Alexander Segal to Rebecca Brickner, 20 May 1958, 6/14, Brickner papers.

83. "Sisterhood—60th Anniversary," 20 January 1970, 8/1, 8/2, and 8/3, Brickner papers.

84. The World Union for Progressive Judaism was founded in England in 1926. 6/11; Rebecca Brickner to Friend, 20 February 1968; "They Adopt a Temple," *The Press*, 23 January 1964, in 9/2, Brickner papers; and Meyer, *Response to Modernity*, 217, 335–37.

85. Joe Pirsky, remarks, "Rebecca Brickner: Luncheon"; Iris Fishman, remarks, "Tribute to Rebecca Brickner," Rebecca Brickner Cultural Day, 22 February 2000, personal files of Brickner; and Lois Cooper, "Honored, Revered on her 80th Birthday," *The Sun Press*, 28 February 1974, in 8/10, Brickner papers.

86. Barry [Friedman] to Rebecca Brickner, 14 February 1974, 8/10, Brickner papers.

87. Lelyveld, remarks, "Rebecca Brickner: Luncheon."

88. "Program Suggestions," 1938, p. 9, 33/2; *Topics and Trends*, September-October 1940, 69/2, WRJ; and NAORR session. George Lieberman served as rabbi of Central Synagogue in Rockville Centre, New York, from 1954 to 1984.

89. Lelyveld, *Omaha Blues*, 171–72; and Reichert, interview. For more on this mentoring role vis-à-vis post–World War II rebbetzins, see below, chapter 4.

90. "Convocation of the Cleveland College of Jewish Studies Proceedings," 13 December 1971, personal files of Brickner.

91. "Commencement of the Cleveland College of Jewish Studies Proceedings," 11 June 1972; "Review of the Cleveland College of Jewish Studies," 1972; and "Prophecy, Ethics and Messianism in the Teachings of Professor Joseph Klausner,"(Hebrew) M.H.L. thesis, Cleveland College of Jewish Studies, personal files of Brickner; 9/5; and "Biography—Rebecca A. Brickner," 8/7, Brickner papers. The title of Brickner's thesis is misleading. She wrote about the development of prophecy, ethics, and messianism, with a special emphasis on Isaiah and Jeremiah. Information on Klausner is limited to chapter 6, which reviews his life and accomplishments and his influence both on Brickner personally and on the Jewish people.

92. Cooper, "Honored, Revered"; David E. Powers to Rebecca Brickner, 18 February 1974; and "Tribute to Mrs. Barnett R. [Rebecca] Brickner," 22 February 1974, 8/10, Brickner papers.

93. Barnett Brickner, "President's Message," *CCARY* 65 (1955): 14; and Silver, *Portrait,* 104. Silver mentioned two other equally capable rebbetzins: Avis Clavitz Shulman and Goldie Adler. Samuel Silver, "A Great Woman," *Las Vegas Israelite,* 16 August 1974, in 8/10, Brickner papers.

94. Brickner, interview; Nadell, *Women,* 137; "Biography—Rebecca A. Brickner," 8/7, Brickner papers; personal files of Brickner; and Interview with Rebecca Ena Aaronson Brickner.

95. Tamar de Sola Pool, "Comment," *Problems,* 224–25.

96. *EJ,* s.v. "Hirschensohn"; and *Who's Who in World Jewry* (1965), 745. *Who's Who in American Jewry* [*WWIAJ*](1938/9) incorrectly lists Pool's date of birth as 1893. Biography, 15 August 1946, "articles, newspaper clippings," folder 2; and Tamar de Sola Pool, "Eliezer ben Yehuda: Personal Reminiscences," presented at the Ninth World Congress of Sociology—Sociolinguistic Section, Uppsala University, Sweden, 1978, *Israel Digest,* 9 February 1979, 15, 1/1, rg 13, HA. The specifics of their formal Jewish education are unclear. As an adult, Tehilla took classes with individual rabbis, including Milton Steinberg. "Shall Jewish Women Have Religious Equality?" undated sermon, 7/2, Tehilla Lichtenstein Papers, AJA.

97. *JWA,* s.v. "Lichtenstein, Tehilla," and s.v. "Pool, Tamar de Sola"; *AJYB* 83 (1983): 360; *Who Was Who in America* [*WWWIA*] 7: 994. "Dear Girls," *Hunter College Bulletin,* 6 June 1917, Tamar de Sola Pool Scrapbook; and Unmarked autobiographical excerpt, "Mrs. Pool Corres. and Misc." box, Pool papers; and Tamar de Sola Pool, "A Page from the Treasure-Store of Memory," *Journal in Honor of the Ninetieth Birthday of Tamar de Sola Pool,* 1/19, rg 13, HA.

98. Pool, "A Page from the Treasure-Store of Memory"; *AJYB* 83 (1983): 361; Secretary, board of trustees to Tamar Hirschensohn, 31 October 1916; unidentified newspaper clipping and certificate, 27 April 1911, "Tamar and David

Engagements letters . . . Other early correspondence, clippings about Tamar's early career, 1910–1917" folder; and Unmarked autobiographical excerpt, "Mrs. Pool Corres. and Misc." box, Pool papers.

99. *EJ*, s.v. "Pool, David de Sola"; *WWWIA* 7: 994; Pool, "A Page from the Treasure-Store of Memory"; and unmarked autobiographical excerpt, "Mrs. Pool Corres. and Misc." box, Pool papers.

100. David de Sola Pool to Tamar, 5 January 1917, "Tamar and David Engagement Letters" folder, Pool papers.

101. Bernard Postal, "Death Sunders Unique Cultural Partnership of 53 Years," *American Examiner-Jewish Week*, 10 December 1970, 8ff, in "Mrs. Pool Corres. and Misc." box, Pool papers.

102. "Dear Family and Friends of Shearith Israel," 22 April 1980, 1/1, rg 13, HA; Sue Gardner, "Tamar de Sola Pool: Daughter, Wife, Mother, Grandma of Celebrities Is Very Much Herself!" *Jewish Week-American Examiner*, 13 May 1979, 28; Naomi de Sola Pool, phone conversation with author, 11 June 2000; and "Addresses Bible Class," *New York Times*, 9 May 1927.

103. Pool, conversation; and Irma and Abraham Cardozo, interview.

104. Pool, conversation; Ellen Umansky, phone conversation with author, 12 June 2000; unmarked personal reminiscences, "Corres. etc." folder, Pool papers; and Lemle, ed., *Precious Memories*, 15–16.

105. 1/2, rg 13, HA; "Food Conservation and the Jewish Diet," *American Jewish Chronicle*, 11 October 1918; and "Home-making in Jerusalem after the War," *Young Judaean*, 356–58, undated clipping, in Tamar de Sola Pool Scrap-book, Pool papers. .

106. Fineman, *Woman of Valor*, 311; Henrietta Szold to Tamar de Sola Pool, 23 July 1924, Pool papers; Louis M. Levitsky to Tamar de Sola Pool, 20 October 1937; Ida M. Cohen to Tamar de Sola Pool, February 1937; [Mrs. Henry J.] Sophie S. Friendly to Tamar de Sola Pool, 12 January 1939; and Juria? to Tamar, 31 October 1939, "Dr. & Mrs. Pool, Notes, Articles , Corres. 1920s–(1972)" box; and "Dr. and Mrs. Pool Lectures" folder, Pool papers. Pool was also invited to give radio addresses on Jewish topics. Radio scripts, Rochester, N.Y., 16 January 1945; and WEVD, 19 May 1946; 1/2, rg 13, HA.

107. Tamar de Sola Pool to Rose [Jacobs?], 17 June 1937; and Tamar de Sola Pool to Rose Jacobs, 20 January 1938, "Mrs. Pool-Corres.-Hadassah" folder, "Dr. & Mrs. Pool, Notes, Articles, Corres. 1920s–(1972)" box, Pool papers.

108. For examples of her articles, see her serial review, "Reminiscences of a Zionist Odyssey" (March 1937): 9–11; (May 1937): 7–8, 16; (January 1938): 76; (February 1938): 98–99; and (March 1938): 117. On Youth Aliyah, see "The Youth Aliyah Conference" (October 1937): 13–14; and the May 1938 issue, which reprints on its cover an excerpt from Eleanor Roosevelt's "My Day" column on Youth Aliyah. On Cyprus, see "Palestine Revisited" (May

1947): 5–7, 31; and "This Barbed Wire—These Bitter Herbs" (June-July 1947): 6–7, 28–29, 32. On the need for women to vote, see "A London Letter" (April 1938): 123–24, 139; and "Zionist Relations and Political Education" (November 1938): 31.

109. Marian G. Greenberg, "Tamar de Sola Pool's Ideas"; and Obituary press release, 1 June 1981, 1/19, rg 13, HA; Dash, *Summoned*, 253; Cardozo, interview; and Pool, conversation. Pool's daughter quipped that her mother was such an effective fundraiser that she could raise money from stones.

110. *Denver Post*, undated clipping, unmarked folder, Pool papers; and Radio Address to the City Chapter Membership Rally, 19 November 1940, 1/2, rg 13, HA.

111. Tamar de Sola Pool, "Exiles on Cyprus," *Highroad* (March 1948): 24–28, reprinted from *Survey Graphic* (June 1947); "This Barbed Wire—These Bitter Herbs," 6–7, 28–29, 32; and "Appeal Made to American Parents to Supply Educational Aid to Homeless Cyprus Youth," *New York Times*, 23 April 1947, in 1/2; letters in response to *Times* article, 1/8, rg 13, HA; Tamar de Sola Pool, "Children to Palestine," *Woman's Press* (June 1948): 6–8, 42; and Cardozo, interview.

112. "Appeal Made to American Parents"; "First Annual Luncheon NYS Committee of the American Mothers Association, Inc." program, 14 November 1968, "Mrs. Pool-notes, family corres.-1970s" folder, Pool papers; Gardner, "Tamar de Sola Pool," 28; and Cardozo, interview.

113. Dear Everybody, 20 May 1959, "Mrs. Pool Corres. and Misc." box, Pool papers; and Mrs. David [Tamar] de Sola Pool to Eleanor Roosevelt, 26 August 1959, 84/1, rg 4, HA.

114. Greetings to Inter-American Jewish Conference, 23–25 November 1941, 1/1, rg 13, HA; "Mrs. Pool Corres. and Misc."; *Daily Mirror*, 7 December 1955; D. Wachs to Tamar de Sola Pool, 7 December 1951; Mavis Morris to David and Tamar de Sola Pool, 27 January 1956; and Invitation, David and Tamar de Sola Pool Duologue, 18 October 1959, "Pool Corres., bulk 1950s," folder, Pool papers. Naomi de Sola Pool recalls her father playing the learned, scholarly role while her mother provided a light, humanistic touch. The power of their stage presence is apparent even in the written scripts. Pool, conversation.

115. (New York: Columbia University Press, 1955); (New York: National Jewish Welfare Board, 1943); and 1/17, rg 13, HA.

116. Pool, *Is There An Answer?* "Author's Note," n.p.; "*Is There an Answer* Corres. and Typescript" folder; and Judy Manischewitz to Tamar, 24 July 1962, "Dr. and Mrs. Pool, Duologs 1962" folder, "Dr. and Mrs. Pool, Corres, Bio, Mss. etc." box, Pool papers.

117. *Book of Prayer: According to the Custom of the Spanish and Portuguese Jews*, ed. David de Sola Pool (New York: Union of Sephardic Congrega-

tions, 1947); and Tamar de Sola Pool to Solomon Gaon, 1 July 1975, "Mrs. Pool Corres. and Misc." folder, Pool papers.

118. A reference to Gen. 2: 18. For more on this phrase, see chapter 2.

119. Pool, conversation; David de Sola Pool to Tamar de Sola Pool, 26 May 1936, unmarked folder; and "Mrs. D. de Sola Pool Coming January 10," *Jewish Post,* 31 December 1954, 1; and "Annual Journal and Purim Luncheon Women's Division, Central Sephardic Jewish Community of America, Inc.," 22 March 1972, "Mrs. Pool Corres. and Misc." folder, Pool papers.

120. *JWA,* s.v. "Lichtenstein, Tehilla"; *WWIWJ* (1965), 596; Pool, conversation; John J. Appel, "Christian Science and the Jews," *Jewish Social Studies* 31 (April 1969): 105; and *Reform Judaism,* 126–27. The latter source gives the date of their marriage as June 1919.

121. Appel, "Christian Science," 114; and *JWA,* s.v. "Lichtenstein, Tehilla." See also Ellen M. Umansky's comprehensive study, *From Christian Science to Jewish Science* (New York: Oxford University Press, 2005).

122. Appel, "Christian Science," 112–13; *JWA,* s.v. "Lichtenstein, Tehilla"; and Umansky, conversation.

123. Tehilla Lichtenstein papers, AJA. The way Lichtenstein's sermons were prepared also reflects the more mundane realities behind the evolution of women's professional lives. Before 1938, Lichtenstein's sermons and addresses were handwritten. After Morris died, his wife must have inherited either his typewriter or his typist, or both. All subsequent addresses are typed, a shift that surely facilitated her preparation. A volume of sermons written between 1938 and 1970 was published separately as *Applied Judaism: Selected Jewish Science Essays by Tehilla Lichtenstein,* essays selected and edited by Doris Friedman (New York: Society of Jewish Science, 1989). This particular collection includes primarily Lichtenstein's universalistic messages.

124. *JWA,* s.v. "Lichtenstein, Tehilla"; *WWIWJ* (1965), 596; Appel, "Christian Science," 114; and Lichtenstein papers.

125. "About Forgiving Yourself," 1948, 1953, 1958, 1/1, Lichtenstein papers; reprinted in *Applied Judaism,* 273–85.

126. "Shall Jewish Women Have Religious Equality?" undated, 7/2; "The Heart of a Mother," 14 May 1933, 10/5; and "The Changing Relations between Men and Women" [1939–45], 1/4, Lichtenstein papers; and Umansky, conversation.

127. "What Jewish Science Has Planned for You," undated, 8/1, Lichtenstein papers; and Appel, "Christian Science and the Jews," 114.

128. Lichtenstein explained that the Society did not join the Union of American Hebrew Congregations (despite the fact that Morris Lichtenstein was an ordained Reform rabbi) because it did not want to alienate members who belonged to Orthodox or Conservative synagogues. Appel, "Christian Science," 106n19.

129. *AJYB* (1983): 361; unmarked autobiographical excerpt, "Mrs. Pool Corres. and Misc." folder; and Duologue, 5 May 1960, Pool papers; and Umansky, conversation.

130. Pool, conversation.

131. Pool, conversation; Kirkley, "'Mrs. God,'" 19; Brickner, interview; interview with Rebecca Ena Aaronson Brickner; and Brickner, "Rebecca Brickner: Luncheon."

NOTES TO CHAPTER 4

1. Margaret Abrams, "Auto-biographical Notes" (unpublished). I am grateful to Jonathan D. Sarna for sharing these notes with me.

2. Abrams, "Auto-biographical Notes." JPS issued a third printing in 1962.

3. Edward S. Shapiro, *A Time for Healing: American Jewry since World War II,* in *Jewish People,* ed. Feingold, vol. 5, 162–63.

4. *I Married,* ed. Bader, 8, 9, 12.

5. Priscilla Wahl Stamm, "Her Church," in *I Married,* 29–30.

6. Ibid., 32.

7. Grace Tilton Shullenberger, "Her Privileges," in *I Married,* 37, 41.

8. Helen Mitchell Gibson, "Her Vacations," in *I Married,* 140.

9. Ruth Wolf Levi, "I Married a Rabbi," in *I Married,* 166.

10. Ibid., 166, 168. For example, Mae Talmadge Pruden, in "Her Special Interests," in *I Married,* 120, advised that "every minister's wife should be an authority in some field of interest or activity, if only that she may thus become more interesting to herself, her family, and her friends."

11. Levi, "I Married a Rabbi," 169.

12. Ibid., 170.

13. Ibid., 171. Ruth Stafford Peale, in "Her Home," in *I Married,* 70, described a similar no-win situation for the minister's wife.

14. Levi, "I Married a Rabbi," 173.

15. Katzoff, "Status," 8; Gerstein, "Reflections," 16–20; Shoni B. Levi, "Don't Look Now," 8, 13; "Another Point," 7; Wilner, "Rabbi's Wife," 9; Kose, "It Feels Good," 5, 9; Barras, "Wraps Off," 20–24; Kripke, "Why Crack Up," 13, 20; and Klaperman, "Heaven Help," 21–23.

16. Katzoff, "Status of the Rebetzin," 8. Katzoff, a rabbi's daughter, earned a Master of Hebrew Literature degree from JTS. Her husband, Louis Katzoff, also a JTS graduate, served as rabbi of B'nai Abraham, Easton, Pa., from 1941 to 1949. He also served as campus rabbi at the University of Pennsylvania and registrar of the College of Jewish Studies in Chicago. "Women's League Notables," *Outlook* 27 (December 1956): 19.

17. Gerstein, "Reflections," 16–17.

18. Proverbs 31: 10.

19. An allusion to higher biblical criticism, which was rejected by traditional Jews and which Solomon Schechter had condemned as "higher antisemitism." See "Higher Criticism—Higher Anti-Semitism," in Solomon Schechter, *Seminary Addresses & Other Papers* (New York: Burning Bush Press, 1959), 35–39.

20. Levi, "Don't Look Now," 8, 13. Her husband, S. Gershon Levi, served as rabbi of the Jamaica Jewish Center, Jamaica, N.Y., from 1947 to 1972.

21. Ibid.

22. "Another Point," 7.

23. Her husband served as rabbi of Congregation Ahavath Sholom in Bluefield, W.Va. Wilner, "Rabbi's Wife," 9.

24. Kinberg, "How Treat?" 8.

25. Kose, "It Feels Good," 5, 9. Elvin I. Kose served as rabbi of Temple Beth Shalom in Union, N.J.

26. Barras, "Wraps," 20–22. Abraham D. Barras served as rabbi of Temple Israel in Wilkes-Barre, Pa., from 1952 to 1983.

27. Ibid., 22–23.

28. Ibid.

29. Kripke, "Why Rebbitzens," 13, 20. Meyer Kripke served as rabbi of Beth El Synagogue in Omaha, Neb., from 1946 to 1974. Both were JTS graduates; Dorothy finished the Teachers Institute in 1936. The Kripkes later gained great wealth and donated $7 million to JTS for the renovation of the tower that now bears their name. In light of this, Dorothy's quip in this 1947 article that she cared little about the nuances of money is particularly poignant: "mouton and mink. . . I don't crave either. As for Cadillacs and Chevys, I can't tell them apart. The things I want passionately are not things that money can buy—with the possible exception of security, where money helps."

30. *Saturday the Rabbi Went Hungry* was published in 1966. Kemelman's first book in the series, *Friday the Rabbi Slept Late*, appeared in 1964. For more on Kemelman's depiction of the rebbetzin, see below, chapter 5.

31. Klaperman, "Heaven Help," 22.

32. Ibid., 22. Gilbert Klaperman, founding rabbi of Congregation Beth Sholom in Lawrence, N.Y., served from 1950 to 1988.

33. Ibid., 23.

34. Barras, "Wraps," 22.

35. Kirkley, " 'Mrs. God,' " 23–29. The captain/service crew metaphor is taken from Welthy Fisher, *Handbook for Ministers' Wives* (New York: Women's Press, 1950), 91, quoted in Kirkley, 26; Greenbacker and Taylor, *Private Lives,* 33–35, 41; and Boyer, "Minister's Wife," 258–59.

36. In 1940, the marriage rate stood at 105 per 1,000 women age 17 to 29, well above the rate of 89.1 per 1,000 for the years 1925–1929. The rate peaked in 1946 at 148 per 1,000 and averaged 121 during the postwar years. Hartman, *Home Front,* 163–64.

37. Weiss, *To Have and to Hold,* 40–41; May, *Homeward Bound,* 87–89; and Filene, *Him/Her/Self,* 187–88.

38. Hartman, *Home Front,* 114–16; May, *Homeward Bound,* 80; Kaledin, *Mothers and More,* 36, 44, 51, 58–80; Rupp and Verta, *Survival in the Doldrums,* 15–18; Weinberg, "Absorption of Wives"; *Women and Work,* 97–98; and Fowlkes, "The Myth of Merit," 347–60.

39. Rona Jaffe, "A Real-life Class Reunion," *Ladies' Home Journal,* June 1980, 142, quoted in Kaledin, *Mothers and More,* 43; Elise Waintrup echoed these sentiments. As she recalled, "I think that many women, doctor's wives, professors' wives, at that period of history and time, lived through their husbands." NAORR session. For more on Waintrup, see below.

40. Cott, *Public Vows,* 193.

41. Kaledin, *Mothers and More,* 61–65.

42. May, *Homeward Bound,* 16–20; Ellwood, *Fifties,* 2–3; Filene, *Him/Her/Self,* 188; Joanne J. Meyerowitz, "Beyond the Feminine Mystique: A Reassessment of Postwar Mass Culture, 1946–1958," in *Not June Cleaver,* ed. Meyerowitz, 232–42; Rothman, *Woman's Proper Place,* 225; and Kaledin, *Mothers and More,* 25–28, 36, 44, 58–82. The Roosevelt quote, from her book *It Seems to Me* (New York: W. W. Norton, 1954), 55, is found in Kaledin on 99.

43. May, *Homeward Bound,* 84–89; Kaledin, *Mothers and More,* 31–33, 91–94; and Meyerowitz, "Beyond the Feminine Mystique," 6.

44. Kaledin, *Mothers and More,* 12; Shapiro, *A Time for Healing,* 159–60; Moore, *Golden Cities,* 1–52; Hudnut-Beumler, *Looking for God,* 7–9; Arthur A. Goren, "A 'Golden Decade' for American Jews: 1945–1955," in *American Jewish Experience,* 2d ed., ed. Sarna, 294–95, 301; Paula E. Hyman, "From City to Suburb: Temple Mishkan Tefila of Boston," in *American Synagogue,* ed. Wertheimer, 185; and *AJYB* 62: 130.

45. Zev K. Nelson, "Special Problems of the Rabbi's Wife and Children," paper delivered at "On Being a Rabbi" Conference, JTS, winter 1964, 1–2, personal files of author.

46. Ibid., 2.

47. Ibid., 1.

48. Genesis 18: 9. This was Abraham's reply to the three visitors who inquired after Sarah's whereabouts.

49. Nelson, "Special Problems," 2.

50. Seminars for minister's wives in connection with their husbands' conventions were already taking place in Christian denominations. Groups of wives also met informally at other times to share ideas. See Shullenberger, "Her Privileges," 37, and Stamm, "Her Church," 27, in *I Married.*

51. Whenever possible, I use the women's first names, but in the meeting minutes transcripts, the women are referred to solely by their husbands' first names, e.g., Mrs. Baruch Treiger.

52. "Summary of Session of Rabbis' Wives," *Proceedings of the Rabbinical Assembly* 11 (1947): 389, 391.

53. Ibid., 390. Her husband, Saul Teplitz, served as rabbi of Congregation Sons of Israel in Woodmere, N.Y., from 1963 to 1991. She was the daughter of Esther Podolsky Arzt and Rabbi Max Arzt. For more on the Arzts, see below.

54. Ibid. Morris Goodblatt served as founding rabbi of Congregation Beth Am Israel, Philadelphia, Pa., from 1927 to 1968.

55. Joan Lipnick Abelson, interview.

56. "Funny"; and NAORR session.

57. Kaledin, *Mothers and More,* 53; May, *Homeward Bound,* 83; and Joselit, *Wonders,* 19–20.

58. Greenbacker and Taylor, *Private Lives,* 41.

59. Simon Greenberg had served as rabbi of Har Zion Temple in Philadelphia, Pa., from 1925 to 1946. Max Arzt had served as rabbi of Temple Israel in Scranton, Pa., from 1924 to 1939.

60. Levi, "Don't Look Now," 8; Miriam Teplitz, interview; Maurine Kessler, interview; and RA session.

61. Teplitz, interview; Kessler, interview; and RA session.

62. Baila Round Shargel, conversation with author, 31 August 1994; and Baila Round Shargel, "The Texture of Seminary Life during the Finkelstein Era," in *Tradition Renewed,* vol. 1, 543.

63. Other rebbetzins who took classes at—and in most cases graduated from—JTS and who married JTS rabbis include: Adina Katzoff, Ethel Barbanel Rothenberg, Zipporah Jacobs, Jeanette Finkel Miller, Esther A. Panitz, Esther Saltzman, Margie Pressman, Miriam Wise, Gilla P. Rubin, Sharon Citron Urbas, and Peggy Kronsberg Pearlstein. "Women's League Notables—They're Worth Talking About," *Outlook* 27 (December 1956): 18–19; RA session; Zipporah Jacobs, interview; Jeanette Finkel Miller, conversation with author, Miami Beach, Fla., 5 January 2000; Esther A. Panitz, "Adloyoda," *Outlook* 24 (March 1954): 27; and Esta Saltzman, "Marjorie Morningstar: Jewish Mute or Mutiny," *Outlook* 26 (December 1956): 17, 26–27.

64. John J. Macionis, *Sociology* (Englewood Cliffs, N.J.: Prentice Hall, 1995), 38. I am grateful to Carol Poll for calling my attention to this model.

65. Eileen Kieffer, interview. Her husband, Melvin Kieffer, served as rabbi of the Old Westbury Hebrew Congregation, Westbury, N.Y., from 1957 to 1983.

66. Teplitz, interview.

67. Greenbacker and Taylor, *Private Lives,* 36–37, 39.

68. "Autobiographical Questionnaire," Cincinnati, Ohio, 1980, in "Wohl, Belle Myers," sc #13150, AJA. Her husband, Samuel Wohl, served as rabbi of Congregation Bene Yeshurun, Cincinnati, Ohio, from 1931 to 1966.

69. Blank's husband, Sheldon H. Blank, served as professor of Bible at the College from 1926 to 1989. Amy Blank was a writer whose poems and stories

on Jewish themes were published in various journals including the *CCAR Journal, Journal of Reform Judaism,* and *European Judaism.* Collections of her poems were also printed privately. Blank also wrote educational materials for the Reform Movement, including *A Passover Haggada for Children* (Cincinnati, Ohio: n.p.,1940); "An Assembly Program for Founders' Day for the Elementary School," arr. Amy K. Blank, ed. Emanuel Gamoran (Cincinnati, Ohio: UAHC, n.d.); and a play about Isaac Mayer Wise. "Blank, Amy K.," nearprint file, AJA.

70. "Hebrew Union College: Constitution, Annual Report, Membership List and Questionnaire of the Students Wives' Club, Cincinnati, Ohio, 1949–1950," sc #4771, AJA; NAORR session; and "Funny."

71. NAORR session; and "Funny."

72. "Hebrew Union College: Constitution, Annual Report."

73. Ibid.; Miriam Wise, response to author's questionnaire, February 2000; RA session; Miller, conversation; NAORR session; Abelson, interview; Eveline Panitch, interview; and Finch, *Married to the Job,* 153–54.

74. "The Distaff Side of Student Life," *Hebrew Union College-Jewish Institute of Religion Bulletin,* April 1956, 11, "Blank, Amy K.," nearprint file.

75. "Future Rebbetzins Gain Their 'Smicha' in Social Relations," *The Commentator,* 4 March 1958, 2. I thank Jeffrey Gurock for sharing this reference with me.

76. He later served as Executive Vice President of the Chicago Board of Rabbis, 1963–95.

77. RA session; and Wise, response to author's questionnaire. Her husband, Aaron Wise, served as rabbi of Valley Jewish Community Center, later called Adat Ari-El, in North Hollywood, Calif., from 1948 to 1979. Many other rebbetzins emulated the behavior of the wives of senior rabbis whom their husbands served as assistant rabbis. Ricki Fenster learned about the role from Hilda Prinz when her husband, Myron Fenster, was Joachim Prinz's assistant. Ricki Fenster, phone conversation with author, 23 December 1993. Edith Kling remembers learning from Bessie Feinberg Halpern, wife of Abraham Halpern of Bnai Amoona in St. Louis, Mo. (1917–62), when her husband served as assistant rabbi. Kling remembers Halpern as a charming, gracious hostess who displayed a lovely table, was a wonderful cook and baker, and had a beautiful home. Kling hoped to emulate these qualities. Edith Kling, interview. Charlotte Rothman idolized Lillian Freehof, whom she got to know when her husband, Martin, was Solomon Freehof's assistant in Pittsburgh, Pa. She recalls her being "glamorous, chic, accomplished—the kind of rebbitzen I could never be." Charlotte Rothman, "Rabbi Honey," unpublished manuscript, [1965–70], 63, personal files of Charlotte Rothman.

78. Helen Tomsky, "I Didn't Marry a Rabbi, but I Answer to Rebbitzen Now," *Outlook* 54 (fall 1983): 12; and Helen Tomsky, response to author's

questionnaire, January 2001. Mervin Tomsky served as a rabbi of several congregations, including Beth Jacob in Pennsauken, N.J., from 1956 to 1959.

79. Reuben Katz later served as rabbi of Congregation Bnai Israel in Freeport, N.Y., from 1949 to 1990.

80. RA session; and Reba Katz, interview.

81. Zipporah Marans, interview. Since 1965 her husband Arnold Marans has served as rabbi of the Sephardic Temple in Cedarhurst, N.Y.

82. RA session; and Miller, conversation. Jeanette's husband, Raphael Miller, served as rabbi of Ahavat Shalom in Lakewood, N.J., from 1958 to 1984. Francis's husband, Joseph Miller, served as rabbi of Congregation Shaare Torah in Brooklyn, N.Y., from 1922 to 1967.

83. Morris W. Graff, "Rebitzen—An Old Title with New Meaning," *CCARJ* 13 (October 1965): 52–54.

84. Jack Wertheimer, "The Conservative Synagogue," in *American Synagogue,* 123–25.

85. But rebbetzins could no longer become national president. Miriam Teplitz remembered being told explicitly while serving as National Vice President of Women's League that she would not be considered for the presidency because it was a lay woman's organization. Teplitz, interview.

86. National Women's League of the United Synagogue of America, Program Scripts, n.d., WLA.

87. For example, see Mrs. David [Bertha] Aronson, "National Women's League Convention Brings *Kashrut* to Minneapolis," *Outlook* 21 (March 1951): 8; Saltzman, "Marjorie Morningstar," 17, 26–27; Mrs. David M. [Rose] Goldstein, "Ten Tests for Effective Sisterhood Programming," *Outlook* 20 (May 1950): 12; idem, "'Blossoming from Healthy Roots': A Report on Judaism-in-the-Home Project," *Outlook* 21 (March 1951): 12; idem, "More about Hanukkah in the Home," *Outlook* 22 (December 1951): 16–17, 30; idem, "Your Summer 'Home Work,'" *Outlook* 26 (May 1956): 9, 25; idem, "Program Service," *Outlook* 19 (March 1949): 13; Mrs. S. Joshua [Priva] Kohn, "Leadership Training," *Outlook* 20 (May 1950): 11; idem, "A Time for an Accounting: Leadership Training," *Outlook* 23 (September 1952): 12; Rebecca Lang, "How Good a Program Chairman Are You?" *Outlook* 16 (December 1945): 10; idem, "What Turn Shall Sisterhood Programs Take?" *Outlook* 18 (September 1947): 14; Miriam Teplitz, "The Homontash that Changed Its Name," *Outlook* 21 (March 1951): 24–25; Panitz, "Adloyoda," 27–28; idem, "The Land of the Bible Exhibit," *Outlook* 24 (June 1954): 1–8; idem, "To Be Fully and Naturally Jewish: A Positive Program for Sisterhood," *Outlook* 26 (May 1956): 17, 28; Mrs. Ben Zion [Kallia] Bokser, "Penina Moise—A Woman of Valor," *Outlook* 23 (May 1953): 6, 9; and idem, "Happy Purim for Susie," *Outlook* 25 (March 1955): 28–30.

88. David and Laura to Edith, undated, Lara Ilse to Edith, undated, Polly

Adler to Edie, undated, and Barbara to Edie, undated, personal files of Edith Kling; Tomsky, response to author's questionnaire; Hilda Greenberg, interview; Miller, conversation; and Abraham J. Karp, "Overview: The Synagogue in America—A Historical Typology," in *American Synagogue,* 25–27.

89. Mrs. Leon S. [Rebecca] Lang, "What Turn Shall Sisterhood Programs Take?" *Outlook* 18 (September 1947): 14.

90. "Summary of Session of Rabbis' Wives," 390.

91. Ibid.; "Hebrew Union College: Constitution, Annual Report"; Kose, "It Feels Good," 5; Katz, interview; Marans, interview; and Gerstein, "Reflections," 17–18.

92. RA session; and Jacobs, interview. David Jacobs has served as rabbi of Temple Beth El in Quincy, Mass., from 1957 to the present.

93. Jeanette Kanter, conversation with author, Miami Beach, Fla., 5 January 2000.

94. Panitch, interview; "Hebrew Union College: Constitution, Annual report"; Hilda Greenberg, interview; Fenster, conversation; and Katz, interview.

95. Fenster, conversation. Her husband, Myron Fenster, served as rabbi of Shelter Rock Jewish Center in Roslyn, New York, from 1966 to 2002; Hilda's husband, Josiah Schnitzer, served as rabbi of Congregation Shomrei Emunah in Monclair, N.J., from 1951 to 1979; and Melinda (Malka) Kieffer, phone conversation with author, February 1, 2000.

96. Jacobs, interview; Gidon, ed., *Adat Ari El,* 20; NAORR session; and Panitch, interview.

97. Marans, interview; Kieffer, interview; Peggy K. Pearlstein, conversation with author, 1 July 2001; personal files of Peggy K. Pearlstein; and RA session.

98. Her husband, Sidney Greenberg, served as rabbi of Temple Sinai in Philadelphia, Pa., from 1942 to 1992.

99. Undated, personal files of Hilda Greenberg.

100. Rothman, "Rabbi Honey," NAORR session; Kieffer, interview; Tomsky, response to author's questionnaire; Abelson, interview; RA session; Joy Fish, conversation with author, 30 June 2001; Charlotte Shanblatt, conversation with author, 30 June 2001; Kessler, interview; Panitch, interview; Bronsen, *B'nai Amoona,* 156; and Kling, interview. In Louisville, Kling followed in the footsteps of Leah Saltzman, wife of Rabbi Joseph Saltzman. Educated at a Russian gymnasium, Leah began teaching at the Hebrew school in the 1930s, where she "carved out a niche as a beloved teacher on her own." Landau, *Adath Louisville,* 50, 79.

101. "Summary of Session of Rabbis' Wives," 391–92; Dorothy's husband, Jacob Kabakoff, served as a rabbi in Philadelphia, Pa., from 1944 to 1948, but then went on to an academic career. Max Nussbaum served as rabbi of Temple Israel in Hollywood, Calif., from 1942 to 1974. RA session; Kieffer, interview; Jacobs, interview; NAORR session; Marans, interview; Miller, conversation;

and Pearlstein, conversation; Sarah Lewis, JTS Tribute Dinner invitation, 16 March 2002, personal files of author; and Sarah Lewis, conversation with author, Miami Beach, Fla., 5 January 2000. Her husband, Albert Lewis, served as rabbi of Temple Beth Sholom in Cherry Hill, N.J., from 1948 to 1992.

102. On her collaboration with Myer on the lattermost book, Dorothy explained that she "felt the need, because of the nature of the subject, for the masculine perspective. Following the example of the masters in the field (on the adult level) [presumably Masters & Johnson], who are a husband-and-wife team, I asked my husband to collaborate with me," 9.

103. *AJYB* (1984): 334–35.

104. Her husband, Solomon Freehof, served as rabbi of Pittsburgh's Rodef Shalom Congregation from 1934 to 1966, and wrote numerous books, especially on Reform Jewish law.

105. "Hebrew Union College: Constitution, Annual Report"; Peggy Pearlstein, e-mail correspondence with author, 3 and 17 July 2001; Open House Invitation, 10 December 1967, Bowie, Md., personal files of Pearlstein; Abelson, interview; Marans, interview; Kazis, conversation; Kling, interview; Barras, "Wraps Off," 21; Kieffer, interview; Fenster, conversation; Hilda Greenberg, interview; Lewis, conversation; Miller, conversation; NAORR session; Hadassah Ribalow Nadich, "The Rabbi's Spouse," *Jewish Spectator* (summer 1985): 17; and Teplitz, interview.

106. Katz, interview; Miller, conversation; Devorah Rosenberg, "Have Pots Will Travel, or How to Make Your Kitchen Kosher" (New York, [1976?], mimeographed), WLA. Her husband, Yaakov Rosenberg, served as rabbi of Congregation Adath Jeshurun in Elkins Park, Pa., from 1960 to 1978.

107. Her husband, Herbert Panitch, served as rabbi of Congregation Agudath Achim in Altoona, Pa., from 1959 to 1970, and of Congregation Beth Israel in Milwaukee, Wis., from 1970 to 1995. Of course, some rebbetzins refused to play into the stereotype and deliberately stayed out of the synagogue kitchen. NAORR session; Marjorie Pressman, response to author's questionnaire, January 2001; Kieffer, interview; Freedman, "Rebbetzin," 150; Lucy Vandervalt, conversation with author, Miami Beach, Fla., 5 January 2000; and Panitch, interview.

108. *Creative Cooking* (New York, 1968), iv–vi. Israel Jacobs served as rabbi of the Jewish Centre of Bay Shore, N.Y., from 1956 to 1984. A review of more than a dozen Reform Temple cookbooks of the period revealed both that they did not discuss Jewish dietary laws and that the rebbetzins rarely played an authoritative role in them.

109. Undated notes; and "Queen for a Day" brochure, 14 March 1966, personal files of Edith Kling. Her husband, Simcha Kling, served as rabbi of Congregation Adath Jeshurun in Louisville, Ky., from 1965 to 1991.

110. Saltzman, "Marjorie Morningstar," 17, 26–27; Abelson, interview; Pressman, response to author's questionnaire; NAORR session; Marans, inter-

view; Pearlstein, conversation; Kieffer, interview; Kessler, interview; Jacobs, interview; and Shanblatt, conversation.

111. NAORR session; Gidon, ed., *Adat Ari El*, 47; *Adat Ari El Bulletin*, 15 March, 1 May, 15 September, 1 October, 15 October, and 1 December, 1949; and 1 January, 15 January, 1 March, 15 March, 15 May, and 15 June, 1950. I thank Joellyn W. Zollman for alerting me to this reference. Lillian Kronish and Bella Lehrman introduced Sisterhood gift shops in their Florida congregations. Moore, *Golden Cities*, 103, 107. For an example of pioneering research in this area, see Zollman, "Shopping for Our Future."

112. Naomi Cohen, interview; and Jacobs, interview.

113. 43:5, 6, 45: 2, 3, 4, Rebbetzin series, arch. 128, Rabbi Israel Mowshowitz Collection, JTSA.

114. "Installation," n.d., 44:3, Mowshowitz collection.

115. Jean Smith, "Cook of the Week: Children Love Her Hamentaschen," *L.I. Star Journal*, 28 February 1955, 44: 5, Mowshowitz collection.

116. Mowshowitz, *Straight Talk*, n.p. [January 1962].

117. Charles Salzman to Libby Mowshowitz, 22 May 1986, 43: 1, Mowshowitz collection.

118. Jeff Benkoe, "Her Career One of Love and Service," *Newsday*, 27 August 1986.

119. "Donor Testimonial," 16 January 1962, 45: 3, Mowshowitz collection.

120. Rose Berman Goldstein, Reuben Berman, Ted Berman, and William Berman, "Sarah and Alexander Berman, a family chronicle by their children," 26 September 1973, 18–21, 48, 51–53, personal files of Jeremy Goldstein. Sarah Berman helped found the Minneapolis Talmud Torah and several synagogues, including Beth El, and served as president of the Talmud Torah's women's auxiliary.

121. Ibid., 54; *JWA*, s.v. "Goldstein, Rose"; and Simon Greenberg, "Rose Goldstein," eulogy, 30 December 1984, personal files of Goldstein.

122. Rose Berman Goldstein, *Songs to Share* (New York: United Synagogue Commission, 1949), 6.

123. Goldstein, *Time to Pray*, 1.

124. Ibid., 10–15.

125. Goldstein, "Program Service," 13; idem, *Time to Pray*, book jacket; Jessie Yoshpe, "A Woman Ahead of Her Time," *Temple B'nai Israel Bulletin* (Sacramento, Calif.), February 1985, n.p.; and Greenberg, "Rose Goldstein."

126. Greenberg, "Rose Goldstein."

127. Ellen M. Umansky, "Paula Ackerman: Reform's Lost Woman Rabbi," *Genesis* 2 (June-July 1986): 18–20; biography, Paula Ackerman, nearprint box, AJA; "Ackerman, Paula," *Reform Judaism*, 1–2; and Nadell, *Women*, 120.

128. *Ethics of the Fathers* 2: 20. Paula Ackerman to Co-Worker, 22 January 1943, 28 January 1944, 17 March 1943, 26 October 1943, 23 January 1945,

and 21 September 1945, 36/2; Report of the National Committee on Religious Schools (1944), Thirty-first Annual Report, 190–92, *PNFTS* 4 (1942–47), box 1; Report of the National Committee on Religious Schools (1944), Thirty-second Annual Report (1944), 74–75; Report of the National Committee on Religious Schools (1945), Thirty-third Annual Report, 136–38, box 1, vol. 4; and Transcript of Proceedings, Seventeenth Biennial Assembly (1948), 50–54, 4/2, WRJ; and Umansky, "Paula Ackerman," 18–19.

129. Paula Ackerman to friend, 12 December 1950; and Paula Ackerman to friend, 9 January 1951, box 68, "Ackerman, Paula," correspondence file, sc #69, AJA.

130. Ibid.

131. *Time,* 22 January 1951; and *Meridian Star,* 21 January 1951, box 68, "Ackerman, Paula" file, sc #69; and Umansky, "Paula Ackerman," 20.

132. "Rabbi Maurice N. Eisendrath Denies Approving Appointment of Woman Rabbi," press release, and [Maurice N. Eisendrath?] to Sidney S. Kay, 30 January 1951, box 68, "Ackerman, Paula" file, sc #69.

133. "Ackerman, Paula," *Reform Judaism,* 1–2; Meridian, Mississippi, Temple Beth Israel minutes and misc. material relating to the activities of Rabbi and Mrs. William Ackerman, microfilm #2041, AJA; Ackerman to Jacob Rader Marcus, 24 April 1979, box 68, "Ackerman, Paula" file, sc #69; Nadell, *Women,* 124; "Rabbi Regina O'Hara?" *American Judaism* 2 (September 1952): 2, 26; and Umansky, "Paula Ackerman," 20.

134. Katz, interview.

135. Panitch, interview.

136. Kessler, interview; Panitch, interview; Abelson, interview; Pearlstein, conversation; Fish, conversation; Shanblatt, conversation; Wise, response to author's questionnaire; Miller, conversation; Nadich, "Rabbi's Spouse," 18; and RA session.

137. Pressman, response to author's questionnaire; NAORR session; and Hilda Greenberg, interview (emphasis mine). Martin Silverman served as rabbi of Temple Beth Emeth in Albany, N.Y., from 1972 to 1992. Leon Kronish served as rabbi of Temple Beth Sholom in Miami Beach, Fla., from 1944 to 84. Dvora Cooper served as editor of the Sisterhood bulletin of Temple Beth Israel, York, Pa., for more than twenty years. *New York Times,* 25 January 2001, obituary.

138. Ross, *Minister's Wife?* 59; Barbara Brown Zikmund, "Challenge to the Ordinand's Wife," 13 May 1979, Barbara Brown Zikmund papers, Women in Theological Scholarship Archives, Union Theological Seminary, New York, N.Y. I am grateful to Letitia Campbell for sharing this reference with me. Campbell recalls her grandmother serving with her minister husband in just this way in several small, rural churches. Letitia Campbell to Shuly Rubin Schwartz, [January 2001]; and Greenbacker and Taylor, *Private Lives,* 61, 308.

139. NAORR session; "Funny"; Freedman, "Rebbetzin," 64; and Nadich, "Rabbi's Spouse," 18.

140. Her husband, Ralph Pelcovitz, served as rabbi of Kneseth Israel, in Far Rockaway, N.Y., from 1951 to 1995.

141. *New York Times*, 23 October 1986, obituary. I am indebted to Annette Muffs Botnick for sharing this reference with me; *30th Anniversary Journal Wantagh Jewish Center*, 1982; and Hilda Greenberg, interview.

142. Kling, interview.

143. Freedman, "Rebbetzin," 150.

144. Kessler, interview. Her husband, Stanley Kessler, served as rabbi of Beth El Temple in West Hartford, Conn., from 1954 to 1992.

145. NAORR session. Agatha's husband, Joseph Glaser, served as executive vice president of the Central Conference of American Rabbis from 1972 to 1994.

146. Greenbacker and Taylor, *Private Lives*, 56–57.

147. Fenster, conversation; "Rabbis's Wives," The *Jewish Journal of Greater Los Angeles*, 22 June 2001, http://www.jewishjournal.com/home/preview.php3?id=7082; Teplitz, interview; and Kessler, interview. For example, Maurine Kessler, who had earned her B.A. in 1947, returned to school and earned an M.A. (1969) and Ph.D. (1978) from the University of Connecticut. Similarly, in 1965, Miriam Teplitz returned to school to earn her MSW from the Wurtzweiler School of Social Work.

148. Dorothy B. Spevack to author, 21 January 2000.

NOTES TO CHAPTER 5

1. Behrmann, "Shrinking Pedestal," 49–53; and letters in *Moment* 1 (February 1976): 50.

2. Farber, *Great Dreams*, 240–41, 254–55; Miller, *Seventies Now*, 18–19; and Langer, *Feminist Critique*, 13–14, 143–63, 167.

3. Kate Millett, *Sexual Politics* (Garden City, N.Y.: Doubleday, 1970); and Chafe, *American Woman*.

4. Doris B. Gold, "Women and Voluntarism," in *Woman in a Sexist Society*, 390–95.

5. The proportion of students graduating from college who were women almost doubled between 1966 and 1984, from 11 to 21 percent. The proportion of law degree recipients who were women rose from 3 to 33 percent between 1960 and 1982; for medical degrees, the jump from 1960 to 1981 was from 6 to 25 percent. McLaughlin et al., *Changing Lives*, 4, 34, 37–38, 201.

6. Marsden, *Religion*, 251.

7. The full story of the history of women's ordination as rabbis is recounted in Nadell's *Women*. On the 1970s and 1980s, see 170–214.

8. Alan Silverstein, "The Evolution of Ezrat Nashim," *Conservative Judaism* 30 (fall 1975): 41–51. The quote is from Martha Ackelsberg, "Women at Rabbinical Assembly Seek Full Religious Participation," *Genesis* 2, 25 March 1972, in Silverstein, "Evolution," 46; Nadell, *Women,* 170–71; and Priesand, *Judaism,* xiv.

9. "Here's What I Think: Readers React to Gerson D. Cohen's Article in the December Issue of *Outlook,*" *Outlook* 44 (summer 1974): 27. A. Joseph Heckelman served as rabbi of Beth El Synagogue in Waterbury, Conn.

10. Alan Silverstein, "A New Image of the Rabbinate," in *The Seminary at 100: Reflections on the Jewish Theological Seminary and the Conservative Movement,* ed. Nina Beth Cardin and David Wolf Silverman (New York: Jewish Theological Seminary, 1987), 427–32. The quote is on 430.

11. Feingold, *Time for Searching,* 143–45; and Shapiro, *Time for Healing,* 100.

12. Polner, *Rabbi,* 156.

13. See, for example, J. G. Koehler, "The Minister as a Family Man," *Pastoral Psychology* 11 (1960): 11–12.

14. Lenn, *Rabbi and Synagogue,* 381–83.

15. Her husband, Jacob M. Rothschild, served as rabbi of the Hebrew Benevolent Congregation in Atlanta, Ga., from 1946 to 1973. Janice Rothschild later authored a history of the congregation, *As But a Day,* and a volume about her husband's involvement in the Civil Rights Movement, *One Voice.*

16. Rothschild, "Rebbetzinhood," 25–27.

17. Polner, *Rabbi,* 154–61. The quote is on 157.

18. This report appeared as Jack Bloom, "The Rabbi as Symbolic Exemplar," *Yearbook of the Central Conference of American Rabbis* [YCCAR] 86 (1977): 105–14. It was released in expanded book form as Bloom, *The Rabbi as Symbolic Exemplar: By the Power Vested in Me.*

19. "Funny"; YCCAR 78 (1968): xix; 79 (1969): xviii; 85 (1975): xxx–xxxv; 87 (1977): xxix; 88 (1978): xxviii; and 89 (1979): xxviii. Marcia Weinberg mentioned that the "subject of clergy family life" served as "one of the main topics" of the 1978 conference. Weinberg, "*Rachel,*" 30.

20. Letter to the editor, *Lilith* 1 (spring 1978): 5; and Mindy Gewirtz, "A Process for Defining the Role of the Rebbetzin," *The Rebbetzin's Letter* 2 (summer 1998): 1–2.

21. Shuchat, "Rabbi and His Family," 177–81.

22. Mordecai Waxman, "The Changing American Rabbinate," in *The American Rabbi,* ed. Gilbert S. Rosenthal (New York: Ktav, 1997), 165–88. For information on his wife, Ruth Waxman, see below and my "Ruth Waxman," in *Yakar Le'Mordecai.*

23. Sundheim, "Personal Equation," 153–57. Her husband, Frank, served

as rabbi of Congregation Schaarai Zedeck in Tampa, Fla., from 1966 to 1985. The following quotes are taken from this article.

24. Four years later, Sundheim gave a similar message in a session titled "How to Make Our Families Healthier," *YCCAR* 94 (1984): 196–99.

25. Freedman, "Stress"; and idem, "Role-Related Stress," 1–8.

26. Raphael, *Profiles,* 69.

27. Sternfield, "Rabbi as Family Man," 5, 99–100.

28. Ibid., 229, 251, 256.

29. Fisch, "Wives of Law," 107–8, 125, 147, 152–53, 170.

30. Tape recording #1195, HUC-JIR Student Association evening symposium on the role of the Congregational Rabbi's wife, n.d., AJA. Though undated, the symposium took place in between 1973, when Troup was ordained, and the mid-1980s, when he had already remarried.

31. Leonard Fein, "Beginnings," *Moment* 1 (May/June 1975): 9; and Behrmann, "Rabbis' Wives," 49–53.

32. Wertheimer, *People Divided,* 118–23; Shapiro, *Time for Healing,* 184–86; and Gurock, *From Fluidity,* 36–38.

33. Selavan, "Friday the Rebbetzin," 39–41.

34. Letter to the editor, *Lilith* 1 (spring 1978): 5. Sherry Levy-Reiner's husband, Fred N. Reiner, served as rabbi of Temple Beth Shalom in Topeka, Kansas, from 1975 to 1982. Since 1985, he has served as senior rabbi of Temple Sinai, in Washington, D.C.

35. Tennenbaum, *Rachel,* 9–11, 191. Her husband, Lloyd Tennenbaum, served as rabbi of the Huntington Hebrew Congregation, Huntington, N.Y., from 1959 to 1969.

36. See, for example, Wisse, "*Rachel,*" 76–78.

37. Weinberg, "*Rachel,*" 25–33. Joseph P. Weinberg served as associate rabbi of the Washington Hebrew Congregation in Washington, D.C., from 1968 to 1986, and as senior rabbi from 1986 until his death in 2002. The quotes are taken from this article.

38. Heller, "The Pulpit Rebbitzen," 12–13, 19–20. Her husband, Zachary Heller, served as rabbi of Temple Emanu-El in Bayonne, N.J., from 1970 to 1998.

39. Cohn, "Please Don't," Allender, "I Married," and Kieffer, "Call Me," 12–13, 17–18, 20–22. Cohn's husband, David White, served as rabbi of Kol Shofar Congregation in Marin County, Calif., from 1977 to 1991. Allendar's husband, Louis Zivic, served as rabbi of Congregation Beth Israel in Lebanon, Pa., from 1983 to the present. Mordecai Kieffer served as rabbi of Temple Beth El, in Troy, N.Y., from 1975 to 1980.

40. Cohn, "Please Don't," 12, 17–18. Several years later, Elaine Kahn wrote an article with the same title in which she also spoke of her resentment at the

imposition of the term. "Please Don't Call Me 'Rebbetzin,'" *Baltimore Jewish Times,* 29 December 1989. I thank Elaine Kahn for sharing this with me.

41. Allender, "I Married," 12–13, 21.

42. Kieffer, "Call Me," 13, 22.

43. Responses: "Response on the Rebbitzens," *Outlook* 53 (fall 1983): 12–13, 19.

44. Tomsky, "I Didn't," 12.

45. Asekof, "What You Will," 12–13. Her husband, Stanley Asekoff, has served as rabbi of Congregation B'nai Shalom in West Orange, N.J., since 1972.

46. Glazer, "Rebbitzens," 13. Mel Glazer served as rabbi of the West End Synagogue, Nashville, Tenn., from 1980 to 1985.

47. Goldberg's "Understanding," 6. Jonas Goldberg served as rabbi of Congregation Beth El in Norwalk, Conn., from 1972 to 1989.

48. Evans, *Born,* 302; McLaughlin, *Changing Lives,* 61; and Shapiro, *Time for Healing,* 244. The Kieffers divorced in June 1993. Allendar and Zivic divorced in 1998. The Glazers divorced in 2001.

49. Greenberg, *Rabbi's Life Contract,* 60, 102; and http://mccoy.lib.siu.edu/illinois/supp-g.htm.

50. Wise, response to author's questionnaire; Rosa and Boris Fitershova to editor, (Louisville) *Community,* 3 April 1998, 2; Yelena Leltser to Edith, undated; Andrew Adler, "Minyan Demystified"; Norman S. Rosenberg to Edith Kling, 5 January 1992; Ruth Greenleaf to Edith Kling, 21 July 1997; *Adath Jeshurun Bulletin,* December 1998, 7; *Community Paper,* 10 September 1999; flyer, personal files of Edith Kling; Kling, interview; Hilda Greenberg, interview; Katz, interview; Tomsky, author's questionnaire, January 2001; NAORR session; and Spevack to author, 21 January 2000.

51. Miriam Wise to author, February 2000; Spouses in Retirement session, National Association of Retired Reform Rabbis Convention, Ft. Lauderdale, Fla., 7 January 2000; and Helen Jacobson and Leona Lefkowitz, "Wives of Retired Rabbis," *JRJ* 34 (summer 1987): 1.

52. Goldstein, "Emotional, Physical," quoted in Freedman, "The Rebbetzin in America," 30.

53. Mrs. Nathaniel Share, letter to the editor, *JRJ* 29 (winter 1982): 57–58.

54. Spouses in Retirement session; NAORR session; "Facing and Coping with the Inevitable," Rabbinical Assembly Association of Retired Rabbis Conference, Miami Beach, Fla., [7] January 1997, in *Hamodia, Rabbinical Assembly Association of Retired Rabbis Newsletter,* July 1997; Debbie Miller, e-mail communication with author, 25 October 1998; and Abelson, interview. Jerome Lipnick served as rabbi of Temple Beth El in Utica, N.Y., from 1946 to 1960. Kassel Abelson served as rabbi of Beth El in Minneapolis, Minn., from 1948 to 1951, and from 1957 to 1992. Another example of a widowed rebbetzin marrying a rabbi is Leah Treiger Schimmel, who remarried in 1961, after the death of

her husband, Baruch, and who was "welcomed with open arms by her [second] husband's Congregation Beth Zion in Philadelphia." Naomi Flax Tepper, "Leah Treiger Schimmel: In Memoriam," *Outlook* 42 (summer 1972): 27.

55. Wilkes, *My People,* 14.

56. Schwartzman, "Still Room," 64–66; and Cathy L. Felix, letter to the editor, *JRJ* 29 (winter 1982): 55–57.

57. Goldman, *Rabbi Is a Lady,* 26.

58. See, for example, Roland B. Gittelsohn, *Here Am I—Harnessed to Hope* (New York: Vantage Press, 1988), 48–50; Reuben, "Two's Company," 37–41; and Arfa, "Rebbetzin."

59. See, for example, Marietta B. Hobkirk, "Some Reflections on Bringing Up the Minister's Family," *Pastoral Psychology* 12 (December 1961): 23–29; and William G. Douglas, *Minister's Wives* (New York: Harper & Row, 1965).

60. See, for example, Lavender, *They Cry, Too!*; Nordland, *Unprivate Life*; Ross, *Who Is*; and Morgan, *Wives of Priests.*

61. Truman, *Underground Manual,* 12, 66, 141, 149.

62. Ibid., 68, 81. Ministers' families experienced the same anguish over the parsonage in retirement and widowhood. Greenbacker and Taylor, *Private Lives,* 88–89.

63. Truman, *Underground Manual,* 159.

64. *Your Church* (July/ August 1977); and Ministers' Wives brochure, personal files of Tomsky.

65. Cott, *Public Vows,* 208.

66. Lorge, interview; Pearlstein, conversation; unidentified newspaper clipping, n.d., personal files of Pearlstein; Marans, interview; Gidon, ed., *Adat Ari El,* 30–31; and Wise, response to author's questionnaire.

67. Herbert A. Otto, "Marriage and Family Enrichment Programs: An Overview of a Movement," 12–17; and Bernard Kligfeld, "The Jewish Marriage Encounter," in *Marriage and Family,* ed. Otto, 129–43; http://huc.edu/aja/ Kligfeld.htm; *New York Times,* 10 July 1999, obituary; Institute of Jewish Learning brochure, box 1, Bernard Kligfield, nearprint biographies, AJA; Michael Kligfeld, phone conversation with author, 21 September 2004; and *The Teachers Institute Seminary College of Jewish Studies of the Jewish Theological Seminary of America: Fiftieth Anniversary Alumni Directory,* 1909–59.

68. Kligfeld, "Jewish Marriage," 129–43; "Jewish Marriage Encounter (Enrollment Lists)," 2/14; Jerry and Marilyn Sexton to Bernie and Julie Kligfeld, 10 February 1976, 4/2; Louise and Arthur Haselkorn to Julie and Bernie, 12 March 1973, 4/1; and Jean Herschaft, "Marriage Encounter Claims Challenged and Defended," *Jewish Post,* 31 May 1974, 2/11, Bernard Kligfeld Papers, AJA; Tomsky, response to author's questionnaire; Wise, response to author's questionnaire; personal files of Pearlstein; Pearlstein, conversation; and personal files of Reba Katz.

69. "Jewish Marriage Encounter (Board Meetings) 1974–1978," 2/12, Kligfeld papers; and personal files of Reba Katz. I thank Reba Katz for sharing these files with me.

70. Fran and Joe Gross to Bernie and Julie, 22 February 1973; and Michael and Ellen Brooks to Bernie and Julie, undated, 4/1 Kligfeld papers.

71. *The Spouse Connection* (New York: Central Conference of American Rabbis, n.d.). I am grateful to Nina Salkin for sharing back issues with me. In the mid-1990s, both movements created e-mail listserves for rabbinic spouses.

72. Alfred H. Katz, *Self-Help in America: A Social Movement Perspective* (New York: Twayne, 1993), 8, 22. Rabbis' wives' groups met for several years in large Jewish communities such as Philadelphia and Long Island. I was a member of the Long Island group in the 1980s. The Philadelphia group galvanized on behalf of Soviet Jews. Teplitz, "Public Persona," *Rabbinics* 4, 8; Teplitz, interview; Edwin H. Friedman, Response to Freedman, *JRJ* 32 (winter 1985): 10; Fran Katz, conversation with author, 12 July 2001; and Agnes Kraus, conversation with author, 29 June 2002.

73. http://www.yu.edu/wurzweiler/m_s_w.htm.

74. Rebbetzin Chana Perel Kotler, Rebbetzin Sarah Yaffen, and Rebbetzin Kaplan in *Torah Profile*, ed. Wolpin, 285–328; and *The Modern Jewish Home: A Unique Perspective* (Brooklyn, 1981), viii.

75. "Funny"; Peggy Pearlstein, e-mail correspondence with author, 18 July 2001; Abelson, interview; Daniel Pressman, e-mail to author, 27 December 2000; Dorothy B. Spevack to author, 21 January 2000; and Kieffer, interview.

76. Much of the information on Greenberg, Waxman, and Jungreis is drawn from my "Ambassadors without Portfolio."

77. Jonathan Mark, "Women Take Giant Step in Orthodox Community," *Jewish Week,* 19 December 1997, 22.

78. Novak, "Talking," 31–32.

79. Blu Greenberg, interview; Novak, "Talking," 14–19; and *JWA,* s.v. "Greenberg, Blu."

80. Ruth Jacknow Markowitz, *My Daughter, the Teacher* (New Brunswick, N.J.: Rutgers University Press, 1993), 12–13; and Rothman, *Woman's Proper Place,* 156.

81. Blu Greenberg, interview.

82. Ibid.; and Novak, "Talking," 25. Her son, J. J., died in Israel in 2002 after a tragic bicycle accident.

83. Blu Greenberg, typewritten notes for an invited talk to rabbinical students, Reconstructionist Rabbinical College, Philadelphia, Pa., [1980s], personal files of Blu Greenberg; and Greenberg, interview.

84. Greenberg, interview.

85. Ibid.

86. Greenberg, typewritten notes.

87. Blu Greenberg, transcription of invited talk to rabbinical students, Reconstructionist Rabbinical College, Philadelphia, Pa., [1980s], personal files of Greenberg. In this quote, Greenberg twice mentions the "richness" of her role. This is an ironic turn of phrase, since Greenberg confessed elsewhere in this talk as well as in the interview that she deeply regrets both her and her husband's naiveté with regard to finances during their years in a congregation. In her travels as a lecturer in synagogues, Greenberg makes a point of counseling young rabbinic couples to be more actively concerned with matters of financial security.

88. Blu Greenberg, interview.

89. Ibid.

90. Greenberg, *On Women,* 30–31; and Novak, "Talking," 26–27.

91. Greenberg, *On Women,* ix–x, 21–37, 44, 99, 142.

92. Greenberg, *How to Run,* 102, 32.

93. Ibid., 68, 226.

94. Novak, "Talking," 34.

95. Greenberg, *How to Run,* 256–57.

96. Greenberg, interview; Novak, "Talking," 32–33; Greenberg, "Will There," 23–33; idem, "Orthodox Feminism," 1–2; idem, "Challenges," 1–2; http://www.jofa.org; and Andrea Levin, e-mail correspondence with author, 1 April 2003.

97. Greenberg, *On Women,* xi.

98. *Black Bread,* xii–xiii.

99. (New York: Simon & Schuster, 1988), 10.

100. The College of Jewish Studies was organized in 1924 by Chicago's Board of Jewish Education to provide opportunities for systematic Jewish studies and teacher training. In 1945, the College was incorporated as a separate institution and became a degree-granting program. *Encyclopaedia Judaica* (Jerusalem: Keter Publishing, 1971), s.v. "College of Jewish Studies."

101. Mordecai Waxman, interview.

102. Waxman, "Focus on Women"; Helene Schachter, conversation with author, 14 August 1997; *Adelphi College Course Catalogue* (New York: Adelphi College, 1948); Waxman and Keller, interview; and Jonathan Waxman, conversation with author, 21 August 1997.

103. Waxman, "Focus on Women"; Schachter, conversation; Hillel Waxman, conversation with author, 14 August 1997; Waxman and Keller, interview; Jonathan Waxman, conversation; Shirley E. Keller, "Ruth," *Temple Israel of Great Neck: The Fiftieth Anniversary Album,* 1992; Mordecai and Ruth Waxman, Temple Israel, interview; Ruth Waxman, "Goldfish," 5; and Florence Kahen, "Petit Memories of Ruth Waxman," written remarks to author, fall 1997.

104. Schachter, conversation; and Jonathan Waxman, conversation.

105. Mordecai and Ruth Waxman, Temple Israel, interview; Rothman, *Woman's Proper Place,* 226; and Jonathan Waxman, conversation. The *Light* was the recipient of numerous annual awards of excellence from the United Synagogue of Conservative Judaism. According to some, the magazine was so superior to any other synagogue publication that after several years, the synagogue was asked to withdraw its publication from consideration in order to give others an opportunity for recognition.

106. Jonathan Waxman, conversation. In the foreword, the author simply expresses gratitude to his "wife, Ruth Waxman, for her aid and advice." Mordecai Waxman, *Tradition and Change: The Development of Conservative Judaism* (New York: Burning Bush Press, 1958), x.

107. Stein, interview; and Waxman and Keller, interview. David and Eve actually met at one of these Saturday salons. This tradition continued when the Waxmans traveled as well. As Kahen recalls, "On trips with her and her husband, first business at any stopping point was to locate a store where she could buy Mordy fruit and other goodies; a nosh to sustain him if the hotel meals presented a kashrut problem. Their hotel room was like the Waxman living room, always replete with sweets and nourishing items as well." Kahen, "Petit Memories."

108. Ruth Waxman, "More Bubbles," 3–4; idem., "Goldfish," 5–6; Waxman, "Focus on Women"; and Mordecai and Ruth Waxman, Temple Israel, interview.

109. *Adelphi College Course Catalogue,* 1947–59; and *New York Times,* 28 October 1996.

110. Jonathan Waxman, conversation.

111. Hillel Waxman, conversation; and Stein, interview.

112. "Statement of Sponsorship," *Judaism,* inside front cover.

113. *New York Times,* 22 October 1996; Lippman Bodoff, interview by author, New York, N.Y., 8 September 1997; Jonathan Waxman, conversation; and Hillel Waxman, conversation.

114. Stewart Hoover, *Mass Media Religion: The Social Sources of the Electronic Church* (Newbury Park, Calif.: Sage, 1988), 20–28.

115. *JWA,* s.v. "Jungreis, Esther."

116. Jungreis, *Jewish Soul,* 15–22. According to the *EJ,* s.v. "Jungreis, Asher Anshel," Asher Jungreis (1806–1872) served as rabbi of Csenger for forty years and gained a widespread reputation for his piety. People turned to him for amulets and cures from ailments, and he was known for supporting widows and orphans. His *Menuhat Asher,* which consists of Talmudic exposition and responsa, was published in two parts by his children after his death (1876–1908).

117. Jungreis, *Jewish Soul,* 25–27 (emphasis mine).

118. Chaya Sora Jungreis Gertzulin, written draft of remarks, Congregation Ohr Torah Sisterhood Dinner, East Rockaway, N.Y., 23 June 1997.

119. *JWA,* s.v. "Jungreis, Esther"; and Jungreis, *Jewish Soul,* 28–29.

120. Jungreis, "Rebbetzin's Viewpoint," *Jewish Press,* 3 February 1967, 26.

121. See, for example, Jungreis, "Rebbetzin's Viewpoint," *Jewish Press,* 27 January 1967, 15, and 7 March 1976, 11.

122. Ibid., 16 June 1967, 29 and 6 January 1967, 15.

123. Peter Rowley, *New Gods in America: An Informal Investigation into the New Religions of American Youth Today* (New York: D. McKay, 1971), 3–4; A. James Rudin and Marcia R. Rudin, *Prison or Paradise? The New Religious Cults* (Philadelphia: Fortress Press, 1980), 15–16; *Smashing the Idols: A Jewish Inquiry into the Cult Phenomenon,* ed. Gary D. Eisenberg (Northvale, N.J.: J. Aronson, 1988), xiii; and David G. Bromley and Anson D. Shupe Jr., *Strange Gods: The Great American Cult Scare* (Boston: Beacon Press, 1981), 3–4.

124. Jungreis, "Rebbetzin's Viewpoint," *Jewish Press,* 22 September 1972, 20.

125. Interestingly, there have been very few Christian women evangelists who became masters of the electronic church. For biographical sketches of a few prominent ones, see Richard G. Peterson, "Electric Sisters," in *The God Pumpers: Religion in the Electronic Age,* ed. Marshall Fishwick and Ray B. Browne (Bowling Green, Ohio: Bowling Green State University Popular Press, 1987), 116–40.

126. Graham, *Just As I Am,* 29–30, 53, 297–324; Marshall Frady, *Billy Graham: A Parable of American Righteousness* (Boston: Little, Brown & Co., 1979); James Schaffer and Colleen Todd, *Christian Wives: Women Behind the Evangelists Reveal Their Faith in Modern Marriage* (New York: Doubleday & Co., 1987), 49–66; Marshall W. Fishwick, "The Blessings of Billy," in *God Pumpers,* 63; Stewart M. Hoover, *Mass Media Religion: The Social Sources of the Electronic Church* (Beverly Hills, Calif.: Sage Publications, 1988), 56–57; and William Packard, *Evangelism in America: From Tents to TV* (New York: Paragon House, 1988), 154–56.

127. Jungreis, "Rebbetzin's Viewpoint," *Jewish Press,* 22 September 1972, 20.

128. April 1, 1973.

129. Jungreis, "Rebbetzin's Viewpoint," *Jewish Press,* 13 October 1972, 18; and Rudin, *Prison or Paradise?* 16.

130. Jungreis, "Rebbetzin's Viewpoint," *Jewish Press,* 16 November 1973, 33. For information on these rabbis, see *Orthodox Judaism in America,* 65–66, 91–93, 202–7.

131. *Jewish Soul,* 37–44; and Barbara Janov, interview by author, New York, N.Y., 5 June 1997.

132. Willa Appel, *Cults in America: Programmed for Paradise* (New York: Holt, Rinehart and Winston, 1983), 11; and Janov, interview. All the booklets were written by Jungreis, edited by Janov, and published by Hineni Publications (New York, 1973).

133. Jungreis, "Rebbetzin's Viewpoint," *Jewish Press,* 10 May 1974, 21. This story is recalled somewhat differently in Jungreis's autobiography. According to that account, the state was California, not Florida, the setting a school not a revival meeting, and Jungreis recalled waiting outside the girl's home in the middle of the night to speak with her. But the message of the story emphasizing Jungreis's power to save Jewish souls remained the same. "It never occurred to me to phone ahead or to ask my husband and children whether they would be willing to accept a new addition to our family. Nor did I consider consulting my eldest daughter, Chaya Sora, who, being the same age, would have to assume a large share of the responsibility. To her credit, Chaya Sora responded by greeting her with open arms." The book notes that she lived with them for two years and was married from their home. An interview with Chaya Sora corroborates the essence of this story, though she recalls the girl sharing her room for three years. Jungreis, *Jewish Soul,* 35–37; and Chaya Sora Jungreis Gertzulin, interview by author, East Rockaway, N.Y., 23 June 1997.

134. Hineni is not funded by UJA/Federation and thus relies heavily on "uniquely individual contributions" and an annual dinner. Janov, interview.

135. Craig Horowitz, "The Vanishing American Jew," *New York Magazine,* 14 July 1997, 32.

136. Ibid.

137. Yisroel Neuberger, "Miracle on 85th Street," *Hineni News,* Passover 1997, [2].

138. Stuart Daniel, quoted in David Gonzalez, "From Pages of the Torah, A Passion," *New York Times,* 23 April 1997, Metro section.

139. Horowitz, "The Vanishing American Jew," 32.

140. Freund, "Standing Room," 16.141. Cathy Kadets, "A Hineni Shabbos: A Special Experience," *Hineni News,* Passover 1997, [8].

142. Galit Chinitz, "Dr. David Smolanoff: From Body Builder to Soul Builder," [4], and Lauren Feinman, "Hineni, My Bright and Shining Star," [6], *Hineni News,* Passover 1997.

143. (New York: HarperCollins, 1998).

144. (San Francisco: Harper, 2003); and Lisa Keys, "Rebbetzin Esther Jungreis, Still Matchmaking after All These Years," *Forward,* 16 May 2003, 15–16.

145. Gonzalez, "From the Pages of Torah."

146. Janov interview, and http://www.hineni.org.

147. *Hineni News,* Passover 1997, [7]; Slovie Jungreis Wolff, interview by author, East Rockaway, N.Y., 23 June 1997; and http://www.hineni.org/askus.asp.

148. *New York Times,* 1 April 1973; Jungreis, *Jewish Soul,* 28; Esther Jungreis, honoree remarks, Congregation Ohr Torah Sisterhood Dinner, East Rockaway, N.Y., 23 June 1997; and Keys, "Rebbetzin Esther Jungreis," 15–16.

NOTES TO CHAPTER 6

1. *Encyclopedia of Women and Religion in North America,* ed. Rosemary Reuther and Rosemary Keller (forthcoming), s.v. "Reform Judaism" and "Conservative and Reconstructionist Judaism."

2. Steven M. Cohen and Judith Schor, "Gender Variation in the Careers of Conservative Rabbis: A Study of Rabbis Ordained since 1985," 14 July 2004, 4–12.

3. Erica Faith Giller, "One Home's Make-over for Passover," *Baldwin Herald,* 27 March 1996; Schwarzbaum, "Rebbetzin"; and Fine, "Rebbetzins Rev." In a contemporary twist, one of the seven rebbetzins included in this article is a rabbi herself, but she is featured because she is married to one.

4. "Rabbis' Wives," *Jewish Journal of Greater Los Angeles,* 22 June 2001, http://www.jewishjournal.com/home/preview.php3?id=7082; *Jewish Journal of Greater Los Angeles,* 6 July 2001, http://www.jewishjournal.com/home/preview .php3?id=7135; Salkin, "She Said," 17; Ketcham, "Pep Talk"; and Stewart Ain, "Identity Crisis," *Jewish Week,* 19 May 1995.

5. Hoyt, "All Eyes," 58, 66; and http://www.fusiondesign.com/our_work_ web_hfnm_womansday.shtml.

6. Kahn, *Fax Me,* 17.

7. Wilkes, *My People,* 67.

8. Internet joke, received 18 January 2000.

9. Milstein, "Husbands of Rabbis"; Scheinerman, "He Said"; Salkin, "She Said"; and Kline, "Don't," 26–28. I am grateful to Robert Tabak for sharing the Kline article with me. James Meier, conversation with author, 29 June 2004. Judith Edelstein currently serves as chaplain of the Jewish Home and Hospital in Manhattan. Meyer, "Rebbitz," 77–78.

10. Salkin, "She Said"; and David M. Feldman, "Her Majesty's Loyal Opposition," *Conservative Judaism* 48 (fall 1995): 41. Jeffrey K. Salkin served as rabbi of the Community Synagogue, Port Washington, N.Y.

11. Gerry Peretsman, "*The New Rabbi* and Temple Israel," *The New Light* (Temple Israel of Great Neck) 45 (spring 2003): 45. In a similar vein, many spouses of college presidents today earn a salary to promote the university. Diana Jean Schemo, "College Leaders' Spouses Gain Salaries as Partners," *New York Times,* 11 January 2003.

12. Melinda Kieffer, phone conversation with author, 1 February 2000; Miriam Benson, phone conversation with author, 19 January 2000; Alisa Rubin Kurshan, phone conversation with author, 18 May 2003; and Jody Wernick, conversation with author, 10 April 2003.

13. Ain, "Identity Crisis"; and Silverstein, "Tribute," 4.

14. Horowitz, *Bostoner Rebbetzin;* Malka Schwartz, *In Her Own Right a Great Woman: Rebbetzin Rivkah, Wife of the Fourth Lubavitcher Rebbe* (Los

Angeles: Schwartz Publishing, 2001); and "Preteen Angst in Sappy Series," *Forward,* 9 October 1998.

15. Sally Charnow, "Seasons of the Soul: Context and Meaning in an Orthodox Girls High School," in *Active Voices: Women in Jewish Culture,* ed. Maurie Sacks (Urbana: University of Illinois Press, 1995), 174.

16. *JWA,* s.v. "Teitelbaum, Faige"; "Faige Teitelbaum, 89, a Power among the Satmar Hasidim," *New York Times,* 13 June 2001, obituary; Steve Lipman, "Faige Teitelbaum, Influential among Satmars, Dies at 89," *Jewish Week,* 15 June 2001; and Zalman Alpert, "The Rebbetzin Who Became a Rebbe: The Chentsiner Rebbetzin," *Chasidic Historical Review* 1 (April 1996): 9.

17. Elicia Brown, "Breaking the Mold," *Jewish Week,* 24 March 2000; Steve Lipman, "Spreading Lots of Purim Joy," *Jewish Week,* 5 March 1999; "Chaplain of the Year Award," *NYBR Bulletin* (December 1997): 6; "Chaplain of the Year Award," *NYBR Album,* [1997]; and Gilbert Rosenthal, phone conversation with author, 25 September 1998.

18. Steinig, "Rebbetzin," 3. Sholom Steinig serves as rabbi of the Young Israel of Bayside in Bayside, N.Y.

19. Lerner, "New Roles," 1–2. Yaakov Lerner serves as rabbi of the Young Israel of Great Neck in Great Neck, N.Y.

20. "Reinventing," 12–15.

21. "The Rebbetzin's Role," Second International Conference on Feminism and Orthodoxy, 16 February 1998.

22. *The Rebbetzin's Letter* 4 (winter 1998): 2.

23. Kessler, "Women Interns"; Zuckerbrod, "Women's Work?"; and Cymrot, "Breakthrough?"; Rebbetzin Mimi Mehlman to the editor, *Jewish Week,* January 2, 1998; and Laurie Goodstein, "Unusual, but Not Unorthodox," *New York Times,* 6 February 1998, Metro section.

24. Rhanni Herzfeld, remarks at the Hebrew Institute of Riverdale Dinner, 15 June 2003. My thanks to Jeffrey Gurock for sharing this talk with me. Shmuel Herzfeld serves as one of the rabbis of the Hebrew Institute of Riverdale in Riverdale, N.Y.

25. Sue Fishkoff, *The Rebbe's Army: Inside the World of Chabad-Lubavitch* (New York: Schocken, 2003), 14–15, 114; and Yaakov Arnold, "Career Women of Crown Heights," *Jewish Week,* 19 February 1999.

26. Fishkoff, *Rebbe's Army,* 88–93; *Total Immersion,* ed. Slonim; Samantha M. Shapiro, "Keeper of the Flame: The Paradox of the Rabbi's Wife," *New York Times Magazine,* 9 September, 2001; Ketcham, "Pep Talks"; and Chaya Teldon, "Chicken Soup for the Jewish Soul," talk, Baldwin, N.Y., March 30, 2000.

27. Sarna, *American Judaism,* 267–71.

Bibliography

ARCHIVES

Adat Ari-El. Jewish Center Archives. North Hollywood, Calif.
Hadassah Archives. New York, N.Y. [HA]
Jacob Rader Marcus Center of the American Jewish Archives. Cincinnati, Ohio.
    [AJA]
The Jewish Center Archives. New York, N.Y.
The Joseph and Miriam Ratner Center for the Study of Conservative Judaism.
    New York, N.Y. [Ratner]
Mishkan Tefila Archives, Chestnut Hill, Mass.
National Women's League Archives. New York, N.Y. [WLA]
Spanish-Portuguese Center Archives, New York, N.Y. [Sp.-Port.]

PERSONAL FILES

Personal files of Balfour Brickner, Shulamith Elster, Jeremy Goldstein, Blu
Greenberg, Hilda Greenberg, Mollie Israelitin, Reba Katz, Edith Kling, Peggy
Pearlstein, Marjorie Pressman, Charlotte Rothman, Hillel Silverman, and Helen
Tomsky.

TAPED INTERVIEWS BY AUTHOR

Joan Lipnick Abelson, Kiamesha Lake, N.Y., May 4, 1994.
Balfour Brickner, New York, N.Y., February 3, 2000.
Irma and Abraham Cardozo, New York, N.Y., May 24, 2000.
Hadassah Carlebach, New York, N.Y., October 16, 1996.
Janet Chiel, Kiamesha Lake, N.Y., May 4, 1994.
Naomi Cohen, Kiamesha Lake, N.Y., May 4, 1994.
Sylvia Geffen, New York, N.Y., February 1, 1994.
Rae Goodman, Kiamesha Lake, N.Y., May 3, 1994.
Blu Greenberg, New York, N.Y., December 6, 1995.
Hilda Greenberg, Miami Beach, Fla., January 4, 2000.
Zipporah Jacobs, Miami Beach, Fla., January 4, 2000.

Reba Katz, Freeport, N.Y., November 11, 1999.
Maurine Kessler, Kiamesha Lake, N.Y., May 2, 1994.
Eileen Kieffer, Miami Beach, Fla., January 5, 2000.
Edith Kling, Miami Beach, Fla., January 4, 2000.
Eudice Lorge, Ft. Lauderdale, Fla., January 8, 2000.
Zipporah Marans, Cedarhurst, N.Y., October 20, 1995.
Hadassah and Judah Nadich, New York, N.Y., December 21, 1993.
Eveline Panitch, Kiamesha Lake, N.Y., May 4, 1994.
Rabbis' Wives session, Rabbinical Assembly Retired Rabbis Convention, Miami Beach, Fla., January 4, 2000. [RA session]
Louise Reichert, Cincinnati, Ohio, March 13, 2000.
Retired Spouses' session, National Association of Retired Reform Rabbis Convention, Ft. Lauderdale, Fla., January 7, 2000. [NAORR session]
Lilly Routtenberg, Clifton, N.J., August 15, 1994.
Jack and Jean Stein, Great Neck, N.Y., November 14, 1997.
Roz Stein, New York, N.Y., February 10, 2000.
Miriam Arzt Teplitz, Lawrence, N.Y., October 20, 1994.
David Waxman and Eve Keller, Great Neck, NY, August 14, 1997.
Mordecai Waxman, Great Neck, N.Y., July 11, 1997.

OTHER INTERVIEWS

Mordecai and Ruth Waxman, Temple Israel interview, videocassette, November 14, 1995.
Ruth Waxman, "Focus on Women," interview by Florence Rapoport, producer and host, TV 22 Cablevision, October 1, 1987.

ON AND BY REBBETZINS

Abrams, Margaret. *Awakened.* Philadelphia: Jewish Publication Society, 1962.
"Another Point of View." *Outlook* 20 (May 1950): 7.
Arfa, Orit. "The Rebbetzin." *Jewish Journal of Greater Los Angeles.* June 22, 2001.
Aronson, Mrs. David [Bertha]. "National Women's League Convention Brings *Kashrut* to Minneapolis." *Outlook* 21 (March 1951): 8.
Asekof, Cecile. "Call Me What You Will." *Outlook* 53 (fall 1983): 12–13.
Badt-Strauss, Bertha. "'Aunt Mathilde': Mathilde Schechter Friend of Youth." *Outlook* 23 (December 1952): 4–5.
Barras, Sylvia A. "Wraps off the Rebbetzin." *Reconstructionist* 22 (15 June 1956): 20–24.
Behrmann, Joan. "Rabbis' Wives: The Case of the Shrinking Pedestal." *Moment* 1 (December 1975): 49–53.

————. Letters. *Moment* 1 (February 1976): 10–11.

Bengis, Esther. *I Am a Rabbi's Wife.* Moodus, Conn.: n.p., 1935.

Blumberg, Janice Rothschild. *As But A Day: To A Hundred and Twenty, 1867–1987.* Atlanta: Hebrew Benevolent Congregation, 1966. Rev. ed. 1987.

————. *One Voice: Rabbi Jacob M. Rothschild and the Troubled South.* Macon, Ga.: Mercer University Press, 1984.

Brickner, Rebecca A. "As I Remember Dr. Benderly." *Jewish Education* 20 (summer 1949): 53–59.

Cohn, Sharon L. "Please Don't Call Me Rebbitzen"; Allender, Julie. "I Married A Rabbi"; and Kieffer, Barbara. "Call Me Rebbitzen." *Outlook* 53 (summer 1983): 12–13, 17–18, 20–22. "Responses on the Rebbitzens." *Outlook* 53 (fall 1983): 12–13, 19.

"Council of Wives of Rabbis." *United Synagogue Recorder* 6 (October 1926): 33.

Crown of Royalty: The Rebbetzins of Chabad-Lubavitch of Seven Generations. Hebrew. Com. Hedvah Segal. Ed. Alter Cohen. Brooklyn. Merkos L'Inyonei Chinuch, 1998.

Cymrot, Deborah. "Is This a Breakthrough? Local Rabbis, Rebbetzins Evaluate New Positions." *Washington Jewish Week,* 15 January 1998.

Davidson, Carrie. *Out of Endless Yearnings.* New York: Bloch, 1946.

Ehrlich, Elizabeth. *Miriam's Kitchen: A Memoir.* New York: Viking, 1997.

Fast, Howard. *The Outsider.* Boston: Houghton Mifflin, 1984.

Feinsilver, Lillian Mermin. *The Taste of Yiddish.* South Brunswick, N.J.: Thomas Yoseloff, 1970.

Fine, Arlene. "Rebbetzins Rev Up." *Cleveland Jewish News.* March 30 and April 3, 2001.

Fisch, Stephen E. "Wives of Law, Medical, and Rabbinical Students: Their Present and Future Role Expectations." Rabbinic thesis, Hebrew Union College, 1974.

Frank, Ray. "If I Were a Rebitzin." *Jewish Times and Observer.* June 20, 1880. http://www.jwa.org/archive/frank/rfreb1.jpg .

Freedman, Carla. "The Rebbetzin in America in the Nineteenth and Twentieth Centuries." Rabbinic thesis, Hebrew Union College, 1990.

Freehof, Lillian S. *The Right Way: Ethics for Youth.* New York: UAHC Press, 1957. Rev. ed. 1969.

————. *Bible Legends: An Introduction to Midrash* I & II. Introduction by Howard Schwartz. Illustrated by Phyllis Tarlow. New York: UAHC Press, 1987, 1988.

————. *The Bible Legend Book.* 3 vols. New York: UAHC Press, 1948, 1952, 1954.

————. *Captive Rabbi: The Story of R. Meir of Rothenburg.* Illustrated by Albert Gold. Philadelphia: Jewish Publication Society, 1965.

Freehof, Lillian S. *Embroideries and Fabrics for Synagogue and Home: 5000 Years of Ornamental Needlework.* New York: Hearthside Press, [1966].

———. *Flowers and Festivals of the Jewish Year.* New York: Hearthside Press, 1964.

Freund, Rebecca. "It's Standing Room Only at Mt. Sinai." *Forward.* March 14, 1997, 16.

"From the Funeral Tribute of Dr. Elias L. Solomon." *United Synagogue Recorder* (October 1924), 6–7.

"Funny, You Don't Look Like a Rebbetzin: Where Have We Been? Where Are We Now?" Spouse session, CCAR Convention, 1989. Audiocassette.

Gerstein, Channa. "Reflections of a Rebbitzen." *Jewish Life* 15 (December 1947): 16–29.

Gewirtz, Mindy. "A Process for Defining the Role of the Rebbetzin." *The Rebbetzin's Letter* (summer 1998): 1–2.

Ginzberg, Eli. *Keeper of the Law.* Philadelphia, Pa.: Jewish Publication Society, 1966.

———. "The Seminary Family: A View From My Parents' Home." In *Perspectives on Jews and Judaism in Honor of Wolfe Kelman,* ed. Arthur A. Chiel. New York: Rabbinical Assembly, 1978.

Glazer, Donna. "Rebbitzens: Supportive and Visible." *Outlook* 53 (fall 1983): 13.

Goldberg, Chelly. "Understanding Your Rebbetzin." *Outlook* 56 (fall 1985): 6.

Goldman, Alex. *The Rabbi Is a Lady.* New York: Hippocrene Books, 1987.

Goldstein, Mrs. Herbert [Rebecca]. "The Jewish Woman as a Force for Jewishness." Jewish Forum 8 (December 1925): 571–73.

Goldstein, Herbert S., and Rebecca Fischel, trans. *Lah-y'-shaw-riem T'hie law.* New York: Bloch, 1915.

Goldstein, Herbert S., and Rebecca Goldstein, comp. *Avodat HaShulkhan: Home Service with Translation and Transliteration.* New York: Bloch, 1921.

Goldstein, Mrs. David M. [Rose]. "'Blossoming from Healthy Roots': A Report on Judaism-in-the-Home Project." *Outlook* 21 (March 1951): 12.

———. "More about Hanukkah in the Home." *Outlook* 22 (December 1951): 16–17, 30.

———. "Program Service." *Outlook* 19 (March 1949): 13.

———. "Ten Tests for Effective Sisterhood Programming." *Outlook* 20 (May 1950): 12.

———. "Your Summer 'Home Work.'" *Outlook* 26 (May 1956): 9, 25.

———. *A Time to Pray.* Bridgeport, Conn.: Hartmore House, 1972.

Gordon, Noah. *The Rabbi.* New York: McGraw-Hill, 1965.

Gould, Mrs. Bernard [Sophie]. "Minnie W. Epstein of Blessed Memory." *Outlook* 21 (September 1950): 8, 11.

Grade, Chaim. *Rabbis and Wives.* New York: Random House, 1982.

Graff, Morris W. "Rebitzen—An Old Title with New Meaning." *CCARJ* 13 (October 1965): 52–54.

Greenberg, Betty D., and Althea O. Silverman. *Jewish Home Beautiful.* New York: Harper & Row, 1967.

Greenberg, Blu. *Black Bread: Poems, after the Holocaust.* Hoboken, N.J.: Ktav, 1994.

———. "The Challenges Ahead." *JOFA Journal* 3 (summer 2002): 1–2.

———. *How to Run a Traditional Jewish Household.* New York: Simon & Schuster, 1983.

———. "Marriage in the Jewish Tradition." *Journal of Ecumenical Studies* 22 (winter 1985):3–20.

———. *On Women and Judaism.* Philadelphia, Pa.: Jewish Publication Society, 1981.

———. "Orthodox Feminism and the Next Century." *Sh'ma* 30 (January 2000): 1–2.

———. "Will There Be Orthodox Women Rabbis?" *Judaism* 33 (winter 1984): 23–33.

Greenberg, Blu, and Linda Tarry. *King Solomon and the Queen of Sheba.* New York: Pitspopany Press, 1997.

Greenberg, Marilyn S. *The Rabbi's Life Contract.* Garden City, N.Y.: Doubleday, 1983.

Heller, Lynn E. "The Pulpit Rebbitzen: Para-Professional? Wife Support System? Career Woman?" *Outlook* 50 (spring 1980): 12–13, 19–20.

Herman, Agnes. "I Am a Rabbi's Wife." Unpublished manuscript, 1984.

Hoffman, Charles I. "Mrs. Schechter as Helpmeet." *United Synagogue Recorder* (October 1924): 7.

Hoffman, Fanny B. "The Use of Leisure by Jewish Women." *United Synagogue Recorder* (October 1924): 2–3.

Horowitz, Raichel. *The Bostoner Rebbetzin Remembers.* Brooklyn: Mesorah Publishers, 1996.

Hoyt, Carolyn. "All Eyes upon Us." *Woman's Day.* April 6, 1993, 58, 66.

Hyamson, Mrs. Moses. "The Rabbi's Wife." *Jewish Forum* 8 (December 1925): 583–85.

———. "Ritual Baths (Mikvaoth)." Jewish Forum (January 1927): 22–25. Reprinted in *Total Immersion: A Mikvah Anthology,* ed. Rivkah Slonim, 100–103. Northvale, N.J.: Jason Aronson, 1996.

"Irrepressible, Unforgettable 'Mama G.'" *Outlook* 51 (fall 1980): 4, 20–21.

Isaacs, Abram S. *Under the Sabbath Lamp: Stories of Our Time for Old and Young.* Philadelphia: Jewish Publication Society, 1919.

Isaacs, Lewis M., and Mathilde S. [*sic*] Schechter, eds. *Kol Rinah: Hebrew Hymnal for School and Home.* New York: Bloch, 1910.

Jungreis, Esther. *The Jewish Soul on Fire.* New York: William Morrow, 1982.

Jungreis, Esther. *The Committed Life: Principles for Good Living from Our Timeless Past*. New York: HarperCollins, 1998.

————. *The Committed Marriage: A Guide to Finding a Soul Mate and Building a Relationship through Timeless Biblical Wisdom*. San Francisco: Harper SanFrancisco, 2002.

————. "Rebbetzin's Viewpoint." *Jewish Press*. Weekly column, 1963–1998.

Kahn, Sharon. *Fax Me a Bagel*. New York: Scribners, 1998.

Kaplan, Sylvia R., and Shonie B. Levi. *Across the Threshold: A Guide for the Jewish Homemaker*. New York: United Synagogue of America, 1959.

Karp, Deborah B. "Mathilde Schechter Comes to America." *Outlook* 72 (summer 2002): 29–31.

Katzoff, Adina. "The Status of the Rebetzin." *Outlook* 15 (September 1944): 8.

Kessler, E. J. "Women Interns to Invade Shuls, Reckons Riverdale's Rabbi Weiss." *Forward*, 26 December 1997.

Kessner, Carole S. "Rosa Sonneschein: The Woman and Her Work." *Tenth World Congress of Jewish Studies*. Division B. 2 (1990): 326–28.

Ketcham, Diane. "Pep Talk for Jews in Nebraska and Alaska." *New York Times*, 25 January 1998.

Keys, Lisa. "Rebbetzin Esther Jungreis, Still Matchmaking after All These Years." *Forward*, 16 May 2003, 15–16.

Kinberg, May. "How Treat the Rabbi's Wife?" *Outlook* 26 (December 1955): 8.

Klaperman, Libby M. "Heaven Help the Rebbetzin." *Jewish Life* 36 (September-October 1968): 21–23. Condensed in *Jewish Digest* (March 1969): 67–69.

————. *The Scholar-fighter: The Story of Saadia Gaon*. New York: Farrar, Straus and Cudahy, 1961.

Klaperman, Libby M., and Gilbert Klaperman. *The Story of the Jewish People*. New York: Rabbinical Council of America by Behrman House, 1956.

Kline, Michael H. "Don't Call Me Rebbitzin." *Raayonot* 5 (summer-autumn 1985): 26–28.

Kohn, Jacob. "The Beauty of Mrs. Schechter's Character." *United Synagogue Recorder* (Oct. 1924), 6.

Kohn, Mrs. S. Joshua [Priva]. "Leadership Training." *Outlook* 20 (May 1950): 11.

————. "A Time for an Accounting: Leadership Training." *Outlook* 23 (September 1952): 12.

Kohut, Rebekah. *My Portion*. New York: Thomas Seltzer, 1925.

————. *More Yesterdays: An Autobiography*. New York: Bloch, 1950.

————. "Personal Memories of Mathilde Schechter." *Outlook* 19 (December 1948): 8.

Kose, Leona W. "It Feels Good to Be a Rebbetzin." *Outlook* 25 (June 1955): 5, 9.

Kramer, William M., and Norton B. Stern. "A Woman who Pioneered Modern

Fundraising in the West." *Western States Jewish History* 19 (July 1987): 335–45.

Kripke, Dorothy K. *Let's Talk about God.* New York: Behrman House, 1953.

———. *Let's Talk about the Jewish Holidays.* New York: Jonathan David, 1975, 1970.

———. *Let's Talk about Right and Wrong.* New York: Behrman House, 1955.

———. *Let's Talk about the Sabbath.* Los Angeles: Alef Design Group, 199.

———. "Why Rebbitzens Crack Up." *Outlook* 27 (March 1957): 13, 20.

Kripke, Dorothy K., and Myer S. Kripke. *Let's Talk about Loving: About Love, Sex, Marriage, and Family.* New York: Ktav, 1980.

Lang, Rebecca. "How Good a Program Chairman Are You?" *Outlook* 16 (December 1945): 10.

———. "What Turn Shall Sisterhood Programs Take?" *Outlook* 18 (September 1947): 14.

Lehrman, Nathaniel S. "The Three Rebbitzens." *Outlook* 53 (fall 1983): 13, 19.

Lemle, Edna Fuerth, ed. *Precious Memories of David and Tamar de Sola Pool.* Pittsboro, N.C.: Town House Press, 1993.

Lerner, Abby. "New Roles of Rebbetzins: Teacher, Halachic Liaison, Counselor, & Friend." *The Rebbetzin's Letter* (summer 1998): 1–2.

Levi, Shoni B. "The Author Has Her Say in Recorded 'Q and A.'" *Outlook* 27 (September 1956): 28.

———. "Don't Look Now—But She's a Rebbetzin." *Outlook* 20 (March 1950): 8.

Marx, Alexander. "The Life of Mathilde Schechter." *United Synagogue Recorder* (January 1925): 11–12.

Marx, Hanna. "Mathilde S. [*sic*] Schechter." *Outlook* 9 (December 1938): 5, 10.

Melamed, Deborah M. *The Three Pillars: Life, Practice and Thought for the Jewish Woman.* New York: Women's League, 1927.

Meyer, Michael A. "On Being a Rebbitz." *Journal of Reform Judaism* 34 (summer 1987): 77–78.

Milstein, Tamar. "Husbands of Rabbis Setting Precedents in Temple Role." *Jewish Advocate* [Boston] (July 1998): 3–9.

Minkin, Mrs. Jacob S. [Fanny]. "Mrs. Solomon Schechter: An Anniversary Appreciation." *Outlook* 2 (December 1931): 2.

Mowshowitz, Libby. *Straight Talk from a Rabbi's Wife.* Binghamton, N.Y.: Gould, 1986.

Nadich, Hadassah Ribalow. "The Rabbi's Spouse." *Jewish Spectator* (summer 1985): 16–18.

Nelson, Zev K. "Special Problems of the Rabbi's Wife and Children." Paper delivered at "On Being a Rabbi" Conference, Jewish Theological Seminary, winter 1964.

Novak, William. "Talking with Blu Greenberg." *Kerem* (winter 1995–96):12–37.

Ollendorf, Paula. "Mathilde Schechter." *Outlook* 5 (December 1934): 7.

Panitz, Esther A. "Adloyoda." *Outlook* 24 (March 1954): 27–28.

———. "The Land of the Bible Exhibit." *Outlook* 24 (June 1954): 1–8.

———. "To Be Fully and Naturally Jewish: A Positive Program for Sisterhood." *Outlook* 26 (May 1956): 17, 28.

Pool, Tamar de Sola. "Henrietta Szold." In *Three Zionist Rishonim in America.* New York: British Rishonim of the United States, 1961.

Pool, Tamar de Sola, and David de Sola Pool. *Is There an Answer? An Inquiry into Some Human Dilemmas.* New York: Thomas Yoseloff, 1966.

Porter, Jack Nusan. "Rosa Sonneschein and the American Jewess Revisited: New Historical Information on an Early American Zionist and Jewish Feminist." *American Jewish Archives* 32 (November 1980): 125–31.

"Reinventing the Role of Rebbitzin." *Yeshiva University Review* (fall 1994): 12–15.

Reuben, Didi Carr. "Two's Company, Three Thousand's a Crowd: Reflections of a Rebbetzin's Husband's Wife." *Journal of Reform Judaism* 33 (spring 1986): 37–41.

Rothschild, Janice. "The Rebbetzinhood." *Central Conference of American Rabbis Journal* 20 (winter 1973): 25–26.

Routtenberg, Lilly S. "Once upon a Rabbinate." *Outlook* 56 (spring 1986): 12.

Routtenberg, Lilly S., and Ruth R. Seldin. *The Jewish Wedding Book.* New York: Harper & Row, 1967.

Rubenovitz, Mignon L. *Altars of My Fathers.* Boston: Jewish Museum, Temple Mishkan Tefila, 1954.

———. *Around the Year in Jewish Ceremonial.* n.p., n.d.

———. *The Boy of Okup: A Day in the Childhood of a Jewish Saint.* Boston: Jewish Museum of Temple Mishkan Tefila, 1952.

———. *The Light of the Centuries and Other Historical Dramas.* Boston: Sisterhood of Temple Mishkan Tefila, 1938.

———. *Winecup and Book: The Story of the Darmstädter Haggadah.* Boston: Jewish Museum of Temple Mishkan Tefila, 1946.

Rubenovitz, Mignon L., and Herman H. Rubenovitz. *The Waking Heart.* Cambridge, Mass.: Nathaniel Dame & Co., 1967.

Salkin, Nina. "She Said: 'It Wasn't All Bat Mitzvahs and Honeycake." *Forward,* 20 February 1998, 17.

Saltzman, Esta. "Marjorie Morningstar: Jewish Mute or Mutiny." *Outlook* 26 (December 1956): 17, 26–27.

Schechter, Mathilde. "A Plea for Jewish Ceremonials." 1904. Reprinted in *Outlook* 17 (May 1947): 5, 17.

———. "A Task for Jewish Women." 21 January 1918. Reprinted in *Outlook* 2 (April 1932): 1.

Schechter, Mathilde, and Lewis M. Isaacs, eds. *Kol Rinah: Hebrew Hymnal for School and Home*. New York: Bloch, 1910.

Scheinerman, Edward. "He Said: 'My Wife Was a Novelty, I Was an Oddity.'" *Forward*, 20 February 1998, 17.

Schram, Penina, ed. *Chosen Tales: Stories Told by Jewish Storytellers*. Northvale, N.J.: Jason Aronson, 1995.

Schwartz, Shuly Rubin. "Ambassadors without Portfolio: The Religious Leadership of Rebbetzins in Late-Twentieth-Century American Jewish Life." In *Women in American Judaism: New Historical Perspectives*, ed. Pamela S. Nadell and Jonathan D. Sarna. Hanover, N.H.: University Press of New England, 2001.

———. "Mathilde Schechter: First Lady of Conservative Judaism." In *Solomon Schechter in America: A Centennial Tribute*, ed. Robert E. Fierstien. New York: Joint Convention Committee, 2002.

———. "Rebecca Aaronson Brickner: Preacher, Teacher and Rebbetzin in Israel." *American Jewish Archives* 54 (2002): 64–83.

———. "Ruth Waxman, 'Our Eleanor Roosevelt': The Role of the Rebbetzin in Post-War Conservative Judaism." In *Yakar Le'Mordecai: Jubilee Volume in Honor of Mordecai Waxman*, ed. Zvia Ginor. New Jersey: Ktav, 1999.

———. "Serving the Jewish People: The Rebbetzin as Religious Leader." In *Jewish Religious Leadership: Image and Reality*, ed. Jack Wertheimer. New York: Jewish Theological Seminary, 2004.

———. "'We Married What We Wanted To Be': The *Rebbetzin* in Twentieth-Century America." *American Jewish History* 83 (June 1995): 223–46.

Schwartzman, Sylvan D. "Is There Still Room for the Rebbetzin Today?" *Journal of Reform Judaism* (fall 1981): 64–66. See also the responses: Stahl, Lynn. "Responses." *Journal of Reform Judaism* 28 (fall 1981): 67–72; Felix, Cathy L., and Myra Yedwab. Letters to the editor. *Journal of Reform Judaism* 29 (winter 1982): 55–58.

Schwarzbaum, Leon. "Rebbetzin with a Recipe." *Jewish Week*, 12 September 1997.

Selavan, Ida Cohen. "Friday the Rebbetzin . . . A Feminist Look at the Rabbi Small Series." *Lilith* 1 (fall/winter 1977/78): 39–41. And see: Letter to the editor. *Lilith* 1 (spring 1978): 5.

Shapiro, Samantha M. "Keeper of the Flame: The Paradox of the Rabbi's Wife." *New York Times Magazine*, 9 September 2001.

Shenker, Israel. "Adele Ginzberg, at 90, Says, 'So What?'" *New York Times*, 16 May 1976.

Silverman, Althea O. *Behold My Messengers! The Lives and Teachings of the Prophets*. New York: Bloch, 1955.

———. *Habibi and Yow*. New York: Bloch, 1946.

Silverman, Althea O. *Habibi's Adventures in the Land of Israel*. New York: Bloch, 1951.

———. *The Harp of David: Legends of Mount Zion*. Adapted from the legends and tales related by Dr. S. Z. Kahana, Curator of Mt. Zion, Jerusalem. Hartford, Conn.: Hartmore House, 1964.

Silverstein, Harry. "A Tribute to the Traditional Rebitzin." *Rabbinical Assembly Association of Retired Rabbis Ha-Modia* (February-March 1998): 4.

Simon, Carrie. "Women's Influence in the Development of American Judaism." Forty-first Annual Report, *Proceedings of the Union of American Hebrew Congregations* 8 (1911–1915): 7688–92.

Singer, Isaac Bashevis. *In My Father's Court*. New York: Farrar Straus & Giroux, 1962.

Slonim, Rivkah, ed. *Total Immersion: A Mikvah Anthology*. Northvale, N.J.: Jason Aronson, 1996.

Solis-Cohen, Elfrida. "Mathilde Roth Schechter: A Biographical Sketch." *United Synagogue Recorder* (October 1924): 5–6.

Soloveitchik, Joseph B. "A Tribute to the Rebbitzen of Talne." *Tradition* 17 (spring 1978): 73–83.

Sonneschein, Rosa. "Women as Breadwinners." *American Jewess* 9 (May 1899): 4–6.

Spouse Connection: A Newsletter for Men and Women Married to Rabbis. New York: Central Conference of America Rabbis.

Steinig, Judi. "Rebbetzin, Wife, Mother, Professional: Striking a Balance." *The Rebbetzin's Letter* (spring 1998): 3.

Sundheim, Adrienne. "The Personal Equation of a Rabbi's Life." *Yearbook of the Central Conference of American Rabbis* 90 (1980): 153.

Szold, Henrietta. "The Lineaments of Mathilde Roth Schechter." 1925. Reprinted in *United Synagogue Recorder* (January 1925): 10–11.

Tennenbaum, Silvia. *Rachel, the Rabbi's Wife*. New York: William Morrow & Co., 1978.

Teplitz, Miriam. "The Homontash that Changed Its Name." *Outlook* 21 (March 1951): 24–25.

———. "Public Persona and Private Person." *Rabbinics Today* 1 (November 1992): 4, 8; 15–42.

Tomsky, Helen. "I Didn't Marry a Rabbi, But I Answer to Rebbitzen Now." *Outlook* 54 (fall 1983): 12.

———. "Pesah Foods for Special Diets." *Outlook* 49 (spring 1979): 13.

Umansky, Ellen M. "Paula Ackerman: Reform's Lost Woman Rabbi." *Genesis* 2 (June-July 1986): 18–20.

Waxman, Ruth B. "The Goldfish in the Big Black Hat." *Temple Israel Light* (April 1957): 5–6.

———. "More Bubbles from the Goldfish Bowl." *Temple Israel Light* (summer 1963): 3–4

———. "Only the Details Have Changed." *Outlook* (spring 1982): 8, 20, 21.

Weilerstein, Sadie Rose. *The Adventures of K'tonton: A Little Jewish Tom Thumb.* New York: Women's League for Conservative Judaism, 1964.

———. *K'tonton in the Circus.* Philadelphia, Pa.: Jewish Publication Society of America, 1981.

———. *K'tonton on an Island in the Sea.* Philadelphia, Pa.: Jewish Publication Society of America, 1976.

———. *K'tonton in Israel.* New York: National Women's League of the United Synagogue of America, 1964.

———. *K'tonton's Yom Kippur Kitten.* Philadelphia, Pa.: Jewish Publication Society, 1995.

Weinberg, Marcia. "Rachel, the Rabbi's Wife." Review Essay. *Journal of Reform Judaism* (winter 1979).

Wilkes, Paul. *And They Shall Be My People.* New York: Atlantic Monthly Press, 1994.

Wilner, Helen A. "The Rabbi's Wife Can Help Herself." *American Judaism* 4 (September 1954): 9.

Wise, James Waterman. *Legends of Louise: The Life Story of Mrs. Stephen S. Wise.* New York: Jewish Opinion Publishing Co., 1949.

Wisse, Ruth R. "Rachel, the Rabbi's Wife." Review Essay. *Commentary* (June 1978).

Wittigschlager, Wilhelmina. *Minna, Wife of the Young Rabbi.* New York: Consolidated Retail Booksellers, 1905.

Wolpin, Nissim, ed. *The Torah Profile.* Brooklyn: Mesorah Publishers, 1988.

"Women's League Notables." *Outlook* 27 (March 1957): 17, 21.

"Women's League Notables—They're Worth Talking About." *Outlook* 27 (December 1956): 18–19.

Zucker, David J. "Rebbetzins and Women Rabbis: Portrayals in Contemporary American Jewish Fiction." *CCARJ* 42 (winter/spring 1995): 1–12.

Zuckerbrod, Nancy. "Women's Work?" *Washington Jewish Week,* 15 January 1998.

JEWISH HISTORY BACKGROUND

Adler, Frank J. *Roots in a Moving Stream: The Centennial History of Congregation B'nai Jehudah of Kansas City, 1870–1970.* Kansas City, Mo.: Congregation B'nai Jehudah, 1972.

Bauman, Mark K. *Harry H. Epstein and the Rabbinate as a Conduit for Change.* Rutherford, N.J.: Farleigh Dickenson University Press, 1994.

Berkowitz, Henry. *Intimate Glimpses of the Rabbi's Career.* Cincinnati, Ohio: Hebrew Union College Press, 1921.

Berman, Myron. *Richmond's Jewry, 1769–1976.* Charlottesville: University Press of Virginia, 1979.

Bloom, Jack H. "The Rabbi as Symbolic Exemplar." Ph.D. dissertation, Columbia University, 1972.

———. *The Rabbi as Symbolic Exemplar: By the Power Vested in Me.* New York: Haworth Press, 2002.

———. "The Rabbi's Family." *CCAR Proceedings* 86 (1977): 105–14.

Bronsen, Rosalind Mael. *B'nai Amoona for All Generations.* St. Louis, Mo.: Congregation B'nai Amoona, 1982.

Cleator, Kenneth Irving, and Harry Joshua Stern. *Harry Joshua Stern: A Rabbi's Journey.* New York: Bloch Publishing, 1981.

Cristol, Gerry. *A Light in the Prairie: Temple Emanu-El of Dallas 1872–1997.* Fort Worth: Texas Christian University, 1998.

Deutsch, Shaul Shimon. *Larger than Life: The Life and Times of the Lubavitcher Rebbe Rabbin Menachem Mendle Schneerson.* Vol. 1. New York: Chasidic Historical Productions, 1995.

Ehrlich, Walter. *Zion in the Valley: The Jewish Community of St. Louis.* 2 vols. Columbia: University of Missouri Press, 1997, 2002.

Eisenstein, Ira. *Reconstructionist Judaism: An Autobiography.* New York: Reconstructionist Press, 1986.

Elovitz, Mark H. *A Century of Jewish Life in Dixie: The Birmingham Experience.* University: University of Alabama Press, 1974.

Feibelman, Julian B. *The Making of an American Rabbi.* New York: Vantage Press, 1980.

Fein, Isaac M. *The Making of an American Jewish Community: The History of Baltimore Jewry from 1773 to 1920.* Philadelphia, Pa.: Jewish Publication Society, 1971.

Feingold, Henry L., general ed. *The Jewish People in America.* 5 vols. Baltimore: Johns Hopkins University Press, 1992.

Fierstien, Robert E., ed. *A Century of Commitment: One Hundred Years of the Rabbinical Assembly.* New York: Rabbinical Assembly, 2000.

Freedman, Leslie R. "Role-Related Stress in the Rabbinate: A Report on a Nationwide Study of Conservative and Reform Rabbis." *JRJ* 32 (winter 1985): 1–8.

———. "Stress in the Rabbinate: A Report on a Nationwide Study of Conservative and Reform Rabbis." Ph.D. dissertation, City University of New York, 1983.

Gidon, Ruth, ed. *Adat Ari El: The First Fifty Years: A History, 1938–88.* North Hollywood, Calif.: Adat Ari El, 1988.

Ginor, Zvia, ed. *Yakar Le'Mordecai: Jubilee Volume in Honor of Mordecai Waxman.* Hoboken, N.J.: Ktav, 1999.

Gittelsohn, Roland B. *Here Am I—Harnessed to Hope.* New York: Vantage Press, 1988.

The Golden Book of Congregation Adath Yeshurun. Houston, Tex.: D. H. White, [1942?].

Goldman, Karla. *Beyond the Synagogue Gallery: Finding a Place for Women in American Judaism.* Cambridge: Harvard University Press, 2000.

Goldstein, Shannie. "Emotional, Physical, and Financial Well-Being of Widows of Reform Rabbis." M.A. thesis, Tulane University, 1986.

Glazer, Nathan. *American Judaism.* Chicago: University of Chicago Press, 1957, 1972.

Gurock, Jeffrey S. *American Jewish Orthodoxy in Historical Perspective.* Hoboken, N.J.: Ktav, 1996

———. *From Fluidity to Rigidity: The Religious Worlds of Conservative and Orthodox Jews in Twentieth Century America.* Ann Arbor: University of Michigan, 2000.

———. *The Men and Women of Yeshiva: Higher Education, Orthodoxy, and American Judaism.* New York: Columbia University Press, 1988.

———. "Twentieth-Century American Orthodoxy's Era of Non-Observance, 1900–1960." *Torah U-Madda* 9 (2000): 87–107.

Heller, James G. *Issac Mayer Wise.* New York: Union of American Hebrew Congregations, 1965.

A History of Kehilath Anshe Mayriv: Congregation of the Men 'of the West. Chicago, 1951.

Joselit, Jenna Weissman. *New York's Jewish Jews: The Orthodox Community in the Interwar Years.* Bloomington: Indiana University Press, 1990.

———. *The Wonders of America.* New York: Hill & Wang, 1994.

Katz, Irving I. *The Beth El Story, with a History of the Jews in Michigan before 1950.* Detroit: Wayne State University Press, 1955.

Kohn, S. Joshua. *The Jewish Community of Utica, New York, 1847–1948.* New York: American Jewish Historical Society, 1959.

Krucoff, Carole. *Rodfei Zedek: The First Hundred Years.* Chicago: Congregation Rodfei Zedek, 1976.

Landau, Herman. *Adath Louisville: The Story of a Jewish Community.* Louisville, Ky.: H. Landau and Associates, 1981.

Lebeson, Anita Libman. *Recall to Life—The Jewish Woman in America.* New York: Thomas Yoseloff, 1970.

Leket Divray Torah: A Collection of Divray Torah from the First 75 Years of Women's League for Conservative Judaism. New York: Women's League for Conservative Judaism, 1992.

Lenn, Theodore I. *Rabbi and Synagogue in Reform Judaism*. New York: Central Conference of American Rabbis, 1972.

Marcus, Jacob Rader, and Abraham J. Peck, eds. *The American Rabbinate: A Century of Continuity and Change: 1883–1983*. Hoboken, N.J.: Ktav, 1985.

Mayerberg, Samuel S. *Chronicle of An American Crusader*. New York: Bloch, 1944.

Moore, Deborah Dash. *At Home in America: Second Generation New York Jews*. New York: Columbia University Press, 1981.

———. *To the Golden Cities: Pursuing the American Jewish Dream in Miami and L.A.* New York: Free Press, 1994.

Morris, Bonnie J. *Lubavitcher Women in America: Identity and Activism in the Postwar Era*. Albany: State University of New York Press, 1998.

Mowshowitz, Israel. *A Rabbi's Rovings*. Hoboken, N.J.: Ktav, 1985.

Nadell, Pamela S. *Conservative Judaism in America: A Biographical Dictionary and Sourcebook*. New York: Greenwood Press, 1988.

———. *Women Who Would Be Rabbis: A History of Women's Ordination, 1889–1985*. Boston: Beacon Press, 1998.

Nadell, Pamela S., and Jonathan D. Sarna, eds. *Women in American Judaism: New Historical Perspectives*. Hanover, N.H.: University Press of New England, 2001.

Noveck, Simon. *Milton Steinberg: Portrait of a Rabbi*. New York: Ktav, 1978.

Olitzky, Kerry M., Lance J. Sussman, and Malcolm H. Stern, eds. *Reform Judaism in America: A Biographical Dictionary and Sourcebook*. Westport, Conn.: Greenwood Press, 1993.

Polner, Murray. *Rabbi: The American Experience*. New York: Holt, Rinehart and Winston, 1977.

Priesand, Sally. *Judaism and the New Jewish Woman*. New York: Behrman House, 1975.

Problems of the Jewish Ministry. New York: New York Board of Jewish Ministers, 1927.

Raphael, Marc Lee. *Profiles in American Judaism: The Reform, Conservative, Orthodox, and Reconstructionist Traditions in Historical Perspective*. San Francisco: Harper & Row, 1984.

Reichel, Aaron I. *The Maverick Rabbi: Rabbi Herbert S. Goldstein and the Institutional Synagogue—"A New Organizational Form."* Norfolk, Va.: Donning Co., 1984.

Rosenblatt, Samuel. *The Days of My Years: An Autobiography*. New York: Ktav, 1976.

Rubin, Saul Jacob. *Third to None: The Saga of Savannah Jewry, 1733-1983*. Savannah, Ga.: Congregation Mickve Israel, 1983.

Sarna, Jonathan D., ed. *The American Jewish Experience*. 2d ed. New York: Holmes & Meier, 1997.

————. *American Judaism: A History.* New Haven, Conn.: Yale University Press, 2004.

Schwartz, Samuel. *Tell Thy Children: The Autobiography of an American Rabbi.* New York: Exposition Press, 1959.

Scult, Mel. "The Baale Boste Reconsidered: The Life Of Mathilde Roth Schechter (M.R.S.)." *Modern Judaism* 7 (February 1987): 1–27.

————. *Judaism Faces the Twentieth Century: A Biography of Mordecai M. Kaplan.* Detroit: Wayne State University Press, 1993.

Sharfman, I. Harold. *The First Rabbi.* Malibu, Calif.: Pangloss Press, 1988.

Shargel, Baila Round. *Lost Love: The Untold Story of Henrietta Szold.* Philadelphia, Pa.: Jewish Publication Society, 1997.

Sherman, Moshe D., ed. *Orthodox Judaism in America: A Biographical Dictionary and Sourcebook.* Westport, Conn.: Greenwood Press, 1996.

Shuchat, Wilfred. "The Rabbi and His Family." *Proceedings of the Rabbinical Assembly* 37 (1975): 177–81.

Silver, Samuel M. *Portrait of a Rabbi: An Affectionate Memoir on the Life of Barnett R. Brickner.* Cleveland, Ohio: Barnett R. Brickner Memorial Foundation, 1959.

Sklare, Marshall. *Conservative Judaism.* Reprint ed. Lanham, Md.: University Press of America, 1985.

Stein, Regina. "The Boundaries of Gender: The Role of Gender Issues in Forming American Jewish Denominational Identity, 1913–1963." Ph.D. dissertation, Jewish Theological Seminary, 1998.

Stern, Frank Elash. "Factors Influencing the Career Decisions of North American Reform Rabbis." Ph.D. dissertation, University of California, Riverside, 1983.

Sternfield, Michael P. "The Rabbi as Family Man." Rabbinic thesis, Hebrew Union College, 1973.

Temkin, Sefton D. *Isaac Mayer Wise, Shaping American Judaism.* New York: Oxford University Press, 1991.

They Dared to Dream: A History of National Women's League. New York: National Women's League of the United Synagogue of America, 1967.

Waxman, Mordecai. "The Changing American Rabbinate." In *The American Rabbi,* ed. Gilbert S. Rosenthal, 165–88. New York: Ktav, 1997.

Weinberg, Robert. "The Absorption of Wives into Their Husband's Work: The Phenomenon, Its Antecedents and Consequences." Ph.D. dissertation, New York University, 1984.

Weiner, Hollace Ava. *Jewish Stars in Texas: Rabbis and Their Work.* College Station: Texas A & M University Press, 1999.

Weinstein, Jacob J. *Solomon Goldman: A Rabbi's Rabbi.* New York: Ktav, 1973.

Wertheimer, Jack. "Pioneers of the Conservative Rabbinate: Reports from the

Field by Graduates of 'Schechter's Seminary.'" *Conservative Judaism* 47 (spring 1995): 53.

Wertheimer, Jack. *A People Divided: Judaism in Contemporary America.* New York: Basic Books, 1993.

Wertheimer, Jack, ed. *The American Synagogue: A Sanctuary Transformed.* New York: Brandeis University Press, 1987.

———. *Tradition Renewed: A History of the Jewish Theological Seminary of America.* 2 vols. New York: Jewish Theological Seminary of America, 1997.

Zola, Gary P., ed. *Women Rabbis: Exploration & Celebration.* Cincinnati, Ohio: HUC-JIR Rabbinic Alumni Association Press, 1996.

Zollman, Joellyn W. "Shopping for Our Future: The Synagogue Gift Shop as Jewish Women's History." Ph.D. dissertation, Brandeis University, 2002.

Zolty, Shoshana P. *And All Your Children Shall Be Learned: Women and the Study of Torah.* Northvale, N.J.: Jason Aronson, 1993.

Zucker, David J. *American Rabbis: Facts and Fiction.* Northvale, N.J.: Jason Aronson, 1998.

MINISTERS' WIVES

Bader, Golda, ed. *I Married a Minister.* New York: Abingdon Cokesbury Press, 1942.

Boyer, Paul. "Minister's Wife, Widow, Reluctant Feminist: Catherine Marshall in the 1950s." In *Women in American Religion,* ed. Janet Wilson James. Philadelphia: University of Pennsylvania Press, 1980.

Denton, Wallace. *The Role of the Minister's Wife.* Philadelphia, Pa.: Westminster Press, 1962.

Douglas, William. *Minister's Wives.* New York: Harper & Row, 1965.

Gifford, Carolyn De Swarte, ed. *The Nineteenth-Century American Methodist Itinerant Preacher's Wife.* New York: Garland Publishing, 1987.

———. *Women in American Protestant Religion 1800–1930.* New York: Garland, 1987.

Graham, Billy. *Just As I Am: The Autobiography of Billy Graham.* San Francisco: HarperCollins, 1997.

Greenbacker, Liz, and Sherry Taylor. *Private Lives of Ministers' Wives.* Far Hills, N.J.: New Horizon Press, 1991.

Hobkirk, Marietta B. "Some Reflections on Bringing up the Minister's Family." *Pastoral Psychology* 12 (December 1961): 23–29.

Jeffrey, Julie Roy. "Ministry through Marriage." In *Women in New Worlds,* ed. Hilah E. Thomas and Rosemary Skinner Keller. Nashville, Tenn.: Abingdon, 1981.

Keller, Rosemary Skinner, ed. *Spirituality and Social Responsibility: Vocational*

Vision of Women in the United Methodist Tradition. Nashville, Tenn.: Abingdon, 1993.

Kirkley, Evelyn A. "'Mrs. God': The Role of the Minister's Wife 1930–80." M.A. thesis, Union Theological Seminary, 1985.

Lavender, Lucille. *They Cry, Too!* Grand Rapids, Mich.: Pyranee Books, 1976. Rev. and expanded, 1986.

Madsen, Keith. *Fallen Images: Experiencing Divorce in the Ministry.* Valley Forge, Pa.: Judson Press, 1985.

Morgan, John H., and Linda B. Morgan. *Wives of Priests: A Study of Clergy Wives in the Episcopal Church.* Bristol, Ind.: Parish Church Library, St. John of the Cross, 1980.

Nordland, Frances. *The Unprivate Life of a Pastor's Wife.* Chicago: Moody Press, 1972.

Research Division of the Support Agency United Presbyterian Church, U.S.A. *Pastors' Wives Study.* New York, 1977.

Robbins, Jhan. *Marriage Made in Heaven: The Story of Billy & Ruth Graham.* New York: G. P. Putnam's Sons, 1983.

Ross, Charlotte. *Who Is the Minister's Wife? A Search for Personal Fulfillment.* Philadelphia, Pa.: Westminster Press, 1980.

Sinclair, Donna. *The Pastor's Wife Today.* Nashville, Tenn.: Abingdon, 1981.

Sweet, Leonard I. *The Minister's Wife: Her Role in Nineteenth-Century Evangelicalism.* Philadelphia, Pa.: Temple University Press, 1983.

Truman, Ruth. *Underground Manual for Ministers' Wives.* Nashville, Tenn.: Abingdon, 1974.

Tucker, Ruth A. *First Ladies of the Parish: Historical Portraits of Pastors' Wives.* Grand Rapids, Mich.: Ministry Resources Library, 1988.

Whybrew, Lyndon E. *Minister, Wife and Church: Unlocking the Triangles.* [New York?]: Alban Institute, 1984.

Williams, June P. "What About Your Wife?" *The Christian*; also reprinted in the *Seminary Quarterly* of Minister's Life and Casualty Union (winter 1970–71).

GENERAL BACKGROUND SOURCES

Blair, Karen J. *The Clubwoman as Feminist: True Womanhood Redefined, 1868–1914.* New York: Holmes & Meier, 1980.

Braude, Ann. "Women's History *Is* American Religious History." In *Retelling U.S. Religious History,* ed. Thomas A. Tweed. Berkeley: University of California Press, 1997.

Brekus, Catherine A. *Strangers & Pilgrims: Female Preaching in America, 1740–1845.* Chapel Hill: University of North Carolina Press, 1998.

Brown, Dorothy M. *Setting a Course: American Women in the 1920s.* Boston: Dwayne Publishing, 1987.

Caroli, Betty Boyd. *First Ladies,* expanded ed. New York: Oxford University Press, 1995.

Chafe, William H. *The American Woman: Her Changing Social, Economic, and Political Roles, 1920–1970.* New York: Oxford University Press, 1972.

Chaves, Mark. *Ordaining Women: Culture and Conflict in Religious Organizations.* Cambridge: Harvard University Press, 1997.

Cott, Nancy F. *Public Vows: A History of Marriage and the Nation.* Cambridge: Harvard University Press, 2000.

Daniels, Arlene Kaplan. *Invisible Careers: Women Civic Leaders from the Volunteer World.* Chicago: University of Chicago Press, 1988.

Degler, Carl N. *At Odds: Women and the Family in America from the Revolution to the Present.* New York: Oxford University Press, 1980.

Douglas, Ann. *The Feminization of American Culture.* New York: Knopf, 1978.

Drachman, Virginia. *Sisters in Law: Women Lawyers in Modern American History.* Cambridge: Harvard University Press, 1998.

Ellwood, Robert S. *The Fifties Spiritual Marketplace: American Religion in a Decade of Conflict.* New Brunswick, N.J.: Rutgers University Press, 1997.

Epstein, Cynthia Fuchs. *Woman's Place: Options and Limits in Professional Careers.* Berkeley: University of California Press, 1970.

Evans, Sara M. *Born for Liberty: A History of Women in America.* New York: Free Press, 1989.

Farber, David. *The Age of Great Dreams: America in the 1960s.* New York: Hill and Wang, 1994.

Filene, Peter G. *Him/Her/Self: Gender Identities in Modern America.* 3d edition. Baltimore: Johns Hopkins University Press, 1998.

Finch, Janet. "Devising Conventional Performances: The Case of Clergymen's Wives." *Sociological Review* 28 (1980): 851–70.

———. *Married to the Job: Wives' Incorporation in Men's Work.* Boston: George Allen & Unwin, 1983.

Fowlkes, Martha R. *Behind Every Successful Man: Wives of Medicine and Academe.* New York: Columbia University Press, 1980.

Gavron, Hannah. *The Captive Wife: Conflicts of Housebound Mothers.* New York: Humanities Press, 1966.

Gerber, Lane A. *Married to Their Careers.* New York: Tavistock Publishers, 1983.

Gerstel, Naomi, and Harriet Engel Gross, eds. *Families and Work.* Philadelphia, Pa.: Temple University Press, 1987.

Glazer, Penina Migdal, and Miriam Slater. *Unequal Colleagues: The Entrance of Women into the Professions, 1890–1940.* New Brunswick, N.J.: Rutgers University Press, 1987.

Ginzberg, Lori D. *Women and the Work of Benevolence: Morality, Politics, and*

Class in the Nineteenth-Century United States. New Haven, Conn.: Yale University Press, 1990.

Gornick, Vivian, and Barbara K. Moran, eds. *Woman in a Sexist Society: Studies in Power and Powerlessness*. New York: Basic Books, 1971.

Hartman, Mary S., and Lois Banner, eds. *Clio's Consciousness Raised: New Perspectives on the History of Women*. New York: Octagon Books, 1976.

Hartman, Susan M. *The Home Front and Beyond: American Women in the 1940s*. Boston: Twayne, 1982.

Helfrich, Margaret L. *The Social Role of the Executive's Wife*. Columbus: Ohio State University, 1965.

Hochschild, Arlie. "The Role of the Ambassador's Wife: An Exploratory Study." *Journal of Marriage and Family* 31 (February 1969): 73–87.

Hudnut-Beumler, James. *Looking for God in the Suburbs: The Religion of the American Dream and Its Critics, 1945–65*. New Brunswick, N.J.: Rutgers University Press, 1994.

Kaledin, Eugenia. *Mothers and More: American Women in the 1950s*. Boston: Dwayne Publishers, 1984.

Kessler-Harris, Alice. *Out to Work: A History of Wage-Earning Women in the United States*. New York: Oxford University Press, 1982.

Langer, Cassandra L. *A Feminist Critique: How Feminism Has Changed American Society, Culture, and How We Live from the 1940s to the Present*. New York: HarperCollins, 1996.

Lerner, Gerda. *The Creation of a Feminist Consciousness*. New York: Oxford University Press, 1993.

Lindley, Susan Hill. *"You Have Stept Out of Your Place": A History of Women and Religion in America*. Louisville, Ky.: Westminster John Knox Press, 1996.

MacPherson, Myra. *The Power Lovers: An Intimate Look at Politics and Marriage*. New York: G. P. Putnam's Sons, 1975.

Marsden, George M. *Religion and American Culture*. New York: Harcourt Brace College, 1990.

May, Elaine Tyler. *Great Expectations: Marriage and Divorce in Post-Victorian America*. Chicago: University of Chicago Press, 1980.

———. *Homeward Bound: American Families in the Cold War Era*. New York: Basic Books, 1988.

McLaughlin, Steven D., et al. *The Changing Lives of American Women*. Chapel Hill: University of North Carolina Press, 1988.

Meyerowitz, Joanne J., ed. *Not June Cleaver: Women and Gender in Postwar America, 1945–1960*. Philadelphia: Temple University Press, 1994.

Miller, Stephen Paul. *The Seventies Now: Culture as Surveillance*. Durham, N.C.: Duke University Press, 1999.

Nieva, Veronica F., and Barbara A. Gutek. *Women and Work: A Psychological Perspective*. New York: Praeger Scientific, 1981.

Otto, Herbert A., ed. *Marriage and Family Enrichment: New Perspectives and Programs.* Nashville, Tenn.: Abingdon, 1976.

Papanek, Hanna. "Men, Women, and Work: Reflections on the Two-Person Career." *American Journal of Sociology* 78 (January 1973): 852–72.

Rosenberg, Rosalind. *Divided Lives: American Women in the Twentieth Century.* New York: Hill and Wang, 1992.

Rothman, Sheila M. *Woman's Proper Place: A History of Changing Ideals and Practices, 1870 to the Present.* New York: Basic Books, 1978.

Ruether, Rosemary, and Rosemary Skinner Keller, eds. *Women and Religion in America.* 3 vols. San Francisco: Harper & Row, 1981–86.

Ruether, Rosemary, and E. McLaughlin, eds. *Women of the Spirit: Female Leadership in the Jewish and Christian Traditions.* New York: Simon & Schuster, 1979.

Rupp, Leila J., and Taylor Verta. *Survival in the Doldrums: The American Women's Rights Movement, 1945 to the 1960s.* New York: Oxford University Press, 1987.

Rury, John L. *Education and Women's Work: Female Schooling and the Division of Labor in Urban America, 1870–1930.* Albany: State University of New York Press, 1991.

Solomon, Barbara Miller. *In the Company of Educated Women: A History of Women and Higher Education in America.* New Haven, Conn.: Yale University Press, 1985.

Wallman, Sandra, ed. *Social Anthropology of Work.* New York: Academic Press, 1979.

Ware, Susan. *Holding Their Own: American Women in the 1930s.* Boston: Dwayne Publishing, 1982.

Weiss, Jessica. *To Have and To Hold: Marriage, the Baby Boom, and Social Change.* Chicago: University of Chicago Press, 2000.

Willard, Frances E. *Woman in the Pulpit.* [N.P.]: Women's Temperance Publishing Association, 1889.

Woloch, Nancy. *Women and the American Experience.* New York: Knopf, 1984.

Index

About the Author

Shuly Rubin Schwartz is the Irving Lehrman Research Associate Professor of American Jewish History and Dean of the Albert A. List College of Jewish Studies at The Jewish Theological Senimary. She is the author of *The Emergence of Jewish Scholarship in America: The Publication of the* Jewish Encyclopedia.